S0-BQZ-786

"Consider infinity. When Hubble gazed into the deep field, staring into what appeared to be a vacancy in the cosmos: the eye of this beholder saw the Light. From a distance it was observed to be a black hole of darkness in the Universe, presumed to contain nothing of any consequence. Focused upon a fixed point in space, this is what Hubble found. A sight for mere mortals to ponder: a wonder to behold; a humbling observation prompting a collective pause for reflection."

"We do not need to see to believe our eyes. We are connected to the cosmos as a speck in space, a ray of light from the darkness, as significant or irrelevant as any other piece of the expansive whole. Incapable of conceptualizing infinity, mortal beings stare into it hopefully, searching beyond ourselves in an effort to find ourselves; seeking contact with our Creator, in pursuit of epiphany: God. We need only peer within ourselves to find the purest essence of our Divinity."

House of Darkness

House of Light

The True Story

Volume One

Andrea Perron

authorHOUSE®

AuthorHouse™
1663 Liberty Drive
Bloomington, IN 47403
www.authorhouse.com
Phone: 1-800-839-8640

First published by AuthorHouse 3/4/2011

ISBN: 978-1-4567-4759-6 (sc)
ISBN: 978-1-4567-4760-2 (dj)
ISBN: 978-1-4567-4761-9 (e)

Library of Congress Control Number: 2011903407

Printed in the United States of America

For my Mother

The Twenty Third Psalm

The Lord is my shepherd, I shall not want.
He maketh me to lie down in green pastures,
He leadeth me beside still waters.
He restoreth my soul.
He leadeth me in the paths of righteousness, for His name's sake.
Yea, though I walk through the valley of the shadow of death,
I will fear no evil, for Thou art with me;
Thy rod and Thy staff, they comfort me.
Thou preparest a table before me, in the presence of mine enemies;
Thou anointest my head with oil; my cup runneth over.
Surely goodness and mercy shall follow me all the days of my life,
and I will dwell in the house of the Lord forever.

House of Darkness ~ House of Light
The Trilogy

Prologue in Prayer
A Proper Introduction

I. A Place in the Country

*let there be light   *frozen stiff   *sounds of silence
*a matter of time   *contact   *a chill in the air
*creature discomforts   *the devil's pets   *safety in numbers
*sword of Damocles   *a very fine how do you do
*familiarity breeds contempt   *cold as stone   *dusk 'til dawn

II. Fire in the Hole

*bless this mess   *close that door   *smoke and mirrors
*spirit matters   *scorched offerings   *apple blossom time
*kiss of death   *omens   *from frying pan into the fire
*blue light special   *an old torch carries a flame
*fire and brimstone   *trial by fire   *lady bug
*burnin' down the house   *feet to the fire   *bats!

III. Wicked Woman...Evil Ways

*demon doors   *knock knock knock   *blown away
*Bathsheba   *a stitch in time   *from insult to injury
*is this the party to whom I am speaking?   *a pain in the neck
*message received   *twisted sister   *solitary confinement
*as the crow flies   *off the hook   *no rest for the wicked
*sink or swim   *a rude awakening   *a fate worse than death

IV. Spooked

*going for a ride   *bed knobs   *broomsticks   *boo! who?
*kindred spirits   *clarion call   *things that go bump in the day
*things that go bump in the night   *reality   *Baker boys
*go away little girls   *told you so   *bloodbath   *shared space

Metamorphosis

V. Ghostly Cries and Whispers

*secrets and lies   *make yourself at home   *comes and goes
*timely manners   *for crying out loud   *rearing its ugly head
*history   *all fun and games until someone gets hurt   *insight
*listen up in smoke   *staking a claim   *making matters worse
*in the closet   *poetry and prose   *chants and incantations

VI. Down the Hatch

*ye olde cellar hole   *beneath the bell stone   *the big dig   *eureka!
*a sense of direction   *fountain of youth   *release the hounds!
*knocked back   *buyer's remorse   *black hole   *dead in the water
*all's well that ends well   *holy hell   *leave well enough alone
*teardrops   *a woman's touch will get a man's attention   *tug of war

VII. Warren Peace

*inquest   *divine intervention   *promises…promises
*tempting fate   *twilight   *hippies, freaks and misfits
*blessings and curses   *darkest before the dawn   *death becomes her
*inner sanctum   *fear the living…not the dead   *continuum
*eye of the beholder   *a little knowledge   *all things considered
*more harm than good   *wrack and ruin   *this too shall pass

VIII. Bless Me Father

*a turn for the worse   *a wing and a prayer   *all in good time
*comfort zone   *common sense   *act of god   *hallelujah
*something sacred   *guess who's coming to dinner?   *joy
*leap of faith   *doubt   *abandon all hope ye who enter here
*clearing the air   *epiphany   *the foreseeable future   *amen

Transformation

IX. Rock On with your Bad Self

*elemental reflections   *windsong   *broken record
*pine forest portal   *cracking up   *season of the witch
*feel free   *if these rocks could talk   *good vibrations
*along came a spider   *journey   *wonders never cease
*to soothe the savage beast   *perfect harmony   *starlight
*a fish tale   *harvest home   *solitude   *welcome home
*stairway to heaven   *highway to hell   *wisdom

X. A Fly on the Wall

*the new paranormal   *right of way   *go in peace
*rites of passage   *terms of endearment   *keep the faith
*manifest destiny   *fond farewell   *carpe diem   *no turning back
*homecoming   *what a relief   *grand slam   *smoke signals
*soul searching   *master of his domain   *escaping unscathed
*ancients and horribles   *photographs and memories
*revisiting the past   *touched by an angel   *mistress of her domain
*darkness and light   *to lift the spirits   *truth be told
*long ago and far away   *collective memoirs   *revelation

Confluence

Epilogue in Epitaph
In Gratitude

Volume One

"When the moon's full those creatures of the full
Are met on the waste hills by country men
Who shudder and hurry by: body and soul
Estranged amid the strangeness of themselves,
Caught up in contemplation, the mind's eye
Fixed upon images that once were thought,
For separate, perfect and immovable
Images can break the solitude
Of lovely, satisfied, indifferent eyes."

~ **the barn at twilight in snowfall** ~

~ House of Darkness ~ House of Light ~

"Because all dark, like those that are all light,
They are cast beyond the verge, and in a cloud,
Crying to one another like the bats;
But having no desire they cannot tell
What's good or bad, or what it is to triumph
At the perfection of one's own obedience;
And yet they speak what's blown into the mind;
Deformed beyond deformity, unformed,
Insipid as the dough before it is baked,
They change their bodies at a word."

William Butler Yeats
A Vision

PROLOGUE IN PRAYER

"Convinced myself, I seek not to convince."
Edgar Allan Poe

The telling of this true story is not intended to persuade the reader of its authenticity. Those who believe in the existence of the spirit world will not require convincing; those who do not believe so will likely remain skeptical. It matters that this tale be told with honesty and integrity. Embarking upon the journey has been scary in its own right. For the past forty years the family involved has remained guarded and exclusive about their mutual experience. Delving into the painful memories has proved difficult; rekindling imagery, disturbing emotions long repressed. Exhuming the dead spawned its share of nightmares and yet it is a tale worthy of telling because it is true; a collective memoir worthy of sharing because of the message a family received.

It is a tale of good and evil, life and death, darkness and light. Evil exists. One need only tune in the nightly news to establish this sad, distressing fact. It is as powerful as invisible. We witness myriad manifestations of evil yet it is essentially an intangible force; an intention to deliberately inflict harm. At times it appears as if evil is winning the battle against what is good and pure, kind and sane in this world. The balance seems skewed. Earth's news is very bad indeed: omnipresent issues of war and peace.

Let there be Light. Truth be told; the human race is immersed in goodness and light. Evil has yet to prevail, though the struggle between them is real. Philosophers and laymen alike, from the greatest minds in history to those merely curious, have wrestled with the concept. Presuming the existence of good and evil, this narrative explores the Nature of life and Transcendence of death. It poses questions yet does not seek answers; nor will it provide any substantive guidance. There are no definitive answers in this realm. For those who lived through it, the mystery remains. It is time to divulge their closely guarded secrets; the time has come to tell the truth.

Acquiring knowledge through direct experience is a blessing and a curse. It defines then redefines. Once something so extraordinary has been witnessed, there is no escaping the imagery impaled in a memory. It cannot be explained and it cannot be denied. There is no legitimate reason to dismiss otherwise consistently reliable senses. Ultimately, we do believe our eyes. We should. Certainty of knowledge informs all else in life, including the inevitability of death and the consequences for souls who linger, suspended in the ether. In the vast continuum of time and space, there are ramifications for mortal and immortal alike.

The following story chronicles this series of phenomenal encounters and metaphysical moments, events which transformed the seven involved in the saga. What the family endured together was absorbed individually, resulting in an intensely personal search as each one discovered their own spirituality, developing a fundamental belief system based upon what they experienced dwelling for a decade in a house alive with death. Those years provided them with hearth and home then gifted them with an explicit knowledge regarding the inherent complexities of life as it intersects the mysteries of death. Each member of the family believes they were privileged to have a powerful truth revealed in their presence, considering what they had shared was nothing less than the stunning realization: there is indeed some form of existence beyond mortal death. Affirming a belief in Spirit, what became their core assumption gradually evolved into simple, certain, steadfast faith.

There is a tendency for time and distance to ease and clarify consciousness; distilling the truth, instilling a sense of peace; replenishing hope where once only torment prevailed. A family's private recollections, intimate knowledge of Spirit is no longer burdensome to them. Instead, they consider it to be an awe-inspiring responsibility, sharing the belief they have kept their secrets long enough; perhaps too long. The writer believes everything happens in its proper moment in time, with purpose and reason; perfection intrinsic to the Universe.

The cast of characters, both living and dead, is extensive yet the house has the lead. Many have come and gone from this place in the country, some far more quickly than others. It has acquired quite the reputation over the years, legitimately so. Some have departed in reverence. Others have reportedly run for their lives, literally and figuratively. Then there are those who were born, spent their lifetime and died in this fascinating farmhouse, some of whom never left it at all. What happens in this house is infinitely more significant than to whom it happens; the essential truth of the story.

The Perron family requested this tale of darkness and light be honestly told. It contains no embellishment; merely a modicum of literary license regarding dialogue, though some is quite precise. Their intention is not to entertain but rather to inform. The writer humbly respects their request yet as daughter and sister, as one of seven dwelling in the shadow of death during an illuminating decade of life, it is a given. This story is something sacred. Amen.

"It's not the answer that enlightens, but the question."
Eugene Ionesco

A PROPER INTRODUCTION

"You are whatever a moon has always meant,
and whatever a sun will always sing is you."
e. e. cummings

During those final desperate moments of her life, was she frightened by her own intentions or steadfast in her resolve? How could the woman of such an advanced age climb a rickety ladder to the hayloft of the barn then reach over to a beam from which to suspend the rope? Had life become so intolerable to a beleaguered old soul, the drastic measure appeared to be her only option for retreat? Perhaps she'd been ill and had suffered too long in her own wrinkled skin. What measure of pain prompts the notion to deliberately end a precious life? Had she carried her woes up that ladder or had she made peace with the concept and her creator? Did she believe the decision was her own privileged one to make, or did this woman suspect she risked punishment from the God who reserves such judgments as His own, unforgiving of those who take this matter into mortal hands? Only one thing is known for certain; far more than a century ago Mrs. John Arnold decided to claim her life at the age of ninety-three and was discovered, cold and gray, as stiff as the wood from which she was found dangling in the rafters of a barn. Now, suspended in the ether just as surely as she was detected hanging at the unraveling end of a makeshift noose, her immortality lives on as the stuff of legend and folklore; a mystery from the ages...for the ages. She may well have considered it her only escape and yet, truth be told, there was no escape for her wounded spirit. Whether as an act of eternal damnation for an ill-conceived exit from a mortal existence, or as the dire consequence of the premature departure, her spirit lingers still, remaining in her old home place in the country; a farmhouse where she once lived out her days then died by her own hand. May Almighty God have mercy on her immortal soul.

This woman is not alone. There are others, many others who share her fate; what some might describe as a fate worse than death. Perhaps she is the one who tucked the girls in at night, the one who'd loved them well and tenderly kissed their foreheads and smelled of flowers and fruit. It was a presence of comfort and caring; one who never meant to frighten or disturb youngsters in their own beds. Instead, she was a light in the darkness of night; someone to watch over them. It was this holy presence which tempered their fear. In the framework of an inexplicable existence for a family dwelling in a house alive with death, it was a welcome presence, a protective influence in an otherwise scary place. She was not the only one. Johnny Arnold, presumably a relative, made the same critical decision to take his own life in the eaves of the house where he remains. As gentle a spirit as this elderly woman was, he too made his presence known. He was an omnipresent spirit, from the day they arrived at the farm, there to greet them in the dark shadows of a doorway, one cast as the figment from another dimension. Leaning back into his perpetual pose, watching, no doubt wondering about a sudden changing of the guard, he too would soon become a familiar part of the new landscape. And then there was Bathsheba...a God-forsaken soul.

Consider this a proper introduction to but a few of the many who still dwell among the living in a house revealing as many secrets. It took some time for the seven mortals involved, decades to realize, ultimately, they were glad to meet them. What they learned was worth it, though it cannot be simply stated as *in the final analysis* because *this* subject will *be* subject to analysis for the rest of their natural born lives. A lone fear remaining among them now is the potential for an unwelcomed postmortem return to the house they abandoned so long ago as each will eventually, inevitably, enter the realm of supernatural life at the threshold of death's door: a fear of being drawn *home* again, there to resolve the questions left unanswered during a mortal existence; a dreaded possibility. Best to reconcile spirit matters in life than to face them in death; or risk becoming one of the restless spirits of a house drawing souls back to a place in the country, as it had done in life, perhaps with purpose and reason.

"Nothing in the entire universe ever perishes, believe me, but things vary, and adopt a new form. The phrase 'being born' is used for beginning to be something different from what one was before, while 'dying' means ceasing to be the same. Though this thing may pass into that, and that into this, yet the sums of things remain unchanged."
Ovid
Metamorphoses

I.

A PLACE IN THE COUNTRY

"And out of the ground made the Lord God to grow every tree that is pleasant to the sight, and good for food; the tree of life also in the midst of the garden, and the tree of knowledge of good and evil."
Genesis 2:9

So it began. Long before Carolyn Perron ever considered picking up that newspaper at the corner market, the wise, infinite Universe began conspiring with elements on Earth to provide an extraordinary pathway for her family. Perhaps it was fate or their destiny. Whatever it was, powerful forces beyond mortal imagination intervened on behalf of those who sought respite from an intense and chaotic existence. During the summer of 1970 cosmic confluence occurred in the firmament; their journey commenced.
Lo! And Behold.

***

Carolyn was at once thrilled and overwhelmed to have all of her children at home again. It was a breezy balmy end of June, a later than usual dismissal due to an inordinately high number of *snow days* spent at home the previous winter. Finally, school was out for the season. Instead of having only one to watch, there were suddenly five. All of them arrived together, report cards in hand, waving like flags in the wind. Bedlam: Each young lady wanted to be the first in line with a piece of paper certain to solicit praise from her mother. Andrea was at the head of the line. As the eldest, an expectation of deference came with the territory; a claim staked. Nancy stepped forward, followed by Christine; Cynthia presumed to be the last. April was the baby, still at home, watching as her sisters begged for the same type of attention she received all day, every day. With a usual thoughtful and kind consideration of each child, Carolyn perused their grades, acknowledging her girls for any efforts made. Education had become a friendly competition in the family, due primarily to a positive emphasis placed upon it. As Carolyn was well aware, the children worked diligently merely to please their parents. In those days there was no such thing as an allowance, at least not in their household. Encouragement and approval meant everything; their greatest reward. The rest of the payoff would have to wait until later in the evening when their father arrived home. His acknowledgements were always more subdued and understated, always a critical mention of room for improvement, though meaningful nonetheless.

As years passed, a young mother noticed summer vacation becoming a less daunting task as her eldest daughter assumed more responsibility, though it remained a fulltime job. The planning of activities became less of a necessity as the girls grew and began to effectively amuse themselves. A mother could relax and enjoy her children. Less a caretaker and more a playmate, she took great pleasure in the company. Within a few days, a good start to the season, what began as a perfectly fine summer holiday was transformed into a mean season of high anxiety and immeasurable pain.

Roger and Carolyn Perron purchased their house in the suburbs in 1964. It was an adequate, modest "Cape Cod" style house with a generous back yard. They had made the deliberate choice based on the quality of the schools their children would attend. Cumberland, Rhode Island held promise as a peaceful and quiet community in which to raise a family. During the summer of 1970 the changing society around them began encroaching, imposing itself upon their idyllic existence. As a result, a childhood innocence was lost, a sense of security was sadly forsaken and everything was about to change.

Within their first few days of school vacation a traumatic loss struck the whole family. A year or so earlier the children had been gifted with a puppy. She was the sweetest, most magnificent creature they had ever known, a rare and exceptional specimen of canine. Her breed was African Basenji. Carolyn was as delighted by her arrival and told her children that such an unusual dog deserved an equally unusual name. After a thoughtful moment she suggested a unique one, apparently coming from the ether. Though it was an unfamiliar name they all liked the sound of it and it stuck: Bathsheba.

The eldest child, Andrea had fallen so in love with the creature, she hardly went anywhere without her. Though the dog had been intended as a gift for all, Andrea felt a special bond with their pet. One afternoon Andrea asked her mom if she could take Bathsheba for a walk. Only ten years old at the time, Andrea had already displayed maturity beyond her years. Carolyn had no qualms about the request. Sisters suddenly popped out of nowhere and the walk became a group activity. Andrea held onto the leash as her siblings followed. They traveled up Mohawk Street to Diamond Hill Road. Without warning, a car loaded with teenagers drove by at approximately the speed of light. The crew must have been cheerleaders because they were shouting out something in unison while shaking brightly-colored tassels from their open windows. Bathsheba was an obedient dog but the tassels caught her eye and, in an instant, she bolted across the road to chase after the car. Andrea began screaming out loud in panic, calling the dog back; a tragic mistake. Standing safely on the sidewalk at the other side of the road, Bathsheba immediately obeyed a command. The elderly couple that hit her never even saw the dog. Her leash got wrapped around a wheel well and the damage to her skull was so extensive, there was no question...no saving her. A passerby drove to the police station about a block away and within minutes a police officer was on the scene. He yelled at the girls to return home and as they ran back toward the house they heard the gunshots, two of them, enough to mercifully finish the dreadful deed. Hysterical, all the girls ran to their mother who soon began sobbing with them; not only was she grief-stricken by the loss, she knew Bathsheba had suffered...and her girls had suffered the sight of it.

The entire family caved in; succumbing to a deep despair which had, at its core, their unspoken pain. The silence on the subject was almost unbearable. Though it slowly passed for the others, Andrea withdrew into a kind of grief reserved only for a guilty conscience. Believing she alone was responsible for an unspeakable loss, no one, not even mom could convince her otherwise. Sadness consumed her. Andrea stopped playing outside, barely interacting with her siblings. Carolyn became very concerned; doing her best to distract her eldest daughter, giving time itself the time to do what it does best. Heal. Meanwhile, during the first few weeks of July, a series of events transpired which would cumulatively become the catalyst for an abrupt and a unilateral decision made by an anxious mother on behalf of her children.

There were many adolescent boys in the neighborhood. That summer they formed a pack. Wild dogs had nothing on them! Evil does exist in the world. As individuals they all seemed to be acceptable but, as a group, they became the personification of what is ugly and mean-spirited in society. Classmates became hoodlums. A number of these boys were familiar to the Perron girls and some of them were considered friends, including the boys who lived next door. As incidents began occurring, no one ever suspected the problem child, the leader of the pack, was lurking so close to home; a wolf in the woods.

A list of minor and major infractions included a number of petty thefts then the gangland assault on their schoolyard playground; from vicious pranks to more threatening encounters with rumors of weapons involved. For the most part bad boys were fighting amongst themselves resulting in a series of black eyes and fat lips. When they began aggressively targeting several girls in the neighborhood, Carolyn disdainfully announced they were toxic; testosterone poisoned. A vigilant mother forewarning her own away from all of them, on the day she was informed of an attempted sexual assault on a young girl who had been gagged, bound to playground equipment at their elementary school, they instantly lost their freedom. Once relegated to the back yard the children began wondering what was going on around them in a place where they once felt so safe. Not one considered they might be the next victims of the sinister souls doing the devil's footwork.

A family vacation had been planned well in advance. Everyone was excited by the prospects of a big field trip. It meant restaurants and swimming pools at motels. It meant shopping for bathing suits and ice cream cones at roadside stands. For all six gals, it meant quality time spent with the man of the house. Most importantly for Carolyn, it also represented a necessary distraction. She enlisted Andrea to assist her with their many preparations. As packing began, Carolyn made arrangements with her mother-in-law for the care of the house and what cherished pets remained. There were four kitties: two very loud but lovely Siamese and two strays which found their way into heart and home.

It was late afternoon when the family returned from what was a thoroughly enjoyable, relaxing trip together. It had only been a few days away, yet the healing effects were remarkable. The Perrons had been restored to a one-big-happy-family status. Andrea started smiling again. When they pulled into the driveway Roger immediately noticed that the door to the sun porch was wide open. His mother had been watching over their house and he assumed when she last came, had forgotten to close or lock it. Then Carolyn saw something lying limp on the picnic table. By the time she could intervene, Andrea was already out of their car, running to greet her normally frisky kitty, Scrunch. Andrea called her by name. There was no response. No movement. The child could not believe her eyes; the gruesome discovery dropped her to the knees. Her precious cat had been brutally killed...murdered. Her skull was crushed; every bone in her body, shattered. It is unnecessary to describe what ensued. Carolyn comforted her while Roger removed the stiffened carcass. He then entered their house to find that it had been thoroughly ransacked; food from the kitchen cupboards poured all over the floor, their furniture overturned, mirrors shattered. A freezer full of food was open, provisions saturated with motor oil. All the cats were missing. With a frantic phone call Roger learned that his mother had been there only a few hours before their arrival and had indeed locked the house. She left their Siamese cats inside and let the other two out to play, as the weather was fine and her son was expected home later in the day. As Roger searched their house, utter despair turned into wild rage. The freezer in the basement, fully stocked with meats, was destroyed beyond repair. Nothing could be salvaged. He peered inside at all the food intended to feed his family, trembling with justifiable anger. The police were there for hours, surveying and documenting extensive damage done; a loss sustained. Their normally rambunctious neighborhood fell eerily silent; a conspicuous absence of movement and sound from the three boys who occupied the house next door. One peered reflectively out his bedroom window.

Carolyn later found Juliet, mother of Scrunch, hiding beneath thick shrubs. The cat had been brutalized but apparently escaped her captors; surviving the ordeal she'd obviously endured. Both Siamese cats were gone. Within a few days a tortured soul arrived at their door. A boy from the next street over had witnessed, if not participated in this horrific attack. With tears in his eyes as the tremendous burden of some unspoken guilt weighed too heavily for the youngster to bear, a conscience dictated this confession. He told Mrs. Perron what had happened and who did it. Apparently it was a twelve-year-old boy who lived next door. He had planned the scheme then initiated the break-in, and when he and his thug buddies were finished destroying their house, they held Scrunch down inside a pothole in the road then beat her to death with a baseball bat. Juliet fought back and finally escaped. One of their cohorts stole then sold the Siamese cats to an unscrupulous woman who never bothered to ask any questions. Carolyn called the police. They went directly to the house and confronted the mother of this boy. She denied everything; lying to cover for her mini-criminal. The officers seemed unwilling to pursue the matter any further then discouraged Carolyn from acting on her own, but she refused to let this rest in peace. She later went back to their house, against the advice of law enforcement, speaking firmly with a woman hell bent on protecting her own. The terse conversation deteriorated into argument and accusation as the responsible party emerged from his bedroom; both arms visibly scarred with scratches, evidence of a cat fighting for her life. His mother instantly ordered him back into his room, wedging her bulbous body between the door frame to block the view but Carolyn was convinced of his guilt; there was as much metaphorical blood on his hands as residual scars on his serrated arms. The next day she and Roger went to the Cumberland Police Department, there to file charges against that juvenile delinquent; an assault addressed as animal cruelty. In spite of the ample evidence these assailants remained on the loose. ***Breaking and entering; Destruction of property***: Demon seeds. Andrea was unwilling to wait for the court or an act of divine retribution. Distraught, she began quietly plotting a vigilante attack on someone who deserved the full weight of her ungodly wrath; a lesson in smiting she learned the hard way.

Andrea had not yet really recovered from the tragic death of her beautiful Bathsheba when a sadistic execution of her precious cat occurred. These two traumatic events prompted a metamorphosis in the child, one nobody would have ever expected or predicted, effectively transforming her from a demure little girl into someone angry, vengeful; she suddenly became as evil as those who had committed a heinous crime. Carolyn had divulged the identity of the culprits as she explained to her girls that they must not have anything to do with those boys anymore. Andrea blatantly defied mother's order, devising a plan of her own when she knew who was responsible. She couldn't get to all of them at once, but truly believed she should punish the leader of the pack. Enlisting the assistance of friends sworn to secrecy she used the telephone to track the whereabouts of her intended victim. It took three days to carry out her plan as she stalked him throughout a neighborhood; poised, knowing the moment opportunity presented she would confront the criminal, causing him to suffer as much as her cat did for the duration of her torturous death. When she located him near the corner of Mohawk Street and Diamond Hill Road, unaccompanied by his bodyguard brother she pounced in a way which would have made her feline proud. Though both youngsters were roughly the same age and size, his was no match for her intensity in the revenge-driven assault. Then there was the infamous element of surprise. He never saw it coming.

Not once in her life had Andrea displayed any type of violent behavior, yet there she was, on the side of the road, beating this culprit bloody. Though her physical strength was equivalent to his, an emotional outburst was something supernatural. Adrenaline coupled with pure, unadulterated hatred: dangerous in combination; a lesson the recipient of her self-righteous rage soon learned. She broke his nose, punching him repeatedly. Once his eyes sealed shut she throttled his scrawny neck, muffling his pleas for help then took aim at every vulnerable part of his body; ribs to groin. After several minutes of relentless, inexhaustible brutality, no mercy bestowed, the witness to this vicious attack came to his rescue, pulling the girl from her prey. "Go! Home!" Reluctantly, she did as he ordered. It was over. Andrea failed: her evil intention had been to commit *justifiable* homicide; planting the demon seed six feet under.

7

The police officer was sympathetic. He had no choice except to file another report. Roger had to handle this problem. Whatever he said on her behalf in a courtroom was sufficient to fully explain and likewise excuse her behavior. Though the charges were dropped, much animosity remained. No longer the quiet and placid neighborhood in which to raise her family, Carolyn began to press her husband about relocation. It was her fervent hope, in fact, adamant intention to remove her children from the negative and unstable environment. She became watchful, distressed by what was happening to her eldest, a child transforming…increasingly sullen and withdrawn. She knew the only way to mitigate an adverse impact on all the girls was to extricate them from such an increasingly volatile place. Their anxious mother decided and then *insisted* her children be raised surrounded by wild Nature instead of wild criminals. She wanted them to have a place in the country.

Roger did his best to placate his wife. He knew they were in no position to afford the expense of moving at the moment. There was hardly any equity in their current home. Likewise, he realized an agitated demeanor complicated matters; disturbing what peace lingered amidst turmoil. Timing is everything in life; though he regretted having to do so, especially considering the events occurring all around them, Roger announced his plan to leave on business for several days, effectively abandoning his spouse to deal with the dilemma: an emergence of a theme. Stress spiked. The man had no choice. He had clients waiting, appointments pending. An astral convergence began as a Universal plan began spinning in perpetual motion, stirring up the cosmos. Change was inevitable; the only constant. There'd be no predicting what was to come.

It was early in the morning on the day of his departure. While Roger and Carolyn stood in the kitchen sharing a cup of coffee, an explosion rumbled through their front yard. It sounded like cannon shot; echoing throughout the community. Alarmed, they raced outside. Carolyn had created a rock garden near the entrance of their driveway soon after they purchased their humble home. Friends often teased her about it, reminding her that the centerpiece resembled a tombstone. They were right. It accidentally did. The only thing missing from the gigantic ice-aged edifice was a deeply chiseled inscription denoting the name of someone using the natural relic as a final resting place.

The man residing below them climbed into his truck that chilly morning. He cranked the engine, had a massive heart attack and died behind the wheel; his lifeless foot collapsing onto the gas pedal. The truck raced up the narrow lane, stopping only when it lodged upon the massive stone; wheels spinning. Roger scrambled to his aid while Carolyn called for help. Mister Curtis was already deceased; nothing Roger attempted would revive him. As neighbors poured into the road, the adversarial mother next door shouted vile remarks toward Carolyn about the *graveyard* on her lawn. Once the police arrived she waddled back inside her house. After the ambulance left with the body, only then did Carolyn break down, spilling tears of grief. Still shaken, Roger had to leave but she wanted him to cancel the trip. The sudden death upset him as much as it had his wife. They exchanged few terse words before he departed. Stress was taking its measure of the man...and the woman.

Carolyn expended a great deal of energy attempting to suppress her grief, a strain causing her to tremble while she prepared a cake for the Curtis family. Bringing it over to their house in the afternoon, she was promptly rejected, dismissed at the door. Returning home, still carrying the cake she'd baked in the worst heat of summer, Carolyn knew it was time to go. Later confiding in her friend Cathi, she explained: Mrs. Curtis actually blamed *her* for the tragic death of her husband; the woman blatantly accused Carolyn of being a witch. That was it. Enough. No more.

When Roger came home, she explained what had happened in his absence. She sat him down at the table. Expressing her heartfelt sentiments about the death of their neighbor as well as legitimate concerns she had for the safety of their children, his wife begged him to reconsider selling the house to leave its whole community behind. Recounting a series of unfortunate events, what became the basis of her conclusion, he agreed; these were serious problems. He empathetically reiterated: they were in NO position financially to make a move, certainly not a sudden one. Carolyn was fixated on getting her girls to a place in the country. The couple spent well over an hour discussing limited options. When they went to bed it was with a mutual understanding; it would take some time to transform this dream into reality. There was no obvious or immediate remedy available. According to Roger, there's no point dwelling on what they could not change. Carolyn acquiesced. She did not mention her distress again. Within the next few days he would leave town on yet another business trip; one which kept him away just long enough for the Universe to intervene on their behalf. A cautionary tale: Be careful what you wish for...

***

While waiting outside enormous doors, examining the impressive façade of **Mount Saint Charles Academy** Carolyn suddenly remembered that she had neglected to bring something to read. Rarely taking Andrea to music lessons, the child usually traveled with a friend who also studied flute. It was only an hour but, in the heat of June in Woonsocket, it was becoming a stifling wait. Seeking a shadier spot, she noticed a newsstand in front of the corner market. There, Carolyn purchased a copy of **The Woonsocket Call**. Having enough time left to scan a few of its pages, she tucked it beneath an arm, crossing the road to meet her daughter as the budding musician popped out from behind one of the massive, ornately carved wooden doors, seeking her mother on the crowded city street.

When they arrived home, the newspaper was temporarily discarded; tossed into a corner of the kitchen counter: Time to make the dinner. Revisiting the newspaper later that evening, once the children had gone off to bed, Carolyn spread it wide on the table then settled back in a chair; it was such a luxury to relax with a newspaper. Nursing a lukewarm cup of coffee, the woman read page after page with nothing on her mind except whatever her eyes fell on at any given moment; she had no ulterior motives or hidden agenda. Arriving in the classifieds, she paused. Only then did the idea occur to her: "No harm in looking." So she did. Knowing precisely what she was looking for, locating a ***"Land and Farms for Sale"*** column, Carolyn began the search, reading one little box at a time. **The Woonsocket Call** was a comprehensive newspaper, covering all of Northern Rhode Island, including rural or remote areas of the state. Though there was substantial acreage for sale she found nothing which included a suitable house for their family. Her eyes continued wandering the column. There it was: the pipe dream. **"9 room colonial farmhouse w/ barn + 200 acres Harrisville $75,000."** It was well past 9:00 p.m. when she spied the advertisement. In spite of the hour, Carolyn called the realtor then made an appointment to view this property the following day. That night she went to bed then laid there, alone in the darkness, unable to sleep; disturbed by the persistent, nagging regret at having made the call at all. What was the point? Roger had been quite clear on this topic. There was no extra money; no hope of moving anytime soon. Carolyn struggled with the idea. In one moment she felt selfish; altruistic in the next. It was for her children that she so longed for a place in the country. As the listing agent, Mrs. Hertzog had been gracious; understanding about the late hour of the call. Carolyn felt fraudulent; tacitly misrepresenting their situation with total silence on the subject; a covert and deliberate sin of omission. During their extended conversation she failed to disclose the fact there was no *Earthly* way they could afford to buy property, yet she made an appointment to view it anyway. Compelled to do so, swept up by the notion of a home place in the woods, the enticements of it evoked intense emotions, over-riding an otherwise formidable conscience. Slipping into the dream, a final conscious thought occurred: "It couldn't hurt to look."

Up and on the phone at first light, Carolyn called upon her closest friend. Cathi was there within the hour. Lingering over their coffee at the corner of the kitchen, the women whispered their conversation as girls mulled around, anxious for some undivided attention. Neither of them wanted to arouse any suspicion regarding a sudden excursion; likely nothing more than diversion: an adventure. Cathi encouraged Carolyn to go and have a good time house-hunting; certain it was pure folly which would culminate in little more than a few welcome and well-deserved hours away from their house. The girls were all more than willing to remain behind with the favorite friend, never asking where mom was going. A chance to be with Cathi meant playtime: **Weebles**!

As a lark, perhaps a lapse in judgment; Carolyn considered her behavior as she drove along, chastising herself repeatedly. It felt like an especially long ride which meant it would probably be the same for Mrs. Hertzog. When she finally met the woman at her real estate office in Harmony, she was, at once, ashamed yet excited by the prospect of seeing a grand old estate up for sale. It would prove to be an historical journey; a whimsical passage through time and space: the ultimate of magical mystery tours. All reticence was about to subside; inner conflict, pangs of conscience about to come to an abrupt end.

Mrs. Hertzog was kind; very generous with her time. Inviting Carolyn into her car, they drove many miles of winding country roads, dodging neglected potholes along the picturesque route. Entering the village of Harrisville from the south, the realtor did a great job pointing out various landmarks: schools, library, theater, town hall and churches. The lush landscape was remarkably uninhabited. There was ample space between its homes; land even within the village proper. *This* was it; the place Carolyn had searched for in mind.

~ The Assembly Theater ~ Harrisville, R.I. ~

Passing beyond the quaint little town, heading north onto Round Top Road, Carolyn became breathless with pure anticipation, longing to view what Mrs. Hertzog had been so busy describing as they traveled their rural route. It was more than magnificent...it was everything she had dared envision in dreams; pastoral pleasure beyond mortal imagination. The farm defied all description: Technicolor in comparison to black and white... Dorothy stepping through an open door, over the beckoning threshold... upon entering the Land of Oz.

Rounding the final corner, Carolyn first saw the barn, then three enormous evergreen trees lining the front yard of the farmhouse set back a considerable distance from the road. As they pulled into its earthen circular driveway, Mr. Kenyon emerged from the house, waiting patiently on the porch to receive his guests. This elderly gentleman: as gracious a host as the realtor. He escorted his company around the property, through the barn, then into the house. She was enchanted. Mr. Kenyon told her what he knew of the history of this old estate. As she admired the lone apple tree, he then explained the Hurricane of 1938 claimed thirteen others from the grounds. He suggested the only reason the barn survived that horrendous storm when so many others did not fare as well was because centuries before, it had been painstakingly constructed by a master shipwright; its solid oak center beams deliberately arched to sway in the wind. Entering the farmhouse, Carolyn instantly noticed how cool it felt in the worst heat of day. Together they strolled from room to room. It seemed gigantic compared with a humble home in the suburbs. Wide-planked floors creaked beneath their feet; hinges on each door seemed to sing a unique tune. She was intrigued by its ancient fixtures; wrought iron latches at every twist and turn; cubbyholes in every corner. So many aspects of it were authentic to the centuries old structure. Carolyn was amazed by the living museum.

Though Mr. Kenyon knew little about the earliest history of the house or its inhabitants, he did tell Carolyn the estate was one of the original **Providence Plantations**; the property deeded in 1680, house completed in 1736. It was a veritable journey through time. She drank it in like sweetest nectar, savoring every sip as if it would be her last. Apparently it was a love potion, working wonders on a dispirited soul thirsting for unbridled beauty, seeking space far from the madding crowd. *This* was the place; her elusive vision of a country home. It beckoned her as siren song does a sailor, disguised as a clarion call. She was swept away...utterly overcome by her own heart's desire.

Walking them over to their car, Mr. Kenyon extended his hand to Carolyn, holding hers gently within his own as he spoke: "This is a wonderful place to raise a family." A singular statement, delivered with sincerity, convinced the young mother her intuition was trustworthy. He departed for the farmhouse. Mrs. Hertzog silently studied Carolyn's facial expression. Reaching into her handbag, retrieving the checkbook tucked discreetly between the leather and a ragged tear in its tattered satin lining, the woman met her realtor's gaze.

"My husband is out of town. How much would it take to hold this place?" Carolyn presented a delighted real estate agent with a check for five hundred dollars, earnest money to seal the deal, effectively emptying a bank account. A single impetuous act secured the farm for her family. Likewise, it all but assured certain conflict would erupt when her husband arrived home. It was worth risking Roger's wrath. Looking back toward the house, she spied Mr. Kenyon pacing the porch, hoping to overhear some good news, no doubt. He raised his hand, holding it in place until she returned the gesture. He knew. Roger would soon breathe the sweetest air and drink the purest water. He too would sip the irresistible nectar and would, in time, ultimately succumb to a potent hypnotic spell cast by the natural beauty of this mysterious, magical place in the country. She need only convince him to come take the tour.

***

A long drive home seemed brief by comparison with an initial journey into deep, dark woods. Carolyn floated euphorically through their front door then grabbed Cathi, embracing her tightly. Shocked by this outburst, she realized what it meant. Oh, my God! What had she done? It was obvious; her dearest friend, the woman who could not even afford to *pay* the babysitter, had done something supremely impulsive. Her suspicions were instantly confirmed.

"I bought it!" Wild-eyed with excitement, she screamed out the news with a whisper the girls could not possibly hear...it was a secret.

"You bought *what*?!"

"The farm!" Carolyn's enthusiasm was almost contagious. Almost.

"With **what**!" Cathi's incredulous expression said the words well before her lips could form or utter them aloud. "You *bought the farm...or you will!* when your husband gets home! You, my dear will *pay* for this!" Her sardonic sense of humor was lost on Carolyn that hot afternoon. Instead, she chose to take these phrases literally, ignoring the intended intimation.

"I put money down on the place."

"How much?" Cathi felt her stomach twist...*knot* such a good sensation.

"Five hundred. Earnest money: a good faith payment to hold the property."

"Five hundred...*dollars*!"

"All we had...well, not *all*; there's enough left to buy milk and bread!"

"Oh, my God..." Cathi's voice seeped out of Carolyn's consciousness. It seemed to trail off into the distance as the ecstatic woman allowed herself the freedom to project into the future, to imagine her family in such a remarkable place. Cathi jolted her back to reality. "Listen to me!" Still somewhere else, lost on a fine piece of property in Harrisville...Cathi persisted. "Carolyn!"

"What! I know...I know...he'll love it! We'll find a way...we will!"

"You *hope* so." To which Carolyn promptly responded, "I *know* so."

The children were all playing outside. Carolyn decided not to say anything yet. Cathi concurred, suggesting she return in a few days to take them all out for ice cream after Roger's arrival home; aware Carolyn would require some private time to discuss this matter with her husband. They concocted a plan. She would call Cathi to come get the girls as soon as he pulled into the yard. While watching kids taking turns on the swing set, staring through dozens of prisms provided by rays of sunlight intersecting water spots splattered on the kitchen window, Carolyn described in full detail where she'd gone and what she had seen on that fateful summer day. Pure delight sparkled in bright eyes; the incredible Lightness of being Carolyn. A broad smile had graced her lips while speaking of its endless walls constructed of stone, rooms which echoed with a whisper; an apple tree gnarled by age and Nature's relentless assaults. Enraptured, the woman seemed all but transported back to the place she had just returned from; a magical, mysterious place on Earth where a barn could survive a ferocious storm by dancing with the wind.

It was love. Carolyn had fallen deeply in love. It is said that love is blind.

Cathi left the house that evening repeating a promise to return after Roger's scheduled arrival. She was as torn as Carolyn had been prior to writing the check. It was a leap of faith, to be sure, but also a serious lapse in judgment. Her downright sensible friend made a unilateral decision which was going to affect her entire family. It was at best, disrespectful of Roger and his position on the matter. At worst, it meant a loss the family could not afford to sustain. Five hundred dollars: a great deal of money; their hedge against a disaster. It became, with the drafting of the single check, the potential root of another; a foundation for upheaval. Cathi had reason to be worried. She traveled along considering the leap and lapse of it all. The impetuous act, so out of character for the mother who would do anything to protect and defend her family, may have placed them all in jeopardy. She likewise considered this was precisely what her friend was attempting to do; protect her young with an effort made to remove them from the place she believed to be unsafe. Carolyn had done something radical. In time and space perhaps it would prove to be as brilliant as any gathering cluster of stars in the firmament. Time would tell the tale.

"I believe in God, only I spell it Nature."
Frank Lloyd Wright

let there be light

"Hope, like the gleaming taper's light, / Adorns and cheers our way; / And still, as darker grows the night, / Emits a brighter ray."
Oliver Goldsmith

Roger was not a bit pleased; his grimace as proof. Neither was he intrigued by his wife's vivid descriptions of this property; his main concern revolving around devising a means of retrieving a check. Carolyn remained unscathed by his objections, her position firmly held: steadfast...resolute, insisting this place was the real estate deal of a lifetime. Roger was purely a businessman. If his wife could convince him of its worth, the intrinsic value of this estate, he might become far more amenable to an otherwise outrageous proposition. Persistently on point, entirely unyielding, her husband relented. He agreed to a tour, though he made no promises during their tenuous negotiations.

A discussion not yet concluded, Roger pressed Carolyn on the issue of her unilateral decision, one made without regard; without his knowledge, opinion or consent. She did not plead her case nor apologize, however she refrained from reminding him of numerous times he'd done the same, expecting her to understand his motivations. What she had done was provocative enough; no need to be defensive. Carolyn simply stated, when she saw the ad it sparked her curiosity so she acted immediately, never imagining one call would result in what she had discovered; something rare and exceptional. His wife made it clear, despite objections, she was determined to begin the process of finding a more suitable home for the children; reassuring him she was as shocked as he was when that search met its end with one single viewing on a single day. There wasn't any way to reach him out on the road and he did not dare refute the claim, having neglected to call home during the trip. Once she'd seen the farm, unwilling to risk losing it to a delay or indecision, she acted; what she considered to be her responsibility: do the right thing on behalf of her family. The funds in their joint bank account were just as much hers as his, as far as she was concerned. In

ANDREA PERRON

his noted absence, as his equal partner in a marriage, permission should be implicit; not required. She did what she did for all of them. This he seemed to understand.

Many months would pass before Mrs. Hertzog could finally reveal the truth of their situation. Carolyn's call had been the one and *only* inquiry she'd ever received on the listing. It had come on the first day the farm was advertised. Nobody else seemed to want a place in the country. It was as if the Universe had reserved it for her. There had been no risk of losing the farm; none at all.

The next morning everyone piled into the family car, a Bonneville with no room to spare once all were present and accounted for; off they went for a ride. Carolyn had deliberately tempered an enthusiasm, never divulging their destination. When they arrived at the farm, Mr. Kenyon was working beside the barn. Carolyn then noticed his height for the first time, towering over her husband as they shook hands. He was a thin, lanky man with deep grooves etched into his face, as pronounced as the ruts in an old wagon road they had walked together a few days before. His watery, pale blue eyes seemed to smile. Delighted by their arrival, Mr. Kenyon warmly welcomed his guests, even though no formal appointment had been made through the realtor. He knew precisely why they had come and could not have been more pleased with the company he kept on a day he thought was destined for solitude.

Instinctively focusing all his attention on Roger, the gentleman realized the significance of this man's presence and the necessity to impress him. Carolyn appreciated an effort being made for her husband, though he'd taken time to interact with the ladies, too. Excusing himself for a moment, he slipped into the house, returning with pockets full of candy. Generously dispersing these sweets, Mr. Kenyon was quite enchanted with their children. Complimenting good manners, he'd included the parents for the job well done. Then without any parental consent requested, suggesting children need freedom, Mr. Kenyon made his own unilateral decision. Releasing the girls to their greatest good, providing unfettered access to his property, he suddenly said: "Go and play!" As explorers in uncharted territory, they all bolted...no compass required; no directions given or necessary. They could *feel* their way around, by instinct.

Carolyn was mortified. She knew a wild child lurked in the heart of each of these urchins. A glance instructed her eldest to maintain a head count at all times. It was understood but it was also impossible. Carolyn reminded all of them to remain within the confines of the yard, inside stone walls, but it was more than six acres of land. Andrea did her best for the first few minutes but such freedom is enticing to youngsters; they scattered like thieves in a crowd of tourists. The polite little girls instantly transformed into raucous banshees. Before long they were swinging from the rafters of a barn, scaling the apple tree, climbing up into the loft of a woodshed and pretending stone walls were balance beams built exclusively for their amusement. Unleashed into such an unfamiliar setting, the girls seemed so agile and able to navigate it with ease. It was strangely familiar to them. As for Andrea the scenario quickly evolved into chaos; quite beyond her ability to control this beautiful but foreign land or those making mischief in it. She chose instead to join her siblings in folly.

As Mr. Kenyon stood beside the young couple, on the hill overlooking the opulent grounds a subtle yet discernible pride snuck in, tucking itself into the corners of his wry little grin. He was so pleased; certain he'd found the right family for this old house. Carolyn gently nudged her husband, prompting his notice of the perfect garden spot. The adults listened as sounds of laughter, a distant music, wafted throughout the valley; a joyful noise evoking echoes of their past. Revisiting their childhoods during those moments, each listened in reverence. His contemplative expression, one of placid repose, betrayed Mr. Kenyon's journey through memories which lingered with him for a lifetime. Back he went to a simpler life: back-in-time travel.

Cordial, eager to entice his prospective buyers, Mr. Kenyon asked Roger if he and Carolyn would enjoy a walk down to the river. They quickly accepted the invitation. Pressed for time, Carolyn had not gone during her initial visit, though Mr. Kenyon had graciously offered to take her there. As if what they had already seen wasn't paradise enough, a soft-spoken gentleman promised his welcomed guests a virtual oasis, respite from sultry summer heat, some shade from a brutal Sun only a few hundred yards away. A whistle from dad called the clan. They all knew a clarion call to assemble the troops and from which direction the familiar signal had come. Fall in! Roger took the plunge.

It was a lovely stroll down to the Nipmuc River. There had been abundant rainfall that year, producing the thick, bountiful grass which cushioned every step of the lush lawn sprawled along three gently sloping tiers. Roger paused on top of its second plateau, turning to reexamine the place from a different perspective. He marveled at the stone walls enclosing the "yard" prompting a comment on the incredible amount of work it must have required... countless hours of hard labor to create those granite edifices. Nearing the bottom of the hill he noticed several stones had been removed, providing a narrow pathway as easy-access to a wagon road leading them onward to the decayed remains of an archaic wooden bridge: a lovely vision of rustic old New England.

As they walked together the air began changing. If possible, it became even sweeter; an aroma more fragrant than any perfume produced by beds of old stock flowers framing the front yard. Pine straw, as slippery as silk, lined the surface of the road. A dark tunnel formed as the heavily laden limbs hovered overhead in loving embrace; their dense outstretched branches had seemingly grown together over time. Approaching what was described as a *creek* during the height of summer, each step was cooler than the last; each breath became deeper within surrounding woodlands. They began to hear running water still at quite a distance. Even though blossoms had passed, fragile dogwood trees gratefully gathered beneath aged oaks. Humbly accepting a protective cover, slender branches trailed off as delicate tendrils, bowing gracefully toward a forest floor sprinkled with lady slippers. Nature's finest features of a season, wild orchids would surely be difficult to avoid should one venture too far off that beaten path. Roger took Carolyn by the hand. As they walked along the steeply descending road, cautiously slowing their pace, perspective changed. Arriving at river's edge, shadows surrendered to light.

Behold! The creek; lined with majestic maples shedding leaves as large as dinner plates. They paused, awestruck by a spectacle. Roger stood quite still; stunned: a breathtaking scene overwhelming his senses. Mounded mountain laurel kept a silent vigil, draped elegantly over both sides of the river bank. It sprung forth from earthen walls, clinging precariously to the moist black dirt, watching over its meandering stream of crystalline water. Drenched, dripping with delicate blossoms, each bush could have been admiring its own splendid reflection. Roger peered over the edge, gazing into the mirror, examining his own startled expression; the picture of youth in a fountain. All signs of stress had been erased from his features, as if cleansed by the cool, babbling brook traveling beneath him. There he found his future smiling back from its glassy surface. Carolyn was quietly observing her husband. He was doing it; sipping the potent nectar of Nature, like bird from bloom. It was love at first sight.

Through the purest water Roger stared at fish, studying the fluid movement of dozens of rainbow trout; the dancing and prancing in and out of cascading spotlights, shifting with the breeze. The markings on each one appeared to be distinctly its own. Patterns emerged. Perceptible traits, characteristics such as those shared among families were enhanced and magnified by this elemental interplay of water and light; perfection: Simpatico in Nature. Each excursion through beams of sparkling sunshine further revealed their essential nature. It *was* magical; something beyond beautiful: Technicolor rainbow fish gliding through a shallow pool illuminated with rays of divine light from above.

This rippling flow was inhabited by a multitude of creatures. Frogs leapt as snakes slithered, skimmers skimmed while minnows paddled by in its muddy puddles. Crayfish scampered beneath flat rocks protruding from the rugged shoreline. Roger could no longer resist it; this call of a cool pool. He quickly removed his shoes and socks then tightly rolled up the bottom of his trousers. His kids begged to follow. He'd denied their request for a legitimate reason, not wanting mud pies leaking in their car. A father already knew in his heart; his children would spend endless hours in this river. Satisfied with "no" they perched themselves along the bank and watched their daddy play; man of the family transforming into a boy, traversing its steep embankment with the full vigor of youth. Wading through shallows, walking along shoals, he inspected multi-colored stones layering the riverbed, worn smooth over time. After an inspiring few minutes he peered upward to find his wife, poised at the center of a single weather-worn beam, precariously placed across the wide expanse, resting on two giants: slabs of granite, facing off from opposing sides. It was a pitiful excuse for a bridge. Roger would later decide to replace it with a far more substantial version. "You be careful up there." Carolyn was a beautiful woman yet, this day her husband gazed at her with a renewed appreciation of grace. She appeared as an ethereal vision; an angel awash in Heavenly Light.

"Roger. Can you believe this? The Lord works in mysterious ways…"

"…His wonders to behold. I see." He was still staring up from the riverbed.

"Look at the water!" She pointed downward. Illuminating the deepest part of the pool was a perfect circle; white hot spotlight. Craving sudden warmth it provided, trout gravitated to the hot spot like heat-seeking missiles. At first it was a frenzied approach, involving a few awkward intersections. Then they all figured it out. The fish began swimming in tandem within the mobile and temporary perimeter established by the instant infusion of midday sunshine. Their synchronized movements created a whirlpool on the surface. Everyone present was mesmerized. As the beam shifted the crowd dispersed, following the light. Roger actually giggled as he scaled the riverbank. He went directly to Carolyn. Leaning toward an embrace she whispered some poignant words. "It's a wonderful way to spend the day." He wrapped her tightly in his arms.

The children ran ahead as instructed, back up toward the farmhouse, each claiming a portion of its grounds as her private pastoral pathway. The couple thanked their host for an exceptionally generous gift received. Roger finally entered the house. He became instantly distracted; lost in space too ample to absorb it all at once. Mr. Kenyon remained in the kitchen. He sent Roger off to explore, offering him free reign to investigate the place at will. Wandering room to room, the indelible imagery of a riverbed impaled an over-stimulated mind. The father of five lingered here and there, attempting to regain a focus fractured. Effectively house-inspecting, he'd continually reminded himself to remain on alert. A checklist: the heating system, plumbing then wiring; make mental notes; questions to ask. It was his job to determine its adequacy; what the house might lack, what it may need in terms of future improvements and of course, what the fixes would cost. Utilizing all the self-discipline he could muster, denying himself the luxury of wallowing in the sheer spectacle of the house, he forced himself to overcome the temptation to simply admire it, to walk it as one would a museum, merely to celebrate its existence. This home offered an abundance of space in which to raise a big family. There would be time to enjoy it later. In the interim, it was Roger's responsibility to inspect it as thoroughly and objectively as possible; to look at it with different eyes: to observe it with *indifference*…as a pragmatic, ***devil may care*** advocate.

Carolyn gathered her children on the front lawn. Exhausted, they collapsed into a pile to rest. She settled in beside them, taking in the aromas, beckoning the supple blades of grass to stroke her slender fingers. Mr. Kenyon emerged from the house holding a tray with a large pitcher of water and four matching glasses, all he had on hand. The temperature was climbing; humidity equally oppressive: Ah, it was summertime in Rhode Island. With the excitement and adventure, everyone was drenched with perspiration, sporting flushed, ruddy cheeks as proof. The young ladies shared, passing glasses, drinking heartily. Carolyn waited for them to replenish their fluids before helping herself. She was startled by the cold pitcher; almost painful to the touch. Filling a glass to the rim, she placed it up against her lips. Shocked, as if jolted by an electrical charge, eyes widened and brightened in equal measure with the first swallow. Never before in her life had she tasted water so frigid or pure, like something straight from the heart of a glacier: Refreshment!

"Mommy! It hurts my teeth!" April, only five years old, was not normally shy about expressing herself. Garbled words were barely intelligible as she'd stuffed a few warm fingers into her mouth, to ease the pain of the oncoming brain freeze. Wrinkling up her face in a disapproving grimace, she obviously took exception to laughter erupting at what she perceived to be her expense.

Mr. Kenyon smiled at the baby of the family, long blond hair plastered to the sides of sweaty cheeks; sea blue eyes peeking out and up at her mother. The cherub stole his heart. In fact, the family's presence brought a sudden ray of light into the life of a lonely old man who feared the darkness of night. He made himself clear in a moment: they were *always* welcome at his home. Carolyn believed she'd rediscovered a long lost friend. His kindness was so endearing, sincerity so compelling, the instant connection she'd felt with Mr. Kenyon when they first met was coming to fruition; a blossom as fragrant as mountain laurel...as delicate as lady slippers. She recalls it as an inexplicable familiarity, as if it were a well-established friendship with a man who was, in reality, a virtual stranger when they were introduced. Neither seemed to feel the initial reticence associated with such an awkward circumstance. Instead, they'd tacitly accepted the feeling with a knowing silence. The sensation they shared did not require any further acknowledgement.

As she sat there observing a man reveling in laughter, an insidious sadness crept into Carolyn. Diverting her eyes so to avoid anyone's perception of the suddenly languid mood, the woman looked down, studying a glass cradled in her hands. Beads of water resembling tears trickled down the face of the vessel, leaving streaks to mark a journey. Chasing the frost from its surface, droplets paced a solitary dirge, tracing icy paths. The vivid, haunting imagery instantly evoked a memory; a somber reflection, one entirely contrary to her formerly uplifted spirit; the pure elation she was experiencing only moments before. Several lines of poetry, pensive words Carolyn memorized in youth, consumed her mind then began escaping her lips. They listened attentively, familiar with the practice as well as their mother's proclivity for drawing on fine literature during more poignant moments in life. Her tone softened; the reverence in her voice stilled the birdsong and stunned their host. It was as if the garden flowers humbly bowed their blossoms as surrounding stone walls knelt in prayer. Reciting the lines betrayed her melancholy mood:

"And still other brothers and sisters,
Linking their arms together,
Walked down the dusty road where once he ran
And into the deep green valley
To sit on the stony banks of the stream he loved
And let the murmuring waters
Wash over their blood-hot feet with a springing
crown of tears."

Mr. Kenyon leaned back, observing the gentlewoman while she spoke. He was visibly moved by her rendition of the poem with which he was familiar; asking what caused her to recall this particular passage when she'd finished. The children remained respectfully quiet for the duration. They all listened.

"Look." Lifting her glass as delicate droplets mournfully descended, "They resemble human tears." Searching Mr. Kenyon's moistened brow and soulful eyes for acceptance; she found only sadness akin to her own.

"It was beautiful, mom: Joseph Langland." Andrea shared an appreciation.

"She says poems like that to us all the time." Nancy directed her comment toward Mr. Kenyon apologetically; apparently the nine-year-old spitfire felt the necessity to expound. Leaping to her feet, hands propped on skinny hips, she made an impatient plea, a rather terse request of her mother. "Can we go back to play in the barn again?" Her precocious stance demanding an equally terse response, if not another form of covert discipline, Nancy was officially bored and everyone knew it; a hard to *little miss* moment.

"I do not *say* poetry, sweetheart. One *recites* poetry." Infinitely patient, the mother had to be so, especially with her second-born, condemned as she was to a life of trial by spitfire.

"No...you *say* it right out of your head!" This persistent pixie had a point.

Having been a poet since childhood, becoming the mother of five left no time for writing it though she conceded to sharing whatever her memory retained.

"Yes. I suppose I do."

"You do." Several spoke in unison.

The familial interaction completely engaged Mr. Kenyon's imagination. He listened intently to every word uttered by a bevy of ladies at rest on his lawn. It was obviously his pleasure to do so.

"So? Can we *please* go back into the barn now?" It was Nancy again.

"No, we have to go home soon. It's getting late." Carolyn had rendered her verdict. Before Nancy could challenge it again Andrea pulled her sister to the ground, planting the child firmly beside her: Argument over.

Roger joined his family and host on the front lawn, discreetly thanking Mr. Kenyon for allowing him such an extensive tour of this property without the presence of a realtor. Gratefully, he accepted the last glass of water.

"Isn't it great?" Soliciting a response, Carolyn realized Roger could not yet speak for gulping. Nancy followed up on the subject in his hand.

"Mommy said poetry about it." Thus, divulging no particular secret to dad.

"She did, huh? I'm not surprised." Patting his daughter on the head, Roger asked Mr. Kenyon the next logical question: "Where does *this* come from?"

"There's a spring…over there." Pointing with pride at a sharply rising hill on the other side of Round Top Road, Mr. Kenyon informed them that half of the two hundred acres was directly across the street. Escorting Roger away from the family, he spoke privately with his prospective buyer. After awhile they rejoined the group; time to bid a fond farewell. Cordially, Mr. Kenyon first extended a firm handshake to Roger; then held Carolyn's hand tenderly in his own while they spoke, not wanting to release her delicate fingers from his grasp. Exchanging pleasantries, their children loaded up as a resounding chorus of **thank you** and **goodbye** rang out from their car. Then pulling onto Round Top Road from the far side of the circular driveway, everyone waved as they passed, leaving dear old Mr. Kenyon standing alone in his front yard. Carolyn looked back longingly toward the sympathetic solitary figure; a man for whom she had developed an abiding affection; an isolated man who now seemed quite frail, somewhat smaller than she had previously perceived him to be. As they departed, Carolyn again became plagued by the same insidious sadness which seized her on the lawn. The vision of him as they drove away infused her consciousness. Committing him to memory, as if he was a poem, the haunting image lingered. Her troubled soul had sensed its own captivity, caught in the clutches of an inescapable remorse she could not comprehend. She could not bear to leave him behind and did not want to leave the farm.

As expected, the girls promptly fell asleep. The parents felt drowsy enough to do the same while traveling at light speed. It had been quite an adventure. Roger kept his eyes focused on the unfamiliar roads, searching for landmarks or memorizing the route, for future reference. He did not utter a sound until Carolyn asked what Mr. Kenyon had said as they walked off together. Roger leaned toward her, whispering, so as not to be overheard from the back seat.

"He wants *us* to have it; he'll do whatever it takes to make that happen."

With a single glance, the light in her husband's penetrating eyes released a surge of adrenaline through Carolyn's veins, causing her to shudder. Though appearing aloof, unattached to the notion, she easily read his tone of voice; Roger wanted the old farm just as much as she did, maybe even more. As the weight of self-doubt lifted, her spirit soared. She was suddenly wide awake. The couple remained silent for the duration of the lengthy ride back to their little house in the crowded suburbs and did not speak of it again until much later in the evening, after their children had gone off to bed.

Having checked in on the girls, Carolyn rejoined her husband in the parlor. Settling in on a sofa together, there was much to discuss. They spent the rest of the night relaying impressions and exploring their options. A conversation began with an unexpected announcement.

"Andrea asked me why we went where we did today; if it was because we were moving to the farm." Exasperated, motherly sighs escaped as her lungs collapsed. Their eldest daughter was known to be precocious and a bit too perceptive at times…and this qualified as one of those times.

"What did you say to her?' Roger was concerned. Neither of them wanted to set their girls up for another loss or disappointment, especially considering the devastating events they had endured that summer. Neither was willing to make a promise they might not be able to keep.

"I told her to get some sleep and we'd talk in the morning. I put her off."

"She knows." Roger appeared distressed, his furrowed brow as evidence.

"She knows *nothing* yet…that's why she asked." Carolyn reassured him.

"*We* don't know anything either…so what are we going to tell them?"

"The truth…" Roger nodded in agreement. "…we'll tell them the truth."

The children had not asked any questions that morning. They were thrilled just to go somewhere, *anywhere* with mommy and daddy. The nature of their excursion prompted suspicion in the eldest as Mr. Kenyon was a stranger to them, not among a group of friends with which she was familiar. Andrea had observed the way he'd spoken with her parents; the way they spoke with one another. Naturally curious, by the end of the trip she was listening for clues, whereas her sisters remained oblivious to the process embarked upon, merely enjoying their day moment-by-moment in that grand and fascinating place, entirely unaware of the significance of their fateful journey into the woods. Resolving to tell all of them the next morning, the couple moved on to other equally relevant issues. This was, after all, a very old house begging for some long overdue attention. To determine the extent of renovations required and at what costs incurred, they revisited their place in the country…in mind.

"The house is dark and dreary and the ugly linoleum has simply got to go!" It had not escaped the woman's notice…several floors covered up in plastic!

"It has *no* insulation; none. The heating system is antiquated, the electricity is original wiring. It hasn't been updated since it was installed in the twenties and it needs a paint job. Then there's the plumbing. That septic system has to be inspected and **ONE** bathroom is totally inadequate for seven people. Did you see the in-house/out-house in the woodshed? Can you imagine using *that* for a bathroom, not *if* but *when* your pipes are frozen up?" They were giddy. They were playful. They were already in over their heads.

Roger was doing his best to be sensible and responsibly critical about this property but he'd been bitten and smitten, like a man who had fallen deeply in love at first sight with a mysterious maiden and was then unfairly expected to point out all of her flaws. He didn't really see them. Love is blind, so they say. In terms of scrutinizing a house with major faults, his heart wasn't in it; yet his heart was in it, envisioning the beauty of a place he secretly longed to call *home*. The man was already invested, having nothing to do with a check.

"You love it as much as I do!" Carolyn felt compelled to state the obvious.

Flustered by her innate ability to see right through his false bravado, Roger pulled Carolyn over to his chest and began stroking her dark, flowing hair as he scrambled for a response.

"I know you want a place in the country." He was placating her again.

"No. I want *that* place in the country." She had pulled away long enough to stare directly into his eyes as she made her request; a veritable demand made of the Universe. There it was: Light. She had seen it down by the river; she'd seen it in their car. Snuggling beside him again, Carolyn paused, awaiting his next argument against the purchase of a farm; but the opposition never came.

"It will be a lot of work." Roger was all business...even in matters of love. "For both of us." No time for a congratulatory pat on the back, no money for the finder's fee, let alone the farm; Roger understood the ramifications of this decision, the nature of the challenge ahead of them. "I don't know if we can pull it off...but we can certainly try." Carolyn squeezed her husband's neck. Those were precisely the words she'd wanted to hear...a lover's leap of faith.

They talked late into that night; preliminary plans being made as potential resources were being reviewed. Ideas explored. A heady conversation began yielding to exhaustion. It was when Carolyn began to divulge having a rather unusual reaction to their return "home" earlier in the evening.

"When we drove back into Cumberland I had the strangest feelings. It was like coming into a foreign land; unfamiliar territory...and yet I knew my way around...as if going somewhere I've never been before but knowing where I was...the *identical* sensation I have at the farm. Diamond Hill Road, Chapel Four Corners, even the Monastery looks...I don't really know how to explain it...*different*. It was as if I was having a déjà vu experience. It was surreal." Her transition had begun: Metamorphosis. Roger listened attentively, without passing judgment, his silence; a tacit approval of her previous observations. He'd grasped what Carolyn meant, though she continued to explain; unaware his experience had been quite similar to her own in many respects.

"When we turned on to Mohawk Street, it was even more bizarre; this road looked so narrow and crowded; these houses seem much smaller to me now." Frustrated by a perceived inability to articulate the sensation, she pressed on: "You know, that feeling you'd have if you left home as a kid, then went back to revisit a childhood home years later; how small it would appear compared to your memory of it. God! We were away from here for less than five hours! *Everything* feels so different now, as if we don't even belong here anymore, like we've already moved on...out to the farm. Isn't that weird?"

Thoughtfully considering her comments, Roger admitted to feeling several oddities all his own. Carolyn was relieved, having been initially reluctant to share these perceptions with her husband. It soon became evident: he too had a reaction; closely akin to her own. He found himself plagued by the aromas of the distinctly earthy scent; the cellar of the farmhouse. It was as if it had been trapped, embedded in his sinuses; an unusual scent strangely enticing to him. He divulged having been distracted by visions; recurring images of the farm, especially by the river. He then revealed his deepest and most personal reaction: he'd never felt so attracted or attached to a place before; so anxious to return: like being drawn into a magnetic field of streams and dreams.

A quiet evening spent together renewed something lost between the couple. Though exhausted by the eventful day, they regained enthusiasm squelched over time by the burdens of responsibilities which come with a large family. Ironically, it was a mutual decision to assume more responsibility which had restored energy and vitality to a withering relationship, by necessity; a union replenished by sipping the nectar: a love potion. Once again, a loving couple with a common purpose, it would require every reserve of strength, resilience and fortitude they possessed to complete this transaction. It may require more than mere mortals could muster; perhaps some Divine Intervention would be called for as an act of God: The Holy Spirit. A Guiding Light as a beacon in the night. A clarion call disguised as the wind; all, calling them home...again.

A single conversation solidified an intention; a commitment to one another strengthened their resolve to do whatever was best on behalf of their family. Providing the children with a secure, wholesome environment, one ordained to foster growth and creativity had become a priority for both. While honing his skills in the fine art of personal communication, Roger paused to reflect, seemingly lost in thought. He made an unsolicited, unexpected statement:

"I hear confession is good for the soul."

"What have *you* done?" Carolyn snapped to attention. "Roger...what."

Mr. Perron had apparently made his own connections with Mr. Kenyon. He told her about the talk they had just prior to leaving the farm that afternoon. They'd struck an agreement; two men reached an understanding regarding an amount of time necessary to pull all of this together. Essentially, Mr. Kenyon had given Roger some breathing room with his "as long as it takes" attitude, insisting he wanted his home to go to their family. Roger admitted making a conscious decision to pursue this property from the moment he'd pulled into the yard, long before he stepped foot across the threshold of a dream house. He had become captivated by an old man and an older farm, thinking it *was* indeed the perfect place to raise a family. Roger confessed his belief in their destiny being revealed. He, too, envisioned them living there already.

"You let me sweat for nothing." Her feigned resentment was transparent.

"It's been a hot day. You'd be sweating anyway." He winked...a sly one.

"Not so hot down by the river." Reminding him of the respite they enjoyed, his wife admitted she *knew* it was a done deal the instant he pulled the shoes off his feet and rolled up his trousers.

"The river." Roger's eyes sparkled like sunlight dancing on its surface. He was enamored with the place; Carolyn knew her husband would do whatever he could to procure the piece of property. While they frolicked there in mind, absorbing magical imagery, it felt as if they had been transported to another dimension, an alternate reality. Describing the sensation to each other as an odd combination of déjà vu and surrealism, they wondered why they'd been so comfortable there. Why did the farm feel so familiar? It was as if they had both been there before, perhaps in another space and time? (A little spooky.)

"I think we found the Garden of Eden. It even has an apple tree!"

"**We** found it?" Carolyn skeptically cocked an eyebrow in his direction.

"Better be careful about eating the fruit." Roger found himself so amusing.

Carolyn settled into total relaxation; a true indulgence for a mother of five. A few more words residing in the recesses of her mind found their way to her lips; private suggestions floating on whispers aimed toward a husband's ear; some shameless hussy remarks regarding Adam and Eve. Roger, embracing a suggestion, along with his wife, they went off to bed, prepared to share more with each other...undercover...cloaked by the darkness of night.

~ Carolyn gazing into a fountain of youth ~

Children eagerly gathered around the table for breakfast as Carolyn did the honors; filling their bowls with maple oatmeal. Roger passed the toast along.

"Did all of you have a good time at Mr. Kenyon's farm?" She had to ask.

"Oh mommy, I loved the barn!" Really? Nancy was bound to outburst first. "All it needs is some horses!"

"And cows!" Cindy thought it could really use some cows.

"It's beautiful." Andrea developed a keen appreciation of nature at a young age and found her true contentment on a lovely trip to bountiful; the farm: a place where she desperately wanted to live and never wanted to leave again.

Spontaneous chatter erupted in the crowd. Carolyn glanced toward Roger. He promptly stood and began wandering the room, reveling in a *Santa Claus* sensation, like watching over the girls while they opened a big gift intended for all of them. He couldn't help himself...he simply had to interrupt.

"How would you like to live there?" Suddenly inundated with flailing arms wrapped around his torso, Roger laughed. "Guess I got my answer." Andrea leaned into her mother; their brief exchange of "I knew it!" and "I know it!" whispered before turning to embrace her father. It was a family reunion, the picture of hope for a brighter future...a place in the country for all to enjoy but not just *any* place in the country. This place was miraculous and they all knew it from the moment their family arrived on the property.

"All right...all right...everybody sit down. We'll have to talk about this." Following directions, the girls reclaimed their seats as Roger took his place at the head of the table. "Your mother and I have decided to *try* and buy the farm. But all of you need to understand that it won't be easy and we might not get it, no matter how hard we try. It's a lot of money. A lot. We promise to do our best and that's *all* we can promise. Any questions?"

April raised her hand. "Are we moving in with Mr. Kenyon?" Apparently she'd not yet grasped the notion of relocation. April was just an infant when the family moved to Cumberland. It was the only home she had ever known.

Their house on Mohawk Street seemed smaller to them, as well. These ladies were enthralled by the property they'd visited. Her mother responded.

"No, honey. Mr. Kenyon would sell his house *to* us then he would pack up all his things and go to live someplace else." Carolyn explained an unfamiliar process to the perplexed child as simply as she could.

"But where would he go?" A logical question: as a follow-up from Cindy.

"I don't know. It would be *his* decision; probably a much smaller house."

"Can he stay there with us if he doesn't want to leave, or if he doesn't have a place to go?" Christine always had a generous spirit...and a keen intuition.

"But he would not be selling the house if he wanted to stay there." Carolyn inadvertently uttered a false statement. The sweet old man was as attached to the farm as anyone on Earth could be and he had already begun the painful process of mourning the loss of it, long before it went on the market. It had been his home for so long he could not imagine leaving it behind.

"Would we get the barn, too?" Nancy was fixated on the rustic structure.

"Yes, of course." Carolyn smiled. Curiosity suddenly seemed a natural trait in all of her children.

"And the river, too?" Chris had most wanted to go wading with her daddy.

Mom laughed. "Yes, the river too...yard and barn and river and much more you haven't even seen yet. The farm has two hundred acres of land, a pine grove, a river, a pond and an old cellar hole to explore!"

"Where's the pond?" Andrea was anxious to explore it in her imagination.

"What's an acre?" Chris was looking forward to mathematical calculations.

Roger fielded this question with words which could be readily understood. "You know how big the yard is, right? If you walk from the backside of the barn and then follow the stone wall down and around to the other side of the house then back up to the road again...*that* is six acres of land." They could not yet conceive of it; could not absorb the idea of having perpetual access to so much space…land overwhelming to the senses…like imagining the size of the Universe! Their faces were flush with excitement, the promise of new life in a virtual paradise, what they perceived to be an extraordinary place…even if they could not yet think that BIG.

"And now for the *bad* news…" Listening attentively as their father spoke, the girls became as sober while searching their mother's face for her reaction to his words of forewarning. It was only fair and they agreed to tell the truth.

"No more trips this summer; no more trips for awhile. No more dinners out or ice cream cones or shopping for clothes, except for school. No more rides at **Rocky Point** or chowder and clam cakes at the **Shore Dinner Hall** and no more boat rides to get there, either. We'll have to sell the boat and that means we have to scrape it down and paint it first." Reality began to settle into their young minds yet there weren't any complaints forthcoming; what their father was saying translated into dollars and good sense. No one felt deprived. They all understood what their parents were trying to do for them. The girls were grateful, confident in the mission. They had faith in mom and dad.

"We will all have to work together." Carolyn spoke. "Your father and I will do everything we can to buy the farm but it means we will all have to make sacrifices to have the home of our dreams. Do you understand?" One of her children took the words more literally than the others had. Nancy would soon reveal her innovative entrepreneurial spirit.

After breakfast, Carolyn phoned Mrs. Hertzog. She arrived that afternoon with the purchase and sales agreement, explaining how she would hold onto the five hundred dollar check until their closing date and could then apply it toward the down payment. The welcome pronouncement took some financial pressure off the couple in the short term but both of them knew, by signing that document, they would be literally signing their life away…life as they'd known it, anyway. In the coming weeks their initial euphoria would subside, replaced by a steadfast resolve involving the entire family. It meant sacrifices made; it meant giving up and pitching in. Everyone was expected to make an investment; no matter how small, it would prove to be significant. The girls put their heads together to develop a plan, including some ingenious ideas.

Roger literally disappeared; lending new meaning to his job description as an "on-the-road" salesman. As it turned out, he was not the only entrepreneur in the family. Several of them were enrolled in a summer activity camp at the elementary school. They took a course in arts and crafts. The house became cluttered with festive wares. Christine had a brilliant smile, platinum blond hair and deep blue eyes the size of cup saucers. Secretly knowing she was an adorable eight-year-old, Chris decided to take her show on the road, just like daddy. Gathering up all the macramé potholders she could get her hands on, she even emptied her mom's linen drawers for good measure; taking aprons and hand towels along with *real* potholders the woman used on a daily basis. Off she went, bodyguard in tow; biggest sister. Nobody in the neighborhood was going to mess with *her* anymore! As they went door-to-door, primarily to neighbors they knew, sisters told their story about the beautiful farm their mother found and how they were all helping to buy it. In a few days, Chrissy was flush with cash...and flat out-of-stock. Of course, the next time Carolyn needed a potholder from the linen drawer she was shit out of pot-holder luck! Though the girls worked feverishly during their last weeks of summer camp, manufacturing as many items as time and materials allowed; the kids simply could not keep up with demand: a not-so-subtle message received? Perhaps.

Piggy banks overflowed into the ginger jar tucked in a corner of the kitchen counter. It was their tangible testament to a commitment made by their entire family. Carolyn was impressed by such moxie: a willingness to work beside their parents with common purpose. They too had a dream; a vision quest in mind, imagining what it would be like to live in an old country estate. Nancy had one particular vision quest: Horses! This is why she took it so seriously, bringing the profession of "door-to-door" sales into another dimension.

Late one afternoon in August Nancy approached her mother in the midst of preparing dinner. Carolyn was distracted; she did not notice that her highly motivated daughter had an ulterior motive while offering to "help" clean up food debris from the kitchen counter. Collecting all the discarded waste from ingredients required for Yankee pot roast, placing them into a brown paper bag, the nasty concoction included an assortment of onion skins, potato peels and carrot shavings, as well as other sundry items: a wide variety of wet and smelly yucky stuff from their kitchen garbage pail. With her covert mission accomplished, she disappeared. Prancing proudly up their street toward the home of her very best customer, a stained paper bag swinging in the breeze, Carolyn thought nothing more of it. She sealed the lid on the pressure cooker then settled down with a cup of coffee. The other girls were outside playing with Cathi. Assuming Nancy was with them, she was surprised as the perky little pixie flew back through the kitchen door, frantically waving a crisp new dollar bill. Big brown eyes all but hidden beneath that windblown mass of sandy blond hair, she had run home so fast, it tangled in the wind she created with friction caused by traveling at the speed of light.

"I'm back! Look what I got, mom!" The girl resembled a sunbeam bursting through a cluster of billowing clouds.

"Where'd you go, honey? Where did you get *that*?" Carolyn was delighted, for the moment.

"From Mrs. Hill!" Glowing with sweat, innocence and certain satisfaction of the sale, Nancy presented her mother with all the profits. "She paid me for bringing her our scraps...for her garden!"

"What?!" Carolyn leapt from her skin...a virtual out-of-body experience. A bit overzealous, Nancy had over-stepped in a way she did not understand.

"She said she *needed* it for the milks pile." Nancy was glowing aloud.

"Her *mulch* pile?" Carolyn's heart began to pound. Her face flushed. What would people think? "Honey, you *can't* sell our *garbage* to the neighbors!"

"But she told me she *needed* them!" Nancy's full lower lip began quivering uncontrollably. "Mrs. Hanaway bought some of it, too!" The child retrieved three more quarters from her pocket then laid them on the table as her sweet little face wrinkled up like the soiled paper bags she had just delivered to the kind-hearted women who lived at the top of the street. Carolyn sighed aloud, "Oh, my God" then quickly hugged a very resourceful daughter, praising her efforts on behalf of the family. Cathi entered the kitchen; she could not help but notice remnants of distress on a good friend's face. A stream of siblings followed. Carolyn gently explained their situation, so as not to hurt Nancy's feelings any further. Cathi's hearty laughter erupted abruptly, startling them. *"Brilliant! Pure profit! A stroke of genius! What outstanding initiative! Hire that girl!"* Nancy's trembling lower lip curled back up into a smile. She then issued a heartfelt plea, promising never to do it again...at least not with the garbage. All was forgiven. (Carolyn would return the money later on.)

Cathi Urbonas was a friend indeed. She had known their family for several years and established an endearing relationship with Carolyn both cherished. Cathi adored the children; the sentiment was mutual. Astonished by Roger's demure reaction to his wife's impulsive decision to purchase the farm, it was the last response she expected. However, since everyone else was onboard, she decided to help. Practically worshipped by them, thrilled to spend time with Cathi whenever possible, she kept kids very busy. In spite of what their father predicted, the trips were *not* over. Cathi moved in for the summer. She took the girls out to parks and concerts, festivals and any other *free* event she could locate in the area. Once, she took all of them to Harvard Yard. On the way through Boston Common another Vietnam War protest was underway. No sheltering them from *that* storm, though she tried to divert rapt attention from that raucous rally. Cathi was a bona fide hippy chick, as free a spirit as they'd ever know in life. Supremely happy, spreading her joyfulness liberally throughout the land of the free, her family was equally inspiring, especially her mother, Elsie. The children frequently spent time at their lovely home in Seekonk, Massachusetts. There they learned much in her presence, instilling an appreciation for classical music and the fine arts in each one of them. The house was much like a lived-in museum; brimming with elegant antiques and fine collectibles Cathi's mother acquired over the years, many of which she'd found displayed on someone's lawn at a yard sale.

What remained of that summer was spent in Cathi's company. If they were not swimming in her pool they were packing a lunch for the beach. Instructed to locate the smoothest stones, the most interesting shells in the sand, Cathi would then gather their load into a towel and bring once-buried treasure back to her house. There they'd spend hours in her mother's artist studio painting faces onto their *pet rocks* or dipping tie-dyed tee shirts. Days passed weaving sandals or bracelets or anklets, making wind chimes from rawhide and shells, drawing *happy faces* and *peace signs* on anything they could sell within the neighborhood of people apparently eager to see them all go, based upon the number of items the girls continually sold around town. What Cathi did over those months was of immeasurable importance. It provided Carolyn freedom to take contract jobs here and there; she did some modeling and knew people in the fashion industry who kept her busy designing for them. Roger was on the road. During the month of August he spent only four days at home. When he was there, everyone hung around with him, so he put them to work. It was quite the chore to scrape and clean; to sand and paint a twenty-four-foot boat. As barnacles are hazardous, especially to tender young skin, Roger took that task on himself. His daughters observed, longing to pitch in. There would be plenty of work ahead. A chore nearing completion, no one felt left out of the process. Over the course of four Sundays the older kids learned and perfected an entire series of skills as the two youngest got their first taste of real labor. They experienced the satisfaction of a job well done. The boat was gorgeous. It had never looked so good and looked far too good to sell; then it was gone. Though they all briefly lamented the loss, the gain was becoming substantial: a down payment kept growing and growing...by some saving grace.

Back-to-school shopping was less extravagant that year. Necessity was the norm. No one complained. The girls studied hard and did their best, excitedly sharing news of an impending move with friends well before they knew for certain they were actually leaving. Roger worked incessantly. Carolyn staged the house to the extent she could. Time to put it on the market; another listing for Mrs. Hertzog, who'd remained helpful in every way she could, primarily with the paperwork involved in this complicated transaction. In preparation, Mr. Kenyon made arrangements for a survey of the land. Things were going along as well as could be expected...or unexpected! No trouble yet, but...

One Saturday morning in early September, Carolyn called Mr. Kenyon. He invited the family up to the farm for a visit. Roger was away but Cathi went along. It was on this day she realized what all of the sacrifice had been for, redoubling her personal commitment to help them acquire the farm. Another splendid day, though considerably cooler than their previous visit, this time the girls were permitted to go jump in the river! The host stood with Carolyn on the bank watching them, Cathi included, playing for an hour or so in the shallows while Carolyn quietly spoke with her gentleman friend. He seemed content, obviously enjoying the sight of his company. A peaceful expression on his face, Mr. Kenyon told her he'd wait until they were ready; no rush, no pressure...no hurry. It was the first time Carolyn suspected he did not want to leave his home. She sensed his grief; a reluctance to part with the place. A difficult decision, one likely made by necessity, due to his advanced age. She likewise sensed hopefulness in the patient man, someone reconciling a loss before it occurred; a faithful belief that *this* was the family to take his place. The bond, a genuine affection between them coupled with a determination to create a new reality from something as ethereal as desire.

All six ladies got filthy! They had come in Cathi's car, so, if it was all right with her, Carolyn did not question the wisdom of taking the plunge. Its water was low; crayfish abundant. Stones were gathered up and stuffed in pockets. All was right with the world. Preparing to leave, Mr. Kenyon held Carolyn's hand a bit too long...again. He loved her. Embracing him spontaneously, her impetuous outburst caused him to blush. Imagine that. No further words were spoken. None were necessary.

That afternoon the girls remained lively; no naps, in spite of all the energy they had expended. It was time for some excited sightseeing. The village was compact but charming, speckled with historic homes and lovely landscaping. Weaving her way through town, Cathi was prone to sudden turns: jerking its wheel, pointing the car toward roads which looked particularly inviting. It was better than a trip to **Rocky Point**; a thrill-ride with the wild woman beat out the *Wildcat*. The library seemed small but the general store appeared to be adequate. It was important to the girls to see their new respective schools. Crossing over the narrow bridge at the waterfall, astounded by the beauty of Mill Pond, Andrea was delighted to see the vintage theater beside it, a place "Now Showing" movies every weekend. Once they were out on the highway again, each sweet urchin began emptying saturated pockets, examining their haul; something to occupy the time during a long haul back to Cumberland. A festive outing, it would be their last before officially moving to the farm. Harrisville would be their destination: a new hometown on the horizon.

The next few months were exasperating for Roger and Carolyn. They had to sell their house at a substantial profit in order to afford to buy their farm. Mrs. Hertzog listed it, repeatedly showing the place. Working diligently to close the deal, her relentless efforts finally paid off; it wasn't enough. Family and friends rallied around the couple. Roger *sold* in his sleep. He then sold back the cash value of his life insurance policy: whatever it took. The down payment slowly accrued. Another expense would suddenly emerge to gobble it up. Weeks passed. Their house in the suburbs was sold; they had to leave! Waiting patiently, Mr. Kenyon kept his word. A survey of the farm came in ten acres short, for some inexplicable reason. Their down payment was *still* coming up short. Reassuring them the land *was there*, Mr. Kenyon offered to lower the asking price, an incredibly generous gesture on behalf of a family. Finally! In mid-December of 1970, they closed on the farm: bought and sold. Hallelujah! Praise the Lord and pass the nectar! They were homeward bound.

As the Perrons celebrated Christmas for their final time in Cumberland, the children were instructed to hang onto all the empty boxes for their toys. That year gifts came from everywhere; seemingly from the ether. Friends close to them *knew* their cupboards were bare, coffers depleted by the purchase of a farm. From an attorney to real estate agent; neighbors to teachers, Santa had some serious competition! Cathi brought gifts…books and more **Weebles**! Family members and friends alike emerged to assist in a *moving* endeavor. It was a glorious celebration; a testament to precious, enduring relationships.

Well beyond weary, an ambitious couple had over-extended themselves in every conceivable way. They decided to take a few days off to rest and relax, spending time with the ladies instead of hovering over notarized documents. Grateful for these many blessings bestowed upon them, it was time to pack; what that entailed was much more than Carolyn could handle alone; Cathi came to help. When she arrived, so did the running joke which had begun the previous summer, feigning the *deprivation* associated with buying the farm.

Kids to Cathi: "What's for dessert?" Cathi to kids: **"J-E-L-L-O… Nothing!"** To this day, it remains the standard answer to the question.

During the second week of January 1971 the real adventure began. All else had been a prelude to it. Snow flurries cluttered the sky that frigid morning, a precursor to the storm to come. Their truck arrived on schedule. By the time it was loaded and all ready to go it had been repeatedly swept clean of an icy, impacted residue. Still, in spite of that maintenance, the driver could not see through a frozen, crystal-encrusted windshield. Roger had to engage flashing lights and lead the way. By necessity, they would be forced to crawl along to their place in the country, no matter how anxious they were to head on *home*. In spite of the trial, spirits were high. At last! The Perron family was moving to the farm; the home of their dreams…and eventual nightmares.

***

Their caravan, including the truck and three full cars, labored through the countryside. Though state highways had remained relatively clear, the same could not be said for the narrow, winding roads ahead of them. It took more than two hours to arrive at their destination, less than thirty miles from that journey's point of origin. A snowstorm is nothing unusual in Rhode

Island so everyone took it in stride. Mr. Kenyon; waiting for them with hot chocolate and cookies, fresh from the oven. It took all day to complete the task but by evening, rooms had been chosen and beds assembled. The whole family went down for a long winter's nap…all except for one.

Roger waited for his wife to fall asleep before rising again. He roamed the place, their new old home as quietly as wooden floors allow. Reflecting upon an eventful day he cautiously made his way through the darkened dwelling, a few rooms still clinging to an echo. Though his mind was racing, the pace of his feet deliberately slowed; obstacles at every turn. Passing by several boxes precariously stacked beside their upside down rocking chair, Roger paused to reflect upon the necessity of having to move something else, anything else at the end of a very long day. He did, and managed to do so without waking the dead. No cause for alarm until the morning when several fast little feet would complicate an equation. Nearly tripping over the toy which had no business being where it was in his path, Roger quickly decided he required more light to navigate a treacherous space. A lamp stood alone in a dim recessed corner of the dining room. Reaching for it; murmuring: "Better to light a candle than to curse the darkness, or the kids." Roger was grateful there was a bulb inside and pulled on its chain. Illumination: Let there be Light. The shadowed space instantly consumed a soft yellow glow it cast into the night. Suddenly Roger recalled the rather ambiguous statement Mr. Kenyon had made earlier in the day, just prior to leaving his lifelong home. It knocked on the closed door in his mind, requesting entry and proper consideration.

The father of five righted an old rocking chair then claimed it for himself. Though the snowstorm had subsided, its residual wind was still howling like wolves in the woods. Motionless, he sat in moonlight filtered by lace curtains which had found their proper windows in day one. Carolyn had worked hard. The happy homemaker was on task inside before their last piece of furniture came off a truck outside; she had already begun decorating. He admired her efforts and her stamina. Though he found the house chilly, undoubtedly due to a brutal cold front plunging temperatures to single digits, he was warmed by thoughts of his family. The girls would now have the chance to spend an idyllic childhood in a place quite different from the harsh city streets he had known as a boy. A father smiled with pride and certain satisfaction. This was a blessing...no curses in sight that night.

Lamplight flickered; tightening the bulb Roger heard Mr. Kenyon's cryptic words streaming throughout his consciousness, forewarning him to leave the lights on at night. It had seemed innocuous enough at the time, even sensible advice regarding a house full of girls trying to find their way to the bathroom in darkness. Still, he had found something troubling about those words. The phrase haunted him, perhaps in its delivery. Just before taking his leave from a home all his own for so long, Mr. Kenyon invited Roger outside for a walk. Horizontally blowing snow would have deterred even the heartiest of Yankee souls and yet an elder gentleman seemed entirely unaffected by the elements. Roger accompanied him, as requested. Though the men had walked together before, this time they appeared to be a single solitary figure obscured by the swirling gusts of icy-white, wind-driven haze. Mr. Kenyon paused prior to issuing a statement as opaque as the air. His thoughtfully considered words were spoken in a foreboding tone Roger found foreign. An unusual phrase; Roger dismissed it in mind, as it made no sense to him at that time. He said: **"For the sake of your family, leave the lights on at night."** With no further explanation forthcoming, without one being requested, Roger presumed it to be entirely benign; the well-intended ramblings of an old man who had lived alone far too long. The suggestion tapped Roger on the shoulder as he leaned in toward the lamp. Raw nerves had been frayed ragged by events of the day. The man was exhausted. He stared at the brass pull chain dangling beside his fingertips. Mr. Kenyon was right. Though moonlight was nice enough, it was insufficient for guidance in the dark of night; it *was* too dark in the house. He left the amber lamplight glowing for his girls then went on back to bed.

Harsh winds whipped and curled around the chimney like a cat in perpetual motion; a dog frantically chasing its own tail: the frenetic sounds of creatures stirring things up, not of those attempting to settle into a comfortable position for the night. The valley cried out in shrill tones, begging for mercy from the relentlessly rushing gusts of icy air. Go ahead. Make yourself at home.

They had entered unfamiliar territory in a house which had a secret. Pulling bare legs in beneath a warm quilt, Roger was far too weary to sleep; his mind preoccupied, riddled with images of the tumultuous day. His over-extended muscles ached and throbbed. The man lay there beside his wife, wondering how they'd actually pulled it off. Closing his increasingly heavy eyelids, he remained quite still, listening to new sounds from within a very old house.

***

Several months would pass before Roger again recalled the cryptic words left with him on this day as two men shook hands, bidding a fond farewell in a snowstorm. It took some time for him to fully grasp the significance of this remark; a legitimate warning. When that time did come he would divulge the content of the conversation to his troubled wife. With a few simple words the dear old man had relayed all he knew or understood about the farmhouse; all he could convey without running the risk of being perceived as a madman by a couple of new friends. It was their initial clue; a foreshadowing of things to come, appearing in the darkness of night... from dusk 'til dawn.

"Think of yourself as an incandescent power, illuminated and perhaps forever talked to by God and his messengers."
Brenda Ueland

frozen stiff

"Let your joy scream across the pain."
Ezbeth Wilder

A family was virtually sequestered for the winter; a merciless season beating relentlessly upon their doors and windows, repeatedly threatening to intrude. During the first six weeks or so, their house felt more like an igloo to its new inhabitants. Blowing snow latched onto its rusty screens, which had not been removed in many years. Neglectfulness created conditions which invited the elements, resulting in a visually stunning, brutally cold whiteout from within. Every morning this thin coating of ice laced their windowpanes with unusual patterns splendidly displayed against a backdrop of sunlight, delicately lining the inside of each pane of glass. Every prism promised another cold day. The children, fascinated by one of Nature's marvels, used their hot little hands to leave their personal imprints behind; a patchwork of palms. Fingertips etched names on the artwork, claiming God's work as their own...until their mother noticed the new pre-school ritual; she was the one who would have to clean those windowpanes with her own fingers, too stiff and sore to move without magnifying her pain. Art class dismissed.

Outside, snowdrifts were trapped and jammed into corners of the structure, stretched upward by punishing winds, then narrowed into shafts resembling fingers, each one appearing to point toward the second story of the dwelling, as if with purpose. Storm after storm, week after week, frosted windowpanes shuddered and shivered and shifted in place. Doors trembling with gusts as each swept through the valley; victims of a blustery and unforgiving wind. It was wild and free: Nature on a rampage. Winter was a mesmerizing event.

Enormous icicles clung to the edges of their roof line, as if in desperation. Attached by balls of ice resembling clawed feet, talons latched into the ridge where clapboard met shingle; each one of dozens dangled precariously, their existence contingent upon the temperature and the angle of the Sun. Many of these ice monsters shared the same circumference as those of a smaller tree, creating a fortress-like effect, surrounding the house on all sides. A veritable fence of swords, equally as dangerous, perched ominously overhead, capable of impaling anyone foolish enough to stand beneath them, with catastrophic damage potential. Roger and Carolyn rarely made demands of their children. This hazard was the exception. Naturally, the girls were intrigued. They were ordered to keep a safe distance, to avoid the façade of the house at all times. It was as non-negotiable a point as was the rigid spike that plunged from the rafters into the ground during one brief thaw, driving itself upright through frozen solid tundra. Carolyn photographed it for emphasis, posting a copy of the picture, a health *hazard* on the refrigerator door as a constant reminder to all; these icy giants preserved for posterity, as some proof of their existence. Otherwise, no one would ever believe it! Not unless they saw how a common icicle could, in time, evolve into uncommon weaponry: a mystery of Nature; elemental interplay of water and air conspiring to create: a wonder to behold.

Their harsh environment isolated them. Most extended family members too faint of heart to brave that bleak mid-winter would wait until spring to come out to the country. Carolyn left that ominous photograph in place to show the cowards what they had missed. Their first winter there introduced many new challenges. By comparison, the clan had been coddled in suburban sanctuary. Having a home hundreds of feet away from the road was lovely and private, *until* it was time to carve out a narrow path to their bus stop; then it became treacherous and exhausting work. "Digging out" adopted some new meaning. Roger purchased several snow shovels, anticipating the necessity for a group effort, especially whenever he was away on business. He could not always be there to heave and ho, hoist and bail them out. Instead, he taught his girls the finer points of shoveling snow. It was drudgery, to be sure, but could still be accomplished quickly and efficiently when maintenance *staff* was properly trained: bend at the knees, use legs rather than arms and the back as leverage. The baby was exempt from the chore, though everyone soon learned valuable lessons regarding teamwork. Their boat had been but a prelude; warming up before the *real* workout. So began the building of muscle mass, and a serious Yankee work ethic. In time, cutting, hauling and splitting of wood developed into another exercise regimen, but that's another story entirely.

Snow: What had been merely an occasional nuisance in Cumberland soon became a ritualistic punishment in Harrisville, with a corresponding penance. Just a few miles north of Providence, Cumberland shared the relative warmth of the Atlantic Ocean; a fringe benefit of their former location had apparently been overlooked. It was almost always five degrees colder and several inches deeper at the farm. It would have been much simpler to remain house-bound for the winter. Seclusion was preferable. Day after day, there remained much to do to transform their new house into an old home place suitable for them. However, reality intruded. Children had to be registered in school; that meant digging out. Roger needed to return to his business ventures. That too meant digging out. They had to bring in an adequate supply of provisions, usually in preparation for the *next* forecast: major snowfall! Parked beside the barn, just getting to her frozen car meant, yes indeed, more digging out. According to Carolyn, a poor old bastard named Sisyphus had it easy.

The bleak season soon became Carolyn's winter of discontent. A pervasive cold, coupled with all the overwhelming work, conspired to create an utterly inhospitable environment. It was the chronic dampness; a chill to the house. It was virtually inescapable, undoubtedly due to the presence of a spring and a deep well in an earthen cellar. A water source which had been so cool and refreshing at the height of summer had become an adversarial opponent in winter. What poured from frosted faucets was unbearably cold to the touch; literally undrinkable until it was warmed on the stove. Imagine being the first one up at dawn only to find a sheet of ice in the toilet: Reality: check it out!

The children seemed to be completely impervious to this ubiquitous cold, spending free time exploring their new old home, albeit swaddled in woolen socks and bulky sweaters. Arranging, then rearranging the bedrooms to their liking kept the blood flowing. They did not seem to notice they were freezing to death, except at night. A sudden influx of heavy quilts helped mitigate the situation somewhat but there were many cold nights

49

when howling wind and bitter temperatures chased the children into others beds, seeking the warmth of a sister who was grateful for the company and an extra body: heat. Andrea had the only full-sized bed among them, able to accommodate two siblings. One rude awakening of a winter season; she rarely woke up alone.

The companionship existing between the children sustained them as they adjusted to new schools and began making friends. Word on the school bus: the power lines were *excellent* for sledding! So was their back yard, for that matter. One glorious day Roger came home with a trunk load of new-fangled contraptions aptly named *flying saucers*; a wild ride better than *anything* at **Rocky Point**. Winter became less daunting; far more amusing. With serious trepidation, Roger and Carolyn took their children up the power lines; father somewhat less reluctant than the mother, knowing children *do* bounce...and bounce they did, straight down the forty-five-degree-angle-hill with enough twists to turn *any* stomach, especially the one tucked inside of their mother, heaving up into her throat with every CRASH! Roger had taken precautions, loading bales of hay into the trunk of the car then placing them strategically along that treacherous route to shield his girls from all those granite boulders dotting a rugged landscape. Survival was a prerequisite. Among five siblings it remains one of their fondest memories of childhood; downright dangerous. Death-defying: The Hill of Insanity! Remembered as *a real scream*; it was a truly slippery slope: good times had by children whose parents would rather forget those adventures and loathe admitting they even allowed it to happen!

On a bright, sunny day in February, Mr. Kenyon arrived unexpectedly for a visit. The children were as delighted as their parents. They all ran outside to greet him as he emptied the pockets of his heavy wool overcoat, bulging with candy. Their gloves had dried, socks were changed, and the wild child crew was about to head out on another ride when he pulled into the yard. Carolyn put on a fresh pot of coffee as she rustled up something sweet for him to eat. Roger joined him in the yard and they stood at the top of the hill, listening to screams of joy. Mr. Kenyon was gratified, at peace with his painful decision to part with the farm. His tired eyes beholding a race to the finish, it was all downhill from there! It was precisely what he envisioned for the family when the time came to relinquish his patch of paradise to those who would become its future caretakers. Though his son had built him a lovely house on his own property, complete with every amenity, it was obvious the gentleman missed his old home place. Roger comforted him with the reassurance of a standing invitation…a warm welcome home, anytime. In heart, it was still his home.

Old Man Winter: Mr. Kenyon appeared to be the personification of this mythical figure. His soft, round brimmed hat was the finishing touch. It did nothing to protect his ears but suited him well nonetheless. Roger asked him to remain for Sunday dinner: Yankee Pot Roast. (Carolyn loved her pressure cooker, especially during the season when it did double duty, functioning as an alternative heat source.) Though gratefully declining their offer, due to a prior commitment with his family, he gladly accepted the hot cup of coffee. With an occasional sip of the steaming brew warming his hands, Mr. Kenyon began their conversation praising Carolyn's efforts. The kitchen had a whole new personality, one he instantly noticed and found quite fetching. Its many window ledges displayed an assortment of miniature glass bottles along with other collectibles she had gathered over time; each pane delicately lined with lace. The flimsy fabric did nothing to keep down drafts but certainly allowed for some light, creating at least an illusion of warmth. Acknowledged as their first official guest, therefore Carolyn's greatest admirer thus far, he smiled.

"No one will come to see us." Carolyn seemed as relieved as disappointed.

"Can't say I blame them." Empathetically; the elder gentleman understood. He too had known isolation and loneliness on the farm during colder winters. "They come in the spring…then *stay* through the summer." A glint in his eyes hinted at delightful memories made in this setting of a lifetime; a place where he'd spent a lifetime creating precious moments worth remembering. No one knew the extent to which Mr. Kenyon longed to return home.

Carolyn mentioned how cold she found the house, expressing regret that all the fireplaces had been sealed tight. Though this process had occurred during his tenure in the home, he was evasive, avoiding any discussion of it. Instead, he shifted focus outside, telling them the story of two men who got caught up in a blizzard while walking from Webster, Massachusetts toward Harrisville. It happened during the early 1800s when an old blacksmith shop still stood at its right front corner of the property. Apparently the storm was a vicious one; wind so intense it created whiteout conditions, effectively blinding both men. They could not make it to the house; perhaps they could not see it was there: a tragedy. Seeking shelter from the storm, these men crawled up beneath the foundation of the blacksmith shop where they'd met a bitter end: frozen stiff. The decomposing corpses were not discovered until a sustained spring thaw, due primarily to the smell of death in the air.

"Oh my God! That's awful!" Carolyn was shaken by the vivid imagery.

"I'm not surprised." Roger, nonchalant about it. "I'm from Rhode Island and I have never been this cold in my life. And the snow...!"

"You're in the Worcester Valley here; it makes Providence feel more like Miami Beach...the kind of cold that can freeze you to death." How ominous.

Mr. Kenyon spoke about other fascinations of their property, including an old cellar hole and a giant piece of granite in the shape of a bell covering the abandoned well. He took them for a ride: on an excursion of the imagination through the pine grove, out to the pond toward the back of the property, just inside a borderline to Massachusetts. He told them other stories, too. Rumors persisted about the house being used as a part of the **Underground Railroad** network; speculation still circulating in the village well more than a hundred years later. Reflecting on the history, what little he knew of it, Mr. Kenyon's expression turned suddenly somber. He looked Carolyn directly in the eyes then asked her an equally direct question.

"Is everything all right here?" She didn't know how to interpret his inquiry. It had a strange ring to it; what felt in the moment like some hidden meaning.

"We're settling in just fine; still a few boxes left to unpack but for the most part, we're done. The girls have work left to do upstairs...its getting there."

"Any problems?" The couple couldn't determine what he was asking them; if the question was one of a concerned seller seeking to be of some assistance or if he had anticipated the emergence of a problem known only to him, one which had not been disclosed. Roger responded.

"Other than being chilly most of the time, we are really enjoying the place. It *is* very drafty. I may need to replace that tired old furnace soon. No matter what we do this house just won't hold the heat...it has some very cold spots." There was nothing remotely critical in Roger's tone or content. He was well aware the house had no insulation long before they bought it.

"Clapboard." The former caretaker absolutely knew how cold it could get. He'd done his share of shivering there.

"The house makes some rather unusual noises, even later at night after the wind dies down." While speaking, Carolyn nudged a Danish roll toward their houseguest. She knew he had a sweet tooth.

"It's old and creaky, just like me." Mr. Kenyon smiled a coy grin they had all come to know: "Swallows in the chimney." His quick wink in Carolyn's direction seemed oddly misplaced, as if she was supposed to understand his cryptic message received with subtle skepticism: "Swallows in the chimney." Fixing his gaze on the mistress of the house, he attempted to covertly express the esoteric comment. Not sure how to read it or how to reply, Carolyn raised another issue instead. She had accumulated a series of questions during their first few weeks in the farmhouse.

"I wish we had a proper set of keys. None of these keys fit any of the locks. I've tried them all." Carolyn conveyed her concerns with some tension in her voice, a reflection of the trepidation she felt about often being home alone.

"Lost, I suppose. Years ago."

"Does your son have a set?" Carolyn sought resolution. He shook his head.

"I never locked the doors. No need. No one will bother you here."

The kitchen door blew open; wind and five snow bunnies entered en masse.

"Straight to the bathroom. Wet clothes into the tub." Carolyn pointed one finger in the direction she wanted them to travel. They dutifully obeyed.

"Close that door! You'll let all the heat out!" Roger was the door police.

"What heat would that be?" Carolyn briskly rubbed her hands together as a brutal gust of wind followed behind her children like an uninvited playmate. "God bless friction. Any advice?" The elder gentleman just shook his head.

"It comes with the territory." He seemed sincere. "Ya get used to it."

Carolyn doubted she'd ever adjust to the chill in the air; a Georgia girl who never quite acclimated to New England, even though she had already lived in the frozen tundra for more than a dozen years.

"It's late. I should go." Mr. Kenyon began slowly rising from his seat.

"Stay a little longer, please. I'm sure the girls want to spend time with you. They do thaw out!" Carolyn had an ulterior motive, as she had yet to pick his brain to her complete satisfaction. Only he knew what was really meant by what he said: "Swallows in the chimney"?

"Are you sure you can't stay for dinner?" Roger was as anxious as his wife. Both cared for the old man and loathed to think of him being lonely.

"Thank you, no. I'll come by again soon…if that's all right with the lady."

Reaching for his hand, Carolyn reassured him: welcome anytime. A blush rushed his cheeks, betraying his heart. Citing a previous obligation as reason for his departure, Roger walked him out while Carolyn went into the pantry, dutifully hovering over the pressure cooker; it did not require her assistance. She was seeking steam heat. Roger entered the kitchen, pausing at the pantry door. She felt her husband's stare then glanced in his direction.

"What is it?" Roger's quizzical expression prompted Carolyn's question.

"That was strange." The man seemed distracted.

"The visit?"

"*And* the conversation." Carolyn agreed. "Swallows? What was that about? I think he knows something he's not telling us." Sounding a bit suspicious.

"I think he just *did* tell us…it was an admission." She was right.

"An admission of what?" Roger's question was oblivious but honest.

"I'm not sure....I think *something* is living in the chimney!"

"I think the old man has fallen in love with you."

"Jealous?" A wicked grin pursed her lips.

"Maybe." Roger was only slightly indignant, not threatened in the least by his competition.

"Good. It'll keep you on your toes!" Carolyn continued the tedious chore at hand, yet another Sisyphean task involving the mindless peeling of onions, carrots and potatoes, which was fine, as her mind was otherwise preoccupied with far more ethereal matters...a persistent vision of swallows in flight.

---

*"Advice is what we ask for when we already know
the answer and wish we didn't."*
Erica Jong

~ **Cynthia tempting fate again** ~

55

sounds of silence

"God speaks in the silence of the heart. Listening is the beginning of prayer."
Mother Teresa

Solitary confinement is frequently utilized as a cruel form of punishment; with purpose and reason. Carolyn spent many hours alone; even though April was at home with her, the baby of the family often occupied her time playing upstairs with *sister* toys while they were away at school. The farmhouse was enormous. Both remained isolated within a shared space. Carolyn sometimes heard April off in the distance, chattering incessantly, dragging her multitude of toys across the floor from room to room through an expansive upper deck. At times an object would get wedged into one of the holes of ornate wrought iron grates installed in the ceiling. Carolyn would answer a damsel in distress call, poking them back through with a broomstick: "Thanks, mom!" drifting down from above; a bright, angelic face appearing in the portal.

For the most part, Carolyn relished this solitude. Once all obligations were met she'd steal some time for herself. It was always time well spent, wrapped up in a warm blanket, cradling a book. The ladies often checked in with each other. It was understood; a reasonable expectation between mother and child. April knew her mom would prepare lunch. They would come together in the kitchen around noontime to share a meal. Mom knew her baby would nap for an hour or so after her belly was full. It was their routine; the calm before the storm which inevitably blew in as gale force wind once four siblings arrived; quite like clockwork, appearing on the threshold each and every afternoon; as predictable as sunrise…sunset… sunrise…sunset. Quickly fly the years.

The house absorbed light and sound. It was a vacuum of sorts, like a black hole in the cosmos. Windows upstairs were rather small; the middle bedroom a beneficiary of only one rectangular light source tucked into the outside wall above the eaves, a window which seemed to belong in the captain's quarters of a great ship. The chimney closet was always warm and cozy. It was space April chose, assembling an elaborate village for the **Little People**; gifts they received at Christmas: a collection of wooden miniatures, each figure painted with primary colors. Combining figures to create a community, during school days April had them all to herself or so thought her mother. With benefit of only one bulb the space a child shared behind a chimney became illuminated. Safe haven: an escape hatch from the cold. From one reality into another: as a rendezvous point where ethereal met corporeal…to play. April had a secret.

As Carolyn stood at the sideboard in the kitchen, she distinctly heard the familiar sounds of movement upstairs. It provided a certain comfort to hear a little one above her, smiling at the thought of her daughter having so much time and space to be a child. At this exact instant, April appeared beside her mother; sound silenced overhead. Bright blue eyes peeked out from behind a mass of blond; a meshed web of shiny strands requiring the stroke of a brush. "Hi!" Carolyn leapt from her daughter, a spontaneous reaction she could not avoid, startling both of them. She peered up toward the ceiling, trying to hear anymore movement. Her immediate thought was of an intruder in the house. She bolted through a hallway from which April emerged; climbing stairs two steps at a time; mind flooding with regrets at an obvious oversight: failing to bring along something made of cast iron…as a weapon. Searching bedrooms one at a time, Carolyn found nothing amiss. Quickly returning to find April, anxious to make amends, as she had frightened the child, they met halfway in the middle bedroom upstairs. Carolyn had been followed. April's unexpected presence again startled the woman, a bit on the jittery side of a new reality.

"What's wrong, mom?" Breathless, April was curious and equally alarmed.

"Nothing honey; I thought I heard something. That's all."

"Maybe you did." An innocent voice: "I hear stuff up here all the time."

"What kind of *stuff* do you hear?" April shrugged her shoulders then took her mother by the hand, leading her out of one bedroom into another.

57

Her heart still pounding from the sprint, Carolyn did not follow up on these remarks at the time. April asked if she could go back into the chimney closet to play but her mother was reluctant to allow her to return. Instead, she took her daughter downstairs into the kitchen where they'd play a spirited game of **Chutes and Ladders**. April won. Her mother made sure of it.

Over lunch, Carolyn inquired about what April had heard in the house. The child had already moved on, other thoughts occupying her mind. She did not respond in any depth of description, only telling her mother she heard noises coming from other rooms when she was in the closet. This was true of all the residents, especially during the night. Whether it was a brisk wind whistling through the eaves or a poorly stacked log in the woodshed taking a tumble or the natural expansion and contraction of the structure, the *quiet* home made a great deal of sound in the darkness; no silent nights there but it was daytime.

Carolyn put April down for a nap. Indulging a cup of coffee, in preparation for the chaos which would surely ensue when her darlings disembarked from a bus in the coming hour, she leaned into the sofa, listening to the house with new ears...looking with new eyes. She began wondering if the seclusion had tricked her senses or bewitched her mind. No. Her senses were working fine.

There was no doubt about it. Their farmhouse was cavernous. As the light dispersed it would dissipate, as if being absorbed. Sounds were warped and distorted within plaster walls; it would either become magnified or be utterly lost in the ether. When amplified, the home seemed to be wired for sound: no privacy in even a whisper. At other times, an opposite effect occurred and the most vehement shout was inaudible at the slightest distance. The house broke all the basic rules of physics, what human beings have long presumed to be a given: Immutable Laws of the Universe. Having never before encountered something so bizarre, she marveled; its acoustics defied logic. Had she been a natural scientist, perhaps it would have made some sense. No longer merely a matter of intellectual curiosity, Carolyn found herself concerned about the welfare of her child this February morning; she could not attribute the sounds she'd heard overhead to anything or anyone, yet she experienced it. Until that morning she had assumed there was a rational and reasonable explanation for everything; a sensible notion being formally challenged. Imagine.

Unique acoustics could not explain the event. Contemplating exactly what happened and when, Carolyn re-created the moment in mind when April was standing beside her. She recalled reverberations in the floorboards overhead. Impossible! Considering what had transpired from every conceivable angle, she could not reconcile the event or comprehend any scenario which satisfied the physical science, short of an intruder being in their house; the fear still at work lurking in her consciousness. So many places to hide, so many different ways to enter; their only security was born of isolation. With April a few feet away on the sofa comfort came in watching her daughter sleep as it had when listening to her play upstairs. A perceived threat prompted visceral reactions: alarm; sensory signal indicating a violation of sanctuary: Fear: the intruder.

For the first time, Carolyn sensed another presence. An odd queasiness, a sickening bile-driven twisting of her stomach occurred, one which she could not ignore. Blaming the coffee, she pushed it away in disgust. This dis/ease persisted for several minutes, a perception that she was not alone. The light was changing. The air felt heavy; thick and dark. Carolyn lowered her head, waiting for it to pass. It did. The pallor lifted as if evaporating and then it was over, as quickly as it had come. Slowly raising her head, as if retreating from a solemn prayer, she distinctly heard her baby breathing softly from across the room. Shaking off an eerie sensation she glanced down at her wristwatch. The girls were due home at any minute! Shocked to realize so much time had lapsed, certain it'd been only a few moments, Carolyn reached for her coffee. It was ice cold, as was the parlor. Glancing up toward their antique clock, it was no longer keeping proper time. It had stopped almost two hours before; about the time she'd put April down for a nap. Disoriented, she stared at the silent timepiece. Roger had relocated it from the kitchen wall because of the same problem. A reliable heirloom he inherited after his father's untimely death, Roger's most prized possession, a familiar tick ~ tock just stopped; its pendulum stilled by some unknown force. Why it kept failing was anyone's guess. Perhaps the walls were uneven; one theory. As Carolyn made her way over to April, bringing a warm blanket along, she gently placed it across her daughter. Soundly asleep, April did not stir, no notice taken of the extra layer being added to her nap. Carolyn was relieved she hadn't awakened while her mother was stricken by whatever it was that had a hold of her. There was no time remaining to consider this anomaly further. The school bus had arrived and she had to head the girls off at the pass before they woke up their sister. Racing through the house yet again, she caught them at the kitchen door. A promise was issued: hot chocolate and cookies if they'd only be *quiet* while April slept. Agreed! While all the ladies gathered around the table enjoying a snack, their littlest sister wandered into the room, wrapped in the blanket her mother had provided. The disgruntled youth quickly confronted her siblings, demanding an explanation: a reason *why* she had been so rudely awakened a few moments earlier! Boo! Who?

"Who shook me like that!?" Rubbing her eyes, the angry pout seemed cute to her sisters and they laughed but Carolyn was not amused. She left the baby behind in the parlor to spare her such an intrusion and none of them had left the kitchen since their arrival. Maybe adding the extra blanket disturbed her sleep, after all. Carolyn pulled her five year old into her lap, comforting the tearful child, speaking softly in her ear; a reassurance *no one* had approached her. Was it a bad dream? No! Adamant one of her mischievous sisters struck, shoved then ran, there was no convincing her otherwise. Her siblings became regretful and equally sympathetic, acknowledging their baby sister's distress. Carolyn, once again overcome by the same sickening feeling she'd struggled to dispel, cringed in disbelief. What...*who* was happening in her house?

Cheerful children spent their evening dour and withdrawn. Whatever *it* was that woke April also scared her; when it came time for bed, she refused to go. Andrea invited her to spend the night but she insisted on staying with mom, and mom agreed, grateful for company. Anxiously awaiting Roger's return, they had much to discuss; she hoped he would shed new light on the matter.

Unable to sleep that night Carolyn sat quietly on the sofa, listening intently, absorbed in the sounds of silence. Moon nearly full, it bathed the house with its soft night light, reflecting off the surface of the snow-laden Earth. Winds were calm; barely audible. Tranquility reigned. A jittery mother had begun to relax, feeling somewhat foolish about her initial reactions to events earlier in the day; episodes which had severely rattled her nerves. Dismissing her own reliable senses, Carolyn began reconciling with herself, coming to terms with her own self-doubt. Any conflict internalized is one always lost. A resolution came quickly once she allowed herself the room to be wrong. Yes. Of course a nimble child could make it down a set of stairs *just that fast*. Yes. All kids have nightmares from time to time, even during the day. She disturbed April herself...the only one to blame. Later, crawling in bed beside her littlest girl, Carolyn finally fell asleep.

Returning home to an exceedingly warm welcome, in spite of the season, Roger greeted his girls as they got off the bus the next afternoon. He arrived earlier than expected, due to a fierce, impending snowstorm which followed him home from upstate New York. Having gone shopping somewhere along the route, he promised his girls, if they would all help him dig out (like it was optional) he would have plenty of snacks available as a reward. A perfect snow day was pending: a day off from school for sure, maybe more than one! A snowstorm held great promise; shoveling, sledding and, oh yes, Twinkies! Long before *junk food* became a common phrase, let alone a staple of the American diet (with the status of *food group*), Carolyn knew what to avoid. She allowed it only occasionally...and this was one of those times. They had a deal. Roger seemed excited by the prospect of being house bound for a day or two. He had just come from a very successful trip and needed some rest. Well aware he had been on the road and away from his family an inordinate amount of time in recent weeks, it was his chance to spend a little time with them before heading back out on the highways, forced to sleep in roadside motels at ten bucks a night. It was one tough way to make a living to be sure, but he was growing a business, affording his family the farm. For this reason alone, Roger found it gratifying. Over the next few days it would be *his* turn to enjoy the place he was working so hard to provide for his loved ones.

Right on schedule: snowstorm blew in with a vengeance. What had anyone done to deserve such an onslaught? It seemed like an explosion of snow. One moment dark, brooding clouds gathered like a gang plotting on the horizon. The next, it was beating on their windows and doors, attempting an unlawful entry. That night Roger did the honors, tucking his girls into bed, presenting each of them with a brand new electric blanket; gifts warmly received. April had forgotten about any trepidation she had the night before, going happily to her own bed with her very new very pink blanket, one with soft satin trim, so bright it seemed to glow in the dark... like a night light!

"Wow! Thanks, daddy! It's better than Twinkies!" Roger was delighted; he didn't even care how much it would cost to heat those cozy comforters.

"As long as we don't lose the electricity you'll be nice and warm tonight." Roger said goodnight to all the girls then rejoined his wife downstairs. She'd been preparing for the worst. Dozens of candles laid out, sprawled across the dining room table, several oil lamps placed on the sideboard in the kitchen, each one an excellent source of light and heat when everything else around them went cold and dark, all but inevitable based on the sound and fury of a howling bitter wind. It proved to be quite a snowstorm; perfect for cuddling. They sat together quietly, listening to the raging storm striking the house like a battering ram. Roger had been sure to catch the evening news. Relaying the blood-curdling message, he bluntly stated, "It has already dropped over three feet in Buffalo...the same in Syracuse. The Berkshires are buried."

"What will it do for us?" Carolyn's sarcastic inquiry required no response. Both knew precisely what it meant for them: digging out, again. Gusts lashed at their house from every direction. Snow was setting up like Plaster of Paris; whiteout conditions beyond windows and doors meant they would play hell getting out of it in the morning. Forget about the shovels; try a chisel instead! Roger's concerns had less to do with a snowstorm and more to do with some snuggling up with his wife. His mood was jovial; his touch, sweet and gentle. She did not want to spoil the moment but Carolyn could not disguise her own legitimate concerns any longer.

"What's wrong?" Roger sensed her distraction.

"Maybe it's nothing, really."

"Really? *Something*, I think."

"Could we just talk for awhile?" Her ardent appeal was lost on the man.

"Well, talking was not *exactly* what I had in mind!" He might as well have been holding a cigar. Having inadvertently married Groucho Marx, his wife pulled away as he rubbed his moustache into her neck, thinking it a far better distraction. Resisting overt advances, Carolyn remained ardent. She hesitated then stared into his eyes as she spoke, searching for an open, honest, *serious* reaction from her husband. She could read the thoughts behind his gaze.

"Roger, I'm hearing strange sounds in the house and seeing strange things. Maybe I'm getting paranoid but it feels like I am always being... watched."

"Maybe **Perronoid**!" A disapproving glance instantly settled his silliness. "The light *is* strange here. It plays tricks with your eyes. I've noticed it, too."

"It's not just the light. Sounds I hear...as if there's someone in the house."

"What do you mean?" Roger was now paying proper attention to his wife.

"Something invisible...like some presence...I don't know exactly what I'm trying to explain...impossible to put the *feeling* into words that make sense."

"You spend too much time alone...and *way too many* nights alone."

"Not *last* night...April was so scared she slept with me. I think *I'm* the one who scared her. I heard noise from upstairs. I searched the house and thought someone was inside the chimney closet." Roger listened. "I could've *sworn* I heard someone. There are no keys for this place. We can't lock a single door and you're gone all the time." Her voice began to tremble. Averting her eyes to hide the fear, Roger tilted his wife's head upward with a lift of the chin.

"You lived in Cumberland too long. Remember what Mr. Kenyon said: no one will bother us here." His voice was reassuring. The words were vacant.

Carolyn regretted saying anything about it, considering it her responsibility to "hold down the fort" whenever Roger had to be away from home. She did not want to complain or worse, to be perceived as some weakling. A subject dismissed as quickly as it had been addressed, Carolyn smiled her reluctance away, reminding herself to relax because *finally* her husband was home. She felt safe in his presence; a pair of muscular arms wrapped securely around her torso. Gazing up into his eyes, admiring a confident grin with which she was so familiar, she plucked at the corner of his moustache. Talk over.

Time for bed: the way to stay warm in a storm on such a bitter winter night. Whatever threat she perceived had subsided with a few words uttered by her fearless husband. No bluster or bother, at least not inside the house. At the time Carolyn had no way of knowing, contrary to appearances, her husband's inability to assist in a crisis would play a leading role as the drama unfolded. Even when he *was* home, laying beside her in the darkness, he would possess no capacity to intervene on her behalf during an ungodly ordeal, one destined to change her life. Abandonment issues abound: his reassurances, no matter how sincere, were utterly meaningless...when push came to shove.

***

What had been merely an anomaly, the absence or magnification of sound in the house would, in time, take on a fever pitch. There would be incidents; serious and terrifying incidents that precluded screaming children from being heard by parents in the next room. It would come to be described as a *sound barrier* and a *force field*; a state of being imposed by the spirits so they could communicate privately with their own mortal of choice: being *in the bubble*. Though sounds they created were solicitous of attention or acknowledgement this uncanny ability to nullify *all* sound within the realm of their presence, including their own, would prove to be miraculous in Nature. Turning off the stereo, lights out, Carolyn went to bed with a favorite song still ringing in her head. *"Hello darkness my old friend, I've come to talk with you again, because a vision softly creeping left its seed while I was sleeping and the vision that was planted in my brain still remains..."* Ah, Sounds of Silence. In a moment of recognition, she smiled...the words finally made some sense.

"One need not be a chamber to be haunted;
One need not be a house;
The brain has corridors surpassing
Material place."
Emily Dickinson

a matter of time

*"How cunningly nature hides every wrinkle of her inconceivable
antiquity under roses and violets and morning dew."*
Ralph Waldo Emerson

Timeless beings; lost in the Cosmos, suspended in the ether. No concept
of their own hereafter-life; not even aware they are deceased. No need
to mourn them...they're not really gone. It was all too much to take in,
to absorb into a mind unprepared to receive their message. A quantum
leap in consciousness had to occur for seven mere mortals to comprehend
what they'd witnessed, to accept the existence of spirits in a shared space;
disbelief in the concept of time was a prerequisite to its understanding.
Human beings seem to process information linearly. The new paranormal
required a substantial adjustment; thinking in an entirely different way about
an otherwise commonly accepted system of measurement. Each member
of the family was being forced to step across the threshold, beyond their
comfort zone; an acknowledgment of truth. It was only a matter of time.

***

TIME: There is no adherence to the notion in the netherworld. Either
they come and go as they please or else they have never left...but the spirits in
the farmhouse were, at the very least, capable of manipulating the continuum.
If time and space exist together or they are mutually exclusive, **whatever**
exists in Nature allows them a certain freedom to manifest at will. Perhaps
in death they no longer suffer this narrow interpretation of a far greater
concept. Yet, these spirits seemed to manipulate mortal time with purpose
and reason; the stopping of an antique clock, seeming to be specifically
intended to coincide with their arrival: apparitions coming and going under
cover of darkness then dissipating with the light of dawn. There had to be
some logical connection. Their behavior appeared to be deliberate.

When the girls began divulging and withholding various experiences,
each had already come to terms with the fact: not everything in life is
at it appears or disappears; each understood she was seeing and hearing

some phenomena unlike anything she had ever encountered before. This fundamental shift had to occur before they could begin describing what they were sensing to others. Once the pervasive skepticism subsided in their father, he too was obliged to acknowledge the truth. His tedious, often obstinate denials made disclosure much more difficult for his family. The girls would turn instead to a sister or mother, but their father was off limits in terms of discussing whatever scared them. The one they needed to protect them did not believe them and he was rarely home long enough to see for himself. Abandonment issues abound.

When they discovered what was happening in the house, in their lives, the Perrons had to make the critical decision of whether or not to remain at their farm. They were all in love with a place which also frightened them. As they watched events transpire in their home each sought refuge away from it and each was blessed with complete comprehension of time as we know it based upon the Nature unfolding around them, season by season, year after year. They lived in a house which divulged secrets of its own as a series of "ages" revealed themselves: a variety of entities dressed in the apparel of another era, another time in history, as if in the Colonial period when their house was built; or as some esoteric apparition appearing to be the same man at various stages of his life. The lines of time were blurred and then erased. The family began to see an open path existed in their home, a passageway; a portal to the past as well as to the future. Essentially, the house is a time machine through which everything passes to everywhere else.

The children were not afforded the luxury of growing up simply accepting the parameters of existence. Instead, they were all compelled to reconsider concepts they had been taught. Prior to moving to Harrisville the lessons they had learned, something as innocuous as how to **tell time**, suddenly seemed so complicated and incomplete in comparison to the information they required to navigate a treacherous voyage through time and space. It was stressful for them as what these girls strived for was some semblance of normalcy in their otherwise chaotic lives. Imagine being tucked in by a spirit! Imagine being forced to listen to voices telling secrets in the darkness; where to look to find their bodies. Imagine getting up in the morning to have breakfast then go off to school, as usual, where what occurred the night before cannot be revealed; a rude awakening, to say the least…and that was all they could say!

To describe these children as isolated is only a small part of the story. They had no choice but to adjust then adapt to an ethereal environment, one totally contrary to what each discerned as *reality*; what they knew of the world had changed abruptly, compelling them to reconcile heady concepts for ones so young. It took time. As human beings have a tendency to tick ~ tock through life, they did the same. Whenever **IT** happened and a youngster felt her body trembling from inside out, time was suspended. It ceased to exist…if it ever did. During these moments, what Cynthia describes as being *in the bubble* occurred; that certain icy tingle, a surge of energy or synergy charges in and everything becomes one thing, frozen in time. No matter how frightening or ugly it is, what is there is amazing. That this happens is miraculous. Stepping through time, feeling its irrelevance is awe-inspiring, a powerful emotional experience. It challenges all former beliefs; questions everything presented as fact, accepted as law. In these mesmerizing moments life feels surreal, like a drama being played out on an infinite stage; its characters showing up at will out of nowhere. Any mortal with a leading role is at once captivated yet free to drift into third-person narrative. As body and mind separate temporarily, so to watch from above, a principle player transforms into audience, as well. As the newly introduced element of reality, it was difficult to discern why the supernatural world intermingled, overlapping with present reality; how could this possibly occur? To comprehend the manifestation of these apparitions, friend or foe, one must first endure a wholly consciousness-altering event.

A wise friend once said: "If you can only speak Chinese then you can only speak Chinese." One cannot understand what one cannot understand. That's how it was for their first few months; inconceivable. It was difficult enough to believe one's own eyes; like an existential nightmare. Initially, all of their encounters were terrifying, simply because they occurred. There was no way to factor in their true significance, the extent of their power or its source. An unknown quantity did not fit into a specific mold or any construct with which they were familiar. An anomaly persisted: Now for something entirely NEW! This aspect of their existence would consume the attention of all concerned mortals, precluding any deeper reflection. They were blown away.

It was only a matter of time before Roger's consistently belligerent refusal to acknowledge or accept their predicament festered into a poisonous pocket of disease in the heart of a marriage; only a matter of time before these spirits became an ordinary part of life at the farm. In time everyone would learn to measure precious moments on Earth according to the sunrise and sunset, the depth of the darkness and lilt of the light. Theirs would not be a conventional pathway to enlightenment; no ordinary journey. It all began with the singular realization...time is not the tick ~ tock of a clock marking the minutes of life but rather an exquisite nothingness; acceptance that time is not what it seems and may not *be* at all. It was an expansive concept for mortals to embrace but it was necessary for each one to do so before anything else could make sense. The mother often reminded her daughters: *"To every thing there is a season and a time for every purpose under Heaven."* Actually, she sang it to them. This realization defined a collective childhood, causing girls to seek time in Nature; going forth into the woods where any concept of time is irrelevant, as when being visited by an entity capable of stepping across this threshold in time and space, through a portal, in much the same way children hop across a creek; a quantum leap into an alternate reality, there to behold the wonder, to marvel at the antiquity and newness of Nature; to worship it as God.

Galileo told humanity to look up; his concept of time and space Universal. Whitman told humanity to look down, describing a single blade of grass as the journey work of the stars. Truth be told, everyone must find their path to travel through life, hopefully one which leads out of the darkness and into the light. As a method of measurement based upon Nature itself, the invention of time was brilliantly conceived and still functions splendidly as the system by which humanity marks its existence: a precise, entirely arbitrary assignment yet, by its mere presence, establishing the concept of past, present and future. It is a calculated attempt to control and manipulate environment, providing a specific structure to be learned, accepted and followed by mortals in search of a purpose and meaning to an otherwise chaotic world. However, when one is close enough to touch, to smell and hear someone else who died centuries before they were born, this contact warps time and skews space for eternity. Nothing is ever the same. Nothing is ever small or compartmentalized again. An encounter of this kind rapidly expands *any* consciousness impacted by a vision that cannot be explained and cannot be denied. It does not fit the mold, that tidy little package of precepts constructed by humanity as the method to tally its toll. When mortals stare into the liquid blue eyes of an immortal soul, all time is suspended, fractured and dispersed into the ether in this moment of recognition. A tingling sensation, this infusion of energy forces any thinking being to reconsider time in a far more expansive context: Alternate Reality. Questions persist. What creates the vacancy at contact? Is there another place in space that has its own time? Does the existence of one preclude the other; functioning in terms like an over-write program superimposing itself on the instant it's perceived? Is time significant, observed or necessary where spirits dwell? Do they attempt to measure infinity? These entities do not seem to adhere to constraints and limitations mortals impose on their own existence. Instead, they manifest in places where they do not belong, at least according to the current occupants. But what if they *do* belong? What if they never left? Suppose it is perfectly natural for them to be there…at home. There was so much to contemplate, as each encounter caused a pause for reflection. It was a stunning realization for each and every member of their family, compelling seven mortal souls to reconsider what time is and is not; to think about what it means to go backward, to have spirits come forward into shared space void of the concept of time, prompting a moment of silence. These ethereal beings are *present* in the world. No matter where they come from or where they are going, they are also here…simultaneously. Do human beings witness them as manifestation of memory? Is thought-energy so vivid, precise and intensely focused that a distant memory is capable of *appearing* in the setting where a thought or an action originally occurred? Is time an illusion, practiced by the illusionists who created it to provide them a creature comfort? Thoughtfully considering the concept, Carolyn explored while her husband continued to be actively uncomfortable with the notion. For Roger, it was only a matter time before he too would be confronted by this inconceivable, unacceptable truth; only a matter of time before he could no longer deny his own Reality.

The simplest solution to this dilemma was also the most obvious; five little girls who could not understand what they sensed, seeking respite and refuge, escaped into the woods. Nature is not abrupt or abusive. It does not come and go; it is. It is patient and passive, teaching its lessons by osmosis. Gradually retreating into four seasons, so to measure their passage of time at the farm, children were blessed to discover a certain timeless quality about the floor of a forest. In the woods, everything made perfect sense: Simpatico in Nature.

"Nature does not hurry, yet everything is accomplished."
Lao Tzu

~ the meandering Nipmuc River ~

contact

"Unless you believe you will not understand."
Saint Augustine

To become one with spirit: to be touched by an ephemeral being, no matter how briefly, is a wholly breathtaking experience; an ethereal journey through time and shared space. It leaves one profoundly and permanently altered. A perpetual questioning of the senses is abandoned over time, replaced with an unquestionable belief as mortal minds are forced to absorb then reconcile an irreconcilable difference between dimensions: alternate reality in new Light.

***

The front hallway connecting the kitchen to the dining room was the most frequently traveled route and least comfortable place in the house. Their dog refused to pass through it, regardless of any enticement offered. Over time it would be recognized and accepted as a veritable hot/cold spot of supernatural activity, though no one immediately understood its full implications. Instead, they'd scurry through this oddly disquieting passageway, ignoring what they could not see. Children moved quickly through that corridor, unconsciously sensing the presence, always feeling *watched* within its dark spaces. Nobody ever lingered long near a cellar door; no tempting fate allowed. It was where two of them had seen this man; a phantom standing in the corner behind the door, on the day they moved into the house. The other three had not yet seen him but felt a natural aversion to that cold dampness; the smell of an earthen cellar seeping through the cracks of the door to avoid. Months later, when the children began comparing mental notes on the subject, each of them reported a specific, identical sensation evoked in the hallway; a need to evade a space. Unfortunately, it was a main route through the house and went to a bedroom upstairs as well. Both of the stairwells posed their own series of hazards.

Cynthia was the first to make contact; physical with metaphysical contact. The school bus had arrived. She was not ready to go. Her books were stacked in a pile in Andrea's bedroom stairwell, clear on the other side of their house, right where she'd left them on her way down for breakfast. All of her sisters were leaving as she rushed through the kitchen, into the hallway, her mind focused on one thing: books. Their driver was beeping the horn: "Let's go!" Cynthia wasn't thinking about a spooky feeling she often had in that hallway, running far too quickly to care at the time.

Perhaps that fact is precisely what left her vulnerable to attack; open to this encounter, as her defenses were down; virtually non-existent in the panic of that moment. As she stepped across the threshold of the kitchen door, Cindy was intercepted by a silky, smoky figure emerging through the cellar door. It placed itself directly in her path. There was no time to stop. No time or react. She'd inadvertently body-slammed the intruder; as she did so, it disappeared, vaporizing instantly. The apparition was indistinguishable, more a mass than an actual form. At point of impact, its intense odor and frigidity all but halted her momentum, knocking her back in her tracks. She breathed it deeply into her lungs with a gasp of frozen air. This sudden, foul influx caused her body to lurch into spasms, coughing convulsively; propelling the girl forward with violent jolts: a reflex reaction. It had literally stopped her cold. As her sisters boarded the bus their driver waited less impatiently, reassured that Cindy was on her way. She'd finally made it to the bus stop but her mother was picking her up from school within the hour. What happened adversely affected the youngster in a way she could not recognize as cause. The normally boundless energy of an eight year old had been depleted, her sprint rudely interrupted; abruptly and inexplicably, by something wicked. When Cynthia fell asleep at her desk, the teacher called the nurse. Carolyn put her into bed and there the child remained, sleeping for the next two days and straight through the night. Nobody suspected anything more sinister than the onset of a cold. In a way, that's exactly what it was. It took time for her to fully recover from a contact which occurred between mortal and immortal one chilly winter morning.

This metaphysical intermingling, though brief, effectively robbed the child of her life force; it required an inordinate amount of time to replenish.

Cindy didn't have a virus or a cold; she had an encounter. Contact was made. It was what they did and how they did it...how they could and would usurp then divert a form of energy for their own nefarious purposes; they *took* whatever they wanted from whatever source was available, so to manifest as form. The spirits drained energy from the house and its inhabitants in a variety of ways but nobody realized it or suspected anything of the kind for months to come. Even when this did occur to Carolyn, she doubted her own intuition about it. This concept seemed entirely implausible and yet it was precisely what was happening in the house. Cynthia was the initial point of contact; the first one to feel the stunning sensation: the passing essence of death itself, stealing and stocking whatever it could as a method of manifestation...as an infiltration.

"There is a land of the living and a land of the dead
and the bridge is love, the only survival, the only meaning."
Thornton Wilder

a chill in the air

"Whenever evil befalls us, we ought to ask ourselves, after the first suffering, how we can turn it into good. So shall we take occasion, from one bitter root, to raise perhaps many flowers."
Leigh Hunt

The frigid dampness of the house could not be overcome. It had an adverse effect on everyone, but Carolyn seemed to sense it most profoundly. Within a few days of moving into the ancient structure, her joints began to throb and ache and her knees began visibly swelling. It quickly became a chronic pain, primarily attacking the joints and connective tissue of this young, strong and agile woman. Attributing her pain to the grueling process of moving, Carolyn had invested countless hours packing...and then unpacking their belongings. The boxes were heavy and she'd lifted dozens of them. Though stiff and sore every morning, she usually ignored it, far too busy to focus on much else but her kids and their needs, especially on school days. She got up and got going. Moving around was its own form of therapy. A hot shower handled the worst of the pain, most of the time. Carolyn thought this was a temporary malady, one which would surely subside once they were settled in. It was an improper assumption to make; thinking it would heal in time and she would have time to heal. Struggling through those few remaining boxes was its own reward. It was a Christmas celebration in February. She discovered a bevy of treasures missing for months and in some cases, years. Several of these boxes yielded memories from her youth, things she'd tucked into the back of her bedroom closet well more than a decade earlier. In spite of all of her stress and strains, Carolyn kept her spirits up, taking pleasure in the little delights; simple gifts. A long lost trinket found, a book of poetry longing to revisit anxious eyes.

In spite of pain, she persevered, certain it would subside. It never did. She would often shake her head and say: "I'm too damn young to feel this old." It was awful; a mean-spirited season. Winter was relentless; no respite. Though physical labor finally came to an end, the pain lingered, gradually worsening. Opting out of chores requiring too much of her joints, especially shoveling, Carolyn began to withdraw into a shrinking form, cocooning in blankets and heavy sweaters; doing whatever she could to avoid freezing to death though she was never really warm. Nothing helped. Eventually, this insidious aching spread throughout her entire being, as if possessing a pulse of its own; a life force, reserving the worst of its cruelty for her slender neck, settling in as if planning an extended stay. Carolyn began to complain: it felt as if something was broken. The local doctor told her to *take it easy and stay warm.* "A total waste of time and money!" was how she described the appointment. Not long afterward she realized this was a strange and different dis/ease; it had nothing to do with muscles being pulled by moving heavy objects. A dank dampness had penetrated her body. She recalls it as an oppressive weight crushing her rigid, frozen joints. The woman was becoming too cold to move and too tired to care. Retiring to the relative warmth of her bed for hours a day, the young mother felt old; decrepit. A fierce primal urge begged to be satisfied; Carolyn required the elemental comfort of fire to survive this ordeal called winter.

Why? A naturally inquisitive woman could not help but wonder why all of the fireplaces had been sealed shut. Why had Mr. Kenyon been so evasive on the subject when she broached it with him? Why were there certain spaces in the house which felt so much colder than others did? How could Carolyn see her own breath when someone standing right beside her would claim to feel perfectly comfortable at the mere mention of this observation? Increasingly agitated by a pervasive chill in the air, she began demanding answers. There had to be a logical explanation; a sensible solution to this problem. It was as though she was being held against her will; forced to stay, to live in a harsh, inhospitable environment with no hope of escape. HELL! She just got there! As if buried alive under snow, trapped in her dream home, it was the first of many nightmare scenarios yet to manifest as her destiny. Try as she might, it soon became evident to all; Carolyn could not dig herself out of this one! In too deep...already in over her head...drowning in despair and discontent.

***

One morning Carolyn awoke to become instantly aggravated. The bedroom was bitterly cold; she shuddered at the idea of removing the covers from her shivering body. Their dream of this supposedly placid and peaceful place in the country was being shattered by the reality of it; the incessant discomfort she'd battled caused her to feel totally defeated. A perpetual pain in the neck had become so intense she began to think something inside of it had snapped; bones too brittle to withstand the weight of a skull on its shoulders.

Her stomach was on fire; a persistent burning sensation undoubtedly due to the vast quantity of aspirin she felt forced to ingest on a daily basis, in order to remain barely functional. Gradually Carolyn's sweet disposition began to sour, presumably altered by chronic pain; the adversity she came to perceive as an adversary, one associated with harsh conditions in an extended winter. Later on she would attribute her woes to the equally strange circumstances in which she'd found herself, living with the dead. Increasingly reclusive, her moods grew darker; a black hole had developed in the cosmos of her soul. A corresponding vacancy appeared in her eyes as it began consuming her spirit. It was time to build a fire. Carolyn craved the presence of light and heat.

That cold spring morning she sent her children off to school. Walking them out to the bus stop, she and April made a pit stop at the woodshed on the way back into the farmhouse. Carolyn stood at the entrance, staring at a solid wall of aged hardwood. Resentful about it; cord after cord of long-seasoned logs languished in its neatly-stacked piles, never put to good use. "What a waste!" was the only comment she could muster in disgust. Roger was again away on business and he would be gone for the next few days. Again, his wife had a moment of divine inspiration. What had been stocked and stacked out in the woodshed would be drafted into service...Carolyn concocted the grand plan. Suddenly frustration had an outlet; a dour mood lifted with the promise of a solution. Later in the day, a rusty crowbar in hand, she decided to expel the demon chill from her home. A broad smile crept to her lips as she vowed **not** to succumb, **not** to surrender but to fight; to vanquish what was haunting her.

Carolyn was about to unleash a torrent of supernatural activity, through no fault of her own. She was cold. Her children were cold. The fireplace called to her in mind. It was still functional, according to Mrs. Hertzog. Apparently Mr. Kenyon had been willing to discuss its status with the realtor, if not the purchaser. Although the center chimney (which once served the kitchen and dining room) had been removed, by necessity, due to its advanced age and dangerous disrepair, many decades before she inhabited the house a smaller chimney in the parlor had also been sealed shut for some inexplicable reason. It offered some hope of warmth and renewal to the woman who felt crippled with pain. The stark absence of heat, the marked inability of an old clapboard farmhouse to retain it, became her primary concern as lingering winter kept churning out one brutally cold week after another in spite of the fact that the calendar said it was spring! Carolyn believed there had to be another way to generate some warmth from what was the most obvious source. She craved the pure heat of fire. She'd needed something to effectively banish the chill penetrating her body to the bone. Staring into the woodshed had provided the point of epiphany. It would not be long before that wood went up in flames.

"I am still determined to be cheerful and happy, in whatever situation I may be;
for I have also learned from experience that the greater part of happiness or
misery depends upon our dispositions, and not upon our circumstances."
Martha Washington

~ woodshed in a winter wonderland ~

creature discomforts

"Adversity is the first path to truth."
Lord Byron

Their family cat wanted no part of her new home. Juliet refused to cross the threshold then had to be carried into the house, in howling, vehement protest. A normally docile, affectionate cat became suddenly hostile and frightened. She chose to hide underneath the sofa for the first few days, emerging only reluctantly when hungry or in a desperate need of the litter box. Naturally, all their chaos and confusion had been quite disconcerting and her distress was understandable. Assuming some type of adjustment would be required of all the new occupants, no one thought much of it at the time.

After a few weeks passed, the lovely feline seemed to settle in to her new digs. It was typical of her to snuggle up with one child or another every night and it was usually Andrea. She would tunnel her way beneath the quilt and purr contentedly until she fell asleep. At least this had been the case when the family lived in Cumberland. Once the ritual, it was no longer; a formerly soft demeanor changed abruptly; radically so. She continued to choose a child to sleep with but their routine was decidedly different. Juliet would cautiously slink into the bedroom and look around before pouncing onto the bed. Then, instead of seeking any attention or affection from her roommate, she scurried beneath the covers, as if in hiding. Once she was under the blanket she would growl and moan for several minutes, moving restlessly before settling down for the night. When morning arrived, the cat would emerge from the bed just as cautiously as she'd entered it the evening before, surveying the room then bolting for the kitchen as if her life depended on it, perhaps seeking safety in numbers. No one could explain it; this sudden change in her personality after moving into the farmhouse. She began avoiding contact with the children and spent most of her time alone, either poised on top of a dresser or up on back of the sofa, high off the floor, where she could better see whatever it was she was watching...and she was always watching something. Fur puffed up, ears slicked back as if tacked to the sides of her head, whatever she thought she saw was frightening the furtive feline. Based on her adverse reactions, it was definitely threatening... something wicked this way comes.

On numerous occasions Juliet would enter a room then literally stop dead in her tracks. The kitty would hiss and bare her fangs, staring wild-eyed into thin air. Then she would go into attack stance, ears plastered down, fur fully extended from her body. Rearing up onto her back feet; horrendous sounds emanated from a petite feline: threatening, ominous sounds which could only be associated with self-protection. Claws fully distended, moaning deeply, she would viciously lash out at **nothing** then run from the room and hide for hours, impossible to locate.

April received a puppy for her sixth birthday and the child was overjoyed, as were her sisters who had mourned the terrible loss of Bathsheba and also longed for another dog. She was a mix of Labrador and German shepherd; a beautiful specimen. Adored by all the girls, Jennifer Rebecca became a truly cherished member of their family. She was sweet and kind, gentle and highly intelligent. However, whenever it came time for her to pass through the front hallway, this normally jovial, cooperative puppy became a different creature. Instantly defensive, Jenny's posture warped, twisting into that of an animal which had been traumatized or abused. She had become absolutely terrified. Jennifer would belligerently lie down on the floor, refusing to move beyond that doorway. One time Roger tried to pull her through and she began to cry: whine and whimper. He pulled a bit harder, trying to coax her through into the kitchen. The dog would have no part of it. Perplexed, he retrieved a steak from the refrigerator, extending it toward her from the kitchen doorway. No response at all. Frustrated, Roger approached their pet. Tugging at her leash, attempting to guide one reluctant pup through the dark hallway, she growled and snapped; behavior totally out of character. Roger released her and never tried again. He respectfully accepted her will, wondering what she knew that he did not, at least not yet. It was one of many incidents involving animals sharing space within the dwelling over the course of a decade. It is said that every creature knows more than any human being; a hypothesis proved beyond dispute at the farm.

There would be more cats and dogs, horses and ponies, a drake named Sir Francis, a rooster named George and two precious bunnies named Trumpet and Flute; Christine's special pets. Pineridge and Royal; Honey and Bessie; Pooh Bear and Lady Victoria, the blue-eyed albino cat. There would be a big, Black Angus bull named Heyboy. The kids loved them, not just peripherally, but principally loved and cherished each one; the kind of love and affection requiring a father to lie to his children when Heyboy went for a ride then the freezer in the woodshed was suddenly stocked with meat the following day. In mourning, they refused to eat until he swore to them he *sold* Heyboy and bought another bull to replace him; a bull they did not know personally. He had to promise their boy was alive and well before dinner could be served. It took more than twenty years but eventually, the confession came. No one has forgiven him yet. It would take some time before mere mortals realized all the critters knew more than they did. What they were sensing was a precursor to an inevitable contact. It was a **heads up** of sorts but no one recognized the significance of reactions occurring in a house where space was being shared by so many souls. Human beings are oblivious. Their animals were re-acting out based upon what they could see, including the dead animals appearing as entities, running through solid walls. Mystery, as well as beauty, is in the eye of the beholder. Their eyes were sharp, their senses keen; they were reacting out of fear, an instinctive response to intrusion. Their discomfort existed with purpose and reason. What they'd sensed and seen was a warning. Best for all creatures, great and small, to pay close attention to messages they may receive from Nature.

Bless the beasts...and the children.

"Fear is a question. What are you afraid of, and why?
Just as the seed of health is in illness, because illness contains information,
your fears are a treasure house of self-knowledge if you explore them."
Marilyn Ferguson

the devil's pets

*"A misery is not to be measured from the nature of the evil,
but from the temper of the sufferer."*
Joseph Addison

Within a few days of moving into their farmhouse, an interesting anomaly occurred. No one thought anything about it at first, other than how strange it was to have houseflies buzzing one's head in the middle of deep winter. The weather was bitterly cold. Nothing could survive outside for very long, so the next logical question was: "Where the hell are *these* coming from?" This was what Carolyn asked of her husband as one of the enormous soaring vermin attempted to land on the top of her head. Swatting and swishing the vile thing away, it returned, repeatedly trying to tangle itself in her dark, flowing hair.

"I think it's in love with you." Roger watched an obsession unfold.

"Kill it!" Doing his best to oblige, Roger grabbed a handful of newsprint (hardly the best tool for the job) from one of the open boxes; quickly rolling it into a weapon designed to finish off the unwelcomed houseguest, his sharp reflexes were no match for the apt agility of the elusive little devil. Instead of fleeing the scene, fearing for its life, this house fly taunted him. The intruder was ugly, its features distinct, especially the eyes. As it kept moving around the room at a deliberately slow and tedious pace, it circled once again…then returned to Carolyn. Something wicked…flies in the face of disbelief.

"Kill the goddamned thing!" The man tried. He could not make contact. As if possessing innate intelligence, the insect managed to escape a vicious swat. Evasive maneuvers engaged, as if anticipating in advance which direction the next strike would come from, it was more than mischievous. It was smart.

"Maybe it likes the smell of your *girly* shampoo." Roger's feeble attempt to lighten the mood backfired before he even knew it. His marked proclivity for escalating a situation applied to all creatures, great and small.

"I've been too damn busy to wash my hair!" As annoyed with her husband as she was by a fly, she glared in his direction.

"Maybe *that's* the big attraction!" Without question: the wrong thing to say at that moment. Making matters worse: a dastardly chuckle escaped his lips, amused as he was by his own juvenile joke.

"Go to hell!" His wife did not share the joy, especially if it came at her expense. The phrase she uttered triggered a response, not in the man... *in the fly.* Unable to expel their intruder, Roger lowered his arms just as the demon dive-bombed her. "Get this goddamned thing away from me!" She leapt from its path. It followed her. She went down to the floor. It followed.

Surrounded by boxes, she was stuck in the center, possessions scattered at her feet. It was like playing Dodge Ball in hell; no viable route for a timely retreat. Forced to rely on her husband, in a critical, accusatory tone, she said:

"You're not trying!" His pitching arm went instantly back into service.

"I am, too!" Naturally, Roger became defensive, due primarily to his wife's sudden loss of a normally good sense of humor. Agitated, he flailed his arms wildly; a madman on a mission.

He really *was* trying and she knew it. They became equally frustrated. She wanted to return to the task at hand and get the job done. He wanted to take a life...or two! Darting between them, neither could reach the evil spawn; not even close enough to wound or disable it. With a concerted effort to do so, Roger accidentally struck Carolyn instead. Oops! She leered at her husband for a moment then recited an appropriate reference; a quotation on her mind: "I'm beginning to wonder if your aim is intentionally *off* target... or is it right *on* target! You know, there's an old Chinese proverb: 'Do not remove a fly from your friend's forehead with a hatchet.'"

"This is *hardly* a hatchet and you're not my friend...you're my wife!" Ah, truer words were never spoken. Even tired and cranky, Carolyn had found it amusing. They laughed, realizing the absurdity of their futile endeavor.

Suddenly it backed away, exhibiting another unusual skill. The fly stopped. It hovered in midair, lingering in place as if suspended on a string. Floating directly in front of her face, almost still, the insect seemed to pause in flight and *watch* Carolyn as if she was some sort of curiosity. It then did precisely the same thing to her husband. The residents had every reason to believe they were being observed; it was how the encounter appeared to the couple. When it finished taking in the sights, the fly buzzed their heads one more time then fled the dining room. Roger watched as it went up the bedroom stairwell.

"Go kill it! Did you see that thing? It is some kind of mutation!"

Roger considered himself above such things as hunting down errant pests; an attitude destined to be altered over time…with a pending infestation.

"It'll be back." He was correct. The villain would return…with friends.

"That's what I'm afraid of! Find it and kill it! Please, before the filthy thing lands on a pillow…or in a plate of food." Carolyn was serious. Roger refused. They didn't speak again for an hour. Before long, morning would be entirely usurped by the practice. Gradually the man would become preoccupied, later consumed by his own relentless pursuit of the devil's pets.

They seemed to come from nowhere…then everywhere. Day after day more flies invaded the house. They all appeared to be the same, perhaps a different visit from the same freaky fly; fat and happy; slow as bumblebees… fast as hummingbirds. Pitch black, the color of coal, their size was uniform: Large. Simply put, these flying things were *not* normal, not average, run-of-the-mill houseflies. In the beginning it was only one or two, here and there, present long enough to be noticed as the oddity they were during that far-from-mild winter. The ubiquitous swarm came a few weeks later. No longer a nuisance, these persistent pests were a problem quickly evolving into a veritable health hazard. No doubt about it…they *must* be breeding in the house.

There was no need for Carolyn to bring the worsening situation to Roger's attention. Their infestation was obvious. It had his full consideration within weeks of moving into the farm. Perplexed by it, Roger and Carolyn discussed their options and potential solutions. What was happening in their home was not just an unfortunate aside or some normal liability of living in the country. They had no choice but to acknowledge the flies as peculiar, their experience of them, noteworthy. They were crafty and sly, covertly insidious, certainly not common, ordinary houseflies trapped and disoriented inside the dwelling. In fact, they seemed quite alert, on their game, but it was more than a game. It was an *occupation* which would soon become Roger's nemesis. After their creepy close encounter occurred while unpacking, the couple took notice of them to a far greater extent. Essentially, they watched them back; not merely pests but pestilence deserving to be as detested as any intruder in their home.

Thoroughly disgusted, Carolyn had genuinely loathed houseflies since her youth; a childhood plagued by the existence of nasty things thriving in steam heat and humidity. Her tolerance had diminished further over time. Having been raised on a farm deep in southern Georgia, surrounded by animals, (the perfect recipe for breeding vermin) she developed this aversion at a young age. According to her, as it was with her mother, flies were to be categorized with all other evils…fleas, ticks, chiggers, cockroaches, mosquitoes, spiders and lice: all the devil's pets. In spite of her reaction to their presence, she was reluctant about the necessity for hiring an exterminator. Treating the house with pesticides was not an option. She preferred instead to use other methods to eradicate a population well before they became a presence beyond control. Roger concurred. Neither wanted anyone exposed to harmful chemicals if it could be avoided; nor did they want anyone exposed to the filth and potential disease such insects introduce into any home. Roger decided to begin with a trip to a local hardware store. He purchased several swatters, enough to outfit every single room of their residence with its own weaponry. A general issued instructions to his lieutenants: **kill on sight**. It was everyone's responsibility to eliminate them at every opportunity. Carolyn's idea of stuffing mothballs in closets and eaves was ineffective, a mild deterrent at best. The following weeks would prove to be a trial by firing squad; the beginning of a war: a test of wills on both sides of the battle.

Even their children, generally oblivious to such things, began to notice the very strange behavior of the flies. In spite of the efforts made, the population increased at a rate which was staggering, yet they were all the same size; no sign of any juvenile delinquents among them. Gathering inside the windows, the incessant buzzing became quite the distraction. Clusters of them huddled together, as if plotting the next move. They seemed to be scheming, devising a flight plan; a strategy for attack. Who'd like to buzz the room next? Whose turn is it to taunt another one of the girls out of her mind? One at a time, one after another, they would soar from the sills of windows only to target a poor soul somewhere in the room; then maliciously torment this individual to the point of insanity: All a part of the plan.

Approaches varied as targets were *not* arbitrary. Everybody had the chance to be picked on then put upon at some point or another during their selection process. As harassment followed, not one member of their family was spared the indignities of a sudden surge, having one of the vile creatures commit the ultimate intrusive antic: an excitable "Charge!" then in the nose or worse yet, into an open mouth. At times passive, at other times overtly aggressive, their movements appeared preconceived; the deliberate actions of thinking beings. The *chosen one* would take flight from the sill and begin buzzing the head of its intended victim. The space invader would begin circling, again and again, making one blatant attempt after another to tangle up in some unruly mass of morning hair; land on a face: wherever there was an enticing surface in sight. Each arrived at its intended destination to have its folly then abruptly retreat. Batting them away proved futile and it was especially aggravating when one would light on a utensil or inadvertently land in a bowl of cereal. Watching an errant fly drowning in milk was never an ideal way to start the day. It was entirely unnerving to hear the recurrent slap of the swatter. Roger monitored the kitchen while his children attempted to eat their breakfast. This practice was unappetizing at best. Though the girls accepted their father's nasty chore as a necessary evil, it was sometimes worse than the presence of pestilence. Their assessment would change over time. As this situation worsened it put a real damper on many a meal. The ritualistic practice of extermination became as distasteful (and fruitless) an endeavor as anyone could have imagined.

Disposing of the carcasses was an equally obnoxious chore. The gruesome task fell to the mistress of the house. As windowsills incessantly littered with the shriveling corpses offered no appeal, their removal became a daily ritual but she learned something in the process. By early afternoon the flies would all die together, en masse. Within minutes, their perpetually humming house would fall silent for a brief period every day, before reinforcements arrived. Windowpanes vibrating with activity in the morning became as still as ghost towns, literal death traps for those who lingered while the Sun made its way across the sky. What light was allowed through etched and icy panes of glass melted frozen prisms in its path. Only then would this curious phenomenon occur. Once the hideous intruders were bathed by the brilliant illumination of direct sunlight, exposed to the radiating heat penetrating each pane of glass, they quickly perished. In the morgue-like atmosphere, silence was more eerie than the monotonous buzzing which came before it. By early afternoon each day what was left, rapidly decomposing remnants appeared shrunken, barely distinguishable. Hollow figures; nothing of substance preserved for posterity. A quick glance revealed the indistinct skeletal remains, mere shadows of the former creatures. Wings disintegrated into ashes. Perforated torsos appeared impaled by bright sunlight. Piles of debris as flimsy as dust accumulated on windowsills; it seemed as though magnified light reflecting through panes of glass burned them to death, cremating their wicked wretchedness where they landed in repose. Within hours their house became inundated again as if each one was a phoenix able to regenerate itself, as if rising from the grave…from the ashes of its own morbid demise: Reborn! It became as predictable as the sunrise or a chill in the air.

After a few weeks of conflicts Roger finally convinced Carolyn it was time for them to seek some professional help. He contacted an exterminator. What the man said was as startling as enlightening. Once he completed a thorough inspection of the premises, he rejoined the couple in the kitchen. Carolyn was disgusted. The one and only time she wanted the flies to make their presence known, to become as obvious to him as they were to everyone in the family, those despicable flies completely disappeared. A conspicuous absence aside, residual evidence remained, making this discovery all the more mysterious. She showed him carcasses; bodies not yet cleaned out from the windowsills. He gasped. His reaction told them something remarkable was happening. His simple, straightforward assessment followed: No BUGS! Other than what he had witnessed languishing in death there was no further evidence of anything at all; nothing breeding in seclusion.

In a quandary, Roger and Carolyn sought his advice. Reassuring the couple no harm would befall the family, he suggested he be allowed to apply a toxic treatment to see if this made any difference. Carolyn remained skeptical but he finally persuaded her; it was the right thing to do. His main concern; flies were breeding in the ancient timbers and though he had not located an outlet for their intrusion, it didn't mean one did not exist. It might have escaped his notice. Room by room, he canvassed the house doing his dirty work. Perhaps it would do the trick; resolve the dilemma. With their thanks, he departed.

Later that afternoon they were back with a vengeance, apparently immune to whatever it was in the chemical tank. The only purpose it had served was to "piss them off" according to Roger. He drove back into town then returned from the local hardware store with something more toxic than anything their exterminator had on his truck: Sticky Paper. It smelled worse than it looked. He went throughout the house, suspending the sappy substance from ceilings then waited for the flies to impact the obstacle in their path. As gravity pulled the spiraling sheets open, each one began capturing its victims in flight. With their gauntlet officially thrown down, an arsenal of weaponry procured then dispatched, it was time to issue a formal challenge: A Declaration of War.

Swatter in one hand, cup of coffee in the other, Roger aimlessly wandered the house for hours…morning after morning. Whenever he was at home, the man would rise before dawn, make the pot of coffee; then await their arrival. Something wicked…indeed. What began as an altruistic attempt to protect a family became much more a demented hobby, evolving into a preoccupation, gradually transforming into obsession. The man of the family took command. Mission: Decimate the fly population. Stalking his prey with single-minded purpose, the killing spree was always well underway by the time his girls got up for school. Focus intensified over time to the point, though his penetrating gaze was in constant search mode he'd stroll past his children, neglecting to greet them as if they were ghosts he couldn't see. He wouldn't respond when spoken to, not because he was being rude or aloof. The man simply did not hear a question or comment posed. His face wore a perpetual grimace during each moment of the hunt. Roger did not merely swat the flies; he crushed and splattered them with a sharp, angry "crack", startling everyone around him. Negative energy oozed from his pores. It was hatred, as evil as the miniature demons he was aiming to eradicate, one at a time; nothing subtle about it.

In spite of all the watching and listening going on, Roger was missing a lot. His children were avoiding interaction with him, especially in the morning. As this transpired over more than three months, the ladies began mentioning their father's behavior to their mother. They were all becoming increasingly distressed and could no longer ignore this problem the same way their father had mastered ignoring all of them. Andrea asked her mother to intervene, to confront him about it. They recognized it: something was wrong with daddy. Likewise, they were all disturbed by horrendous sights and sounds of a slow, impending, inevitable death. The sticky paper was beyond gruesome; it was downright cruel. Objections flew from the beginning as these noxious fumes emanating from the strips permeated the household. It seemed to attract then disorient the flies, as did the vision of others struggling to escape their tomb. Those still free would repeatedly circle, approaching out of morbid curiosity or perhaps a desire to liberate their comrades. In so doing, they would fly too close to the prison wall, becoming its unwitting victim as an intended target. Witnesses soon became captives of this toxic substance; mortal witnesses of their torture were victims of it, as well. Death itself was the only mercy; their only escape from a Hellish-on-Earth existence; a tedious, lingering demise. It took time for them to die, if not from the poison, then from sheer exhaustion of the struggle. Their protests were vehement; loud, angry buzzing became a maddening sound vibrating throughout the dwelling. These creatures fought relentlessly for release from glue-based death traps offering only the promise of a miserable end. They continued to fight through various stages of death. It seemed to take *forever* for them to die. They languished for hours before being silenced by its poison. After weeks of the disgusting sights and sounds, revulsion for everyone concerned, Carolyn removed all the sticky paper. She could no longer condemn her enemies to such an evil end. This was immoral: Unethical. According to a compassionate soul, there **had** to be a better way!

Roger returned home to challenge her decision. Carolyn remained resolute, in steadfast opposition to a gross method of pest control. He acquiesced only after she'd agreed to allow another treatment of pesticides. The exterminator sprayed poison liberally throughout the eaves, the cellar and the woodshed. Even the foundation got a dose of the destructive contaminate, to no avail. A bad attitude emerged as: *"Kill me! THOUSANDS will come to my funeral!"* Employing kamikaze tactics; flying their erratic patterns, evasive maneuvers more aggressively than ever before, the insects resorted to surprise attacks: a strike-from-behind approach. Belligerent creatures developed an obnoxious case of oppositional/defiant disorder; re-acting out by attacking all at once. Communicative by nature, this peculiar anomaly persisted. All knew of their displeasure, as if they were claiming the house from mortal intruders: Ironic.

It is important to note, as all of this transpired over their first few months in the house, other events were happening with such frequency that it made this chronic problem seem virtually irrelevant by comparison. Dynamics altered. Perspective was gained. Anxiety levels heightened. Roger and Carolyn began this odyssey believing the flies were a natural, albeit irritating occurrence. As time passed, minds changed regarding the Nature of the aberrant existence in the farmhouse. It was far more than infestation. It was manifestation.

Incapable of recognizing or identifying this odd disorder, ill-equipped to treat a malady, Roger's all-consuming crusade to conquer the flies continued unabated, resulting in a rather ugly altercation. One morning, early in spring, (glorified winter in Rhode Island) the girls were seated around their kitchen table when Carolyn entered the room, appearing to be exhausted. Roger was swatting at pests with abandon as she pulled out a chair then sat down beside her children. Andrea went to pour her mom a cup of coffee. Frustrated by his pointless task, Roger abruptly and gruffly announced his intention to call the exterminator back to have the house treated again. It was the trigger. Carolyn exploded, firing in his direction...her aim, dead on:

"No more! They'll poison my kids with that shit! I don't want it in this house! I'd rather have the goddamned flies!" Slamming her fist down onto the table, a room went deathly quiet. Even roly-poly-fat-black-demon-seeds hushed! Roger was blown away, shocked into silence by her vulgar outburst. Children choked a breakfast down, several with teardrops on their eyelashes. None of the kids had ever heard their mother yell like this before, as Carolyn simply did not talk that way, certainly not ever in front of her children. It was venomous, coming like the sudden strike from a poisonous snake, as toxic as any chemical on the planet.

"Roger! Put that thing away! Give it up! You're *so* neurotic!"

"What the hell is wrong with you?" Roger's comment was issued more as a statement of fact, not posed as one might a question or matter of concern. He was absolutely furious, embarrassed by her harsh assessment of his behavior. A confrontation between them appeared inevitable...what next?

Children scattered from the kitchen, grabbing their books and coats, fleeing the scene, racing for the bus stop. Escape. Carolyn escorted them to the door, apologizing for her sudden outburst; her uncharacteristically foul language. They all understood. Embracing each of them, sincerely remorseful, sending her girls on their way, the woman stood alone in front of the fireplace. She'd have to return to the kitchen, there to make amends, though she stalled for a few minutes, allowing some time for Roger to calm down. It later occurred to Carolyn, considering the many shrew-like symptoms she had been suffering; this chronic condition, her reaction was a direct result of both mind and body under siege, overwhelmed by anxiety and stress. It had everything to do with what happened while her husband was away. She determined the time had come to tell him the truth; tell him about what was occurring in their house, things he knew nothing about because he was always gone. He was like the spirits: out of sight but never out of mind. A baby girl approached her mom.

Propping April up on an oversized pillow directly in front of an episode of **Sesame Street**, Carolyn returned to the kitchen. Roger had cooled off. He'd been sitting at the table, holding a cup of coffee in hand; no swatter in sight. She sat down beside him. They remained silent for a time as she attempted to gather strength; organize her thoughts. She had a story to tell.

"I'm sorry." Carolyn began crying, something she was not frequently prone to do. After several frazzled minutes she talked with her husband for nearly an hour, detailing the many events she had deliberately kept from him. Once confessing she'd called their attorney Sam to express her concerns, it added credence to her otherwise outrageous claims. Carolyn would never have told Sam she thought they'd made a terrible mistake buying their farm; not unless she really believed it. Roger listened attentively. Based on the subject matter, he too had something to divulge, mentioning the conversation he'd had with Mr. Kenyon on the day of their arrival... an ominous welcome home.

Her gentle intervention ensued. Carolyn explained to her husband that his seemingly maniacal hunt was disrupting a family and profoundly distressing their children. Each was forced to reconsider things neither of them had ever been confronted with before, compelling them to explore concepts beyond the realm of any personal experiences. Conclusions eluded the couple; logic failed them. How does one make common sense of an uncommon dilemma? A presence, demonic in Nature, was exposed by this necessary conversation; acknowledged and empowered in the process. They were utterly unprepared.

***

During the following week everything changed. Inexplicably, the phantom flies disappeared. Years later a woman would arrive and explain that the flies were there with purpose and reason, as the harbingers of things to come. She would look Carolyn in the eyes and speak from her heart. "You can't really kill what's already dead." The woman who would see that ugly truth of their situation and share these quiet words of wisdom was someone familiar with what was an essentially malevolent onslaught; painfully aware of its darkest point of origin: Mrs. Lorraine Warren. She'd come a long distance to observe their household and *all* of its occupants...to observe; like a fly on the wall.

"To know the road ahead, ask those coming back."
Chinese Proverb

safety in numbers

"Who can hope to be safe? Who sufficiently cautious?
Guard himself as he may, every moment's an ambush."
Horace

All the children learned quickly to gather and travel in groups. Their house was spooky enough, cavernous in comparison to where they had come from. Their first little house in Willimantic, Connecticut was practically a glorified apartment when juxtaposed to the farmhouse in which they'd come to dwell. Echo chambers abounded as shadows danced within its light. Bedrooms were gigantic. The woodshed was like having a second home attached to the main one. There was plenty of space to explore but all of the girls had the feeling it was shared space and after their first few days there, none of them traversed it alone, unless absolutely necessary. Though no one spoke of it aloud, all of them had the in-common sense: they were **not** alone. Children are perceptive, sensitive and vulnerable to the spirit world. As this was their initial point of contact, no one knew precisely what to make of it, but they knew something was around them all the time…and sometimes it was something wicked.

Peculiar children, they would go off to school all day long then come home and "play school" together for several hours. They owned an enormous slate blackboard on its solid oak swivel frame; Andrea's most prized possession, adorned with all the accoutrement: chalk of every color, erasers: the works. Andrea was their teacher. She would instruct her sisters, show them whatever she'd learned that day in class. Though most of it was too advanced for them, some of it stuck; her own personal **Head Start Program**. Class convened in the middle bedroom during the winter but this location became problematic so when inclement weather finally broke, they moved it out to the woodshed. Adjusting to the new paranormal took time; it required an inordinate amount of patience. Some scoundrel spirits from the Netherworld did not appreciate having to attend school and would play nasty tricks on mortal children who took **their** studies seriously. Andrea became distressed when her chalkboard was repeatedly smeared, often erased. Detailed sentence diagrams would be lost. History lessons wiped clean away. Tediously transcribed lines of music were smudged beyond recognition; irretrievable. She wondered privately if it was mischievous activity or malicious in Nature, but never said a word.

There was an unspoken Golden Rule in the house: **Do unto others as if you were the others.** No one was ever sent off alone because no one would want to be sent off alone. If the children were playing school and someone needed to use the bathroom then "recess" was declared and everybody went along. Not always, but often when they returned to the *classroom*, their lesson was destroyed. At times, the chalkboard was wiped completely clean; pitch black again, as if it had been swabbed with a wet rag then allowed to dry. In most instances the board was so marred with streaks the information was illegible and could not be preserved. Andrea would have to finish erasing it and begin again. Oddly, nobody remembers discussing this anomaly when it happened. Andrea would re-enter the bedroom and heave a heavy sigh; sisters remained silent on the subject. Everyone could see what had occurred in their absence and *knew* it was none of *them* who'd done it, but no one ever spoke about it. Part of the new paranormal: accept it and move on.

Disgusted with all this unnecessary repetition, Andrea enlisted her father's assistance. One spring day they moved the chalkboard out to the woodshed. He seemed puzzled by her desire to set it up elsewhere because he did not know about their numerous class interruptions. It was quite heavy. Carefully navigating it back down her winding bedroom staircase then out through the summer kitchen, they located the level spot on the wide planked floorboards. School was in session again. He made certain it was secure then went to open the large sliding door. Let there be Light! The children enjoyed the warmth; breezes and bright sunshine while learning their lessons well. Satisfied with the effort, Roger returned to a former chore and a class re-commenced. April did not grasp most of what they studied but she wanted to participate anyway as she was alone so much of the time and wanted to be *in school* like her big sisters. The smallest chair was in front, for her. After several days of peaceful sessions, with no interference from beyond the grave, Andrea was relieved. It was her idea and had been a successful one, or so she thought.

Respite was temporary; relocation had virtually no effect. One afternoon as waning sunlight began casting shadows upon the surface of their chalkboard Cindy announced she was starving, having skipped the afternoon snack to get to class on time. Everybody was hungry and wanted something to nibble on before dinner. Traveling in a pack, they all went back inside the house, intent on spoiling their appetites. Returning to the woodshed, about twenty minutes later, the girls found the chalkboard completely smudged; twisted at a ninety degree angle. Andrea became visibly upset; her frustration, palpable. Angry, struggling to replace it in its proper upright position, erasing smeared lessons from the surface, she finally abandoned the effort in disgust: Class dismissed.

Four children went outside to play in what light lingered of an evening sky. Remaining behind to close the woodshed door, Andrea uttered a vulgar curse beneath her breath. Thinking she was alone, unable to resist the temptation to speak her mind on spirit matters, she expressed her opinion with a naughty phrase, especially for someone so young. Having learned a few new words at school, she put them into practice. Confounded, Andrea truly hoped moving the chalkboard would resolve their dilemma. She was wrong on both counts. No. It didn't matter *where* it was placed and yes, someone *was* listening.

Several more days passed uneventfully; the children played well together. Andrea revised her strategy. Whenever someone needed to leave the group, *one* sibling would accompany her for protection. It worked: their chalkboard was left undisturbed. Someone always stayed out in the woodshed to protect IT from being tagged; a unique form of vandalism. Having determined their offending presence was only *present* during school; lessons were no longer being defaced due to an absence of mortals. Is everyone satisfied? Hardly.

One weekend the family had chores and plans so school was not in session. Roger went out to the woodshed to gather their trash for a trip to the dump, a bi-weekly ritual. He yelled to his eldest daughter who dutifully answered the call, assuming her dad required some assistance. When she entered through the door of the summer kitchen, Andrea gasped. Her father was staring at the mass of wood and slate smashed to pieces in a pile on the lower level of their woodshed. She ran down the stairs, touching fragments of slate shattered like glass, its spindles snapped off at the base, its solid oak frame splintered into kindling. There was nothing left to salvage. Roger was as stunned as she by the shocking sight, a loss sustained; he did not accuse anyone of anything. It was obvious none of the girls would have or could have destroyed the object. None of them were even capable of lifting the chalkboard, let alone heaving it the twenty feet it had traveled; an act as malicious as it was mysterious. He knelt beside his daughter, warning her away from hazardous shards, carefully placing each fractured piece inside a paper bag for a safe disposal. Her heart was as broken as their chalkboard. Tears obscured the path as she ran into the house, seeking then finding comfort within the arms of an equally-perplexed mother. The logical question was: "What the hell happened?" Hell happened; an evil intention to deliberately inflict harm: damage done.

Gathering together on the front lawn, watching Roger load its remains into the trunk of a car, by then all the children were crying. No one could believe their eyes. How *could* this have happened? *Who* would have done such a vicious thing? For what purpose or reason? Why hadn't any of them heard a crash? So many questions…so many tears. This mean-spirited, destructive act effectively robbed five children of their favorite pastime. The chalkboard had been a very expensive gift their parents could no longer afford to replace.

A painful lesson learned.   Class dismissed.

*"Experience is a hard teacher because she gives
the test first, the lesson afterwards."*
Vernon Sanders Law

sword of Damocles

During her original tour of the property, Mr. Kenyon had directed Carolyn into the barn. He was so proud of it, as he should be; a magnificent structure which had weathered the worst storm on record in New England history. The Hurricane of 1938 claimed many historic buildings, even that far inland, but not the old barn up on Round Top Road. It survived. The master shipwright who built it was a genius. Carolyn marveled at the hand hewn beams, finely bowed arches visible to the untrained eye. However, she had no recollection of seeing that hand scythe hanging overhead, dangling precariously from its highest beam more than thirty feet from the ground. This barn was very dark. Perhaps she had not noticed it before. Perhaps it was not there at the time.

A few weeks after moving in, while the children were in school (except for April, who was taking her nap), Carolyn slipped out of their house for a few minutes to admire their beautiful barn. She had been fantasizing about using it for the purpose intended...maybe getting a pony or a horse for the children, and she wanted to see if it was properly outfitted to receive an animal or two. Entering from the smaller side door, she'd left it wide open to provide some additional light. Standing in a vacuum-like cavity, having been cleared of all Mr. Kenyon's accumulated tools and its machinery only a week or so earlier, she listened to the echo of her footsteps as her boots struck the wide planked floorboards. The old barn was brutally cold inside; the air deathly still. It was eerily silent, completely quiet within the structure. Carolyn could hear herself breathing...could hear the beating of her own heart. She wondered why it felt so much colder inside than it had been outside; as warmly dressed as she was with a thick cotton turtleneck, a woolen sweater and her heavy leather flight jacket, Carolyn shivered. Cold swept through her delicate frame, seizing her attention. Even though her choice of clothing seemed utterly inadequate to effectively cut the chill, failing to keep frigid air from penetrating her body to the bone, ultimately that outfit would serve her well, protecting her in a way she could never have anticipated. Quaking, Carolyn quickly determined the building was perfectly acceptable; quite suitable for welcoming any resident of the four-legged variety...with a fur coat. Anxious to return to her sleeping child and relative warmth of the farmhouse, at least when compared to a barn exposed to the elements, she turned around to exit the building. In so doing, she distinctly heard a strangely disquieting sound above her head, magnified by still, silent air. Heads up!

Could a bird have become trapped? Had one entered that cavernous space when she opened the door? It sounded just like the frantic fluttering of wings. The rapidly repetitious noise startled her: "whoosh whoosh whoosh" slicing through acrid, stagnant air. A disconcerting sound, Carolyn located its origin. Was it an owl? No. A hand scythe (a sharp, rounded tool used for cutting and baling hay) was flying directly toward her. It resembled a kind of boomerang thrown with velocity, spinning in circles, whirling like a dervish...again and again. This object appeared to be hovering overhead, literally defying the law of gravity. Suddenly it plunged toward her; the woman was in grave danger. She watched. It flew precisely in her direction, yet Carolyn could do nothing to rescue herself in the moment. She was frozen in place, unable to move her legs, incapable of stepping aside. A dangerous airborne device; weapon fixed on its intended target: vital to brace for impact.

Carolyn recalls becoming instantly transfixed, mesmerized by the object as it approached. She was paralyzed, unable to retreat. Though her mind was as provoked as her body, speaking to the subject of self-preservation, trembling legs would not cooperate. Carolyn stood there, rigidly in place, watching the trajectory of the scythe. As it struck her slender form, its blade slicing hard across both her neck and shoulder, the violent force of a blow she expected was stunning nonetheless. There it lay, beside her boots, on frozen planks of wood, as still as the air, its momentum stifled; its threatening tone silenced by the strike. Carolyn stared at the wayward tool as she slowly reached up to touch the wound, fearful of what she might find in its wake. It was then she'd realized the multiple layers of clothing she had worn as protection from cold morning air had proved to be a blessing in disguise; nothing less significant than her salvation. That bulky, cumbersome outfit literally saved her life. In spite of its accurate aim and high speed, the strike of the scythe was unable to penetrate leather, though it left quite a gash. The jacket was destroyed but it was the scar it had left on a mind which would become troublesome. Equally frightened as fascinated by this strange event, she stared at it, in shock, then picked up the hand scythe, latching it onto a protruding nail nearby.

Taking a moment to recover and re-establish equilibrium, she was stymied by her own reaction (or lack thereof) to the occurrence. Even though a surge of adrenaline still pulsed wildly through her veins, the chill of the air began to claim her attention, consuming her being. It felt as if she was frozen stiff, barely breathing, incapable of standing upright. It was surreal. She had been raised in the swamps of Georgia and, in spite of those numerous hazards, had never come so close to death before. Gazing at splinters of wood beneath her feet created by the tool as its tip impaled the wide wooden plank where she stood; Carolyn knew instinctively just how close she had come to a disaster. Finally regaining her composure, she raced out of the barn and back into the house and checked in on April, still soundly asleep, entirely unaware of what happened to her mom. A chill overtaking her in the barn apparently traveled home with the shaken soul. As she sat on the sofa, cocooned in a blanket, she quivered; incapable of controlling her breathing for quite some time. Unable to shed the imagery or dispel the fear, haunting sounds of the close encounter rang out in her mind. It could have been much worse. Considering a thought; it could have conceivably robbed her children of a mother. Awestruck by an incident she could not comprehend; her thoughts became mired in questions, riddled with one deeply disturbing concept: It could have been a fatal blow.

Carolyn was consumed with curiosity, asking herself many questions she could not answer, primarily among them: Why had she been unable to move, to simply step out of the way of a hand scythe? How on Earth was it *possible* that such a dangerous tool had been placed so far out onto the narrow beam, suspended more than thirty feet high? How could it have possibly achieved that rate of speed or the accuracy of its aim without having been deliberately thrown by someone? Carolyn was the only living soul in the barn at the time. Most puzzling; how could merely stepping inside a barn expose her to such an incongruous situation; involving imminent peril? A decidedly horrifying circumstance, yet Carolyn did not feel the full impact of it nor bear the real burden until much later. She did not sense the perceived threat immediately. Actually she was far more amazed than frightened by it. What are the odds of something like this happening to her...to anyone! In time, she'd fully realize the danger she was in; came to appreciate a saving grace in moments of peril. What happened to her had been no accident.

The girls returned from school to find their mother shivering, bundled up in a blanket on the sofa. She was entirely preoccupied...lost to them... lost in thought. If she could have she would have been responsive to their greetings. Instead, there was only a vacancy there, a blank stare, startling to all of them. Their mother was incoherent; incapable of communicating. She had begun to process this incident, acknowledging what happened. Carolyn didn't notice a few children had entered the house. Essentially, they were left home alone.

Several months would pass before she finally disclosed these events to her husband, along with a number of other equally disturbing episodes. A bizarre incident: contrary to accepted laws of physics; Nature. As Carolyn began to grasp the true gravity of it; being in jeopardy...inside an old barn, eventually she understood what had befallen her was a legitimate threat, the warning of impending doom. Targeted by a supernatural force far beyond her cognitive ability to interpret, it was the visceral triggering of an internal alarm system. Instinct; intuition told her she was not wanted, unwelcome in her own home. The deep bruise on her shoulder would heal in time though it left an invisible mark; a permanent scar on her psyche. Perhaps it was an omen; an ominous harbinger of things to come. It served its purpose well; attention being paid.

Years later Carolyn would learn of Mrs. John Arnold; the woman who died by her own hand, found hanging in the barn on precisely the same beam from which the scythe had fallen. The looming threat remained, hovering above. Next time, it would appear to be the face of evil itself. Heads up! Attention! A myth? True after all; the proverbial Sword of Damocles does indeed exist.

"One of the greatest pains to human nature is the pain of a new idea."
Walter Bagehot

a very fine how do you do

*"I see her not dispirited, not weak, but well, remembering
that she has seen dark times before; indeed with a kind of
instinct that she sees a little better in a cloudy day."*
Ralph Waldo Emerson

Intrigue mounted; an evil chill seeped deeply into Carolyn's bones and then
it crept into her soul. Roger complained incessantly about exorbitant electric
bills. As the price of heating oil went up their thermostat came down. Strange
sounds persisted in the night. Flies attacked at will. As tragic violence raged
on in Southeast Asia, very bad news became too difficult to watch. She had
absorbed too much too fast, souring her mood further. The miserable woman
finally snapped. It had been, without question, an intolerably mean season of
snow and bitter temperatures in and out: the winter of Carolyn's discontent.

***

Pacing the house, a rusty crowbar in one hand, a cup of coffee in the other,
Carolyn knew the fireplace in their parlor would bear the brunt of her wrath.
This chimney appeared to be entirely intact. It was the logical choice; where
their family most frequently gathered together. As she pried the face from the
molding, careful not to damage the original mantel or wainscoting during the
arduous process, a certain satisfaction replaced a resentment and frustration
she'd harbored for months while she shivered and stared at the woodshed full
of free heat: going to waste! It was a sin. It was a crime against the humanity
she knew as her family. Why should they suffer cold? Why not do something
about it if one has the tools at hand? Where there's a will…there's a way!

"What a mess!" Once the front panel was removed, Carolyn was no
longer chilly; puddles of perspiration beading up beneath the rim of her
glasses. At the task with pure vengeance, tearing the face off a fireplace with
energy and enthusiasm she thought had been lost to her, what it revealed
was daunting: bricks, horsehair plaster, newspaper and twigs. Whoever
sealed the hole used anything and everything at their disposal to do so. As
the room began filling with debris, April was enlisted to assist in this effort,

filling up garbage bags one at a time…up to her knees in trash! Bag after bag accumulated, piling up like an instant landfill in the parlor, requiring both of them to drag the heavy load off into the woodshed. Soon April was just as hot and filthy dirty as her mother. Together they stood, examining results of their efforts. This tag team had made great progress in a relatively short amount of time.

"Bless this mess!" The child made the sign of the cross…backwards. Later in the afternoon, as her sisters arrived home from school, April relinquished her duties. She went to take a hot shower then a well-deserved nap. She was exhausted. Her mother was just getting started. They all labored well into the evening, breaking for dinner with the unspoken hope of an early bedtime.

Carolyn was not allowed to touch food until she'd hosed off. While Andrea warmed leftovers, her mother, beyond messy, went to take a shower. A sight to behold: the woman's dark, flowing hair was encrusted, matted with white plaster; corners of mouth pasted shut. Bless *this* mess! Peeling filthy clothes from her moist, sticky skin, she stepped into the soothing shower, grateful to her eldest for pulling a dinner together. She dared to relax. Had she realized, by disturbing a long-sealed fireplace, she'd inadvertently trigger a deluge of supernatural activity in the house, she would have definitely left it alone and would certainly not be alone in the bathroom.

While Carolyn was preoccupied, there came a knock at the kitchen door. It was a neighbor, Mrs. Pettigrew, the mother of five boys; a lovely woman in every way. She had called earlier, learning of this massive project underway down on Round Top Road. Knowing Roger would be out of town for several days and Carolyn was quite busy, she had kindly baked a cake for the family, a truly thoughtful gesture. Andrea invited her in then cracked the bathroom door open to announce a pleasantly unexpected arrival. She then put a fresh pot of coffee on to brew before her mother even asked; a conditioned reflex. Duly informed, Carolyn stepped out of the shower and went directly into the "warm room", a term affectionately used by the girls to describe cozy closet space off the bathroom, formerly occupied by an enormous center chimney, the one original to the farmhouse. When a significantly smaller replacement was installed years before, serving only to vent the furnace in the cellar, this space effectively trapped heat, creating a dry environment; providing escape from unrelenting chill: a private spot in which to change clothing in relative comfort and ease.

As she began removing her robe to dress, a large coat hanger *lifted* from the rack beside her then struck the woman repeatedly on her head and neck. Carolyn began to scream; an alarm beckoning everyone in from the kitchen, including their houseguest. Entering the bathroom en masse, they witnessed a vicious attack…nobody believing her eyes. Once that beating subsided, the coat hanger fell to the floor. Those gathering around stood in stunned silence. Carolyn too, was muted…in a stupor; only the vacant expression in her eyes spoke of the ordeal. Slipping the robe back over her wounded shoulder, she quickly moved out of the space where the attack occurred, ushering a crowd back toward the kitchen, securely closing the bathroom door behind her.

This was a traumatizing event for all involved. Carolyn appeared to be in a state of shock. She sat at the table, fidgeting with her fingers, trembling from the effect of adrenaline still surging through her body. Andrea returned to the stove in the pantry, staring into a sauce as she stirred it, wondering what just happened and how it could have possibly occurred. Mrs. Pettigrew remained quiet, perhaps attempting to absorb over-exposed images. Her ruddy English complexion deepening to an auburn tint, the hue matching her hair; once she was reasonably sure Carolyn had sufficiently recovered she decided to forego coffee then politely excused herself. It was so upsetting. Carolyn had been so anxious to find a friend; and now this? They walked into the parlor together. Before departing, Mrs. Pettigrew leaned closely toward Carolyn and uttered a rather esoteric message of her own, forewarning: "The Kenyons always kept the lights on overnight: All the lights…every night." Reaching for Carolyn's hand sympathetically, after she left, Mrs. Pettigrew never returned again.

The children began asking questions which their mother was incapable of answering. Eventually they gave up, finished dinner, did their homework and went to bed. This was beyond anyone's ability to comprehend though each of them had, to a certain extent, become its unwitting victim, as well. That night they all slept together in groups, anxious and frightened, wishing their father was home. Carolyn did what she could to be a calming influence, to no avail. They'd each witnessed something bizarre; something of supernatural origin. Though their children were too young to understand what had happened, they all knew it was something phenomenal...something wicked this way comes.

Concerned about her mother, Andrea crept downstairs after her sisters had fallen into an uneasy slumber. She found her near the bottom of the bedroom stairs, gazing into the hole she had cleared out earlier in the day. Embracing her daughter, Carolyn tried to reassure her eldest, but there was no comfort to be found in their dark and dreary house that night. Andrea helped replace the wood enclosure over the face of a vacant space, so to cut down on any drafts. They studied the abandoned bird nest. It had fallen from inside the chimney during demolition. Having rescued it from the pile of debris, Carolyn placed the specimen onto the mantelpiece for all to admire. At her mother's urging, Andrea reluctantly returned to bed: no rest promised...none gained.

Sensing an intrusive presence, Carolyn remained alone in the parlor, as sole guardian of the dwelling. A mother considered what happened; the impact it made on their children. She then examined the obvious bruises on her body, having been struck in precisely the same place where the scythe hit her a few months earlier. Certain her husband would surely insist on there being some "reasonable explanation" she decided not to tell him, forced to reconsider the position when she realized the girls **would** divulge the incident. It was time to have a talk with him, to describe recondite events; time to suggest perhaps an "unreasonable explanation" existed instead. It was so obvious. She was being targeted; *she* was the one unwelcomed in her own home. Sitting in silence on the loveseat, ignoring the book propped in place against her knees, Carolyn began to pray. Tears welled in her eyes as she contemplated the possibility of being expelled from a place she wanted for her children. No longer an issue separate and distinct from the family, they too were now being exposed to an insidious malfeasance, the likes of which, begrudgingly sharing its space.

Carolyn hesitated to confront Roger with these disturbing allegations. Her suspicions confirmed: they were not alone in their house. Leaning back into a soft pillow, she observed two ominous flies-in-residence entering the parlor, buzzing in a circle, one perching itself on the binding of her book. It stared straight at a woman too weary to swat it away. After a moment, the intrusive, contemptible creatures flew, presumably returning to the place from whence they'd come, though their specific point-of-origin still remained a mystery: an undisclosed location. A very fine how do you. Overcome with a sense of dread, Carolyn felt bereft; void and vulnerable to attack. Exhausted, fighting the sleep her body and mind desperately required, she slowly closed heavy eyes with an intention of doing so for only a minute, awakening hours later at the break of dawn. First light flirted with her sight. Gray and gloomy was all the morning held as a promise for the day. Acrid odor stung her nostrils. The house was something more than cold; it was absolutely frigid. Her body had stiffened beyond measure or movement. Wrenching herself up from the sofa, Carolyn walked directly toward the thermostat. Nope. No way. There was no conceivable way the device could be correct. The heat was blasting; its gauge read seventy-two degrees, yet it would be warmer if every door and window were opened, which is precisely what Carolyn did to vent a powerful stench, attempting to rid the house of its putrid fume which had evidently permeated the dwelling while she'd slept. Disoriented, unable to dispel the smell or the penetrating cold holding her captive, Carolyn knew something was with her; an evil presence she could not see or hear, but felt. There it was; right there at the crossroads of night and day. It was in the parlor. There was no denying it, in spite of the fact that nothing was visible to this bleary-eyed beholder. She felt an unmistakable, inescapable sense of false imprisonment, the sensation of a being in certain peril, grave danger; evoking a response primal in nature, that visceral human reaction of fight or flight. Her children were all sleeping upstairs. Defiant; there she stood, firmly holding hallowed ground, preparing for something to rear its ugly head. Protective instincts deeply entrenched, like soldiers in a ditch, weapons drawn; laying-in-wait prompted the timely retreat of her unwelcome companion. It swept from the room as the whisk of a broom at the flick of a wrist. Clearing the air, temperature rising steadily, it was there and then it was gone, precisely at the break of dawn: wake-up call.

"At first cock-crow the ghosts must go
back to their quiet graves below."
Theodosia Garrison

~ **a pause for reflection** ~

familiarity breeds contempt

"In time we hate that which we often fear."
William Shakespeare

Spring refused to arrive on time. It stalled; delay tactics coming in the form of snow and sleet, freezing rain and biting bitter winter wind. A season toyed with the fragile emotions of those waiting with pressed patience; a virtue that was wearing thinner than cold night air. Breathe deeply, my dear. Breathe in.

***

An adversarial marriage has repercussions throughout an entire household; a low level hostility which tends to vibrate through children. Both Roger and Carolyn did not seem to notice what they were doing; it came naturally. The girls were paying close attention; reading moods, gauging every interaction in comparison to everything else they'd known of their parents prior to this time. Quiet when it was not loud; a study in extremes: darkness and light.

Based on personal reflection of those involved, it appears the root ball was born of an insidious, deep-seeded contempt; this core issue remained buried beneath fertile ground; fertilized with quips, sarcasm and subtle imagery: an eager comment ignored, a shy smile left as an unreturned gesture. Silence, as much a weapon as words, created distance; marriage seemed a mere illusion. It was the root ball of a relationship beginning to rot, kept perpetually moist, drenched with tears. Over time it would turn black in the darkness, deprived of light and hope in the place where no one could watch it die...where no one saw it disintegrating from within. In retrospect, it was a blessing in disguise.

Plagued by normal aches and pains associated with a major move, Carolyn was certain it would subside. It never did. Over time, it worsened, spreading through her being like the wild rivulets remaining after a flood; outstretched fingers trickling over a landscape attempting to return to its source in Nature. A once vital woman was rapidly deteriorating, becoming crippled, struggling through each and every day as the cold infiltrated her bones, her psyche then her soul. Formerly firm muscle mass was compromised; elements conspiring against her caused joints to throb, a wounded heart to break. The strong, agile woman began aging at a remarkable rate...well before her time: Frightening. It altered her demeanor; a soft disposition began to harden, primarily because her husband was convinced it was all in her head.

Why had the farm felt so familiar? Why did this place call to her then reject this woman in every conceivable way? Carolyn routinely wondered about it; somewhere lost in thought, pondering questions plaguing her as much as the pain. It seemed grossly unfair. The longer she lived there the less she liked it; its charms becoming easy to overlook; too many challenges... too many souls. She began to perceive the pain as cruelty; punishment: as part of the process of dismissal. Carolyn felt as if she was being run off her own property. It was obvious; something or someone did not want her there: contempt born of a familiarity growing stronger and stranger by the day.

During their first several months in the farmhouse so many awful incidents occurred, it became difficult to keep track: spooky sounds, a fly infestation, disturbed animals in conflict with invisible foes, demonic doors opening and closing at will; mind-numbing manifestation, finger-numbing cold. What was one to think? Noxious odors: the smell of death. Coat hanger and scythe: an omen or two of animosity shared in kind. Carolyn was under attack. It would soon become evident she was the target of someone's disdain. How to defend against those which cannot be seen? How to face one's fears in the midst of the battle? Uncommon valor was called for in circumstances so preposterous, it was impossible to identify the enemy in a war with no end. Existence at the farm functioned as a metaphor, its description suited to ongoing conflict over in Southeast Asia. Vietnam had become a major point of contention between Carolyn and Roger. Juxtaposed positions on the war spawned many a heated debate often culminating in discordant argument. She loathed Richard Nixon. He wholeheartedly supported the president and would vote for him again. As bad news grew worse, Roger became utterly belligerent about it, defending indefensible positions; poor political decisions escalating as the bloody body count continued to rise unabated: rabid Republican versus staunch Democrat. Theirs was a mixed marriage; not a political love fest, by any measure. It was just another reason to fight. Their relationship became even more adversarial over time; uncivil discourse, one symptom of the disease with no cure. It was an element of a combative nature between them. At its center, a presumption in both camps: the enemy is ignorant and misguided; incapable of admission or compromise…issues of war, no promise of peace.

Carolyn had hesitated to discuss spirit matters with her husband. Initially, she could not believe it herself so there was nothing to convince him about. However, as strange incidents accrued a body of evidence grew substantially. Sam Olevson offered a unique perspective; his opinion factored in, lending credence to Carolyn's speculation, creating less dark space for dispute. Still, in spite of his respectful appreciation of Sam's position, Roger continually questioned her perceptions, maintaining what he'd considered to be a healthy skepticism…for years. His stubborn streak was magnified by the subject. He remained suspicious; not a person ever easily persuaded. This point of view served to antagonize Carolyn further. She considered it highly disrespectful, especially because she'd never given him any cause; no reason to doubt her voracity on any subject in the past. A level of honesty and personal integrity she brought to a relationship from the inception was being overtly challenged by disbelief, as though her opinion was entirely irrelevant, her recounting of events, fraudulent. His doubts and the accusations, implicit and explicit, were leveraged as weaponry throughout a campaign founded on a mutual distrust. Moving to the farm altered them as individuals. In the beginning, well before Roger saw the Light, as luminescent as any which danced upon the surface of the river when he first made the trip to water's edge, he simply did not, *could* not believe her. Then he began to blame her. Carolyn felt abandoned in their marriage, unwanted by a house and husband alike; rejection on all fronts. An ugly war of words was being waged. Casualties were all but inevitable. As an increasingly fiery relationship fed the beast within, flaming passions stirred up the spirits. What they really needed was less heat and more light.

"You don't believe a goddamned thing I'm telling you…" Carolyn shook her head in disgust.

"It's not that…"

"Yes it is *that*! You think I'm delusional…I'm making all of it up just for the HELL of it! I have *never* lied to you, Roger. Not *once* in all these years have I ever told you anything but the truth…and you know it! How *dare* you question me now! How dare you suggest…"

"**I don't** *believe* in ghosts!"

"Roger, you don't get it. Your belief or disbelief has absolutely no bearing on their existence whatsoever. They don't give a damn what you believe!"

"There *has* to be some logical explanation for it…"And so it went, until the root ball was rotted and nothing would grow.

By the time Roger finally became a *believer* it was too late: needle and the damage done. A sharp point of contention evolved into the muck and mire of irreconcilable differences. Though they'd remain together for many years to come, a couple was no longer together in spirit. They shared a life, a house, a family and even a bed, yet a deep chasm of resentment developed in between them; no bridge wide enough to cover that expanse. No meeting one another half way. The more familiar Carolyn became with Roger's bad attitudes and predispositions the less likely she was to try communicating with him on *any* subject. The abyss gradually widened, attaining a dark, immeasurable depth, like staring into what appears as a vacant black hole in the Universe. The Big Bang Theory: a huge explosion then silence and darkness. No sign of Light.

What a shame; a very sad turn for the worse. The negative energy seethed, oozing from every pore whenever Roger was confronted by that which he'd resisted a belief in; gradually transforming him. Unfortunately, his anger was not reserved for the supernatural culprits but spilled profusely onto anyone else in his path. By comparison, Carolyn tempered a reaction she could not disguise but frequently muted (for purpose of keeping the peace) by adopting an insouciant demeanor intended to counteract Roger's irascible nature; her passive approach, measured and deliberate, to offset his own fiery outbursts. Recognizing the union as one of diametrically opposed forces, a war wife did anything necessary to avoid further enflaming the passions of her husband.

She was not the only one changing. As the months passed everyone in the family was adversely affected by manifestations and reactions alike. Anxiety and dread became a paranormal part of life; fear, an ever-present emotion. It was layered like phyllo dough used in a recipe for disaster: Roger was afraid his wife was losing her mind...then *more* fearful that she was *not* losing her mind but was instead *really* seeing what she'd claimed to witness. He feared for her health and well-being, mentally and physically. Her deterioration was increasingly evident to all; a specter far more frightening than anything their house had yet to muster. Carolyn's rapidly aging and shriveling form was the most horrifying apparition of all...one everyone witnessed...all of the time.

Both feared for their children; Roger, because he sensed they were quickly becoming motherless and Carolyn, because of what these children might be observing. She was terrified; the incidents colored her world: shades of gray. Impenetrable shadows did not yield to the light. The more familiar Carolyn became with the characters of various entities, the less she understood about the true Nature of what was happening in this house. Roger would not listen; he did not know how. Resentment brewed; each stirred the curdling cauldron of incomprehension. It festered at the surface while coming to a boil. Toxic bubbles: not fit for human consumption.

All of the children feared for their mother and likewise feared their father's unpredictable moments of spontaneous combustion, as it was Wrath of God: "This house smells like death!" exploding from within him more than once; they'd tremble when he yelled, hide when he hollered, becoming as invisible a presence as those with whom they dwelled. As the two of them fought their own battles the war of words escalated. Seven mortal souls got caught in the midst of an immortal experience, all ill-prepared for their transformation. It spawned a host of unholy emotions; reactions which threatened to intrude on a family which had been, prior to arriving at the farm, a rather peace-loving clan who enjoyed life together. Their idyllic setting was a mirage; the pursuit of happiness merely an illusion. A marriage riddled with conflict and distrust colored their landscape black. A pastoral tapestry Carolyn once admired was being torn to shreds, unraveling before her eyes, and yet she could not see the invisible manifestation: the changeling did not sense her own transformation. An exhaustive attempt to understand the many subliminal messages received incrementally began taking a toll on her soul. Too gradual a decline in assets to feel the fee being assessed... too distracted by the culprit to realize she was being robbed. Like common pickpockets, they were...thieves stealing youth from a beautiful woman one terrifying moment at a time.

There were some whimsical moments of clarity, such as the day all of her children gathered and began to sing a song Carolyn found poignant; perfectly appropriate to their situation. Andrea was teaching her sisters a tune she had learned in **Chorus**, staging a mini-musical production of **"The King and I"** on their expansive front porch; a wonderful scene. Words rang out as music through the house, beckoning a mother from the kitchen. Spring had arrived, allowing for open windows. Proudly peeking through from the dining room, Carolyn saw her chorus standing in a circle, shaking hands on the downbeat, as directed. Each one sang an assigned phrase; sweet and simple lyrics with a profound interpretation, as the subtext had not escaped an observant woman. During a few moments of childhood innocence playing out, while leaning on the windowsill, applauding her theater troupe, an insidious concept crept into Carolyn's consciousness...a notion few parents ever have need to consider.

Resenting the intrusion, a grimace belied her joy; that glimpse of a shadow cast from the Light: Evidence of an intruder. As it leapt through her mind she dismissed it. An attempt to expel it from the class failed. She reconsidered its presence, wondering if it had come to watch the lesson learned, or teach one. Carolyn recalls feeling conflicted, plagued by negative thoughts which came in the most unexpected moments, yet mindful of the messages received. The lyrics said it all: *"Getting to know you...getting to know all about you..."* had struck an ominous chord. Why wasn't she free to merely appreciate the moment? Why must its light be colored by darker thoughts? What purpose did they serve? Truth be told, she *was* getting to know *"them"*...getting to know all about them...like it or not. Smiling, she shook it off and sang along.

***

Fear is the only mortal emotion more powerful than love. As every member of the family continued to witness manifestations of souls with whom they'd shared space in a house alive with death; Carolyn's terror turned into a hatred of souls past, and one present. Fear transforms what it touches, for better or for worse. Among dead and living alike, fear conquers love. Lesson learned:

In quarters too close for comfort, familiarity breeds contempt.

"It is not necessary to understand things in order to argue about them."
Pierre Beaumarchais

cold as stone

*"In faith there is enough light for those who want to believe
and enough shadows to blind those who don't."*
Blaise Pascal

Spirits do not always seem to be aware of their surroundings, as if they're just passing through on their way to somewhere else; as distant as they are present: remote, disinterested beings. When they did engage members of this family it was brazen; a dramatic spectacle, sometimes threatening in tone and demeanor. An attempt made to entice a girl to *come along* for a dimensional journey through time and space was no small spirit matter. Though negligible intrusions occurred frequently, just a part of the new paranormal, when major manifestations occurred it was quite enough to make mortal blood run cold, especially considering the fact that an appearance was often accompanied by a brutal chill associated with the passing essence of an immortal soul; Death.

Even after years in their presence no one in the family ever knew what next to expect; a visit could be highly disruptive, moderately annoying or entirely benign. With their inexplicable power to manipulate objects at will they often received acknowledgment and attention...simply by lifting up the telephone receiver or sweeping the bristles of straw brooms across a floor which clearly required some attention of its own. Disapproval was quite a common theme; sometimes it was a blatant reaction. One of the spirits preferred their kitchen be kept a certain way; another one preferred the musical genre of the 1940's, singers and standards; *not* Rock n'Roll. Theirs was an omnipresent influence, even when it remained relatively quiet for extended periods of time. It was a strange way to live and let die; always sensing something unseen just beyond the shadows...afraid to look more closely...afraid of what might be there.

Nothing would happen for weeks, even months at a time, unless, of course an argument erupted. Such discord inevitably provoked some responses from the other side; the darker side. A few harsh words; all it took to unleash *some* reaction. Most of the spirits hated these altercations. One of them apparently thrived on this upheaval; the uglier, the better. It was not necessarily an overt acknowledgement in that moment; not a manifestation as entity. Instead, an object would suddenly fly across the room, perhaps as shock value to break up a disturbance *or* to prompt its escalation. No one was ever certain of their underlying motivations. Ultimately, it proved irrelevant, as any interruption served its purpose, altering the focus of an argument, silencing it completely. Often just sensing a presence was enough to quell a brewing storm; a sudden chill in the air, cold as stone in winter. The odorous whiff of death infiltrated; it lingered, functioning as a calling card of sorts…enough to redirect the rapt attention of those involved in any dispute, regardless of the subject matter.

Reconciliation eluded an unhappy couple; they'd frequently allow weeks to pass before properly addressing an argument with an eye toward resolution; hostility became an unwelcomed state-of-being during this difficult period. They maintained a certain physical distance, passing in silence like ships in the night; extending little else than a cold shoulder. At a perpetual impasse, no meaningful conversation occurred. Their house muted; a shrouded hovel. Roger would crash on the sofa or find a good reason to hit the road: Be gone! It was the kind of quiet known to shatter the nerves of children, keeping them fearful of saying the wrong thing, afraid of creating any disruption at all. A sad irony as side effect: they too hid in the shadows to avoid detection.

During these most tempestuous of moments, one familiar spirit repeatedly appeared. He would intently observe this household and its many occupants. An innocuous figure lurking in shadows behind an open door in the hallway, becoming the shadows as his translucent form disappeared in the moment of mortal recognition, as soon as somebody saw him he would vanish and then return when everyone was preoccupied. It was Manny; the spirit Nancy spied the day the family moved in; he was perched inside a doorway, watching Mr. Kenyon finish packing. Cindy caught a glimpse of him as well. Obviously he was not a threat but was instead a kind and gentle spirit; his mild expression was always one of bemusement or concern, depending on the circumstances. He was peaceful; a benevolent apparition who stood constant vigil, keeping a watch over mortals in his presence. Even though he never once attempted to directly contact anyone in the family or intervene in any dispute, his warmth transcended the pervasive chill of death constantly surrounding him. Manny was a sympathetic soul; his goodness evident to all who sensed this presence. Though he'd always seemed aloof and unattached to the places and spaces in which he appeared, visually distinctive facial expression indicated an interest in those he was observing. It was a passive/aggressive interaction; overt in its actual manifestation but placid once present. The girls were never frightened of him, considering him a rather protective influence, someone to watch over them, which he did with considerable frequency. As years passed, this warm, especially unobtrusive entity became a peripheral member of their family. He seemed to belong there; seemed to fit in the larger picture: as if in a portrait.

His was not the only integration which occurred, though, for the most part, the other spirits were more circumspect, far removed from those with whom they shared space, as if *mortals* did not exist. The Baker boys never noticed the presence of human beings. Not once. Not that they were evasive. Instead, they were oblivious to the family with which they shared common ground. It was strange to encounter them, usually on the landing of the bedroom stairs. They'd stare straight through those who witnessed them as the father and son serenely surveyed their fine property from the portal disguised as a window. Carolyn would soon *be witched* by their passive/aggressive behavior in her own bedroom, in the form of a chant and incantation delivered before dawn, intended to taunt and terrify; the threat issued by those who did not seem to notice the victim they haunted. Cold, they were, while carrying flames aloft.

***

Carolyn was often found brooding upon the hearthstone, on a solid slab of granite. As her heart became as cold as the stone beneath her feet, the woman considered a tear in the fabric, the shredding of a marriage, acknowledging a stark vacancy: black holes exist. Distance she felt from

Roger had nothing to do with proximity or his travel schedule; it was as omnipresent as the spirits. Ultimately, she concluded the dissent between them was a matter of faith. He had no faith in her. In time, his disbelief would be countered with a mutual, identical sentiment. She had no faith in him: An overt alienation of affection.

"There is in every true woman's heart a spark of heavenly fire, which lies dormant in the broad daylight of prosperity but; which kindles up, and beams and blazes in the dark hour of adversity."
Washington Irving

dusk 'til dawn

*"A sensible man will remember that the eyes may be confused in two
ways — by a change from light to darkness or from darkness to light;
and he will recognize that the same thing happens to the soul."*
Plato

Twilight was often when it began; a time of day when it becomes night
and there will be no halting this natural conversion of light to darkness.
Better to embrace an inevitable transition. It was the same time when the
spirits began crossing over, in and out of sight as shadows cast by a soft,
waning sunlight. Incidents frequently occurred as it became difficult to
distinguish what it was one witnessed, as if spirits were taunting mortals with
their obscure presence. Apparitions: cries and whispers from beyond; beings
who flirt with darkness: beings who exist somewhere, and everywhere, just
beyond the speed of light.

Those who made their presence known during the day were mischievous
or simply oblivious to the mortals they spooked. Sometimes the manifestations
were deliberate in nature, intent upon making a point; sweeping their kitchen
floor or changing the station on the stereo. Sometimes the visitations seemed
entirely arbitrary, as if they were passing the time by passing through time.
The farmhouse; their place in the country, was nothing less than a portal
for the immortal. They didn't seem to have any concept of time in the same
way human beings measure existence. Apparently they have no more need
of it. However, they did seem to acknowledge the measurement on *this* side
of the Universe, stopping a clock at a precise time coinciding with their
appearance. Perhaps their marking of time is based upon its significance
in their former lives, to the extent that it is used by them as a marker in
death.

The one who often made her presence known at night came specifically
to frighten; delivering her messages as a warning to those left alone
in the dark. **Mortal fear** is ancient and primal; the visceral reaction
exclusive to humans who are terrified by that which they cannot see, due

primarily to absence of Light. Yet, in retrospect, the mere existence of these tortured and torturing souls *is* the Light, the proof of something beyond this realm. In light of day and dark of night, they are the source of all Enlightenment.

Night becomes day…then becomes night. A journey the Perron family took through space and time, night and day, year after year, changed each of them in fundamental ways they couldn't fathom. Becoming increasingly sensitized to their supernatural environment, these individuals assimilated experiences incrementally; accumulating then storing information in memory: the more shocking the encounter, the more vivid the imagery retained for posterity. It becomes a matter of history, even when recalling what one would rather not.

Every upstairs bedroom had a different, rather unique hue, at precisely the same time of day: twilight. All three of the rooms had distinct personalities. The windows were small and each gave the bedroom a quirkiness all its own. Regardless of the season or angle of the Sun, the bedrooms glowed at sunset. Depending on the weather, light at dusk or dawn possessed a magical quality. It was not of this world; it was a Holy Light. Often it appeared to signal their arrival. A vision of a beautiful child wandering through, as if lost in eternity: a mournful soul in search of comfort, calling for her mother. Her pitiful cries brought tears to the eyes of a mortal child who witnessed her pain and could do nothing to help lead her home. Perhaps she *was* home, in another time and space: in another dimension. Could it be a memory so intense, it is capable of transporting her back to the time and space she once occupied in the midst of a life lived in torment? At dawn, with the first glimmer of light at sunrise she would emerge as an opaque shadow huddled in a corner of Cindy's bedroom, silent and motionless, as if waiting for something or hiding from someone; and then she was gone. Then, at dusk, she would reappear again. What was it about this time of day becoming night and night becoming day which opened a portal to the past as windows into other dimensions? There is no answer to this question, yet it is worthy of posing simply for the sake of exploring those impossibilities which routinely occurred in the house, often on a daily basis.

As the cycle of day into night revolves in perpetuity, momentum by design, dictated by the natural rotation of Earth in the cosmos, something mystical is revealed at the point of transition: at the intersection of life and death. Is this flickering hue of twilight some signal from beyond the grave as spirit travels across the Universe, dancing upon fringes of shadows cresting the horizon? It may be when an intermingling of Spirit occurs, as a molten melding of souls; the time between night and day when corporeal souls become aware of being inextricably entwined with ethereal disincarnates, in loving embrace of those who came before; entangled with and indistinct from one another, yet whole. During these moments a confluence of darkness and light known as dusk and dawn may be precisely what mortal eyes require, so to behold what is always there, just beyond the speed of light, otherwise obscured by a lack of vision.   Integration: So I see.

"Courage is resistance to fear, mastery of fear — not absence of fear."
Mark Twain

The Incendiary

You are completely free of affectation:
silent you sit, watchfully tense,
just as silence itself pretends to nothing
on a starless night in a fire-gutted city.

Consider that city—it is your past,
wherein you scarcely ever managed to laugh,
now raging through the streets, now sunk in self,
between your insurrections and your calms.

You wanted life and gave it all your strength,
but, sullenly spurning everything alive,
this slum of a city suffocated you
with the dreary weight of its architecture.

In it every house was shuttered tight,
in it shrewdness and cynicism ruled,
it never hid its poverty of spirit,
its hate for anyone who wasn't broken.

And so one night you burned it down
and ran for cover, frightened by the flames,
till chance produced me in your way, the one
you stumbled on when you were fugitive.

I took you in my arms, I felt you tremble,
as quietly your body clung to mine,
not knowing me or caring, but yet,
like an animal, grateful for my pity.

Together then we sallied…where did we go?
Wherever our eyes, in their folly, took us.
But intermittently you had to turn
to watch your past ominously burning.

It burned beyond control, till it was ashes.
And I remain tormented to this day
that you are drawn, as though enchanted,
back to that place where still the embers glow.

You're here with me, and yet not here.
In fact you have abandoned me. You glide
through the smoldering wreckage of the past,
holding aloft a bluish light in your hand.

What pulls you back? It's empty and gray there!
Oh the mysterious power of the past!
You never could learn to love it as it was,
but yet you fell madly in love with its ruins.

Ashes and embers must be magnets too.
How can we tell what potencies they hold?
Over what's left where once she set her fire
the incendiary cries like a little child.

Yevgeny Yevtushenko from: **Stolen Apples**
Translated by Stanley Kunitz with Anthony Kahn

~ a mother keeping vigil on the hearthstone ~

"*Life is not separate from death. It only looks that way.*"
American Indian Proverb

II.
FIRE IN THE HOLE

"He was a burning and a shining light."
John v. 3

With her usual curt impertinence, Nancy stood rigidly in place, hands upon her scrawny hips, deliberately located, so to make a grand proclamation with more panache. "Dad is gonna freak out!" Then for emphasis, as if staking her claim of a position: "Yep! He is just gonna freak!" Shaking her head in total opposition: "I know it, mom. Dad is gonna…"

"*Going* to freak out. I heard you. Now, if you are going to say it at all, then please, try to say it properly!"

"Okay! GOING to freak!" Scanning the parlor, throwing her hands into the air as morning light revealed what dusk in twilight hue had hidden from sight the evening before: dust was everywhere. The parlor was coated; smothered by the thin pale white residual debris it wore like a shroud.

Carolyn was in no mood for any criticism; what she would have normally found adorable did not amuse her in the least after such a difficult night.

"Save it for the stage, babe. You can go to the bathroom through my room. Please close the pantry door on your way." Having already closed the pantry door a few times that morning, she did not know whom she should blame for leaving it wide open again. As far as she knew, Nancy was the first one up on a dreary Saturday perfect for sleeping in. No one was busy doing laundry.

"What died in here? God! It smells so bad!" Nancy wrinkled her little nose while shutting the pantry door very quickly…with a grand slam.

"I don't know. Put a sweater on. I had to open the windows."

"I'm not cold…it just stinks in there!" The comeback kid had spoken.

"Put a sweater on, young lady. Get one from the warm room."

"I'm *not* GOING in the warm room!" The petulant child had a valid point, based on the legitimate fear of an incongruous image lodged in her mind.

"Then get a sweater from your bedroom. You can probably find one in that pile of clothes on your floor!"

Carolyn instantly softened her stance, recalling how frightened her children had been by an assault they witnessed the evening before. Nancy stood there, staring at her mother as if confused, anxious to remain with her in the parlor. She appeared to be terrified. Suggesting her child retrieve something warm to wear from inside the laundry room, (the pantry with a door suddenly opening of its own volition), Nancy snatched the bathrobe then fled the stinky scene. Carolyn saw her close the door and secure the latch...again. The two of them went into the kitchen together. Mom prepared breakfast for her early-riser. A few minutes later she returned to the parlor to continue the cleaning process which would claim many hours of her day. The room was ice cold. It smelled like something dead. The pantry door was open...again.

Roger returned from his road trip later that evening. Carolyn was relieved to have her husband at home. It meant she could get some peaceful sleep. It also meant she would have to deal with the inevitable fallout; his reaction to her ongoing project. As he walked in through the parlor door, children all but mauled the man; apparently their job, as the greeting committee, to keep their father feeling loved and missed, and then kept well-informed. They were all talking at once, which made it impossible to understand any one of them.

"Look! Mommy...WE all opened the fireplace!" The baby chimed in first.

"And she got beaten up by a coat hanger in the closet!" Nancy *had* to tell.

"Mrs. Pettigrew saw it happen, too!" Christine felt the need to validate her sister's impetuous disclosure.

"I saw it, too." Andrea's somber tone reflected concern...in a whisper.

"Can we please get a horse?" No one knew where *that* question came from but it had been on Cynthia's mind and since her daddy was in a great mood, it seemed as good a time as any to ask.

"Hold it!" Roger was overwhelmed by the attention; too much information. "Girls! I just walked through the door! Give the old man a break!" Reaching out to haphazardly embrace his eldest, standing on the sidelines, she'd been unable to penetrate the madding crowd. "Okay, everyone relax. Calm down. Did you save me something good to eat? Hope so...I'm starving!"

They had indeed. Roger was hungry and exhausted. He'd been driving for many hours and only wanted to do what he had suggested his kids do: relax. Andrea went into the kitchen to retrieve a bowl of beef stew from the famous pressure cooker. Carolyn escorted Roger into their bedroom, closing the door behind then began to unpack his suitcase. She'd worked all day to clean up a mess in the parlor. Dust traveling the air settled everywhere; to infinity and beyond! Removing sheets from furniture just minutes before his arrival, she was pleased and satisfied with the results: quite an achievement. The parlor looked great; Roger hadn't noticed. Instead, the road-weary traveler stretched out on their bed, kicking the shoes from his feet.

"You look so tired." Carolyn glanced up from the task at hand, responding to his comment with a deflated expression then her sparse share of whispered words, indicating a willingness to speak with little energy left to do so.

"So do you." She abandoned the task and sat down beside him, running her fingers through locks of his thick, black hair. He was a handsome man, easy on the eyes, especially so that chilly spring evening. She was grateful to have him home. He needed to know what had occurred in his absence.

"It was a really good trip. I can afford to take a few days off. Now, what's all this about a fireplace, a coat hanger and a horse?" He smiled, prepared to indulge a lengthy diatribe, if necessary.

Carolyn had cleaned the parlor so thoroughly her husband did not notice: it was **different**. Likewise, she had effectively vented the putrid smell from the house. Assuming its presence was primarily due to disturbing so many years of accumulated debris from a chimney which had seen its fair share of birds and bats (and Lord knows what else had gotten trapped in the narrow shaft); as he had not detected an odor she didn't even mention it. Instead, she began her explanation of the fireplace by exclaiming the *free* wood in the woodshed was going to waste, something he'd been well aware of; a point upon which they agreed. Roger was not the least bit upset with his wife's initiative taken in the matter. In fact, it sparked his interest. A drowsy man rose from his bed with renewed vigor, returning to the parlor to examine a hole in the wall.

As she removed its wooden façade, exposing the black hole, Roger's face spoke of impending firelight; he glowed like kindling igniting the flames of desire. Never expecting to find a pristine enclosure suddenly at his disposal, Roger crawled up inside to assess it from within. It appeared the flue was in excellent condition though he presumed they would need a chimney sweep to be properly prepared. Roger was literally awe-inspired. He had not thought it through, having yet to consider just how many months of his life would be spent tromping through the woods, out in cold and snow, a chainsaw roaring in his hands, once their ample supply of wood was depleted. He did not think of all the work involved...the former Boy Scout wanted to build a fire.

Pointing out the splendid beehive oven, when prying it open, a piece of the paint chipped away. Carolyn picked it up to study. Dense and multi-colored; layer upon layer of paint had been amply applied to the mantel board and its wainscoting, undoubtedly gorgeous wood beneath. Suggesting they strip the paint and restore the fine colonial specimen, she was surprised when her idea met with no resistance. Her husband was not only willing to see a huge chore accomplished, he was more than willing to pitch in. Likewise, he suggested they remove the old hearthstone replacing it with granite. A plan set in stone. The salesman took a full week off road; he stayed home, there to transform a fireplace into an amazing centerpiece of a farmhouse, if the **Zip Strip** fumes did not prove to be the death of him.

As the couple stood gazing into the open façade, discussing what to do and how next to proceed with this project, they heard the distinct "click" behind them; wrought iron against wrought iron. Turning to see the latch had again dislodged from the pantry door, it slowly drifted open...of its own free will. Roger was puzzled; Carolyn, exasperated. She clearly did not appreciate the exposure of a messy, musty laundry room detracting from their parlor. It had no heat or particular charm and the house was drafty enough!

"Now *that's* a problem. Ever since I opened the fireplace this pantry door *refuses* to remain latched. I've been blaming the kids. You saw it. There's no one else in here. The door opens by itself." The woman was disturbed by it.

Roger considered the dilemma for a moment: what could have caused it to happen? He then calmly and methodically explained his theory...as there *is* a logical explanation for everything.

"I think when you yanked all the stuffing out of the fireplace it shifted the balance of weight in floorboards. It's probably why...I'll tighten that latch." He'd closed the door, looking it over in the process. The piece fit snugly into its groove; a mystery. He reopened it, stepping back abruptly as if stricken, overcome by a sudden nauseating stench, prompting his sour expression.

"Jesus Christ! Do you smell that? What the hell died in there?" Slamming the door, Roger jammed the latch down; wedging it into its place. He fled the scene with his usual dramatic flair. "It's awful! Something *is* dead in there!"

"Maybe a mouse got trapped in the pipes. I don't know. The house reeked this morning, the *same* odor; not something I would forget. It must have been coming from the pantry. The door was wide open when I woke up and it has stayed that way ever since. I had to open doors and windows to get rid of it. At least I *thought* I got rid of it. Did you smell anything when you came in?"

"No. *That* disgusting stink I would have noticed right away!"

Moving quickly out of the parlor, in a futile attempt to escape the pungent odor, they noticed a drastic plunge in temperature; each could *see* the breath of the other as they spoke. Roger was already annoyed. He marched over to the thermostat to inspect the *next* problem while his wife shivered, grabbing a nearby blanket as she followed her husband into the dining room. As if the space around them had suddenly sunken into a deep freeze, a chill dissipated as rapidly as the stench once they both acknowledged it. One moment it was there and then, in the next, it was gone.

"I think the thermostat is broken...the same thing happened this morning." Carolyn wrapped herself snugly inside the blanket; the joys of haunted home ownership. Seating herself at the table, Andrea arrived with the large bowl of beef stew for her father. Waiting for Roger to join her, he was pacing again.

"I've lost my appetite." He'd scowled at the food then changed his mind as the aroma wafted up, drifting into his nostrils, replacing the formerly horrid smell trapped there, lingering too long. Andrea disappeared into the kitchen, attending to the chores her siblings had artfully avoided. Carolyn remained with Roger. There was another subject to raise. He did so before she could.

"What's this about a coat hanger?" His appetite indeed returned. Indulging himself, Roger listened with only mild interest as Carolyn tried to explain.

"Yesterday I went into the warm room to change after taking a shower. As I walked in, I was attacked; something beat me with a coat hanger." Her tone was somber but direct.

"You were what?" She had his complete attention. "What did you say?"

"I can't figure out what it was...how it happened. A hanger lifted up off the rack then struck me; hit me again and again. Everyone saw it, including Mrs. Pettigrew. She stopped by to visit. I yelled out from the shock of it. Everyone in the kitchen came running. It's not my imagination, Roger. It didn't **bounce** off me. It *hit* me, hard; over and over again. That is exactly what happened."

The incredulous expression on his face spoke of doubt about the incident as described. He could not believe his ears. His eyes might convince him.

"You *accidentally* knocked a coat hanger off the rack and it hit you before hitting the floor: Gravity." There was no question in his mind. He understood the cosmic laws of the land, or so he thought. *That's* what happened. Period. No need for further discussion: speculation. As the world's leading authority, he stated his claim as a matter of fact then returned to the stew in earnest.

"You weren't in the warm room, Roger. You didn't see it happen." Having anticipated his reaction, Carolyn was no less defensive simply because she'd known what was coming. He would need to be persuaded to think about this incident in a different way. Carolyn allowed the throw around her shoulders to slip back over the chair. She began unbuttoning her shirt.

"What are you doing?" He glanced at her suspiciously.

"Offering proof: So you don't believe me? Then look at this." Peeling back the fabric hiding the wounds from sight, Carolyn exposed the bruises on her neck and shoulder to the man who'd questioned her voracity.

"Oh, for Christ's sake!" He stared at her then stood to examine the bruising more closely. "You must've done this while you were opening the fireplace. There is *no way in hell* a coat hanger could have done *this* kind of damage!" He'd reached down to touch the tender spot but she pulled away from him, to avoid contact or any further pain: Inspection over. Carolyn buttoned her shirt and gingerly reached behind to pull the blanket back over her cold shoulders. Roger assisted his wife, not knowing what more to say.

"I broke three fingernails opening the fireplace, not the blood vessels in my neck. I didn't want to tell you in the first place. I *knew* you wouldn't believe me." The disgust in her voice instantly put Roger on the defensive. "I am not a liar. After thirteen years of marriage you ought to know that by now. I have *never* lied to you and I'm not about to start now."

"It's not that I don't believe you. I think you're confused." He was certain.

"I'm *not* confused. I'm convinced. Something happened in the closet that I can't explain and neither can you but since you weren't there to see it, don't bother trying." Those sharp words and harsher tone told Roger to save all the theories and skepticism…and swallow them down with his stew. "Go ahead. Finish your dinner. It's getting cold…little wonder in *this* house!" Carolyn stood abruptly, prepared to abandon her husband…so to return the favor.

"You're being ridiculous." The irascible one had to make matters worse.

"Oh, really? Fine. You can eat alone *and* sleep alone. Welcome home."

Metal against metal, a "click" echoed through the room, silencing a debate.

"Your turn." Pivoting in place, Carolyn left the room, joining her eldest in the kitchen. Assisting with evening chores, she stewed as long and hot as the sumptuous meal she'd prepared for her family. Hoisting the heavy stainless steel pot from the surface of the stove, it occurred to her: a *pressure cooker* was becoming a metaphor of her marriage. A symbol. An omen.

Bolting back into the parlor, Roger found the putrid stench overpowering, spoiling his dinner and souring his foul mood further. He saw the pantry door propped wide open as if it had been pushed back rather than drifting open as before. Slamming it shut, wedging the latch down into its slot, Roger glanced behind him while walking back toward the dining room, sensing a disturbing presence...one other than his own. Of course, it was only his imagination. A startling chill swept through his frame, stilling him en route. Contact. Fear. It seized him. Roger knew of only one reaction to have to fear and frustration; anger. All his huffing and puffing appeared in the air, visible as mist from his lips; a jolt of unfamiliar sensations caused a shaken soul to pause, reflecting upon the circumstances in a feeble attempt to identify an unidentifiable force. A power beyond mortal recognition had claimed him for a moment. Thinking someone just touched him, Roger swung around as if to take a swing at the intruder but she was out of sight, yet not out of mind; his mortal eyes did not behold her. Dismissing it as so much nonsense, he sat down hard in his chair, punishing *it* for being there, no doubt.

To this point, the dining room had been remarkably free of flies, especially so considering the presence of fragrant food. This was no longer the case. An absence went unnoticed until their presence filled the void. Buzzing his head with a vengeance, Roger swatted it away; worse yet, one of the evil demons perched itself on the rim of his bowl, effectively squelching his appetite, this time, permanently. It taunted him until the man exploded. Pounding his fist on the table...good aim; crushing his tormentor into the surface. Pushing the bowl away, he raged through the kitchen then into the bathroom to wash his defiled hand. All the overt grumbling beneath his breath was barely audible. Carolyn and Andrea remained in the pantry, grateful they could not hear the words flowing from this disgruntled man. As he passed through the kitchen again, Andrea peeked around the corner of the pantry to observe. Returning to her mother's side, a nervous child asked what happened. She had vaguely heard an altercation; details escaped her at a distance but no one had missed the impact of his fist on solid maple. Andrea whispered her question.

"Mom. What's wrong with dad?" The inquiry was sincere, full of concern.

"Well, now *that's* the million dollar question." Carolyn could muster only the weakest smile. "I think he's having a temper tantrum. Don't worry. He'll calm down. All boys do in time, usually by the age of fifty...though that's not true in *every* case!" she forewarned.

Attempting to make light of the situation, Carolyn was well aware her little Libran abhorred discord of any kind, especially in the home. Obviously upset by the ongoing dispute, a mother felt the need to reassure her eldest child.

"Is he mad about the fireplace?" Andrea's dewy eyes tugged for an answer.

"No honey. He's just MAD." By lobbing a dollop of soapsuds on the tip of her daughter's nose, Carolyn indicated she did not care to discuss it further. While scrubbing the thick steel wall of a bulky pressure cooker she lifted it from the sink, wincing as its weight pulled against damaged shoulder muscle, reminding her of the REAL issue on the table.

Unaware of the extent of the injuries she sustained, Andrea was concerned and gently pressed her mother for some answers.

"Are you all right, mom? Does it hurt much?" Her alarm was evident.

"I'm fine." She raised the arm above her head to prove she could. "See?" It relieved some tension in the muscle...and in the room.

"Let me see." Andrea longed to comfort, sensing her mom's vulnerability.

"It's my heart that hurts right now, not my shoulder."

Based on the child's reaction Carolyn regretted making a somber comment; in lieu of sharing too much she suggested it was almost time for bed. Having divulged her sadness, something she'd tried to avoid, Carolyn decided, rather than risk any further inquiry, to instead send Andrea on one last errand; to collect a bowl from the dining room table. She would use this time to gather herself. Her daughter dutifully retrieved it, discovering the napkin had been thrown, shroud-like, over the remains of a fly. It explained a loud sound she heard, as well as her father's race to the bathroom sink. She'd cleaned up the mess he'd made, kissed her mother goodnight then went off to her bedroom. Carolyn abandoned her efforts in the kitchen: Lights Out. She made her way through the house finding her acrimonious husband sound asleep on the sofa. There she left him, securing the pantry door one more time as she passed it.

Roger was up with the flies. Based on his cheerful demeanor, no one would have suspected he had a less than pleasant encounter with his wife the night before then slept on the sofa. If he did come to bed, Carolyn hadn't noticed. In any event, he was up and very busy well before she emerged from beneath the relative warmth and comfort of their quilt. When she finally entered the kitchen, she could not believe her bleary eyes. Roger had already prepared a pot of oatmeal and the girls were gathered around the table, devouring their scrumptious gruel in peace and quiet. Their father had forsaken the morning murder and mayhem regimen in favor of joining his children for breakfast, monitoring the surrounding area from his seat. He glanced up and smiled as she came into the kitchen then winked. Carolyn knew it was as close as she'd ever come to a formal apology, though she found herself gratefully accepting it nonetheless; another kind gesture to follow, her husband then rose from his seat to get her a hot cup of coffee. He was making an effort to make amends. Carolyn acknowledged it. He gently placed his hand on her bruised shoulder. She reached up to touch him, patting his fingers, releasing an almost audible sigh of relief. Then, as if nothing had happened between them, as if nothing happened at all, an odd couple chatted about restoration plans. Each guilty of ignoring an issue they could not comprehend, their discussion was a prime example of the tendency. Problem was, in that house, dismissing an anomaly never resulted in its disappearance. Deciding on three slabs of granite for the hearthstone, Roger suggested they first prepare the space. It meant removing the existing rocks, piece by shattered piece. Then they should go to a nearby quarry to choose a more desirable stone. Carolyn agreed. (Note: prerequisite of living in New England requires having a well-developed appreciation for granite.) As they'd done so many times in the past, the family made a project of it, working as a team. Once breakfast was finished, everyone got dressed then hard labor began. **The Bugs Bunny / Road Runner Hour** kept the kids entertained as they toiled. Late in the afternoon Carolyn excused herself from the project, going off to begin another chore: dinner. Everyone else remained on task until that dirty job was done, revealing the gaping hole in their floor, nearly two inches deep. Two-by-six feet across: all that remained where the once cracked, damaged-beyond-repair hearthstone had rested undisturbed for decades, if not for centuries. *Well done* according to Roger; an enormous but well-worth-the-effort restoration project was only partially complete.

Congratulating themselves over a hearty meal, the girls were exhausted and went to bed early, leaving their parents behind to admire all their handiwork. Even with a massive removal effort, a shifting of weight, Carolyn noticed the pantry door had not been a problem. It stayed closed and latched throughout the day. Though she kept it to herself, she felt a certain sense of satisfaction, a realization: Roger's theory of "unbalanced floors" had apparently been shot straight to hell. No animosity; just vindication in her grin.

Though everyone else had the chance to hose off before dinner, Roger was the only one yet to enjoy the many benefits of a hot shower; ladies (and more ladies) first. When his turn finally came Roger was grateful there was any hot water. He left his wife standing in front of their fireplace…smiling. When he returned to the parlor several minutes later, her mood had abruptly changed. In the brief time he was away the room had become frigid, the air had turned rancid and the pantry door had, in death, taken on a life of its own. Carolyn stared at the man in silent desperation.

"What's the matter?" He waited for her response. Standing rigidly in place, only the movement of her eyes indicated *the matter*; her gaze shifting slowly toward the door. It was swinging open then closing, as if fanning an invisible flame. Roger rushed over to it, stopping the momentum, pressing his weight against the wood then holding it still in the frame. He secured the latch with a small piece of cardboard from the nearby desk, wedging it tightly in between the fixture. Once he'd jammed the paper into place, a fit so snug it wouldn't budge, he went back into the kitchen, there to locate the roll of twine in the sideboard drawer. Winding the string around the latch, over then under again, he tied a knot that would have made any sailor at once envious and proud: A Navy man. The recurring chill and odor dissipated in the time it took him to traverse the farmhouse back and forth then back into the parlor again. Roger wrapped the latch then wrapped his wife protectively in his arms, as secure an embrace as twine binding a latch; her gaze fixed on the door...what next?

"That'll do it." Yep, that oughta do it. Treat the symptom...not the disease.

Shocked as much by the fact that he had virtually ignored the odd behavior of a pantry door (as doors don't normally have *behaviors*) as she was by the episode itself, she could not believe he'd virtually dismissed blatant evidence of supernatural activity in the home. The man acted as if it was nothing at all; perfectly natural. Actually, this was perfectly *super*natural! With his silence, Roger refused to acknowledge or discuss it. After the news they went to bed.

The following morning Roger rose early, up before dawn. He opened their bedroom door and could not help but notice the mounded pile of twine on the parlor floor. That pantry door had opened again...sometime during the night. The room was flooded with a foul, acrid odor he had become all too familiar with in recent days. The awful air was thick with a stench attributable only to decomposition; the aftermath of death. Roger's angry heavy sigh appeared as mist in the frigid room. Fighting fright which swept through him like a wave of nausea, Roger stood before the open door, staring down his demons. What was tormenting them apparently fled the premises. It was beyond his mortal comprehension. Instantly, the laundry room became as warm as sunshine and smelled of detergent; a clean, fresh aroma penetrating his nostrils. The twine at his feet had been shredded into thousands of tiny threads, as if having been clawed at for hours with sharp fingernails. Did their cat do that? A tight knot woven to secure that latch the night before was virtually indistinguishable; its thick cotton twine resembled a wad of sewing thread. No way.

By the time Carolyn awakened her husband had emptied the laundry pantry of all its contents, except the washer and dryer. Those had been disconnected then dislodged, so he could examine the dead space behind them. There was nothing there. They had not lived in the house long enough to even build up the predictable lint often found behind such appliances. Roger was stymied. There were no rotting carcasses in the room, no evidence of mice or anything else, for that matter. Just the flies, alive and well, buzzing his head while he worked. Pausing long enough to splat one whenever he could, Roger decided to trap them inside the long, narrow pantry by closing the door behind him, effectively trapping himself in the process. It was an opportunity to wipe all of them out at once. No exit. Roger *did* think twice before closing that door. The man was officially spooked.

An ungodly racket disturbed Carolyn's deep and restful slumber. She rose to find Roger vacuum cleaning in the pantry, cornering flies in windowpanes, sucking them in and pulling them down through the hose attached to a bag of dust, there to slowly but surely suffocate; to go back to their father, the devil. Roger clearly derived some sadistic pleasure from the effort, engrossed as he was, taking aim at those who had so often taken aim at them.

"Jesus Christ!" He did not hear Carolyn opening the door behind him and her sudden, unexpected presence shook him to the core. Touching his elbow, Carolyn got Roger's attention, all right; then she witnessed terror in his eyes. Such an adverse reaction was quite unlike her husband. He was not one to be easily startled. To her knowledge, the man feared nothing. According to him, there was nothing to fear but fear itself; apparently his attitude had changed. In the instant prior to mortal recognition of his wife he looked at her as if she was a ghost; an unholy apparition manifesting through dim morning light.

"Sorry! I didn't mean to scare you. What are you doing in here?"

"Look at this." He stepped out of the pantry to show her the pile of twine.

"Did you do that?" Carolyn had already sensed the answer to this question. Roger shook his head in disgust then picked it up to examine it more closely. "If you *didn't* do this…then who did?" His expression told the truth. Afraid: Be very afraid. He did not know who shredded the knot of twine overnight. "I'll go make us some coffee." Carolyn headed toward the kitchen.

The children got up to watch cartoons, only to discover the sofa space was taken by whatever had been formerly stacked on all the pantry shelves. From bleach bottle to blankets, washcloths to linens, every seat was spoken for this Sunday morning. It was a day much like any other; bright and full of promise as any spring morning could be. The Sun crept up over the tree line, peeking in through their kitchen windows as breakfast was served. Roger entered the kitchen. He looked pale and drawn, tired before the day had begun. Sitting quietly at the table for a few minutes, he made a declaration no one expected, suggesting the girls finish eating then go upstairs and get dressed for church. Carolyn was as stunned as their children. It had been quite awhile since they attended services, having had a falling out with the parish priest at the church in Cumberland. He'd been a brutal, abrasive man; unkind to several children attending catechism. As reports of this abusiveness began running rampant in town, finally reaching Roger, this resulted in a serious confrontation between the Father of a church and the father of a family. Mr. Perron withdrew them as parishioners from Saint Aiden's Parish. Not since then had there been any mention of returning to any place of worship; not until that Sunday morning. Carolyn knew precisely what prompted him to make the abrupt statement; as rapid a reconsideration of an issue as she had ever heard from him before.

Rather than parking in front of a television; within an hour all of them were packed into a pew at Saint Patrick's Church located in beautiful downtown Harrisville. As they'd entered the quiet church every head turned, not simply because they were so late for Mass, but also due to the sheer volume of them! Approaching the family afterward, the kindly priest welcomed them into the church and then invited them to join the congregation. Roger and Carolyn gratefully accepted on behalf of their family...as a way to leave the Light on.

After several more days of labor-intensive restoration and a visit from the chimney sweep, their fireplace was ready for burning. Carolyn found all the necessary hardware tucked in a corner of the woodshed, as well as a wooden box covered by a tarp. It was finally time to dispel the chill from their home. The children gathered around their father while he layered kindling so dry, it splintered between his fingers. Carolyn stood on the hearthstone beside him, anxious to feel the burn destined to be welcome respite from cold unlike any she'd ever experienced in her life. Fire was more than elemental...a blessing and a curse of Nature. It was the promise of comfort, the release from a kind of pain unfamiliar to Carolyn, made all the more daunting by her inability to control it. Now she would possess the means of escaping what she perceived had been haunting her: relentless unforgiving cold. With the balmy, bountiful spring season poised on the horizon, Carolyn had, at last, allowed herself to sense the pleasure of relief. It was nearly over; winter was almost gone. This was a false sense of security, but one which she relished. With a single strike of a match, Roger created a towering inferno. Whoosh! Flames crackled and sputtered, leaping up to lap at the logs. "Fire in the hole!" He was so pleased, pride beaming as brightly as the blaze. Scouting skills had not been lost with time. As long-seasoned wood burned fast and hot, permeating the parlor with its welcome-home warmth, it was the first time Carolyn could recall feeling completely comfortable in the old farmhouse; at times, too close for comfort! Worth the work but not the wait; for months she endured sub-zero conditions outside and sub-human conditions within. While baking a body to the bone, this grateful woman spoke her mind. "The swallows just lost their chimney." Perhaps so; maybe Mr. Kenyon knew, when he'd closed that fireplace, it had something to do with bizarre sights and sounds manifesting within the house. Maybe he knew something more than he shared. There was purpose; a reason why he sealed it shut decades before they arrived; a decision made with some intention. When a portal once closed is reopened, some say it creates a crack in the Cosmos; presumably, following logically, that's how the Light gets in.

"Hope is the feeling we have that the feeling we have is not permanent."
Mignon McLaughlin

bless this mess

"Feed your faith and your fears will starve to death."
Author Unknown

Comfort finally found its hearth and home in which to dwell. Carolyn kept the home fires burning, day and night. Though the fireplace was deeply inset, Roger bought a screen as extra protection from its flying embers. It freed her; she could leave the parlor without worry though she'd never leave it for long. Forever gravitating toward this constant source of heat, she'd evolved into a veritable fixture on the hearthstone; as *there* as the slabs of granite beneath her feet, inlaid with her own hands. She was a part of it... it was a part of her: Simpatico in Nature. At times, it required a chisel to remove the woman from her post, her station in life...pain, her cross to bear.

Inspired by their restoration project, Roger insisted upon doing it right: life lessons for those who paid attention in his class. Days of lifting and hauling, sanding and scraping revealed its essence: an original Colonial mantel board. A masterpiece: It was simply beautiful. There was nothing ornate about it; no fancy carving or inlaid tiles. An authentic specimen, it was a treasure hidden in plain sight, buried beneath countless layers of paint and many decades of neglect. A project beyond Roger's mortal imagination became his gift, more than he could have ever hoped to discover. A vision: A wonder to behold.

Contemplating their next big project, he already knew what he wanted it to be: kitchen ceiling. It was quite low and made the room feel smaller and look darker than it should. Carolyn agreed with him, especially because a pestilent infestation they battled might be revealed in the process. The mere possibility of flies breeding in the ceiling was reason enough to tear it down. Exposing the beams was secondary to resolving the more pressing problem. The couple actually agreed on something twice in one week; a milestone. It would be the next priority on the long list of needed *home improvements*. One suggestion yet to be included on the list: treat the damned house for ghosts!

Amazing what must first be destroyed in order to restore, then recreate, an era lost in time. They were only beginning this process, destined to consume years of their lives. Debris fields expanded; every room in the house would eventually be transformed, along with everyone in it. Before he could begin, Roger had to restock his wares then hit the road for several days. He'd been home for nearly a week and had to get back to work so they could afford to demolish their kitchen. A few customers in Connecticut and New Hampshire were due for a visit. He made the customary trip into Providence; a quick pit stop at a supplier's place in Cranston, then left the city: a beautiful drive, due west on Route 6 into Hartford. No major highways existed between the two New England cities at that time. The scenic route was literally the *only* route.

The family dys/functioned in make-it-and-spend-it mode, a hand-to-mouth method Carolyn found extremely disconcerting. Though as patient a woman as possible, she was anxious to begin; so, deluding herself into believing it may be helpful to get a start without her husband, Carolyn brought the ladder into their kitchen and proceeded with the demolition. A theme was emerging: wait for Roger to leave home then buy a farm and pick up a crowbar. Within a few minutes she had punched through the corner nearest the front hallway, creating a hole: two feet wide and nearly a foot deep. Dust rained down upon her head followed with chunks of plaster, accumulating at an alarming rate at the base of the ladder, scattering as it hit a hard floor. April wandered in the room to see what all the commotion was about. The cherub appeared angelic; yet never more so than she did with her mother that morning. Carolyn gazed down on her daughter as April looked up with pleading eyes. The small child seemed otherworldly in the gauzy white haze, her delicate features strikingly beautiful in natural light filtered through floating specks of a weightless dust, motionless, suspended in the air.

"Again, mommy?" By the tender age of six, April already knew what *work* looked and felt like and how to pitch in and help...but this was one chore she longed to avoid. Her mommy had every intention of letting her off the hook.

"I'm getting a head start for dad...not the whole ceiling...just this corner."

"Your hair is all white again...just like when we did the fireplace." Nothing like pointing out the obvious: "You looked so funny that day!"

"Ah, yes...I remember it well. We sure did work hard, didn't we, honey?"

"And we made a really bad mess...remember? It was everywhere!"

"I know, baby doll." Carolyn laughed then spit out what fell into her mouth while she spoke. An effort to enhance the house literally backfired in her face again; same results. "I think *this* will make an even *bigger* mess, if possible! I guess we'll see, won't we? If I keep at it...I won't be able to *see* anything!"

"Do I have to help clean it up this time?" Clearly, April wanted nothing to do with the task. She'd had her fill of it with the fireplace and was certain her day could be better spent working hard at play.

"No. I want you to go into the parlor so you don't breathe in all this dust."

"Okay!" As April turned to make her great escape, she paused then turned back toward her mother. "I know how I can help you!" Closing her eyes, the child solemnly bowed her head, placing her hands together as pudgy fingers pointed upward toward the desired destination. Uttering a few Heaven-bound words, they spilled awkwardly from her lips as she mimicked what she heard during her first memorable trip to church the previous Sunday.

"Dear God...bless this mess!" An ethereal creature: making the sign of the cross...backwards, by mistake. "The Father, the Son...and the Holy Ghost!" Eyes reopened, glowing with pride. April raised her head, shouting, "Amen!" toward a ceiling...with an enthusiasm generally reserved for Southern Baptist revivals. Her mother was delighted by the blessing of the mess.

"Very good! Now scoot!" Carolyn watched as she took off, bolting through the house as if it were her one and only chance to abscond from the worksite; hence the nickname *Scooter*. It stuck like plaster to hair moist with sweat.

Having the forethought to tote a flashlight up the ladder with her, Carolyn peeked in through the hole to examine the enclosed space. She could not see any evidence of breeding flies; no signs of life at all. So where were the little bastards coming from? Running out of theories, at least a curiosity had been satisfied; they were *not* coming from inside their kitchen ceiling. Descending the ladder, she felt a sudden shiver traveling her legs then distinctly heard the crack of a door; the suction seal on a refrigerator door, so assumed April was rummaging for a mid-morning snack.

"What are you doing, little miss nosey?" No answer. Carolyn's back was to the appliance as she stepped down the sturdy ladder, closely watching at her feet, checking her balance, due to steps suddenly covered with debris; pieces of plaster and slippery dust. Once safely on the floor again she turned to look around the kitchen. The refrigerator door instantly caught her attention, as it had been left opened. Agitated, Carolyn pushed it closed, shedding whatever she could from her hair before launching a search for the culprit. Based upon the faulty assumptions made, a mother was seeking a child who knew better than to behave this way. She found April in the middle of the parlor floor, in front of the fireplace, playing with Nancy's stash of Barbie dolls; a plethora of miniature accessories scattered around her on the rug: fully engaged.

"Why did you leave the fridge open? And why didn't you answer me?"

"When, mommy? I've been in here playing dolls…wasn't this okay to do?" Her innocent voice was filled with the truth, as was her quizzical expression. April had not been in the refrigerator and had not gone into the kitchen at all. Dropping the subject, Carolyn did not want to arouse any suspicions or try to explain something she could not, frightening her daughter in the process. An odd sensation: Alert. Her internal alarm system rang. *Something* opened it!

"Sure honey, that's fine…my mistake." Patting her baby girl on the head, a mother asked, "Do you have your sister's permission to play with her dolls?"

"Nancy *always* lets me play with them as long as I *don't* lose their shoes!"

"All right." Glancing down upon squalor, Carolyn said, "Bless *this* mess!"

Gathering several dolls and all of their stuff together, hastily loading it into its carrying case, a giggling little girl closed then latched the lid with a single, sweeping motion.

"*What* mess?" A budding sense of humor officially entered into evidence.

Carolyn grabbed then dumped the case of dolls upside down. "*That* mess!" They played together for awhile...dress up instead of clean up.

Reluctantly returning to the kitchen, Carolyn again found their refrigerator door wide open. A chill in the room had nothing to do with cool air escaping from inside the appliance. *That* kind of cold was something else entirely, of a different sort: a signal, a clue or perhaps an announcement. It was the kind of cold which told her she wasn't alone in the room; a sensation with which she was becoming all too familiar. Deciding to simply ignore it, (a lesson learned from her husband), Carolyn closed the door and folded the ladder then out to the woodshed it went. Later on, she'd bravely venture back into the kitchen to find its morbid chill dispersed and the refrigerator door securely fastened. Whatever *it* was, it was gone...over for the moment.

Looking up into a substantial hole she created in the ceiling, Carolyn could plainly see one of the hand-hewn beams she'd exposed with the effort. It was beautiful. Though tempted to keep going it was time to clean up the mess left behind by this demolition. At least Roger would see: if flies *were* breeding in the house it was happening elsewhere, in an undisclosed location, yet to be determined by the process of elimination. Having taken the same initiative as with the fireplace, Carolyn felt good about the project, in spite of the fact that she was not alone doing it. Whatever deliberately distracted her was likewise working on her nerves. While dragging a canister vacuum across the kitchen floor, pulling up pieces of plaster wedged between planks, she remembered watching Roger attack intruders inside a laundry room, suction his weapon of choice. Staring at the hose, considering the possibility she just might have the stomach for it, she lifted it to the windowsill. Carolyn soon discovered Roger was right. It was good *unclean* fun, if a trifle sadistic, sucking all these filthy beasts into a hose, down a pipe; going for a helluva ride toward certain death. She thought it strange they did not protest, resist or even evade their attacker. No fear. They didn't flee the scene. Fly away you go! It was as if they agreed to willingly go...back to where they came from. Why? No matter: spiritually speaking. Her conscience, as clear as windowsills; sucking it up, she obliged. No need to feel guilty about it. You can't really kill what's already dead.

"The beginning of knowledge is the discovery of something we do not understand."
Frank Herbert

close that door

"God made Truth with many doors to welcome
every believer who knocks on them."
Kahlil Gibran

Their house was coming to life. Not only was the pantry door in the parlor refusing to remain latched, the demon door beside it (an alternate route to the cellar) began some shenanigans of its own. Opening at will, it filled the room with an earthy, acrid odor. The door no one *ever* opened, (an order, due to its unsafe stairwell) kept opening over and over again, throughout the course of the evening. It unlatched then drifted a few inches, stopping in the same spot, as if someone was peeking into the parlor. A cellar as creepy as any on Earth was on the other side of it; down the dark corridor and a rickety set of stairs. The anomaly began after dinner, once Carolyn built a fire.

Squatting on the hearthstone, she struck a match, snapping it sharply across the cold, dappled surface of granite. In a flash the kindling caught, ignited by the flames of a single piece of paper stuffed beneath a grate. It is no chore at all to make a fire when the wood is well-seasoned, the kindling dry to brittle. Heat baking her cheeks; she felt its warmth folding into flesh as she smiled. Whoosh! There it predictably went, up in smoke and flames, as it had done every other night since the completion of the fireplace. Its restoration brought elemental comfort to an otherwise dreary dwelling as fire in the hole blazed. Though generated from the compact space, it seemed to heat the entire house every time it burned, proving to be the only means of dispelling an insidious chill too cold to be imagined; the sensation too weird to be explained. Having been plagued by it for the duration of a brutal winter, this family welcomed a respite long overdue, even though it officially arrived in springtime.

Click. The cellar door unlatched behind her back. Carolyn didn't even turn to see what happened, presuming the pantry door to be the culprit. She felt a rush of air at her feet; its smell gave up the ghost. The scent from their cellar was distinct unto itself, unlike anything else from anywhere else. She turned to confirm her suspicions. Indeed, the cellar door was open, only an inch or so, just wide enough to flood the parlor with an unmistakably pungent aroma. Rising to walk the few feet over to the errant door, a sensation swept through her, one she identified as fear. Mustering courage required, Carolyn opened the door further, peering down into the black hole. Being void of life did not mean the space was unoccupied. Nothing and no one was visible. She closed the door, securing the latch, as it had been prior to the recurring incident. She could not fathom the idea of it dislodging without considerable assistance. Of the many doors in their house it was the only one with hardware so warped it was a struggle for human hands. As with most antique wrought iron latches, relics of the past, they are authentically rustic, quite charming, but have lost some function with age. On those few occasions this cellar door needed to be opened, Roger's strength was required to accomplish the task. After the third time it happened during the evening, a normally jammed shut latch released with ease, she did the only thing she could to resolve this problem, soliciting help from above: her eldest daughter upstairs.

"Mom, it reeks down here!" Arriving from her stairwell, emerging through a barely perceptible white-to-grayish vapor, she was moving far too quickly for it to interfere with or halt her momentum. Instead, Andrea felt cold waves passing through her body, dispersing its natural heat. She knew the smell of death. An instantly identified odor permeating the fog she'd intercepted kept her moving; straight to the fireplace to warm the cold, saying nothing of it.

Without disclosing the reason, Carolyn convinced her to help remove the antique desk from her bedroom, placing it directly in front of the cellar door. Andrea hoisted her half without question. Once properly situated, she went to retrieve her homework, returning to stake a claim at the desk. Carolyn was so grateful for some company. As the parlor warmed again, Andrea found it far toastier than it had been at her own desk upstairs. The rancid smell seemed to fly up then out the chimney. Carolyn stoked a crackling fire. Neither of them spoke about what they'd both sensed in the space they were sharing.

Click. Laundry room: its cranky door cracked open. The pantry: making its presence known, again. Andrea glanced at her mother for a reaction. Carolyn hid her frustration well. There were no words to explain it. She possessed no ability to attribute it to anything; clearly something she did not comprehend. Still, she knew it was *not* floors "settling" in a house which was, at this time in its history, nearly two hundred and forty years old. Carolyn didn't want to have her girls exposed, especially by her own acknowledgment, to whatever cryptic oddities kept occurring in the house, as if that could be avoided. Their mother had, by necessity, learned how to control a household and yet, there she stood, feeling decidedly out-of-control in an old farmhouse, to the extent that it did not feel like *home*. It felt frightening and hostile, complicated and inexplicable; as if the incongruous household was instead controlling her.

"Dad says it happens because of the floors." Andrea leaned over and closed the door. It was a relief to her mother, not knowing what to say in response to the question in her daughter's eyes: "Is that true?" She could hear the thought as if it had been spoken aloud.

Opting for silence, Carolyn nodded in agreement. Of course; certainly that was the reason...it must be. Andrea returned to her homework while Carolyn remained close by, peeking over her shoulder, seeking a progress report. Her nonchalance was becoming a substitute emotion as a passive, benign defense mechanism utilized in lieu of experiencing supernatural activity for precisely what it was: bizarre. Instead, Carolyn resorted to minimizing it, dismissing it entirely if need be, as a skill; as a means of coping with whatever she did not understand. In fact, she deeply resented *feeling* anything at all in the house, especially one persistent, nagging sensory perception: the feeling she was not alone. It rattled her nerves; made her angry whenever she sensed a presence. It caused her to repeatedly question herself and that made her uncomfortable. It was foreign; made her skin crawl. Those who knew this woman considered her as an intellectual: a deep thinker. She found visceral sensations a cerebral intrusion into an otherwise staid and orderly mind. Though she had no notion of it at the time, her negativity was feeding that which dwelled among them. As she became increasingly preoccupied with disturbing thoughts she found it necessary to keep them private, as if ashamed...as if there was something wrong with *her*. Feeling guilty, having been the one who lobbied to buy this place, her girls were now in an environment she was incapable of controlling. They'd seen a coat hanger flailing in midair. They heard noises and watched doors open at will. Their house expressed itself in a wide variety of ways and it was just the beginning of their odyssey. Carolyn's angst began burgeoning; her protective instincts remaining on high alert. Not caring to seek validation from the skeptical husband for her sake, it brought Carolyn no comfort to see their children running to him, divulging what they had seen for themselves, as was the case in the aftermath of the warm room incident. Clearly it would be her preference to keep them sheltered from the cosmic storm. But if they were so terrified they went to their father, then he simply *must* believe them. Carolyn did not yet know the truth. Without exception, all the girls had been approached, each one enduring a close encounter of one kind or another with whomever it was dwelling within those ancient walls.

None of the girls disclosed these incidents to their parents or to each other, for that matter. Like mother, they'd kept it to themselves. Eldest to youngest knew of a presence. They knew something shared space with them and each had been touched by its mere existence; each was equally motivated to keep secrets for personal reasons. Carolyn didn't want these suspicions confirmed; *wanted* to be dead wrong. Andrea wanted to ease her mother's stress. Nancy thought it was "kinda cool". Christine resorted to a "planned ignore" strategy and Cynthia was too frightened to breathe, let alone speak of what she'd seen and heard. April did not want to disclose a newfound playmate. Deliberately withholding vital information kept their astounding discovery quiet. Each of them used specialized survival techniques and developed coping skills which kept the peace and kept special secrets safe. Roger seemed oblivious to what was happening to his family. Though he privately harbored suspicions of his own, they were of an entirely different nature. His fear was rooted in the real possibility his wife was facing some sort of a breakdown; transformation. All of them eager for spring to arrive, anxious to escape the confines of a spooky old house, they craved a peaceful and boring existence. It was not to be.

Lingering in front of the fireplace, Carolyn considered her own words. She felt guilty. Having used them frequently, at times accusatorily regarding the doors of the farmhouse, "Close that door!" had become more a mantra than a phrase. She had repeatedly blamed her children for something they had not done wrong and it was this realization troubling her deeply. If they were not the *irresponsible* party, who or what was responsible? She silently vowed to avoid it in the future. Click. Appearing reflexive, without looking away from her homework, Andrea reached over, closing the pantry door. Like mother, like daughter: she'd learned her lessons well. Carolyn turned around to throw another log on the fire.

It was getting late; the dutiful mother went to the stairwell then hollered up, "Time for bed!" Yet another familiar, if unwelcome phrase often uttered by a mom. Within moments she heard the shuffling of feet overhead accompanied by the sound of dresser drawers opening and closing. In pajamas, the motley crew came downstairs all at once to say goodnight.

"Did everyone finish their homework?" Nods all around; Chris had hers in hand as proof of the assertion.

"Not yet." Andrea's hand went into the air though her gaze remained fixed on a notebook at the center of the desk.

"Not yet!" April's hand went in the air. She often mimicked her big sister.

"You don't *have* homework, silly." Chris sweetly chastised the littlest girl.

"She could do mine for me!" Nancy was a bit too quick with the suggestion meant to be humorous, arousing some suspicion.

"She would probably do a better job!" Cindy's quip; too close to the truth. Nancy had quite a reputation for flying through her work on her way to play. Mom needed to inspect it to be certain, so requested a hard copy as evidence.

"Why me? You never ask anyone else!" Instantly defensive, Nancy knew it was *not* finished; a string of heavy sighs trailing behind her as she went back upstairs, returning to her desk. "I'll check it over first."

"Sure, Nance. That means you'll finish it now." The deadpan comment had come from beneath her breath; Andrea closed a notebook. She *was* finished. Everyone else began to giggle because *everyone* knew it was true. Nancy had earned such scrutiny. Carolyn sent her girls off to bed with grins on their lips and a hug around the neck. Nancy grumbled all the way back upstairs where she would spend another thirty minutes completing her assignments. Andrea went along to help. After awhile Carolyn made the rounds…a normal nightly walk-through to which her children were accustomed and especially grateful for since moving into a spooky old farmhouse. Lingering for several minutes, checking over Nancy's work, she found April, fallen fast asleep. Chrissy and Cindy were chatting but both appeared drowsy and would not be long for the world. Andrea was still reading in bed. Pausing to thank her for helping with a desk downstairs and a homework situation upstairs, Nancy was grateful for the help, too. Mom was passing the message along. They spent a few minutes discussing the book she was into and then, before heading down their narrow stairwell a mother cautioned her daughter not to stay up too late. Returning to the parlor, Carolyn stoked the fire then took up with a good book of her own. Girls in bed, it was time to relax and settle in for the night. The house would be infinitely more peaceful and quiet, or so she'd assumed. Click.

"Let him who desires peace prepare for war."
Flavius Vegetius Renatus

smoke and mirrors

"Death, the sable smoke where vanishes the flame."
George Gordon, Lord Byron Childe Harold's Pilgrimage

The fireplace was so warm and lovely. It burned with a brilliance reflected throughout an old farmhouse infusing it with something it had lost over time. Banking its auburn ashes against the back wall, Carolyn placed the screen in front of it then prepared for bed. The night had been long and the woman was weary. Her usual routine involved the walk-through, first upstairs to tuck the girls in and then around its ground level to turn off the lights. Emerging from the bathroom into the kitchen, the odor rushed her nostrils: the eerily familiar aroma. Her sensory perceptions were fine. It was her extrasensory perception working on her mind. In spite of the fact that she had, just moments earlier, passed through the front hallway, finding it quiet, nothing unusual, Carolyn sensed it was where she should look. The cold scent in the room indicated a door had opened somewhere. It was not the intensely pervasive cold she had begun to associate with some unwelcome guest. Crossing the kitchen then turning the corner into a dark hallway, Carolyn found the cellar door propped wide open as a draft of some velocity swept up the stairwell, reeking of damp earth, old and moldy horsehair plaster. Spoiled air infiltrated her nose as she tightly closed the door. There was no point in asking their girls; it would only alarm them. A mother *knew* none of them had been out of bed; no one snuck downstairs to open the cellar door. No tricks being played by mortals on that night or any other night, for that spirit matter. Nefarious forces were at work: something wicked this way comes, arriving as a chill in the air on the drafts from below, accompanied by an unmistakable aroma; too close for comfort.

Securing the door, she returned to the parlor to check on the fire once more before retiring for the evening. The seasoned wood burned fast and hot; by that time, only a few glowing embers remained. One quick stir told her it was just about out. With a screen for protection, Carolyn went to bed, closing the pantry door as she'd passed by. Her bedroom was just off the parlor, the only bedroom on the first floor; an adequate vantage point for

155

monitoring a house. She could see into the parlor and could hear anything going on overhead. As was her habit whenever Roger was away from home, she'd always leave her bedroom door open. Cuddling up beneath her ample quilt, Carolyn had yet to close her eyes when she'd distinctly heard the sound of ignition, that curious "Swoosh!" made by kindling when fire and air collide with wood. She leapt from bed, peering out into the parlor, directly into the fireplace, a distance of no more than fourteen feet from where she stood. It was not even smoldering and had gone completely dark; no sign of firelight. It was then she realized; a threatening sound she still succinctly heard, a horrible crackling, combustible noise was coming from behind her...from inside her bedroom.

Wrenching her torso around in a panic, Carolyn saw the top of her dresser erupting into flames. It was ablaze with light: sparks jumping from a fireball, the core of which burned so brightly she could barely gaze into it. Off-shoots sprung from its center, appearing like wild sparklers out-of-control, pinging then popping in every direction. Paralyzed by an all-consuming fear, she was literally scared stiff. Describing the shock of this moment as mind-bending, Carolyn tried to react, tried to bolt; tried to breathe. Her mind was as frozen as her body. It remained fixed on the fire and five children sleeping upstairs. For the duration of this episode, Carolyn thought of nothing else. She could only watch as the fire and light intermingled, dancing with its own reflection in the mirror, magnified by the glassy surface, threatening to claim her entire family. In abject horror she watched. It continued unabated for what Carolyn describes as more than a minute, though she would be the first to admit, time becomes distorted or suspended: altered by terror. It felt like eternity. Flames catapulted through the night across the room, searing the darkness with light; a splayed spray of fiery shards flying toward lace curtains, dropping onto the quilt, bouncing off the wooden floor as do the remnants of fireworks hitting a roof. The pulsing surge of adrenaline vibrated through the veins of Carolyn's trembling body; an overwhelming rush. Observing in stunned silence, unable to draw a breath, her eyes burned from staring into the spectral light. It hissed like a snake and flew like a bird. Moment after agonizing moment fire hurled itself around the room and then, in a mere fraction of a second, it was gone. Carolyn fell onto the floor as if having been suspended then released from an invisible wire: an intentionally captivating encounter. She cannot recall how long she remained there before recovering enough to stand up. It took quite awhile to collect herself. Rising slowly from the floorboards, then fumbling around in the dark for the switch, once a light was on in her room the woman was able to regain shaken bearings; sitting on the side of her bed, sliding her quivering fingers across the surface of the quilt. Glancing into the parlor, she could see the fireplace was dark; fire completely dead. Whatever happened to her had nothing to do with shooting embers or an errant reflection of flames.

Though her lean legs remained as limp and liquid as over-cooked pasta, an unbelieving soul who did not trust her own eyes righted herself to the extent she was able. Wandering around the bedroom, searching for debris; a spot of singe, *some* indication of fire, Carolyn found no evidence to substantiate her claim. No lingering odor of smoke; no residual spots: nothing to signify this event occurred. Impossible: lace curtains escaped unscathed; the cotton quilt, bearing no visible signs of injuries to its pearl-colored patches of fabric, lay sprawled above the sheets. Rounding the bottom of her bed, approaching the large dresser at the far side of the room, she was certain there would be some evidence of this event where it had manifested. Fixing her stare on its broad, flat surface, Carolyn detected only a thin sheen of dust on an otherwise clean, undisturbed piece of furniture. Dragging fingertips across it, this motion left streaks behind, a telltale sign of her presence; not the elemental force of fire. Until this instant, that surface remained untouched. She was certain of it. No soot or signs of burn holes on lace doilies. No marks on the mirror. No scars on the wood; apparently no effect from an explosive ball of fire shooting off sparks from the surface of maple veneer. Roger would *never* believe this!

Overwhelmed, Carolyn wandered into the parlor, allowing her weary bones to collapse onto the loveseat directly across from the fireplace. Her mind was still racing as her body shut down. Sleep would elude her this night. Instead, she would spend the time reliving the ordeal in an attempt to resolve it; find a logical explanation for it. Questions loomed along with a foreboding sense of danger. She'd begun to believe a presence had awakened something dormant, something evil in their house: the presence of her family. Carolyn rightfully perceived an ominous event as a threat. Hour after hour, as thoughts wrestled with perceptions, conflict was taking a terrible toll on an increasingly fragile creature. Dread consumed her: afraid to close her eyes, afraid to deflect rapt attention; fearful of lighting the fire. In spite of fear, still cold and trembling, shivering beneath a blanket, she steadfastly rose to meet the threat. Carolyn rekindled the fire, fully extinguished, certain it had not been the source of the spectral display in her bedroom. There she remained, alone on a hearthstone, keeping vigil. Studying the brilliant flames, watching and wondering how to react to space invasion which **must** have been an optical illusion, a mirage in a mirror, Carolyn was cautious yet equally curious. She began to examine the angles, distance; the reflection of light in the parlor. Poised in the doorway of her bedroom, she measured the distance between a dresser and fireplace then gazed at its mirror. There was no reflection of flames leaping up and lapping at chimney walls, no hint of a hue or its golden glow; no sparks of light at all. The height of the mirror precluded a direct reflection of the fireplace. Even if the mirror had been propped on the floor the location of their bed would have blocked its path, refusing to allow the surface of glass to mimic the firelight dancing around a dark parlor: Inconceivable. This harrowing episode was not a natural event. It was supernatural in origin; defying all established laws of physics. It defied all human comprehension. During her pause for reflection, despair began to settle into a mortal Soul.

Bundled tightly inside the blanket, Carolyn returned to the loveseat, staring suspiciously at the fire, as if watching over some naughty child who claimed to be nothing but goodness and light but was instead an omen, a threatening display of darkness and death. She found a disquieting comfort in acceptance of her circumstances. Primal instincts kept the woman awake: the protective urge dictated an unwavering maintenance…a state of alert in consciousness. It was **not** a nightmare; not some smoke and mirrors illusion. It was a threat. It was real and true and it was time to tell. As those few final glowing embers surrendered to the darkness of night, Carolyn reluctantly closed her eyes.

***

Another theme emerged: Fear of fire. Carolyn was well aware of the threat. Their house was a virtual tinderbox. Nobody took it more seriously. It was an omnipresent notion. What better way to scare a mother right out of her mind? What better threat to issue? It had not been an illusion or a nightmare but was instead, a harbinger of things to come; the first, though certainly not the last time spirits would be caught like naughty children playing with fire and light.

Where there's smoke...

"Our time consumes like smoke, and posts away;
Nor can we treasure up a month or day:
The sand within the transitory glass
Doth haste, and so our silent minutes pass."
Rowland Watkyns

spirit matters

At first light Carolyn stirred. Her limbs were weak. It was a difficult task to steady her gait on her way to the bathroom. Though she expected a different outcome, all the doors in the house remained securely fastened. Staring at her image in a mirror on the wall, the young woman was startled by how her face had aged overnight. If she did not know better, she would have thought she'd been asleep for twenty years, awaking as a much older (and wiser) soul.

The house was still. Actually, it was strangely silent. While Carolyn put on a pot of water for oatmeal, she listened intently, noting the absence of sound, unable to discern the nature of it. The dwelling felt warmer than usual though the Sun had yet to crest the tree line. Sitting alone at the kitchen table, alone with her thoughts and a hot cup of coffee, the truth was she was never alone. A steaming brew did nothing to mitigate her exhaustion. Only an intravenous infusion of undiluted caffeine would make any measurable difference. Sleep deprivation caused her to feel rather punch drunk; she had to shake it off fast. Getting the children up and ready for school was the immediate priority.

Carolyn was desperate for help. Rising abruptly, she marched over to their telephone, centered on the kitchen wall between two windows. Only then did she realize why the room was so eerily quiet: there they were, lined up along the windowsills, staring at her. Haunted houseflies were no longer buzzing as usual low-level racket. None of them were flying. Barely moving, they stood as still as statues, as pillars of stone in miniature, observing every move she made as if they somehow knew she was about to rat them out. Carolyn dialed the number from memory. Sam was not only a well-respected attorney but he was also a close personal friend. He had always been their greatest advocate, encouraging the couple to buy the farm from the moment he saw the place in the country; a piece of paradise, he said. Though his office in Providence was empty at such an early hour of the morning, she called him at home, knowing she would be instantly forgiven for this way-too-early intrusion of reality.

"Sam, I'm afraid I have made a terrible mistake." Her hushed tone and the fact that she had just dragged him from a deep sleep caused Sam to hesitate a moment as he identified the distant voice.

"Carolyn?" Though she could hear his grogginess, he could hear her panic.

"I believe I have made a grave error in judgment." She sounded so serious; downright grim. He could hear the tears in the back of her tightening throat.

"Hold on a second." Coming to attention, Sam sat up in his bed.

Recounting everything which happened the previous night, Carolyn's voice trembled as she spoke. It terrified her to relive it, if only in words. When she finished this story she moved on, without affording him any time to respond. For the next few minutes she whispered into the receiver, trying not to wake the children overhead. Listening intently, Sam reserved judgment of his own. She told him about the scythe and a flailing coat hanger and doors opening at will. She leered at those nosy flies as she attempted to describe their intrusive existence in her house. Sam Olevson was pure gentleman; a supremely kind, understanding soul. She felt safe sharing these fears and suspicions, without any reservation. She told him about her ordeal: fire in the hole; then spoke of smoke and mirrors, feeling threatened and unwanted, the *feeling* she was not alone. Describing a pervasive cold and repugnant odor often accompanying such perceptions, when she finished, the depleted woman took a deep breath, relaxing into a chair...awaiting his response. For a moment there was silence then a single statement spoken with the utility of an attorney's own language.

"Sweetheart, sounds to me like you've bought yourself a haunted house."

Carolyn was shocked. In all the time invested thinking about this dilemma, her boggled mind had yet to fuse two simple words together. He was right. It *was* a haunted house.

"You think so?" Her voice was as small as that of her youngest child.

"I do."

"So, you *do* believe me then." An element of self-confidence emerged from Carolyn's voice as she posed the normally probing question as a statement of fact. She trusted the man implicitly, relying upon his objectivity as well as an overdeveloped sense of justice; his more than fair share of common sense.

"Of course I believe you! My house on the East Side is haunted."

"Really? You've never mentioned it before."

"You learn to live with it. In time, it gets less shocking, more *para*normal."

"Sam, what should I do about this?"

"Nothing, dear. When in doubt, do nothing. Fear the living…not the dead."

"My mother used to say that. I never understood what it meant, until now." Smiling at the distant recollection, she asked, "Can't you file some kind of a lawsuit against this THING and *make* it leave the premises?"

"Afraid not; these are *spirit* matters. No court in the land will hear our case. On second thought, *maybe* a judge would issue a Restraining Order!" Sam's warped sense of humor had apparently awakened with him. Carolyn laughed, having been put oddly at ease; comforted by the conversation. Sam promised to visit that weekend; the news of his pending presence, a welcome relief.

Their privacy was suddenly jolted to an abrupt conclusion by the sound of alarm clocks chiming overhead. It took all of her strength to make it through that day. Carolyn fed her children then sent them off to catch their bus. Then she had to get April settled in before she could rest. By the time she allowed her body to drop onto the sofa it was mid-morning. Pure dread kept her eyes from closing. She did not want April out of her sight. After the incident only hours before, the terror still so fresh it was palpable, her baby had to remain close by and her eyes *had* to remain open. She was afraid of falling asleep. What she most feared was something happening to her daughters. (Too late!) Sam told her not to be afraid but she did not know how to dispel the fear she had not conjured. It was *not* her imagination. Instead, it was a reaction to the phenomenon she had never before encountered and could not comprehend. Though disquieting, fear seemed the natural reaction to these circumstances. When her husband did arrive, she would offer no apology for her emotions or corresponding mood. He could not get there soon enough. Her eyes began to close. Resisting the urge, deliberately rising from the chair fast becoming too comfortable, Carolyn wanted out. She wanted to sell the house.

The school bus arrived on schedule; still no trace of her husband, in spite of assurances made: he'd be coming home that afternoon. Carolyn resented his absence. It was all too much to handle alone. Placing April in the care of her eldest sister, the weary, brooding mother sent her children out to play. Shrill screams of delight announced their father's presence in the driveway, though their mother remained quite calm, waiting for him in the parlor. When Roger entered the house, surrounded by his flock of little lambs, her eyes, two dark orbs, stared disdainfully in his direction. She did not care if he was tired from a road trip; she was exhausted, having been on a journey of her own, one he could not imagine. She didn't care about anything except getting some sleep.

"You're in charge." It was all Carolyn said while rising from the sofa.

"Well, that's a very fine how do you do!" His wife did not respond. "Some greeting! What the hell is the matter with you?" Roger became belligerent. She said nothing more, passing him by as she went straight into the bedroom. Closing the door firmly, the man wasn't welcome to follow. April pulled him down to kid level to whisper in his ear. As an authority on the matter, having spent the day with her mother, she explained to the best of her ability:

"Mommy doesn't feel good. She's really tired and in a *really* bad mood."

Roger wondered what the problem could be but did not pursue the issue. If his wife was not well, best to let her sleep undisturbed. Instead, he got busy in the kitchen preparing dinner and catching up with his girls. Nobody spoke of their mother's dour mood. Instead, they hovered around their father, each seeking some form of favor. April brought their most recent renovation to his attention. Roger stood directly beneath it, staring into the gaping hole in the corner of the kitchen ceiling. Knowing he must be curious about it, the baby tugged at a daddy's shirtsleeve again telling him how she had blessed a mess, showing him how she'd made the sign of the cross; backwards, by mistake. Too damn cute to correct, he let it go, all the while wondering about his wife: So, what the hell is the matter? Spirits: They form and substance and matter.

"Mistakes are the portals of discovery."
James Joyce

scorched offerings

"You can discover what your enemy fears most
by observing the means he uses to frighten you."
Eric Hoffer

Roger became distracted and burned the food; not too badly, but enough to taste the scorch from the bottom of the skillet. They ate without complaint; a few (faux) compliments bantered about to spare his feelings. Some food was put aside, in case Carolyn woke up hungry, but that night she never came out of their bedroom; the girls had him all to themselves. They enjoyed spending time with dad; observing as he'd built a fire like a pro, gathering in front of it as the evening chill began settling in. Spring was quite young though it had, thus far, proved no warmer than winter. Watching television, volume down, so to avoid waking their mother only a room away; after about an hour it was time for homework then off to bed. April reminded him to tuck them all in. It was his pleasure, having been gone for several days. Finally, Roger was able to relax, stretching out on the sofa where he promptly fell asleep.

Waking just before dawn, the man's body was stiff and sore. The fire had burned out hours before; he had weathered a cold night without the benefit of a blanket. Rekindling the flames around one large scorched log left behind, piling on a few pieces of dried splinters for good measure, Roger warmed up and thought about his wife. Their bedroom door was still closed. The pantry door was open. He closed it but could still smell the scent of stale cellar air. He felt a draft as he sparked a fire. Glancing behind while leaning toward the fireplace, Roger noticed the cellar door, barricaded by a desk, was now open about an inch; displacing the desk by the same distance. He had not asked the girls about it the night before, assuming Carolyn simply rearranged, creating extra space in their bedroom. It never occurred to him that she did so to keep a door, difficult to open, from doing so on its own. Kindling ignited as usual. Swoosh! Roger closed the cellar door then secured it. Hoisting the desk back in place, the crackling of fire disguised the *click*. From the corner of his eye Roger watched the latch lift up then snap back down in its slot. A shiver went through him, having nothing to do with the temperature in the parlor. Perhaps his wife could shed some light on the situation. He opened the bedroom door and found her bundled beneath the quilt, still fast asleep. Rather than disturb her rest, Roger stoked the fire with a few logs, replaced the screen then went into the kitchen. Once the coffee was perking he put a pot of water on to boil. Examining the hole in the ceiling, he considered it a good start and wondered if the flies might be breeding above. (Far more likely: *below*!) There the little devils were, perched on the windowsill, poised and waiting for him. Agitated by the sight, Roger grabbed the swatter, resuming his task, obliterating every insect he could contact; a fruitless attempt to decimate the population. It was *their* decision when to vacate these premises…not his…the man had much to learn. Children began emerging from their bedrooms; a line, quickly forming at the bathroom door. While patiently waiting her turn Chrissy inquired about breakfast, secretly hoping it would be something her father could not burn, a hamburger from the night before still sitting like a stone in her stomach. He'd been distracted; tired from his long trip, out of practice in the kitchen (mom was the *regular* cook) so the sin was forgivable. Christine was destined to be an accountant; quietly calculating the odds of eating scorched oatmeal, then suggesting they have cold cereal instead. Dad agreed. Turning off the burner as water boiled away, fogging up the pantry windows; steam heat it provided was warmth welcomed by all. Casually resuming his self-imposed charge as the local exterminator, while the girls ate their breakfast, Roger patrolled the kitchen, coffee in one hand, fly swatter in the other. Splat!

Carolyn staggered out of bed, dazed and a bit disoriented. Gathering her wits, she realized, amazingly, her extended nap had passed entirely uninterrupted. Momentarily lost in time, she sat down on the bed again, bare legs dangling, studying the clock. She did the math. It had been more than fifteen hours of deep, restful sleep. Opening her door, a fireplace beckoned. By this time the wood was fully engaged in flames; the warmth of its embrace spreading over her like layer upon layer of blankets. She could smell the coffee and hear her children. As the sharp slap of the swatter intruded, Carolyn remembered her husband was home...and apparently back on task. Though her sleep had been undisturbed, the same could not be said for her waking. This habit of his was something more than irritating. She considered it to be an unnecessary evil. Her expression distorted as Carolyn thought about the girls trying to eat their breakfast in peace. The sounds of assaults impaled her mind like tiny bolts of lightning striking at the peaceful silence. What a way to start a day. Carolyn followed it, prepared to do whatever necessary to make it STOP!

From the look on her face everyone knew something was wrong with mom. Claiming her spot at the table, Andrea went to get her mother a cup of coffee. Roger chose this opportune moment to announce, in his typically aggravated tone, it was time to call the exterminator back again.

Carolyn exploded: "No more! They'll poison my kids with that shit! I don't want it in this house! I'd rather have the goddamned flies!" Pounding her fist on the table, the kitchen fell silent. Children were mortified by their mother's hateful, contemptuous words; her spontaneous outburst not quite concluded. "Roger! Put that thing away! Give it up! You're *so* neurotic!"

"What the hell...is the matter with you?" He stared at his wife as if he had seen a ghost. A ~ who are you and what have you done with my wife ~ look.

What had begun as an ugly altercation one chilly spring morning ultimately resulted in the first meaningful communication between Roger and Carolyn on the difficult, complicated subject. It had indeed become a pressing matter; spirit matters...requiring immediate attention and necessary acknowledgment. It would prove to be rather tense, even terse talk, but one which had to occur. Carolyn had a story to tell. Roger did as well. It was the end of the beginning.

The children quickly finished breakfast in silence then bolted for the door, grateful to have someplace else to go. Their remorseful mother escorted them into the parlor, apologizing for the rude eruption which occurred at the table. Hugs and kisses all around, forgiveness was as much in their nature as it was in her own. Setting April up on the corner of **Sesame Street**, she returned to the kitchen. It was time to tell the truth. Carolyn sat down then stared into her coffee cup, unable to lift it to her lips. A soft humming of wings fluttering in glee provided a queer soundtrack in an otherwise silent kitchen. The flies had come alive again. They seemed delighted by the reprieve *or* the explosion of hostility, suspending certain death sentences for all who made their presence known. Roger was awaiting an inevitable exchange. Examining Carolyn at a distance, keenly aware she had become deeply disturbed by something more than his nasty little habit; he joined her at the table. Trembling with distress, a wife turned abruptly toward her husband, noting his cold, hard expression.

"I'm sorry." The tears came against her will. Carolyn rarely cried; in many ways she was as pragmatic as Roger was, so she struggled to maintain a stoic composure. Tears ruptured a secure seal on the well of loneliness and misery; another chronic pain. Isolation and self-doubt had plagued her for months. It was the release of all she feared and all she felt. Roger did not know how to react. For once, there was no overreaction.

"Tell me what's going on with you?" His tone was an odd mixture of harsh and tender; raw emotion twisted into a knot tightening in his stomach. Roger wanted to be sensitive to his wife yet she had deliberately humiliated him. He was deeply offended by her earlier accusation.

"Night before last the dresser in our bedroom caught on fire."

"What?!" Alarmed by the scary image Roger became transfixed, prompting her for more information: Details. "What do you mean? How did the dresser catch on fire...did you leave a candle burning?" Question posed as demand.

"No. I don't know what happened. There was a fire...and then it was gone. It was a fireball on the dresser, bouncing around; shooting sparks off in every direction. I was terrified out of my mind! At first I thought it was a reflection in the mirror from the fireplace but it *wasn't*...it was a ball of fire, leaping all over the bedroom...and it didn't leave a single mark on anything it touched."

"You were dreaming." He relaxed, smiling knowingly. Judgment rendered. Issue resolved, at least as far as he was concerned.

"I was standing in the middle of our bedroom, Roger. I was wide awake!" Carolyn was not smiling. Apparently she did not *know* as much as he did.

"You had a nightmare." He was convinced, based on her description of it.

"I called Sam." Carolyn finally sipped her coffee. She knew disclosing the situation to their mutual friend would finally get Roger's attention. It did.

"You did what? Why'd you do that? What did you tell him?" Roger closely scrutinized his wife. He did not want the subject discussed, especially outside of the family, but Sam *was* family. Roger knew it must be serious if Carolyn felt compelled to tell him about it. Perhaps he should learn to listen up!

"Everything; I told him everything." Her torso heaved a sigh of relief.

"What do you mean by *everything*; what did he have to say?" Curiosity got the best of him; he *had* to pay attention to Sam, if vicariously through her.

"He said calm down…*be not afraid*…nothing to fear but fear itself; he said *they* couldn't hurt us and then he quipped: *'fear the living, not the dead'* and suggested I go get some sleep. He said his house on Benefit Street is haunted, too." (The East Side of Providence has a well-deserved reputation within the corporeal and spirit worlds alike. They *all* know how to party on the hill.)

"*They* can't hurt us? I do not believe in ghosts." Roger withdrew, suddenly as rigid in demeanor as was his staunch denial of her claim. He didn't believe in ghosts, ergo, he didn't believe his wife. If he denied them they didn't exist.

"Well you know what? I didn't believe in ghosts either, not until we moved into this house. I thought dead was dead and that was it. I was rather looking forward to it…a nice long nap! Imagine MY disappointment! Over the past few months I have seen enough, heard enough and felt enough to know that *something bizarre* is happening in this house! I don't know *what* or *who* it is but I am telling you, Roger, its real, its evil and it doesn't want *me* around!"

"You're being…" He almost went there again.

"Don't you *dare* say I'm being ridiculous!" Her hackles, expectantly up.

"It could be your imagination…"

"No! I don't know what this is but I *do know* it is *not* my imagination! Sam believes me, so it seems you are the one with a problem here…odd man out."

"Lower your voice!" Roger pointed in the direction of their youngest, who was engrossed in an episode of a favorite show. She couldn't hear them from such a distance but her father was taking no chances. Roger suddenly rose to close the kitchen door; a precautionary measure. No need to frighten a child. Neither parent considered what strange and wondrous stories their children could have told had they only been given the opportunity; had they not been excluded from the privileged conversation. Time would tell their tale as well.

"Wait. I'll go check on her. I'm sure the fire needs some tending anyway." Carolyn began to rise. Roger volunteered to go instead. Settling back into her chair, staring at streaks of gray light slicing the table in half, her mind drifted back to the incident in question.

"Get another cup of coffee. I'll be right back." He'd left her alone with her troubled thoughts: the recurrent theme re-emerging in morning light.

When he returned to the kitchen a few minutes later Carolyn appeared as a figure set in stone. Fixed and motionless, she remained in place at their table, gazing into her empty coffee mug. Held captive by the contemplation, as she was by their house, startled by her husband's arrival, she hadn't noticed his presence until he reached in to retrieve the mug wedged tightly in her hands. As he turned toward the pantry she gave voice to a winter's silent discontent.

"I want to sell the house." Transfixed; six words uttered in a whisper stilled her husband. He had to stop and think…what to say…how to react. It could have so easily erupted into an argument. "I want out of here." Her eyes found his as pleading as her own, for different reasons. Roger promptly returned to the table, lifting her into an embrace; a good decision made in the moment.

"Now sit down and tell me what you told Sam." No longer placating, when Roger realized their situation had escalated beyond his perceived control, he had to reclaim it, as if he'd ever had any control of it, anymore than she did. "What did you mean by *everything*? What haven't you told me yet? Really, isn't it at least a *possibility* you were having a nightmare when, as you say, you saw a fire on the dresser?"

Carolyn's body stiffened, adopting a defensive posture again. She *knew* it! She just **knew** he would not believe her! "Please let me go." He obliged. She dropped into her seat, momentarily defeated. In the next moment, Roger was seated beside her again, this time ready to listen...and listen he did. Carolyn proceeded to go through the litany of experiences, beginning inside the barn, detailing instances in which she'd felt another presence; every time she'd felt threatened, harassed or otherwise put upon. The diatribe was a dissertation of sorts, delivered as a lecture to a skeptical student who'd finally have to admit the teacher had an all too real grasp of the material. He sat quietly. There was much to absorb, but were they lessons learned?

At its conclusion, Carolyn slumped back in her chair, intensity diminished by exhaustion. Roger was speechless. He rose very slowly then crossed to the window, searching his troubled mind for a response while gazing through the panes of glass. After a minute or so, he came up with something perfect:

"So you *really* don't think it was a nightmare." An attempt to shatter a dark spell cast met with some success. Carolyn allowed herself to grin. She looked at him and simply shook her head at his incorrigible, impenetrable skull.

Roger turned toward the window again, recalling what he had meant to tell her long before that morning, remembering this event while surveying their property with tired eyes. "You know, the day we moved in, old man Kenyon said something very strange to me."

"No. I *didn't* know." No. He had not mentioned it to her before.

"He asked me to go for a walk...in the middle of a snowstorm...a walk."

"I remember. I could barely see the two of you standing out on the hill."

Roger sat down beside her again. She sensed his seriousness; on the verge of divulging something relevant to the difficult discussion though she didn't expect what she heard. "He stopped me, took my arm then said, 'For the sake of your family, leave the lights on at night.' That's all he said." His wife was astonished; intuition validated. Mr. Kenyon did know more than he revealed; his statement confirmed her suspicion.

"He knows. Why didn't you tell me this before now?"

"I didn't think it was important. It didn't make any sense to me at the time. He's an old man." Roger had not deliberately withheld such crucial evidence though he had failed the math portion of the test: 1+1=2.

"Mrs. Pettigrew said the same thing, after she saw the coat hanger hit me." An equation quickly coming together: "She told me the Kenyons kept all the lights on...all the time. All night...every night. *That's* why he was asking us questions about the house. 'Swallows in the chimney' my ass! He should've told us the truth *before* we bought this place!"

"Should've told us what? 'Oh, by the way, this old farmhouse is haunted.' You can't blame Mr. Kenyon."

"The hell I can't! If he knew it had spooks then he should have told us so!"

"Spooks?" Roger was perplexed by her reaction. "Did it ever occur to you he may have some doubts of his own? Maybe he asked questions because he thought he'd gone around the bend, living here alone for so many years after his wife died. 'Swallows in the chimney' may have been how he explained it to himself for all we know. You can't blame him about it. He's a good man."

"I know he is; I care about him too. But for God's sake, we have children!"

Roger paused to take it all in. The man began questioning his perceptions.

"The desk you moved into the parlor...it was pulled out...or pushed away from the cellar door this morning; while I was moving it back the latch lifted. I had just closed it. I really don't think it's a matter of the floor being warped. This house settled a long time ago." Roger briefly reconsidered his position.

"Thank you." Though tempted to gloat, Carolyn kept it sincere. "All of this is pretty **unsettling**, if you ask me."

"I've always assumed there was a logical explanation. Maybe there *is* and I just don't see it yet."

"Well, Roger...if ghosts actually *do* exist...then it *is* a logical explanation."

"So, what do you propose we do?" Roger was genuinely seeking a rational suggestion, acknowledging something strange, though still unidentified.

"I want to put it on the market. I don't think we're safe here...any of us."

"We have zero equity in the place. We can't afford to be impulsive again."

"Is that some kind of slam? I put money down on this because I thought..."

"Stop it. I know what you thought and I know why you did what you did."

"We should leave lights on at night; maybe it's what keeps them away."

"We can't afford it. The bill is already three times higher than it should be, for some ungodly reason." Truer words were never spoken.

"Sam is coming this weekend. He told me to relax. I don't even know *how* to relax anymore! I'm a nervous wreck all the time...waiting for whatever is coming next! Last night was the first good night's sleep I've had in weeks."

"So, what else did Sam have to say?" Roger held his friend in high esteem, always taking the sage advice freely offered in abundance. He was willing to listen to anything Sam had to say but Roger was very surprised to hear of his belief in the spirit world. They had known each other for years but it was not a subject which ever found its way into one of their numerous conversations. Roger looked forward to the promised visit as a point of clarity.

"You learn to live with it. That's what he said. I don't know if I can learn to live with this and I told him so. He said, 'When in doubt, do nothing.'"

"Now *that* sounds just like Sam." Roger grinned, nodding as if knowing a secret and keeping it. "We should follow his advice. When he comes we will take a walk and have a talk together...the three of us. All right?"

"Don't leave. I feel safe when you're home. I can sleep when you're here."

"So I've noticed!" It was not a mean-spirited comment. "I'll work this area for awhile; pick up some local accounts. I'll be home every night; maybe late but home." Carolyn was visibly relieved; a welcome appeasement.

"Thank you." Grateful for a promise she knew he'd keep, it meant freedom from worry, safety in numbers and another set of senses bearing witness to events beginning to redefine a family. It meant her burden relieved by half.

"I had a really good trip. Tell you what; we'll all go out for dinner tonight. **The Purple Cat.**" An evening spent out at an upscale restaurant was Roger's salve for every mortal wound, at least an adequate distraction, as if prime rib was delicious enough to make them forget they were living with dead people.

"I'm a mess. Take the girls...and please don't bring the fly swatter along."

"And what was *that* about! You never talk like that. It scared the kids."

"It's what you do every morning while you're home which scares the kids! Imagine how unnerving it is for them to have that thing flinging around their heads while they're trying to eat? It's worse than dealing with the flies!"

"I'm *so* neurotic?" The terse question causing Carolyn to pause while her husband reflected on her previous comments: "So...you're a psychoanalyst?"

"Roger, this compulsion is very unhealthy behavior."

"Well, it certainly is unhealthy...for the flies! Remember when you told me to kill them? You got pissed off because I wouldn't chase them through the damn house, track them down and kill them. Remember? Do you recall when you told me how *unhealthy* it was to have them around the kids... how you didn't want them to land on a pillow or in a plate of food? So which is it?"

Roger was right. She had vilified him for doing precisely what she'd asked him to do in the first place. Oh my God! He *was* listening to her, after all! As Carolyn softened her tone then lowered her eyes while speaking difficult but honest words, he expected an apology. "You're obsessed with killing them."

"Obsessed? Now I'm obsessed?" The dynamic had shifted, taking a sudden turn for the worse. Incumbent upon Carolyn to alter the nature of this uncivil discourse immediately, she did not have enough energy to argue with him.

"I really am sorry about that. I should not have said it in front of the girls." Their joust required nothing less than an act of contrition on Carolyn's part, something meaningful to quell the brewing storm; trooper to the rescue.

"You shouldn't have said it at all." Roger was stern with his mate.

Carolyn obliged, removing brisk wind from the billowing sails of a mighty warship. No bellowing allowed. An abrupt change-of-subject was called for; at least there were no flies breeding in the ceiling! Moving on...

Suggesting he take a week off to work on their house, finish what had been started overhead, Roger pointed up at the gaping hole leering down on them. Carolyn smiled, her sigh of relief subtly diverting a warship off course.

"You have no idea what a mess it made! The dust went everywhere! It was worse than the fireplace...this plaster is so old, when you touch the stuff it literally disintegrates! It turns into talc...but no flies up there. I looked."

"So, we'll clean up the mess...and April will gladly bless it afterwards."

"She showed you? Did she do it backwards?" Roger nodded. Both laughed.

Once completing the thought, Roger's facile mind focused on where to go with all those dangling wires. He realized there would be no place left to hide them once the plaster was gone, beams exposed. He began devising a plan. In a minute it was figured out...smart cookie. Roger left to check in with April and the fireplace while Carolyn brewed another strong pot of coffee, certain it was what kept her conscious. There was much more to discuss.

The fire had burned down to cinders and the kid was nowhere to be found. Roger looked around downstairs then followed a voice heard from a distance. Climbing the bedroom stairs, the sounds became more pronounced. Entering the middle bedroom, he paused, listening to his youngest; at play. April had apparently relocated and was now inside the chimney closet, at the far end of the room, its door left slightly ajar. A sliver of light shone through the crack, illuminating the floorboards of a darkened bedroom, creating the narrow path for him to follow. Quietly approaching, he could distinctly hear April happily chatting, explaining how this piece of one toy fits into another; how they lock together. So sweet: a charming child. Rather than interrupting her, he left his imaginative daughter to play being *teacher*. It never occurred to him that she might actually have a student with her...one discreetly hidden in the closet.

"Modern man's besetting temptation is to sacrifice his direct perceptions and spontaneous feelings to his reasoned reflections; to prefer in all circumstances the verdict of his intellect to that of his immediate intuitions."
Aldous Huxley

~ a tree of life as the lone survivor ~

apple blossom time

"Some tension is necessary for the soul to grow, and we can put that tension to good use. We can look for every opportunity to give and receive love, to appreciate nature, to heal our wounds and the wounds of others, to forgive and to serve."
Joan Borysenko

An expected arrival, spring was painfully slow in coming; so long overdue. Even though the days became warmer, the nights were often frigid by dawn; frosty. Grass still crunched beneath their feet as the girls ran across the lawn, sliding their way all the way to the bus stop. Leaving their house bundled in coats, by the time they came home in late afternoon, the outerwear had been shed and it was time to wear shorts and pretend spring had sprung, including some playtime before dark; sunset a little later every evening: a blessing.

The mother's mood lightened and brightened with each passing day. Roger kept his promise. He was returning home every night, even if he had to drive a hundred miles to do so. She felt a burden lifting, comforted by knowledge her husband would be there. For nearly three weeks, Roger had been like a fixture in the house. He stayed very busy, spending several days trashing the kitchen floor with debris from the ceiling above. It was the project promised, and then some. Enough time had lapsed for a skittish mistress of the house to develop a false sense of security as something far more dangerous took root: complacency. She'd thought of herself as impervious to any threat of harm, if her husband was there for protection. She was sadly mistaken: abandoned.

During this period a fascinating phenomenon happened. At the time of year normally reserved for common houseflies to *begin* emerging for their annual siege, those who had tormented the family all winter long suddenly vanished. They all died or disappeared in one day; the same day Carolyn confessed her experiences to her husband; a rather uncommon occurrence. The sound of an eerie silence was haunting; an absence noted. Though an in-depth discussion triggered changes, neither expected the outcome. By evening the windowsills were littered with carcasses, as if an overt acknowledgment of a predicament brought one aspect of it to an abrupt end; dispelling harbingers of doom and gloom, banishing the beasts back to hell to dwell with their father, the devil. Perhaps it was a coincidence. Perhaps their work was done.

Sam's visit was delightful, as usual. After greeting the children he went for a long walk with their parents under the guise of touring the enormous barn. Carolyn showed him the antique scythe, pointing up to the spot from whence it came during her too-close encounter. He spoke with his friends about their house and its inhabitants, both living and those presumed dead, in his typical deadpan manner. He told ghost stories about an old haunted house on the hill near Brown University in Providence, his own home; informing them about his neighborhood, atwitter with supernatural activity. He used language with which they were entirely unfamiliar: *poltergeist*, *apparition*, *entity* peppered his description of an otherwise benign residence. Roger remained aloof. He did not consent to these hocus pocus theories posited by his learned attorney. Consistently maintaining his staunch opposition, his "there *must* be a logical explanation" approach, Roger was startled when Sam abruptly announced it: "There *is* a logical explanation. You live with a ghost; at least one spirit and maybe more than one." (Where had Roger heard that before?) Sam dismissed his skepticism as naiveté, declaring him unsophisticated on the taboo subject he knew nothing about. Then he did his best to reassure Carolyn; if the house *was* haunted, the spirits posed no threat to her or the girls, finally concluding: if the ghosts intended to inflict harm on anyone, they would certainly choose Roger as their primary target! The extensive tour continued. Strolling along, Sam paused to marvel at the sheer volume of blossoms laden upon branches of the lone survivor of the storm of '38; the apple tree halted his momentum. Carolyn told a story of her own, one borrowed from Mr. Kenyon, explaining how a dozen others just as lovely did not survive the ravages of an incredible hurricane, one which left most of little Rhode Island in shambles. She told an old friend how the barn was spared by dancing with the wind; a saving grace.

A jolly man, Sammy sought then found the best in every soul and situation, scattering his natural joy like blossoms on breezes wherever he went. He had always attracted females in droves, including the five girls clinging to him as he began singing a sweet, old-fashioned tune, dancing with his fair maidens beneath the apple tree. *"I'll be with you in apple blossom time / I'll be with you to change your name to mine / Church bells will chime / And you will be mine in apple blossom time!"* A grand old song, each child was charmed beyond measure, as was their mother. Why Sam was so happy mattered not; it rubbed off like chalk dust on all he encountered. It had been a marvelous day. Carolyn smiled warmly, watching her friend while he sang with April in his arms. Then, as any perfect dance partner would, he invited her to stand on his feet while Sam took the lead. All of them were ardently in love with this short, stout, jovial little gentleman, including Carolyn. He finished his round with the ladies in dappled sunlight shining upon the grassy dance floor below its resplendent branches, his lyrical voice ringing throughout their secluded valley. His was a full, deep voice; a pure tone rich in texture and nuance, one in perfect harmony with Nature. For all souls involved in this festive family outing beneath an apple tree, it was a lovely memory to make; a keepsake.

Staying for the day, Sam had a chance to leisurely enjoy all the farm had to offer. His walk to the river convinced him; no matter what was happening in that old farmhouse it was worth tolerating to have the rest of many blessings. His assessment of these spirit matters was based upon his own experiences. Therefore he was unaware of the true personality of the problem. Essentially, his ghost was peaceful and innocuous; mischievous. Sam's error in judgment came in the form of advice imparted, borne of the assumption that he knew more than he actually did on a complicated subject. He told Carolyn to relax, not to worry; to simply ignore the problem. Later in the evening after dinner, Sam sat on the porch with his hosts discussing their plans for the future, all the while insisting they should not, **could not** sell this wonderland he'd spent the day exploring; it was inconceivable to him how they would even consider parting with the place. He had no idea of what would come if they remained. None of them did; circumstances provoking a fear of the unknown.

Carolyn had great faith in their friend. Accepting his encouragement she let her guard down. If she could only let go of this fear, her omnipresent anxiety, everything would be fine. Sam was certain of it. She had been making herself a nervous wreck in a constant state of agitation anticipating the next incident, with good reason. Carolyn agreed to dismiss the notion of selling the place, at least for the time being. Yet, lingering doubts, pure dread she attempted to dispel or suppress would continue to haunt a reticent mortal soul, working on her mind in destructive and insidious ways.

The sweet aroma of apple blossoms saturated the evening air. Sam became intoxicated by it as they'd walked the grounds again, returning to his favorite spot beneath the canopy of an apple tree. He plucked a few fallen petals from dew-laden grass, souvenirs to take home: always the hopeless romantic.

"Carolyn, you've purchased the **Garden of Eden**. Promise me you'll never let it go." Had a Jewish man been more familiar with precepts of Christianity he might have extrapolated some deeper implications based on this analogy. According to scripture the garden was not only beautiful; paradise on Earth. It was more complicated: a place riddled with danger, the evils of temptation; something wicked having to do with mortal desire, an apple tree and a snake. Carolyn stooped beneath the specimen, bursting with blossoms, preparing to bear its sweet fruit. Perhaps the tree of knowledge bore all the lessons she did not care to learn in this life…or the next, for that matter. God only knows.

"What are you looking for, my dear?" Sammy was willing to help.

"The proverbial snake; you know, the one supposedly lurking in the grass." It is important to retain one's sense of humor, especially when under duress; during times of trial and tribulation. So it is written. So it's been said.

Twilight: Sam had to leave before dark, *fearful* of being lost in the woods. How ironic! While humming the same heartfelt tune he'd sung for his ladies, Sam scattered petals he gathered, blossoms reclaimed from the tree of life, all over the seats inside his Mercedes, departing with a promise to return soon. He had come to be with them at apple blossom time and his heart never left.

_____

"There is nothing in the world more peaceful than
apple-leaves with an early moon."
Alice Meynell

kiss of death

"Prayer is the soul's sincere desire, uttered or unexpressed; / The motion of a hidden fire / That trembles in the breast."
James Montgomery

Another week went on by with no further interruptions; no incidents. Doors remained latched when closed. Flies: all gone. Everything was peaceful. The kitchen ceiling was a chore and a half but once complete looked spectacular. Hand hewn beams were exposed and the room felt larger, more welcoming; job well done. Roger worked the immediate area, seeking out new clients for his wares in quaint little villages scattered along the coast of Southern New England. Making his way home to Harrisville every night, Carolyn made no secret of it; she'd been comforted by his presence in the house. Spirits lifted. Her mood improved dramatically, much to the relief of her children.

Sam reassured them; attitude was everything when it came to spirit matters. She was beginning to believe him, absorbing sage advice into consciousness as spring days began blending together. Life became what she envisioned for her own the day she found their place in the country. Relaxing into a routine, everyone began taking for granted; this was how it would be. Mom: cheerful. Dad: home. It wasn't Norman Rockwell but something resembling normalcy.

One balmy evening Roger surprisingly suggested they find a babysitter and go out on a date. Neither of them could even remember the last time they had done anything together as a couple. Dinner and a movie? A distant memory. Carolyn graciously accepted his invitation and began scouting for a sitter. A local teen came highly recommended by their neighbor. Carolyn made a call, grateful the young lady was available, especially on such short notice and on a Saturday night. Arrangements made, the excited woman chose a nice outfit from the closet, hopped in the shower then had a fine time putting on makeup for the first time in...forever. Five fascinated girls intently observed as their mother pillaged through a rather sparse collection of cosmetics, playing dress up alongside her at a mirror. She powdered their noses and painted their lips. The bathroom became crowded, loud with laughter; a rambunctious crew at a festive event: all the girls playing together…making up a fond memory.

Margie missed their driveway three times before pulling into the yard. Her father's old beat up Chevy truck was full to brimming with junk, like a tinker carrying his wares in a covered wagon in olden days. It was Margie Bailey! Andrea was thrilled. They had spent time talking on the bus. Margie brought her guitar then taught Andrea how to play it in one night; a quick study. They became close friends over time. Margie was safe; someone who could always be trusted to keep a secret…a person of good character and stellar reputation: a great choice for a friend. The eldest child required a confidante.

Italian was the most romantic food. Roger was willing to see whatever film Carolyn desired, a deference she appreciated as they had such contrary tastes. Roger knew it probably meant seeing something British or even, God forbid; a "foreign language" film with subtitles. He considered it a risk worth taking, determined to provide Carolyn with a memorable evening. It was destined to become just that but for an entirely different reason. Carolyn does not recall where they dined and what film they saw that night, but she will never forget what happened when they came home. Date night had only just begun: a date with destiny for a mistress of the house…but with which one?

It was a quarter past midnight when they walked through the door. Margie was doing some homework. Gathering her books, the mother asked typically parental questions, inquiring about their kids' behavior and the like. A good report eased her mind. Roger paid the charge, offering to drive Margie home, due to the late hour. Declining this offer, she reassured the couple she lived a mile away and would be fine. They could hear her rattling through their yard, tools sliding, crashing together as the rusty truck navigated through deep ruts in an earthen driveway…then she was gone.

Though their day had been long, this night would prove longer, still. Roger was sleepy due to a lengthy drive. From the farm *anywhere* promised to be a long journey. Rhode Islanders are provincial people. A ten-minute long ride always prompts a complaint of five minutes too far. For Roger, it always felt as if the place in the country was light years away from civilization as he had known it all his life. A city boy...forced to make the necessary adjustments. He crawled into bed while Carolyn went upstairs to check on their children. All was calm; very quiet. They were sound asleep, as was her husband by the time she'd returned. Within moments, she too would fall deeply asleep. Rest, dear woman, for you will need your strength.

Unaware several hours had passed; Carolyn stirred to a distinct vibration of footsteps crossing the wood of her bedroom floor. Sensing a presence beside her, presuming it to be one of the girls, she began to extricate herself from a heavy slumber, softly muttering: "What's the matter, honey?" Stretching her arm out toward the sound, knowing she could instantly identify the child by touch, by the whisper of a voice in the night; there was no response. Opening her eyes, pale dawn light revealed the grotesque figure of a woman hovering above her. Carolyn was staring directly into the torso of an apparition which had usurped the bureau beside the bed, standing in its place. The sudden rush of terror pulsed throughout her body, jolting the woman awake; sending one horrified soul scrambling for cover beneath a cotton quilt.

The image of it leapt through her eyes into her mind, impaling her memory with a spectral wonder so vivid and compelling, it had to be processed in tiny patterns and fragments. As still shots...appearing in a series of freeze-frame photographs slicing into her consciousness; inescapable split-second imagery bombarding the senses, creating the complex memory from scraps and shards of a gruesome vision. Immobilized by fear; its petrifying cold cut like a blade to her bones; its noxious odor: utterly repulsive. With staccato-like precision, an incongruous concept underwent rapid-fire conversion into language as the overwhelmed woman absorbed details of an entity she observed; perceptions unfolding in mind. Exposing itself solicited scrutiny while breathing abject terror and loathing into its victim, forcing its putrid stench deeply into her breathless lungs. A description conjured was beyond mortal comprehension:

the dress rusty green jersey handmade hand-dyed fabric belt cinched at the waist with an oval buckle covered in same fabric vintage clothing a being from another time ugly beehive head a hornet's nest broken neck snapped hanging to the side no eyes no mouth grey mesh cobwebs no hands no feet just floating above me cold so cold can't breathe vile evil death no bureau gone coming closer cold can't breathe so close too close wants to touch me don't touch me head draped at an angle wants a kiss dear Lord Oh my God

There it stood, its cockeyed head leaning sharply forward at a crooked angle, broken neck; no question. Standing *inside* the bureau beside their bed, a solid wooden object, it had fused with the furniture for its own nefarious purposes.

The hideous creature approached silently, as if closing in to steal a kiss or claim a life. Carolyn heard herself shrieking as the spirit drew nearer but still, not a sound would come; nothing but a squeaky whimper would penetrate the frozen knot of vocal chords lodged within her throat. Digging her feet deeply into the covers beneath their quilt, Carolyn kicked Roger repeatedly, scraping his shins with her toenails. It drew closer. One black stick of an arm flopped down across her pillow as the entity leaned over, its head curiously cocked to one side, as if it was studying her. Terrified of being touched, Carolyn's first instinct was to hide; an inclination to cower beneath the quilt, though she had kicked her share of it too far beyond reach. Breaking backward, frantically scampering away, Carolyn catapulted up against the headboard of their bed, crashing it into wrought iron hardware on the doors directly behind it, loudly enough to wake dead and living alike. Eyes sought a face…there was no face; only a swirling, rancid mass of rotting flesh resembling a desiccated hornet's nest, covered in what appeared to be a mesh of blackened cobwebs; flimsy wisps of wiry hair clinging to the crown. Grabbing a fistful of disheveled hair Carolyn jerked Roger's head severely back and forth in her desperate attempt to wake the motionless man. His body was limp…lifeless. His wife was sick inside, certain her husband was dead. Uncontrollable panic ensued, believing the intruder had killed him and was about to claim her; an intention to stop her heart: to literally scare her to death. An evil entity stalking its prey began moving in for the kill. As a spontaneous reaction she slammed her body up against the headboard. Sliding aside, she landed on Roger: fighting for some distance… fighting for her life. The woman's silent screams were deafening; her mind manufacturing at full volume what her body had refused to provide. The wretched being floating cloud-like above her, inches away; becoming a part of whatever was in its way, on its way to a target. Aversion so intense, its repulsive odor overwhelming, it caused her stomach to heave reflexively. Carolyn fought for control; taking shallow, panting breaths, forcing out fine mist from her lips, obscuring the appalling view of what she presumed would be her bitter end. In those few dreadful moments it never occurred to her that she might survive this ordeal. The ghastly apparition aligned its hellish head with the face of its intended victim. In the last instant before contact Carolyn whispered the only words she could form or utter in a moment of pure panic. "God help me." Gasping for air, grasping an edge of the covers with gnarled fingers trembling, she braced for impact. Yanking the blanket toward her had caused it to shift, falling off of Roger, revealing his torso; the shocking sight, momentarily diverting her rapt attention from the imposing apparition. She'd ceased breathing, her mind shrieking in horror; his back and shoulders, even his ribcage was scored; deeply abraded with scratches, as if he'd been clawed to death by a wild animal. Seeking out the entity, she knew she was next.

It was gone. Proving to be a powerful prayer, no matter how quiet or brief, Carolyn saved herself with a faithful request of her Savior. Having had the presence of mind to invoke the presence of God in such a moment of crisis, murmuring words possessing potency enough to cause an intervention on her behalf, "God help me" vanquished the evil spirit, the menacing manifestation imposing itself upon her at dawn. During those stark moments spent awaiting her own pitiful demise, Carolyn could do nothing but hold her breath, clench her fists and pray for salvation; a plea for tender mercies.

ANDREA PERRON

She cannot recall how long she remained locked in position. Roger began to moan, trying to move beneath her. Relief startled her back to life with him. As she slid off his body, Roger rolled toward the edge on his side of the bed and went instantly, deeply asleep. The disgusting smell began to dissipate. A mind-numbing cold suddenly escaped her sense of it. She'd found the room emptied of tortured souls, save her own. What Carolyn witnessed had a hold on her still. Knowing then she would never recover and could never forget what happened to her just before dawn on a spring morning, grateful to God for rescue and respite, she touched Roger's chest to be certain he was *really* breathing. It took time for her mind to correlate the fact; he was actually still alive. This had been the most harrowing experience of her life, to date. The woman could barely move, as if all of her energy, the life-force of her being had been drained. Weak; as if all of her muscles atrophied while languishing, twisted and contorted up against the headboard, awaiting a horrible end.

Though the worst of it was gone, a distinctly foul odor remained embedded in her sinuses; she could not evade a nauseating stench. It lingered internally. The cold went with the apparition, yet Carolyn could not escape its grasp. To her core, she was frozen stiff. A persistent sensation of bloody chunks of ice adrift in her veins caused the shaken soul to quake. Stumbling into the parlor, dragging a blanket along, she struggled to wrap inside it. Disoriented, unsure of her surroundings, she needed rest; the loveseat caught her frame as it fell. Head spinning, limbs quivering…chatter in her mind could not be silenced; rivaled only by the sound of her chattering teeth.

There was no time to waste. NO time to think. She *had* to write this down, draw it; record what she'd seen. It was a compelling imperative; critical she have something scribed for her husband, something to prove her claim. In the aftermath of this ordeal, Carolyn realized she had been to the precipice. By the grace of God, she survived. No question in her mind. Carolyn *did* believe her eyes. Over time, she would grapple with various concepts regarding the haunting in her house but the reality of it would never come into question. A compulsion to provide evidence for her husband resulted in Carolyn standing too quickly. Crumbling like stale cookies, she tumbled onto the loveseat; too soon to walk on scared-stiff legs. The urgency of it was motivation enough to carry her wobbling frame to the desk. Retrieving a pencil and the notebook usually reserved for grocery lists and lines of poetry, Carolyn scribbled and scrawled words as they'd come into mind: *a hornet's nest cobwebs vermin* Huddled up on the sofa, she continued: *no eyes no mouth sprigs of hair no facial features gray ancient corpse* It pained her, every word of it. Fingers crippled with the cold; her handwriting was practically illegible. Carolyn was struggling to write, fighting to describe the grotesque, mutilated apparition; increasingly difficult as she went along, not because the imagery eluded her. Quite the contrary, visualization permanently penetrated her consciousness, it infiltrated her memory; details as vivid as the instant in which they occurred. There would be no escaping the imagery...not in this lifetime. The difficulty came in feeling forced to relive it; revisiting moments during which Carolyn believed she would surely perish from this Earth.

Pressing on, the process made her queasy, like having a hot plate of rancid food thrust before her, something she was being forced to consume but could not digest: a recipe for disaster. This sensation magnified as minutes passed, like staring into the white-hot core of a fresh, gaping wound: it was raw. Intense. Bloody hell. The adjectives chosen paled in comparison to the event, appearing foreign and inadequate as a description of her too-close encounter. She tried to steady her grip. Out-of-body...watching her own hand...writing:

Vile evil decomposing flesh repulsive stench decay putrid odor - need to vomit - want to scream oppressive diabolical not of this world - what is this thing? Bureau gone! Roger dead! Hovering over me breathing into me studying me head cocked neck broken - fighting to breathe can see the mist

Carolyn's heart convulsing, it raced with her fingertips while she scratched words onto the page: *a green brown jersey dress plain long w/ pockets on both sides of bodice/ arms but no hands dress went to the floor but no feet floating above threatening / intimidating wants to kiss me wants to kill me wants me dead this thing killed Roger demonic cold can't move can't speak jaw locked desperation grief fear no evil not a head / an orb a beehive not rounded/oval snapped sideways hanging off sunken hollow shoulders over a high collar vermin crawling a mass cobwebs alive with death despicable to take me away from my children saw his body gasped turned back again to see the bitch from hell gone! No nightmare - this was real! God help me.* Furiously etching the words sideways across lined notebook paper, the pencil tore at it as she wrote, until its point snapped. Her breathing labored, delicate features dripping with perspiration, chronicling this event had been another ordeal all its own; recounting the moments so painfully clear in her memory.

As dawn light seeped into a dim, dusky parlor, no warmth accompanied it. Quivering, Carolyn laid the notebook aside then went over to the wood box. Though legs stabilized her mind remained flooded with images too gruesome to recall. She had no choice. There was no evading or avoiding this intrusion. Glancing nervously around, it suddenly occurred to her; the apparition might return. Thought of it unleashed another violent surge of adrenaline; ravaging fear raging throughout her body. Hands trembling, Carolyn loaded the wood onto the grate then tried to strike a match. Looking back behind she saw the antique banjo clock, the timepiece Roger had moved to the parlor, claiming the walls were too uneven for it to work properly anywhere else in the house. It had stopped. No chimes. No familiar tick ~ tock. Startled, she peered at her wristwatch. The time was fast-approaching 6:30 a.m. Their vintage clock had stopped at precisely 5:15 a.m. Carolyn did the math concluding the timepiece ceased when the apparition first arrived. It had been working fine when they went to bed and had fallen silent since. The same peaceful chimes that sung her to sleep this fateful night went quiet at dawn. Was it a clue, an indication of a presence powerful enough to suspend time itself? Time itself would tell.

A tenuous tranquility had been irrevocably shattered; nothing would ever be the same. Coffee. She needed coffee. As quietly as possible, she made her way into the kitchen. While a strong brew began sputtering along in its pot, a cauldron of caffeine, she sat alone at the table, head in hands. Something was missing: Cigarettes. Where had she left them? On the desk. Returning to the parlor, her approach was halted by a dreadful sight. Andrea was staring at the open tablet she'd left behind on the desk, beside a broken pencil and her pack of cigarettes. No! Carolyn's heart sank, instantly doubling the weight of her body where she stood, settling into her feet.

Naturally curious, Andrea stared at her mother with a peculiar expression, one difficult to interpret from a distance; strangely sedate, even serene. She then fixed her gaze on the scrawled images and scribbled words scarring the pages of a notebook as they had her mother's mind. The otherwise innocuous spiral bound tablet contained all the sordid details of that terrifying incident, an unholy encounter Carolyn had *never* intended to share with her children. Surveying its contents, examining rough sketches, it was too late to stop her. Andrea had passed beyond mortal recognition on the pathway to epiphany.

"Mom, I *know* her. I dreamed this; it woke me up. She wants to hurt you."

"I'm fine, honey. Let me have this, please." Carolyn rushed to her side.

"What is this? Was it a bad dream? I had a nightmare, too. You were there. She was, too…hanging over you. It woke me up but then I couldn't move. You were screaming and I couldn't come to help…but I could hear you."

Feeding the beast at first light, Carolyn felt pure hatred rising up from her soul; sheer contempt for whatever it was which had touched her life and was now threatening her eldest as well. It would not stand. Consumed with anger and frustration, exuding a negative energy almost as palpable as the fear, the woman was furious. At this instant she wanted to rattle the rafters of a house possessed, to scream out loud: *"LEAVE MY KIDS ALONE!"* Carolyn knew she'd have to disguise her emotions in those critical moments so to rationally address Andrea's experience without divulging too much of her own.

Her mind was riddled, tormented by the thought that somehow, some way, one of her girls was exposed to this heinous creature from beyond the grave. Desperate to achieve balance, to establish some semblance of control before engaging in discussion with the youngster who'd surely see through anything other than the truth, Carolyn began breathing deeply. Mother's intuition told her what Andrea experienced was not a dream at all. This entity approached her at the same time! Centering herself, in spite of a presumed inability to do so, Carolyn reached over and removed the tablet from her daughter's hands; taken from a youngster who had already seen too much.

"Let me have that." Andrea relinquished the notebook without question. It belonged to her mother. Carolyn placed it back inside the desk drawer then invited her eldest to join her in the kitchen. Over coffee and hot chocolate the ladies conversed about an encounter they had shared on some cerebral level, attempting to make sense of it all. Carolyn could not lie to her about this. She didn't know how to tell a lie, especially to one of her children; it was foreign to her nature and would have certainly been revealed on her face, should she even try. Instead, the twelve-year-old, capable of grasping complex concepts, described her intrepid journey through the darkness of a dream in disturbing detail. Carolyn did not consider it responsible to converse in kind, unwilling to frighten her child further. Rather, she simply listened to Andrea processing the event aloud. Withholding her sordid details may have qualified as a sin of omission though Carolyn did not consider it such; not a lie: more of a secret. Keeping her own counsel, a shaken woman had reason to withhold. In lieu of divulging her **nightmare**, Carolyn speculated about the nature of "dreams" and what, if anything, it meant. Calm and collected; blunt in her assessment:

"I have no idea what happened…to you or to me. Sometimes when people are really close, connected to each other, they think the same thoughts or feel the same emotions at the same time. It's as though we share a mind. It makes sense because you're a part of me. Maybe that explains it."

"Mom, were you scared, too? I was scared *for* you!"

"Yes, Annie. I was frightened by it, too." Any other response would have been unacceptable…and unbelievable.

"I see things sometimes…I hear sounds…spooky things happen here."

"What have you seen?" Carolyn's probing eyes searched her weary face.

"I see shadows in my bedroom, even when the moon is small, in the dark." Andrea spoke in whispers; telling secrets. "Sometimes I hear voices before I go to sleep. I can't understand what they're saying to me. I don't like to be in the bathroom alone. It feels like I'm being watched; like I'm being looked at while...you know. It's embarrassing! Stuff moves around on my desk while I'm doing my homework...and you *know* what happened to our chalkboard! Mom...you can tell me the truth. Do we have ghosts?"

Carolyn became increasingly alarmed with each passing statement uttered, culminating in a revelation punctuated by the shocking question. She did not want to answer it, especially for her children, or even for herself. Asking yet another question in reply; "How do you know about ghosts?"

"I told Margie about some things I have seen and she says we have ghosts." Innocence in her voice belied the knowledge she had attained in life thus far; the perceptive youngster was too open, too willing to share her thoughts. An anxious mother knew it was best to avoid discussing the topic with others but it was too late to forewarn her eldest; the damage done. She was too young to be jaded by the skepticism of adulthood. Andrea harbored no preconceived notions and was unaware of the stigma attached to supernatural phenomenon. Children are supremely receptive beings, frequently observant, accepting of the world as they find it, including the netherworld. Far more often than their adult counterparts, children *do* believe their eyes. They should.

"There are many people who don't believe in ghosts."

"Why not? The priest at church talks about God and the Holy Ghost as the greatest spirit of all. At least all Catholics believe in ghosts, don't they?"

"Annie, I don't know how to answer your questions. It's really a matter of personal faith. I'm afraid it is more complicated than what the priest said."

"Okay, mom; I'm really tired, anyway. I need to go lay down again."

"Go rest. When you get up we will have a nice breakfast together, all of us. Honey, I think it would be best not to mention anything about this to your sisters. It would only scare them...no need."

"All right." Embracing her mother, Carolyn escorted the girl to the bottom of her stairwell. There they encountered the wide-eyed, tear-streaked face of another child running downstairs, frantic to find her mother.

"Mommy! I had a *really* bad dream. It was terrible!"

"Oh, my God." Carolyn scooped Cindy up in her arms.

Andrea searched her mother's eyes, kissing her little sister on the forehead before going back upstairs to bed. Carolyn led Cindy to the sofa, listening as intently to an eerily similar rendition of a nightmare she had heard described with identical detail only moments before. Reassuring her that it was all over, she tucked her into the soft corner of the sofa where she promptly fell asleep. Rising to tend to the fire, Carolyn paused, staring into the flames. Retrieving her tablet from the desk drawer, she stared at the figure she had sketched in some haste; an issue compounded by its discovery. The obsequious dilemma worked on her mind while she sifting through the pages of a notebook which needed to remain well-hidden. *Milk Bread Salt* Coming across a recent grocery list, Carolyn took comfort in its normalcy, reminding her of how life used to be. *Mayo Butter Coffee Sugar Flour Cheese* Standing on the hearthstone, she examined what had been nothing more than a notebook the day before. Yet, with this inclusion of her incoherent scribbles and sketches, scraps of words, notes and images transcribed onto its lined pages of paper, it was inadvertently transformed into an object of some significance.

Feathering through its pages with her fingertips, she continued perusing the manuscript. Delving the depths of a tablet, she found a hodgepodge of notes and lists and lines of poetry. Addresses, phone numbers, dates to remember peppered the pages with ink spots: a series of drawings, from apple blossoms to dress designs, a list of home improvement ideas filled pages; pipe dreams. Carolyn picked up another pencil. Beneath "Replace the kitchen sink" she wrote, "Get rid of the goddamned ghosts! *That* will improve the home!" Her disdain of an evil fiend duly noted beneath its proper heading, she moved on.

Myriad images scattered in no discernible pattern, juxtaposed against most recent entries in the register, caused her to pause and reflect on the journey. It was surreal. Metamorphosis occurred on two fronts, permanently altering her concept of reality as well as the formerly utilitarian status of the simple spiral notebook. In Carolyn's hands lay a tablet of secrets, as precious as any diary, considering the sensitive nature of insights contained within. From mundane to morbid, silly to profound, she held a virtual treasure trove which, with the lone admission of a single event, became an object to hide, covet and protect.

With the turn of another page, Carolyn came across a few precious lines of poetry which touched her heart years before; lines she would unconsciously commit to paper during moments lost in thought, giving a hand something to do. Reading the words again, it suddenly struck her; these were the lines she had recited while sitting on the lawn with Mr. Kenyon, watching as beads of water trickled down the side of a glass, resembling teardrops.

"And still other brothers and sisters,
Linked their arms together,
Walked down the dusty road where once he ran
And into the deep green valley
To sit on the stony banks of the stream he loved
And let the murmuring waters
Wash over their blood-hot feet with a springing crown of tears."

Carolyn closed the notebook. Lodging it toward the back of a drawer inside the desk, well aware she'd need to find a more secure place for safe-keeping, there was a more immediate concern. That staggering fatigue she battled had returned with a vengeance. She again sought salvation in the kitchen; another cup of coffee...this time with a cigarette.

Head hanging heavily over a steaming cup she considered her predicament. The lethargic stupor she suffered was something beyond fatigue: Exhaustion. No. It was beyond exhaustion. Not natural; supernatural in Nature. It was the same kind of tired she had seen on her eldest daughter's face before the child went back to bed. She recognized it. Andrea left her that morning appearing as if she'd aged overnight: a burdened soul. Cindy emerged from a stairwell in a panic; in pure desperation. Had they been the only ones? What had three other children endured in the night? Was this truly a family affair?

During her unexpected report, Andrea divulged hearing her mother scream in a nightmare of a wakened dream. Carolyn was certain she had been unable to utter any audible sounds in the midst of this crisis. Perplexed, wondering if the girls had been witness or participant, (perhaps both simultaneously), no question remained in her mind. Her children had been approached. Residual waves of nausea crashed against her stomach. This perpetrator committed, at the very least, a psychological assault, detrimental to all of its victims. These thoughts evoked an oppressive sense of foreboding; a sense she feared would be forever. This was not over…not by a long shot. Carolyn began humming a sweet song Sam left behind, his rendition of *Apple Blossom Time*. It was her futile attempt to recapture the life she once knew; naïve. Perhaps her troubled mind went where it was most comfortable; a pretty place in a happy moment, longing for a time before abject terror informed, colored and time-warped her world. Carolyn's perception of everything changed. It happened so suddenly, so drastically, she barely recognized herself in the midst of this new life in an old farmhouse coming alive with death. How to preserve a memory against a vicious onslaught? How to restore sanity to an irrational situation? How then to protect the kids and defend herself? It was war. Peace was an illusion.

There was no solace in suspicions confirmed. Carolyn lifted the cold cup of coffee to her lips, unaware so much time had lapsed while pending dilemmas brewed in her thoughts. Startled by the sensation, she drank it down anyway; bitter but potent. Needing all the help she could get during these trying times, she struggled to reconcile rapidly expanding perceptions of Life and Death.

She was cold…frozen stiff. Carolyn could barely lift her body up from the chair. As she did, carefully, deliberately, as if crippled by frigidity, thoughts occupied her mind which would haunt her consciousness for years to come; the duration of her lifetime. Each time she looked into a mirror a mother was forced to bear witness; the result of an aging process inexplicably accelerated while living in a farmhouse she had chosen, a place which would insidiously rob the young and lovely woman of her youth. "So this is how decrepit feels. This is what it looks like, feels like to be old." Her beauty was the sacrificial lamb destined for slaughter upon an unholy altar. Transformation had begun.

Carolyn dragged her body back to the fireplace. A pile of ashes and embers required more kindling, which she slid beneath the lone charred log: Ignition. Seeking the warmth so often eluding her, Carolyn put her feet to the fire. Too close...she always stood too close to the flames. An attempt to warm oneself from without when the chill comes from within poses hazards to one's health as a thoughtless, distracted act; like playing with fire. Leaning forward to rest her head on the mantelpiece, Carolyn allowed her eyes to close momentarily. She knew what had dispelled the demon in their midst. It did not go away on its own. An entity departed, not of its own volition; only because something even *more* powerful had intervened on her behalf at dawn. Bowing her head against the ancient wood, as though seated in the darkness of a confessional, she'd closed her tired eyes in search of Light, seeking the Holy Spirit of God. Silently engaged in a private fireside chat with her Creator, perceived as her savior, a contemplative woman felt utterly depleted, though her gratitude was entirely pure; sincere. Lamb of God... who takes away the sins of the world; have mercy on us all: A mother's prayer...for her children.

"Jesus Christ!" Roger was awake. Due to this outburst, so was Cindy, still bundled on a sofa. No one took offense, except perhaps for God. His frequent proclamation was presumed by all to be his exuberant form of prayer; as an overt request for help. Opening their bedroom door, he emerged, battered and bruised; raw, bloody abrasions stinging in the cool morning air. Rubbing his tender scalp, Roger demanded to know what the HELL had happened to him! Hell happened. Turning her back toward a fire Carolyn stared at her husband. He found her eyes vacant; orbs void of hope, as cold as the hearthstone upon which she stood. Appearing calm and composed, she peered directly into his angry gaze, indicating the presence of a child in the parlor, informing him in silence with a nod. It wasn't the time or place for any indiscretion on his part. It was clear; a serious conversation was called for, but it would have to wait. Instead, Carolyn quietly issued a proclamation of her own, a singular demand made of a man distraught and confused; one who did not want to understand what was occurring in the house, in their own bedroom, for that spirit matter. These words, as did her eyes, pierced the light of sunrise with their darkness, telling him all he needed to know at the moment.

"Get dressed. We're going to church."

***

Some date night: A date with destiny. A date with death. The kiss, bestowed. Roger's night out with his wife struck a chord in the Netherworld; the timing of it, too suspect. Good and evil in bed together. Carolyn wasn't the only one to experience an encounter too close for comfort, but her husband had been spared the curse of consciousness in the midst of evil. His wife: not as lucky. Roger dared to take a lady out to dinner and a movie and there would be hell to pay when he got home. Only a date: but with which mistress of the house?

"Oh God, early in the morning I cry to you.
Help me to pray and gather my thoughts to you, I cannot do it alone.
In me it is dark, but with you there is light;
I am lonely, but you do not desert me;
My courage fails me, but with you there is help;
I am restless, but with you there is peace;
In me there is bitterness, but with you there is patience;
I do not understand your ways, but you know the way for me."
Dietrich Bonhoeffer

omens

"Hope is some extraordinary spiritual grace that God gives us to control our fears, not to oust them."
Vincent McNabb

Nearly another year passed before Carolyn was visited again. In the interim much transpired. Roger did his best to stay as close to home as possible but their emotional turmoil kept driving him away, literally, for periods of respite under the guise of doing his job. There were times when it seemed as though all of his business was elsewhere...*anywhere* else! His spouse was no longer concerned about having him around as a protective presence; he had virtually no influence or power to prevent an assault sustained and could not even help himself: as it was one thing to be lulled into a false sense of security but quite another to be lulled into a coma. Rescue came from a higher power. Touched by a benevolent spirit which vanquished an evil presence in darkness before dawn, Carolyn had become forever changed. She did not need him anymore.

***

Though the entity vanished, perpetual fear of it remained. A constant sense of dread tormented Carolyn, as if the stunning apparition were omnipresent; merely invisible. It occurred to her: she had no viable options; all she could do was wait to see how powerful her prayers had been. Was an evil presence gone for good? Did she dare to hope it was over? Was the home repair prayer a real fix...or a temporary patch job? Anxiety proved a thief in its own right, depleting her energy and stealing an enthusiasm for life. Partnering with fear, together they had spawned a toxic environment; a persistent, low-level terror. The terrorist among them won initial battles of this war, as success in conflict is measured by the attack...likewise by its aftermath. A terrorist takes certain satisfaction by instilling the permanent sense of foreboding within the psyche of its victims; establishing an expectation of future attack: what next? When?

Stress was magnified further by the pressing need to keep a secret. Carolyn had to be discreet; exclusive, reserving her supernatural suspicions for only a few close personal friends. It was critical she be selective, choosing souls she trusted implicitly; Cathi Urbonas and Samuel Olevson: a short list to be sure. Roger was duly informed, provided with all the gory details of the encounter, pictures as proof. He claimed to accept her account of events at that time, his body bearing the evidentiary scars, having been subject to a *nightmare* of his own. Secretly, he blamed her for his wounds...and vice versa.

Carolyn had rightfully perceived the visitation as a warning and a threat; an omen. Wandering the house in light of day, certain knowledge cast a constant shadow over her consciousness. Awake and watchful in the dark of night, she kept a constant vigil. Withdrawn and withering away, Carolyn made a valiant attempt to disguise the all-consuming fear devouring her. Insidious thoughts became a perpetual distraction, plaguing her, depriving her of the happiness she sought: joy interrupted. Flashbacks to trauma lurked within her troubled mind, traipsing through it, running like an incessant series of film clips. The girls knew; something was wrong with mommy. Andrea knew precisely what that *something* was yet had to abide by her mother's wishes. Keep the secret. Play pretend. It proved a futile effort. Spirits who dwelled among the living were revealing themselves in death, haunting all the inhabitants of the house. The phenomenon had effectively touched every mortal, sometimes literally, at one time or another. They'd simply neglected to talk about it, but that was about to change. Within weeks of the manifestation there would be no more secrets kept; disclosures forthcoming with a stunning rapidity. Sisters began approaching the eldest among them, offering anecdotal evidence; disturbing revelations: cause for alarm. A clarion call to arms prompted by a truth being told, the girls were seeking nothing less than validation. Enlisting a sister, her role as a formal representative on their behalf, they sought relief but were all hesitant to burden their mother further. No parent could ever be prepared for what they would share in confidence...they all had a story to tell.

***

"Sam. You were dead wrong."

"I beg your pardon? Who...is this...Carolyn?"

"You might be keeping Casper as a pet in Providence but I've got a serious problem here, one in particular. She's mean and ugly and wants me dead just like she is...and this is nothing to ignore!"

"Why do you...you sound so...different."

"I *am* different. I will never be the same again. No one ever could be after something like this. Sam, you don't understand."

"Carolyn, what the hell happened? What's wrong?"

"Hell happened. Something terrible, something evil happened in this house and everything is wrong; I have seen things that changed my mind... my life, forever. Sam. We have to sell this place. We have to get out now."

"Calm down, dear."

"She's dying to live in my house...she practically crawled into my bed!"

"I know you're upset." Sam could barely wedge his words in between hers.

"The bitch can have it! And if she wants my husband so badly she can have him, too. I'll take my kids and go!"

"Take a deep breath. I'll be there in an hour." Click.

Having received some bad advice from an otherwise good attorney, she'd prepared for Sam's arrival; her spiral notebook ready...something tangible to enter into evidence. Sam would consider it proper documentation; hard copy regarding an infinitely harder event. Common knowledge: lawyers prefer to have something in writing. Friends see with blind faith eyes; vision based on personal relationship; she wanted him to see what was etched on those pages with the eyes of an attorney; no personal validation required. Carolyn sought understanding instead. If he grasped the notion, perhaps he too would change his mind, realize this threat as posed; recognize the gravity of their situation: Nothing cute or friendly about it. She required his help. Sam was enlightened by the darkness of a story she told; yet another rude awakening at dawn.

As promised, he was there within the hour. She sat him down at the kitchen table with a cup of coffee and stale sweet roll. They had some privacy to talk. April was in the parlor, engrossed in the Letter **B** and the Number **3**. Big girls had gone off to school. Roger was on the road, again. Carolyn had waited as long as she could; a few days, before phoning a friend. It took time to absorb what happened; to process before attempting to discuss. Morning light sliced across the table, landing on the tablet with laser beam precision. Sam studied its tattered surface, cloth stained by many years of handling. Pencil streaks and doodles adorned the shabby cover; its cardboard base bent at the corners.

Fighting to maintain her equilibrium, bracing against fear, Carolyn opened the notebook to precisely the pages revealing her secret, as if marked for easy access. There it was, hiding in plain sight: the deeply disturbing images of an entity which qualified as something wicked; infinitely shocking, yet more so when it was in her bedroom and in her face; an up close and personal affront.

"Here you go; now you have it in writing. As I told Roger…I'm not insane. Sam…I am *not* a liar."

"Carolyn. No one has thought or said anything about you being either."

"Roger doesn't believe me. Not a word of it."

"He *said* that to you?"

"He doesn't *have* to say it; not in those words. I know how he feels about all of this. He thinks I'm to blame…somehow all of *this* is my fault!"

"I'm sure he doesn't think you're responsible for…"

"I'm sure you're wrong. Look at this thing. The smell of it was nauseating. See the head? Well, it really wasn't a head, more like a mass of rotting flesh, all gray covered with a mesh of darker cobwebs. Like a hornet's nest; flimsy paper held together with this…stuff. Look how it hangs off the side, a broken neck I think and there were arms but no hands, only wisps of shredded fabric and broken bones. The dress was greenish brown, a slender belt here with the same fabric on the buckle. There were pockets, here…and on the bodice and here, a narrow ribbon of lace at the top of her collar."

"Amazing detail…Carolyn, this is remarkable." Genuinely impressed with her rendering; Sam saw a memory captured on paper for posterity and proof.

"Not something I could forget…from the moment she was in my face."

"This has to be the most fascinating breakfast conversation I've ever had."

"Smartass! Listen up! There's something to learn here." Class: in session.

"I assure you, my dear. You have my undivided attention."

"Sam, there is *something* beyond death; beyond life as we know it. Here is proof." Carolyn sharply snapped her fingers against the page. Sam appeared grim. He studied the illustrations, pulling the notebook closer, using glasses for a better look. It took nearly twenty minutes to tell her story. Difficult as it was to relive, she had to share the sordid details with him. When finished she felt assaulted all over again. It left her squeamish. Cold: a vivid description, chilling. Sammy suggested they gravitate toward the warmth of the fireplace. Tucking the tablet into a dark crevice of the sideboard, Carolyn's companion lead the way; a gentleman escorting the mistress of the house. Heartened to leave the heavy air behind, he sighed, feeling each thickly laden molecule of it weighing upon him; the density of reviled imagery evoked with sketches, a few words. She'd stoke the waning fire while Sam greeted April. Throwing herself at his belly, she held on tightly to his suspenders while he kissed her on the head. Click. The pantry door unlatched. Still in his arms, she turned to watch as the door drifted slowly open, its rusty hinges whining mournfully.

"Something bad happened in there." The child returned her full attention to Sam then back to **Sesame Street** as if nothing had happened; a commonplace occurrence. Her simple words were telling. Exchanging glances with Carolyn told the rest of the story. Shivers passed through him; the gentleman, visibly shaken. Carolyn knew then; Sam did understand. Having observed her as she crossed the parlor, closing the pantry, Sam could not help but notice how her vibrancy had severely diminished; her youthful glow was gone. Stooped over while tending to the fire; a beautiful woman suddenly seemed so much older: an equally disturbing realization. Five months since his friends purchased the home of their nightmares...at his urging and with his assistance.

After several minutes huddled near the fire, Sam was sufficiently warm and ready to go. Overwhelmed by what he had seen and heard during their hastily arranged visit, Carolyn did not press him further, knowing the man had been inundated with information. It would require time to digest, as it had for her. She helped him with his jacket then embraced the man, the one she trusted; the one who could help her...if anyone could. Carolyn walked him outside.

"I'll do some research. We may be able to void the contract and get you out of this deal and out of this house...on the basis of a failure to disclose."

"Anything you can do. I can't just live with it, Sam. I can't. I won't."

Before leaving, he gathered up more blossoms from beneath the apple tree before they passed for the season. It occurred to him it may be his last chance to collect the delicate treasures. They could soon be gone; an escape from the evils of paradise. He seemed sad as he departed; distracted by the thought.

Once Sam was gone, Carolyn retrieved the notebook, tucking it discreetly, secretly away into a dark hole she had chosen specifically for its safekeeping. Her only other friend destined to see it was in Nova Scotia for the summer. Cathi fell madly in love with Canada on previous trips, deciding to explore as much as possible during the few months a year when it was easier to navigate the frozen tundra; she was due home later in September. Though they stayed in touch, Carolyn had not disclosed details of the ordeal, deciding instead to wait for her return. It was not the kind of information which lends itself well to a letter; necessary to have an "in person" conversation with a friend. Their time would come. Having shown this notebook to Roger, as her evidence, he would later disavow his initial reaction, claiming to remain unconvinced. In Sam's presence, Roger would again describe their encounter as a **nightmare**, discounting the real wounds he'd sustained in battle, as if they never existed, explaining in his usual patronizing manner how Carolyn was the victim of a vivid imagination: Told you so, Sam.

Roger was afraid to believe her. His disbelief was no reflection on his wife but she did not see it that way, taking great exception to his doubt and denial. Relocating the sacred text far from the prying eyes and curious minds of their children, the tablet would come out of hiding only twice before disappearing forever. Carolyn showed it to Cathi when she returned the following autumn. In the interim, it kept space and time inside the beehive oven, buried behind a stack of antique books the children knew they were *not* allowed to touch; an off-limits area where they were not allowed to go. Carolyn was quite clear. It was a non-negotiable closet; warm, dry and dark: a perfect place to hide. For three years this notebook remained there undisturbed. Nobody knew where it was, not even her husband. The highly principled woman never attempted to lie about it...but she knew how to withhold; learned how to keep a secret.

***

Cindy crawled in bed beside her big sister. She was just a peanut, really; a little girl with concerns of her own. Andrea threw back the receiving blanket, warmly welcoming her, inviting Cindy to sleep over on another chilly night. It was late. Cindy was trembling. The child was scared to death.

"Annie, I keep seeing things in my bedroom. My toys all move around. If I run downstairs to go pee or tell mom something my toys are all moved when I come back. I know it's *not* April doing it. The last time it happened I was the only one playing up here. Everyone else was outside the whole time. We have ghosts. They talk to me. I see them. I can feel them all the time."

"I've seen strange things, too. Don't worry. Do you want to tell mom?"

"No. I want *you* to tell mom."

"Why? Do you think she'll believe me more than you?"

"No. You talk better than I do. Tell her about the lady who comes after she tucks us in, how she leans over me to kiss me but I never feel the kisses.

It's **not** mom. I **know** it's not. She smells different than mom does...mom smells like soap but this lady smells like flowers and fruit. But then, after she leaves another lady comes late at night. It always says threes on the clock when she wakes me up. I feel her first. She makes me so cold and then the room stinks! She's the one who hates mommy. I saw her in my bad dream when mom was screaming and the ghost wouldn't let me go help her. I saw it happen."

Testimonials began within days of the manifestation in Carolyn's bedroom. One after another, the girls came to their eldest sister, reluctant to share their many unusual experiences, feeling safe to do so with her. Their stories were disturbing; everything from vibrating beds to shadows crossing through their bedrooms to multiple voices whispering in tandem at night. It was one thing after another. Andrea was concerned knowing what happened to their mother was **not** a nightmare. This was something else: something wicked. She didn't want to distress her any further but these confessions could not be ignored or dismissed; she could not keep anymore secrets. Time was fast approaching to have a serious conversation about what was occurring in their home; again.

Andrea waited impatiently for the right opportunity. She felt guilty having to burden Carolyn; a necessary evil. One evening in early June, the first real hint of pending summer warmth carried softly, like a promise on the breeze, Andrea went to her mother, asking to speak with her privately. It might have been a tone in her daughter's voice or a secret they shared which caused her to drop everything and follow her lead. They went onto the porch together.

"Mom, I really hate to tell you this but I have to do it anyway." Remorse in her voice was telling: very bad news...nothing a mother wants to hear.

"What is it, honey?" Carolyn knew. She could feel it like cold in her bones.

"My sisters keep coming to me. Everyone except April has told me about it and I have to tell you. They are scared about what they have seen or heard in the house. They're scared, mom. I know what happened. I *saw* it happen and I couldn't help you...I couldn't even move. I know it was *not* a nightmare."

"I know. What have they been telling you?" Carolyn felt her heart race; her face flushing with blood. An internal alarm triggered. Fear of the unknown.

"To tell you the truth, mom, it's more than I can even remember. I'm pretty sure Cindy's the one who sees them the most; I'm so sorry to tell you this but we have more than one ghost...they need to tell you about all of them."

Carolyn stood abruptly. Remaining in place for a moment, frantic thoughts muddling her mind, she considered what to do next. Instructing Andrea to go and quietly gather her sisters, except for April, then meet her in the kitchen; a message received. Let the baby sleep...sweet dreams.

During the time required for the eldest to collect three of her four siblings, the blood drained from Carolyn's face. She appeared gaunt; a ghostly shade of pale. Sitting alone in silence, waiting at the table for the girls to arrive, she cursed a demon beneath her breath, angered by this intrusion; the disruption its deathly presence was deliberately creating. Infuriated by the thought of it, the mother wanted to know how this bitch from hell could approach innocent children. An odd question; as if something essentially evil might possess any decency or conscience at all. Of course it would *want* to exploit those among them who are most vulnerable! Logical! Overcome with a sense of urgency, panic brewing in the mental cauldron Carolyn realized she'd imbued a corpse with qualities it couldn't possibly possess. Another thought occurred to her: ***What the hell are you thinking!*** Far-fetched as the concept of having a ghost was in the first place, to then attribute it with mortal characteristics; to assign it an intellect and emotion was absurd. The journey of discovery upon which Carolyn had embarked would yield many revelations over time. In stressful moments, anxiously awaiting the arrival of her girls, she chastised herself for entertaining ludicrous notions which were summarily dismissed. Carolyn had no idea how precariously close to the truth she had come.

Clasping her hands together, she implored God to help her endure whatever she might hear from her children. Carolyn felt defeated before it began. That a group discussion was even necessary was upsetting enough in its own right. Unprepared as she was to receive their news, reactions all around would be curious indeed. As her girls entered the kitchen from several directions, they all remained calm and quiet. Each child claimed her familiar spot at the table then waited for her mother to initiate the conversation; an apprehensive and awkward moment for all involved.

"Annie tells me you've all noticed strange things happening in this house." Silence. "It's important to tell me what's been going on." Silence. "If there is anything...if something is frightening you, then I want to know about it." An ordinarily loud, rambunctious bevy of kids had fallen suddenly mute. "Well, I hadn't planned on telling you about this, but I've seen a few things myself." It was the key...unlocking the floodgates. Carolyn was blown back, swept in then swept away by the deluge: torrential information spilling into her mind.

"My toys move around all the time." Cindy was perturbed. "I'll set up all of my **Weebles** and the **Little People** in the village and the farm animals too, and they'll all move around when I leave, even if it's for a couple of minutes, like when I come down to go pee; the airplane goes up under my bed and the bus goes into the closet. It's why I used to blame April, because that is where she plays all the time...but it's *not* her doing it because the village gets set up all over again, *a whole different way*, and it happens *really* fast! Faster than any of us could *ever* do it. The farm and all the animals, too. It's impossible! Mom. For it to happen that fast is...well, it's impossible!"

"I keep hearing footsteps. Loud and heavy." Nancy was unusually subdued. "In the closet...but also on the stairs to my bedroom...always coming *up* the stairs...but then it stops at the door. I keep thinking the door will open...the waiting...that scares me the most; not knowing who is on the other side of it. Sometimes when I'm in my room the closet door opens all by itself. When my stuff is missing I find it in weird places...where I *know* I didn't leave it."

"How *do* you know? *Stuff* is all over the place!" Chrissy had a valid point.

"Because I *know*! When that door thing happens it gets cold and it stinks!"

"The smell could just be a sandwich under your bed." Chris was quick with the wit and so pleased with herself because of it. Nancy got instantly pissed! Her defensiveness drew nothing more than a coy, dismissive shrug from her not-much-younger sis. Letting it go, relishing the pure satisfaction of having said it at all, Christine decided to divulge her own experiences in their middle bedroom, quite similar to what Cindy described about the space they shared.

"My trolls and my glow-in-the-dark finger puppets move, too." Christine had a pragmatic way about her; making a hands-folded-matter-of-fact statement, just like her father...as no apple falls far from the tree of life.

"It feels like I'm being watched all of the time!" Nancy said. "When I look there's no one there but I know *someone* is in the room with me. It creeps me out...*especially* in the bathroom. I always make Cindy come in to guard me. I *never* go in the warm room without her!" Finally, a reference made.

"She does it for me, too." Teasingly tugging at her guardian's robe, Cindy added, "Unless she gets an *important* phone call...and then I'm on my own!"

"Yeah, the phone!" Nancy recalled what she'd seen. "I was running down my stairs and when I came around the corner I saw the telephone was off the hook, up in the air at least *this much*; when I walked in here it dropped down so quick the cord kept on swinging back and forth. I saw it just plop down on the hook...but nobody was in here to see it *with* me, so I didn't tell 'til now."

"And the fridge opens by itself and stuff spills out of it!" Cindy chimed in.

"*All* the doors open whenever they want or slam in my face right when I'm trying to go through into another room!" Punctuating the previous comment, it was obvious Nancy was equally exasperated by the supernatural activity in the home. "I see shadows on the walls in my bedroom at night; a black cloud. I cover myself up with the quilt and pray to God to make it go away!"

209

"Why does it get so cold only in one room; when that *creepy feeling* leaves it warms back up again. I saw a cat running through the bathroom door and it wasn't *our* cat and the door was closed!" Cynthia was growing more anxious by the moment. Her voice began to tremble. "Sometimes my bed shakes and moves around. It wakes me up. Chrissy helps me put it back in the morning." Cynthia began to cry as she spoke to her mother. "I know you always tuck us in at night but so does another lady, too. She leans over to kiss me goodnight. I never feel her touching me but I know when she's there. It's not you, mom. She smells different than you do...like flowers and fruit. Then someone else, another lady comes late when everyone's asleep. She makes it stink *so* bad in the room...*really* bad...like something died. When she leans over me it feels so cold but when she leaves it gets warm again. That's how I know when she is gone. I hide under the covers and pray. She looks at me for a real long time whenever she comes. I don't know why...then there is a little girl who walks through my bedroom crying for her mommy. Her voice is so sad it makes *me* cry. Maybe *she's* the one who plays with our toys. She can. It's okay by me."

Carolyn felt faint. In the midst of the visceral reaction twisting her stomach inside out, she could taste bile in the back of her throat. A mother stricken ill, head spinning; sickened by what she was hearing from her dearest daughters.

"That's it! We're selling this God-forsaken house!" Adamant: no discussion.

Instantly, the last thing Carolyn expected to happen did. A chorus of "NO!" rang throughout the kitchen; girls voicing one vehement protest after another, in unison. She could not hear who was saying what because all four of them, in concert, were whining at once. "No mom! We love it here! I don't want us to move! I have new friends here, now! We don't want to leave our farm! No mom, I love my room! We can make them go away; it will be all right, you'll see. You promised we could have a horse! I love my teacher! I'm not scared! They won't hurt us. We'll be all right. Please don't sell our house, mommy." Carolyn was stunned by a collective outburst. Observing pained expressions, listening to their pleas, she knew this was entirely sincere; heartfelt from all. Awestruck, she couldn't comprehend why they would want to remain behind in a farmhouse which offered them little else than a promise of numerous and unwelcome intrusions. She thought they'd want to leave a spooky old house. Quite the contrary, they were more than willing to make an unusual sacrifice; prepared to share; to co-exist with spirits to keep their place in the country.

"How long have these things been happening?" Awaiting a response, their mother suspected the answer as they glanced around the table at one another.

"Since the beginning, from the day we moved in." Cindy confessed the sins of omission with some shame and regret; secrets kept: a failure to disclose.

"Six months! This has been happening for six months and nobody told me about it before now? Why didn't any of you trust me? I am your mother!"

"It's not that, mommy. We didn't even tell *each other* for the longest time, you know; what we were feeling in the house or the barn. I guess we thought we were just seeing things." Nancy's explanation was not yet finished when her mother abruptly interrupted.

"You *were* seeing things...*things* you should have *told* me about!" Carolyn was persistently on point. "What about the barn; what happened in the barn?' Her focus on Nancy; an immediate reply expected.

"Stuff...mostly up in the hayloft. It shakes and hums like it's singing when we play up there. It makes me feel kinda queasy...like I'm falling down. The tools move around and jingle like bells and sometimes our things go missing; toys we bring out there to play with...then we find them later someplace else in the barn or sometimes we find them back in the house! It's so weird!"

"Nobody goes up on the hayloft again; no one. Do you understand? In fact, I want all of you to stay out of the barn."

"Aw, come on, ma...that's not fair!" Nancy could whine like a steel saw in a Kentucky bluegrass band. "You *know* it's my favorite place in the world!"

"Absolutely not, young lady."

"Tell her about the chimney." Cindy whispered these words to Nancy, as if it were still a secret kept; one about to be told. "Tell mommy what happened to you in the borning room…when you got stuck behind the chimney."

"What happened in the borning room?" As disconcerting as it was to hear, Carolyn remained vigilant, in relentless pursuit of information. She needed to know everything. Clearly, Carolyn underestimated the dramatic impact these events were having on her family…they had only just begun.

"We were all playing hide 'n seek, and I went to hide behind that chimney. Then, all of a sudden I got frozen stiff. It got *wicked* cold! I couldn't move at all! It felt like something was squeezing in against me while I was standing there and I couldn't breathe…like I was locked in a bubble with no air inside it and it was pushing on me from every side. I was stuck there for a long time and the bubble didn't burst until Cindy came to find me. God! It was so cold and dark in there! It smelled so bad and I was being crushed and thought my bones were gonna break! I got really scared and started to cry…tears poured down my face but I couldn't make a sound. I could hear myself screaming in my head but nothing was coming out of my mouth! But Cindy heard me!"

"I think they play their own kind of hide 'n seek…now you see them… now you don't." Cindy was so perceptive…out of the mouths of babes; she knew there was more than one spirit afloat. "I felt her…I *knew* she was in trouble."

"Jesus Christ." Carolyn hung her head, whispering a holy name as a prayer; another call for help, spoken with reverence, unlike her husband's pleas.

"Remember when you yelled at dad for pulling a chair out from underneath me when I tried to sit down?" Cynthia triggered a bad memory. "It happened right here! We came in from sledding and I still had my hat and coat on and I went to sit down in my chair and then, all of a sudden, it got pulled out from underneath me…straight away from me…and you blamed it on daddy."

"I remember it. I was *furious* with your father!" Her grimace confirmed it. "Well, it was a stupid thing to do! A nasty rotten trick. You hit your head!"

"Daddy didn't do it, mom. I was sitting here, too. I saw what happened. He didn't do that." Nancy felt obliged to state the obvious. "You were *so* mad!"

"I had my hat on. It didn't hurt. Well, it hurt my bum a little. I was okay."

"Mom." Andrea's turn to interject. "I was standing over there..." pointing toward the alcove near the entrance of the bathroom. "I saw what happened. Dad didn't do it. The chair pulled away from Cindy. It moved all by itself."

"Mommy, haven't you noticed how we hold our chair when we sit down?" Christine, the problem-solver in the family: devising a solution after she too, had become the unwitting victim of the terrible taunt...or haunt.

"It has happened to all of us since we moved in; a rotten trick but it wasn't dad who did it. He wouldn't do that, mom." Cindy felt the need to defend her father. "Maybe it's the man who stands over there; in that corner. He watches us all the time." Cindy's comment was subdued; it almost got lost in the fray, though it was heard...followed up by another one of Nancy's outbursts.

"Yeh! Maybe it *was* Manny who did it! I saw him, while Mr. Kenyon was packing, on the day we moved in. He stood right behind the door with his leg up and he has a funny smile." Competitive in every way, Nancy *had* to claim credit for the first official sighting. He lurked in darkened doorways, moving as shadow throughout the house from the moment they crossed the threshold. "Cindy saw him, too! We both looked at each other when we saw him but we didn't say anything about it. You saw him too, right?"

"I did...but I don't think he's the one pulling the chairs out. He's not mean like that. I think he was there to say goodbye to his friend. He didn't look at us at all but he smiled at Mr. Kenyon." No false accusations allowed.

"I named him Manny 'cause he's a man! I think he's cool. He's not scary!" Far be it for Nancy to dislike a man, in this dimension or any other.

A lethargy which plagued Carolyn suddenly dissipated, replaced by panic:

wide-awake and fully alert, her mind reeling with images and fresh insights into what had been going on in her home, with her children. Though she said nothing further about selling their house, she remained determined to do so; resolute. As they discussed a variety of outrageous episodes occurring within those walls, Carolyn refrained from divulging her own experiences. Nobody used the word "ghost" to describe or assign an identity to any apparition. The ladies were relieved, having disclosed something so unusual; having shared secrets kept too long. It was getting late. Carolyn suggested she escort them to bed. All her children were tired yet their mother felt an inexplicable rush; kinetic energy pulsing through her temples, as if her mind had absorbed more than it would hold and was throbbing…about to burst through her cranium.

Tucked in with kisses, their mother asked four of the five to keep her well-informed; immediately notified if April should say anything to anyone about this, requesting they not discuss it with her unless she says something first. It was Carolyn's fervent hope that her youngest be spared the sights and sounds the others had endured. It would be another thirty-eight years before Carolyn learned the full extent of the impact on her youngest daughter; the truth about a haunting which touched her baby girl; what April revealed broke the hearts of everyone who learned of a secret kept for decades.

"Mommy." Cindy approached, speaking solemnly. "It's not God-forsaken. God is here all the time. It feels like living in church. God is always with us."

"What do you mean, sweetheart?"

"You said this is a God-forsaken house. It's not." Leave it to Cindy to point out a common misperception among mortals; the adult variety. Explaining it as simply as a child would, she continued. "God is here. Can't you feel it?"

"Yes, feel the presence of the Lord. You're right. Go say your prayers."

"Just because someone is different doesn't mean they're bad. If God is the one who made everyone, then didn't He make our ghosts, too?" There it was; Carolyn kissed Cindy goodnight; a kiss she felt all the way to her heart.

Wandering aimlessly through their house, sleep was not an option. A weary woman disturbed by multiple assertions, had much to reconsider. Knowledge of these episodes changed everything. No one even mentioned the incident in the warm room. As shocking an event as it was at the time, it was treated as old news in comparison with so many other occurrences.

The fire burned hot well past 2:00 a.m. and still, she shivered and could not get warm enough to save her soul. It was June and Carolyn sat huddled on an icy hearthstone; hard to feel warm on the outside when the cold comes from within. Finding the inner strength to heave one more log on the grate, she did so pondering a future free of spirits; free of fear. Wondering what had drawn her there, what called to her; the curiosity was building. Why did it appear as some grand conspiracy, as a virtual gift from above? Why had all the pieces of the puzzle fallen so perfectly into place, one in the country? Good fortune befalls few in a life often riddled with disappointment. What seems too good to be true: she was living proof of the theory. Could such a rare happenstance be purely coincidental? Her ambivalence was magnified four-fold by a single conversation. Why would her children beg to stay in a space filled with fear? Why did they love it? It was so damn cold: Dark. Why would they want to be there; to remain in a farmhouse they had no choice but to share? Hoisting her burdened body up with some assistance from the mantel board, Carolyn went upstairs one more time. Beginning this night, another ritual; to be certain the girls were safe and sound asleep: second time around. They needed to know someone was there to watch over them; someone mortal.

Upon returning to the parlor, Carolyn allowed her head to fall into the soft center of a pillow. In spite of its comfort, much-needed rest eluded her. The scenario seemed implausible; she could not fall asleep. Frustrated, up within minutes, pacing again; her body ached and her mind reeled in equal measure. Rather than considering this grave subject, Carolyn chose instead to reflect upon things of somewhat less import. Her children were becoming lazy with the language. She'd noticed. Catching mistakes during their group exchange, she chose to postpone usual corrections or mild admonishments due to a need to listen closely to content. Determined to address lapses in syntax and some poor grammar skills at breakfast in the morning, Carolyn drifted off to sleep.

Awaking before dawn, a singular thought occupying her mind, their mother was marveling at the bravery of her children. She could still hear little voices speaking in tandem: "We love it here!" Good God; what were they thinking? "We don't want to leave our farm! Please, mom!" Pleas for mercy: it wasn't something Carolyn thought she could or should have to handle alone. When would her husband be home and why hadn't he called? Out of sight…out of mind? Feeling powerless, she required a conference: a meeting of the minds in the home of the brave, minus five children much too young to make such a life-altering decision based on raw emotion. (Ironically, her criteria as well.)

Roger arrived along with the electric bill. He plucked the mail from the box as a delivery truck drove on down Round Top Road. Several days had passed since Carolyn's disturbing conversation with her children. Roger called only once during a week away, though his wife told him nothing of her encounter with their girls in his absence. He walked in through the kitchen, throwing a pile of bills into the center of the table. Having tucked April into bed for the child's usual afternoon nap, Carolyn was making her way back to the same room from the opposite direction, with a load of folded laundry in her arms, destined for Nancy's bedroom, there to reside in yet another pile on her floor. Literally walking into her husband, an armload of neatly-tended clothing hit the floor earlier than anticipated. It startled the woman so badly she shrieked; an automatic, if spastic response to one's own mate; to be sure. No hugs. No kisses. Quickly picking up the clothes, Carolyn threw them onto their dining room table then had to sit down to recover from the fright of this encounter.

"Well! That's a very fine how do you do!" Roger was just as startled by her reflexive reaction as she was by finding him in the house.

"Sorry. I didn't expect you home yet."

"What's wrong with you? You're beginning to act like the cat!"

"I have reason."

"What reason is that?"

"What do you think?" Carolyn leapt into a defensive posture. "You're gone more than you are home! Roger, you have *no* idea what has been happening with your own family! You leave me here, all alone, night after night to fend for myself and the girls, on a wing and a prayer. I don't even dare fall asleep; *someone* needs to watch over them." She went into the kitchen. He followed.

Retrieving the stack of mail from the table, he sought a particular envelope.

"I'm *gone* so that when I *do* come home I can pay the bills...like *this one*!" Roger ripped open their electric bill, presenting it to his wife by flinging it in her general direction. He jerked it back then read the charge. "*Look at this!*" Plunging the invoice toward her face as if it *was* all her fault: "I guess I am *not* home enough to keep you from running it up through the roof!"

"Really? So I'm to blame! Roger, take a walk through this house right now. It's a morgue in here. Cold and dark. It is eighty degrees outside, bright blue skies and sunshine all around this house...but in here? Nothing but an unholy tomb! Go ahead! Take a walk. Inspect the place! We live in a cave, but if you see any sign of light you'll be sure to snuff it out! *Find* a bulb burning. *Show* me where I can conserve anymore than I already do. Check that old furnace while you're at it. Go see if we used any oil while you were away. Just don't wake up April. She's sleeping in our bed...I don't sleep there anymore and you're hardly ever home so I suppose it should get some use."

"Will you please calm down? *You'll* wake her up!"

"You come in here accusing me of wasting the money *you* earn; you blame me for *everything* when all I am trying to do is keep this house comfortable; some place fit for human habitation!"

"I don't understand this! Kenyon showed us his utility bills. They were less than half as much! Month after month...they keep rising!"

"He was alone in this house. There are seven of us. Big difference."

"Not *this* big. Something's got to be wrong here. He kept *all* these lights on *all* the time...day and night, according to every neighbor I've talked to since we came. Something's wrong here!"

"Call the electric company. Have them check the meter. Simple enough."

Carolyn's energy was spent; her venomous tirade...over. Standing abruptly, she turned and walked out the kitchen door. Her husband remained behind to study the power bill which made absolutely no sense. Months of complaints regarding their use of electricity; it was bound to erupt as pressure mounted. It was equally frustrating for Carolyn to watch the bills come in and have no money to pay them. She recognized the gravity of their situation and knew it was becoming volatile. Based upon Roger's demeanor, his trip had been long and woefully unproductive: Time to hit the road again...in another direction.

Energy is as invisible as evil. Roger and Carolyn had no means of knowing the negativity they were exuding toward one another was fanning a nefarious flame. In moments of supreme volatility, emotional outbursts were occurring more frequently; the making up was getting harder to do. There remained an obvious distance between them, even when appearing affectionate with each other. Acrimonious matrimony breeds distrust; enflamed passions functioned as incendiary devices. Anger spawns resentment spawns contempt. During a difficult first year at the farm they began to alienate one another, to such an extent, the couple separated emotionally. The two fought about money; from utility bills to groceries. They argued about politics; routinely confronting the other: issues of war and peace. The conflicts they willingly engaged in were detrimental in ways they could not yet imagine. Carolyn became increasingly remote, eventually untouchable. She perceived Roger as disengaged with his family and intended to return the sentiment in kind. Distance was preferable to ongoing debate: mouth-to-mouth combat. Disdain could not be disguised. It was volcanic in Nature, bubbling to the surface; molten lava with nowhere to go but up and out as hostility seething from words they used as weaponry. He no longer cared what she thought. She no longer looked into his eyes.

"What could you possibly want?" Carolyn's terse response to his cautious approach was not unexpected. He knew he had to make amends, if she would only allow him to do so...the times that try men's souls.

An unyielding figure against the malleable landscape, Carolyn stood rigid; in her place at the back of the house, overlooking the property from her perch along the foundation wall above the garden spot, plans abandoned, the good Earth left fallow for yet another year; a nightmare in its own right.

"I thought you wanted to plant a garden."

"I *wanted* to do a lot of things." The words were crisp and sharp, lashing at him like a whip. "I had sweet dreams for this place."

"Then I'll plow it up and you can plant...it's not too late."

"What's the point? We won't be here for the harvest. We can't stay here. It is not safe for any of us, especially the kids. It's too dangerous."

"This again? How many times do I have to remind you we're in no position to sell this house? Where do you think we will go? There's no profit here yet. None. We couldn't break even in the best of circumstances."

"If you were home now and then you'd know I'm not the only one seeing and hearing things in this house. Your children are being affected by it, too."

"What the hell have you been telling them?" An accusation levied against an innocent victim...one of planting seeds; no doubt.

"What the hell are *you* suggesting?" Carolyn became instantly enraged by a thoughtless comment. "I haven't told them anything! It's what they've been telling me! You think I am unaware of how impressionable children are; it is at the root of my concerns. Look at this garden spot, Roger. That's what kids are...fertile ground. When you plow it up and plant seeds, this land will grow whatever you plant! It's why I've kept as much from them as possible. They all saw the coat hanger incident and there was nothing I could do to avoid the outcome of it. Andrea knows what happened in our bedroom. She never said a word about it to any of her sisters. They came to her."

"How does she know about that?" He was clearly disturbed by the thought.

"She *saw* it happen."

"What?" Roger's own alarm system chimed in. "What are you saying?"

"She thought she was having a nightmare but when it woke her, Annie said she couldn't move. She could *hear* me screaming for help. She saw an entity; an apparition *identical* to what I saw! When she came downstairs, she looked at the notebook and recognized the image; the figure I drew. I can't explain it and neither can she. We can't begin to understand how it happened but it did. We talked about it afterward. I *didn't* tell her what happened; she *knew*…and what she saw she has kept to herself. A few days ago I found out what's been happening with her sisters. They've been going to Annie, all of them, except for April…so far. Roger. Listen to me. We cannot stay here."

A beautiful day belied the darkness in her stone cold heart. Carolyn openly divulged critically important information and expected a series of questions; anticipating that a concerned father would solicit further details pertaining to the experiences of his children. Instead, Roger continued to perseverate about an electric bill, still in hand.

"Something's wrong here. Old man Kenyon showed us all his utility bills. This is almost triple the amount of his highest month in January…in the dead of winter! I don't understand what the problem is here; this doesn't make any sense! There has to be some reasonable explanation!"

"What the hell is wrong with you?" Carolyn glared with contempt, directly at her obtuse spouse. "Didn't you hear a single word I said? Our children are in danger and all you can do is bitch about electric bills. '*Something's wrong here*'? You're goddamned right…something's wrong here!"

"No one is in any danger. Stop it. You're putting ideas in their heads."

"You're an idiot! Get away from me!" Carolyn's rage was so powerful, it silenced her adversary. He left her to gaze at their unturned garden spot.

While Carolyn stood alone contemplating the cosmic secrecy of seed, the school bus pulled up in front of the house. Roger was making his way to the kitchen. The girls saw his car in the yard. Leaping down the steps of the bus, running straight for their father, the long-awaited reunion was short-lived. By the following day he was gone again. There was an exorbitant electric bill to pay. Roger was away for more than a week. He did not ask his wife anything more about what she'd already told him regarding their children, as if he was not even interested. They didn't discuss much before his departure and didn't address it again until his return. By that time, there was more to tell.

It was true. Mr. Kenyon had provided an ample supply of utility bills for an anxious couple of prospective buyers to peruse. Yet, as months grew warmer, even as the season shared far more natural light, the bills continued spiraling upward, as if the house was being deliberately drained of energy. There was an incessant, low-level humming they could not identify. Long after all of the flies disappeared, omnipresent sounds of them lingered in the still chilly air. It was an unusual anomaly occurring during the last week of school.

The vacant garden spot haunted Carolyn as much as any apparition. It had been a part of the appeal of the place, a reason why she longed to buy a farm. Lamenting the loss, she would often stand out behind the house staring at the unturned earth, imagining what it would have produced for her family. It had been years since Carolyn knew the divinity of such toil. Nothing pleased her more than the aromas, the sensation of cool dirt between her fingers. It was a significant loss for a woman having some difficulty measuring the gains of a major investment made on a place quickly losing its charm.

***

During the last few days of the school year, typically a time when kids find they've got way too much time on their hands, Margie approached Andrea. While chatting on the school bus, Margie asked if anything had **happened** to them lately. Their brief conversation was inadvertently overheard by several students who quickly spread the word. In no time Margie was being routinely questioned about the Perrons and the house where they lived. It was common knowledge in the community; Mr. Kenyon always kept the lights on. He got a pass because of his advanced age then because he was alone so much of the time. No one inquired or gossiped about him; the sweet old man who lived in that spooky old house up on Round Top Road. Margie kept the confidence.

Children are intolerant of others; some possessing what appears as a natural predisposition toward cruelty. Whispers persisted throughout the summer. As ghost stories were fabricated, blatant lies were told. By the time the Perrons returned to school the following autumn they were infamous; lives altered by rumor and innuendo. All five, ostracized and shunned by kids they had called friends the year before. Though their house had a reputation for ages prior to their arrival, it was no more than a smoldering story; where there's smoke, an unholy fire is often fueled by indiscreet comments fanning nefarious flames. Eventually it burst into a powerful pyre. In time, it would burn out of control. Fear the living…not the dead. Sage advice: Words of wisdom.

***

None of the girls were aware of what was being spread around about them. So, on their first day of summer vacation, spirits were high. Everyone was up early, making big plans. After breakfast the girls scattered, except for Cindy, who went upstairs to play with the toys her sisters abandoned for the call of the wild. An excursion through wonders of imagination was an all day affair. Many hours passed without her realizing; it was nearly dinnertime when she recognized the gruesome creature tormenting her mother, having seen her in a *dream*. Squatting on the floor, Cindy had all the figures spread out; her rapt attention fixed on farm animals, finger puppets, trolls and the **Little People**. It didn't occur to her anything was amiss. The bedroom was suddenly awash in a soft glow associated with twilight, still several hours away. As the closet door opened Cindy assumed it was someone coming to fetch her for supper. Preoccupied, she did not look up immediately. A companion remained quiet. After a moment of silence, a quick glance upward instantly paralyzed Cindy. Frozen in place, the child was in shock. Directly before her eyes an entity of substance slowly approached, floating above the surface of a bedroom floor. Horrified, an eight-year-old could not move, could not breathe the putrid air. Steam escaped her lips; the result of a sudden rise in heart rate, coupled with a sudden drop in temperature. Appearing as some form of a solid mist, Cindy identified the apparition as a woman by her garb. She had no features, only a grayish oval mass cocked hard to one side. She drifted across the room, arms outstretched, extended toward the terrified child. Speaking sweetly, tenderly, with a solicitous voice Cindy could clearly hear in her head but not actually inside the room: she was petrified, in the bubble, unable to burst free of it. "Come here, little girl. Come to me."

Time was suspended. It ceased to exist...if it ever did. The object of desire was mortified. Odor accompanying this spirit was atrocious; as grotesque as the approaching image itself. A matter of seconds felt like hours trapped with something dead. As it drew closer, she could see stark details of the figure. A white handkerchief dangling from beneath the ruffled edge of a shirt sleeve; the gray flannel blouse with pockets synched tightly at the waist by a flowery apron covering a full-length skirt. No feet. It positioned itself directly in front of her then began leaning in toward her, closer and closer; she came. The air pressure was stifling, pushing on her from every direction. Anticipating the contact, Cynthia begged God for release from an imposed captivity: Granted. She bolted from the bedroom, running through Andrea's room then down the staircase. Losing her balance, she fell, bouncing over the last few stairs; off the wall then straight into the arms of a startled mother standing at the foot of the stairs, about to come up and get her daughter for dinner. Tears streaked the soft skin on her flushed face. Cindy clung to her mom...for dear life.

"Good Lord! What's going on?" Carolyn knew it was something wicked.

"A lady came through the chimney closet door and she tried to take me!"

"What? Calm down. Breathe. I can barely understand what you're saying!"

"She came into my room while I was playing...and tried to take me away! She tried to hug and kiss me and then take me with her!" Cindy's words were frantic; almost indistinguishable, as vocal tremors vibrated through her torso. Wrapping the youngster securely in her arms, sheltering the traumatized soul the only way she could, Carolyn escorted Cindy over to the sofa. Once there, she tried to calm the girl, still unsure of what occurred. When she noticed her elbows were both scraped and bleeding, Carolyn lifted her shirt to find other abrasions along her back, sustained in a hard fall down the narrow stairwell. Bless her heart. Cindy got hurt. She had not escaped unscathed; not this time.

"Breathe, baby. Breathe in and out. It's all right. I've got you." Carolyn felt sensations rising she could barely contain; heat on her cheeks, nausea in her stomach. With all the calm she could muster, Carolyn took her daughter into the bathroom, there to tend to physical wounds; uncertain what to do about a psychological impact. While busy with a necessary task, a mother listened as her child choked out hysterical words. Bathing her wounds, applying gauze bandages as needed, Carolyn faced what few mothers ever do. Astounded by the vivid description, she soon realized her daughter's encounter shared eerie similarities with her own. Head: resembling a hornet's nest, encased in dense mesh of cobwebs. The smell. The cold. The kiss of death. Floating on the air; hovering over its intended victim. Sleeves with no hands. A skirt but no feet. No features. No face. Snapped at the neck. A desire to be close to its victim; precisely what her mother remembered so well: not something she could ever hope to forget. Time does not heal all wounds. Motivation for the unexpected visit was what seemed quite different, yet proved equally disturbing.

"She loves me, mom!" The words impaled a mother's heart. Gazing into an innocent face, her child's wide-eyed-with-wonder expression; Carolyn knew this was something profound: Significant.

"What do you mean…she loves you?" With a voice weakened by her fear, Carolyn softly inquired; by this time she was trembling, too.

"She wants me to be with her." Terror still dwelling within her daughter's bloodshot eyes, Cindy was silently pleading with her to make it go away.

"My God." Carolyn suddenly reached for the side of the bathtub, lowering herself slowly to its porcelain surface; feeling faint. Stunned into submission, she steadied her body and readied her mind, preparing to receive; needing to know if Cindy had anything further to reveal. Was this spirit evil in disguise or had she encountered a benevolent soul; a spirit lost in the ether? She need only listen to know.

"She wants me, mommy. She told me so. She wants me to go with her!"

"*How* did she tell you this?"

"In here." Cynthia touched the center of her forehead. "And here, *inside* my ears. She talked to me inside my head. I could hear her...I could *feel* it all happen inside me...then the bubble burst. It was *real* strong. She loves me!"

"Well, she can't have you!" Instantly threatened, a mother began shedding tears of her own; Carolyn's outburst startled the child. Cindy quickly went to her side, this time to provide some needed comfort: a reversal of misfortune.

"No, mommy! She *can't* have me...I'm yours!" Holding her mom's hand, the sweet little girl was too precious for words. Carolyn clinging protectively to Cindy; it was a moment shared. She was frightened for all of her children; at an impasse with a spouse she was beginning to despise. Having patched up the external wounds, Carolyn took Cindy into the kitchen. They spent the rest of the evening together. That night Cindy slept with her mother, as if that bed was any safer a place to be than her own. Truth be told, each of them were equally susceptible: both in jeopardy. Carolyn waited until the children were asleep before telephoning Sam. While sitting alone in the parlor, preparing to call, it occurred to her; she had failed to ask Cindy the most obvious question of all: *Go where*? Where did this entity want to take her? Perhaps a question she was too fearful to ask. Be afraid. Be very afraid.

Sam promised to come the next morning and when he arrived, had his two daughters in tow; the mistress of the house was shocked. Considering a story she'd told him the night before either he did not perceive the threat described or it was empirically true: the man feared no evil.

"Sam. I'm telling you, this bitch wants to run me off and take my kids!" As Carolyn revisited the hellacious story, she became emotional. Sam took her hand then walked her away from the house. His girls were off playing with Nancy, Christine and April. Andrea was playing school with Cindy. The day was glorious. Sam and Carolyn strolled out beneath the shade of an old apple tree, revisiting a happier time and place, by then laden with its supple leaves; blossoms having passed for the season. He had some news of his own.

"I'm glad you called; I wanted to tell you in person. There is no way for us to pursue a case...no way to null and void this sale. Unfortunately, you have no legal recourse in Rhode Island. It has no disclosure laws pertaining to the supernatural. I'm sorry, dear. I know you were counting on it."

"So you mean we can sue for a leaky roof or demand restitution for a faulty plumbing job but we can't do a goddamned thing about *this*?"

"I'm afraid not. There's nothing on the books. These are spirit matters. Our courts won't touch it; can't litigate what the court won't acknowledge exists. There are several attempts on record. All of them failed; refused a hearing."

Disheartened, Carolyn hung her head. "I don't want to put my girls to bed at night. Weeks go by when nothing happens at all and then, all of a sudden, I'm catching a kid as she flies down the stairs, terrified out of her mind. This is no way to live. I am trying to provide my children with a normal life in an abnormal environment. It's out of my control. Everything is out of control! I can't predict what the next day holds or the next night, for that *spirit* matter! I don't know where my husband is most of the time and I don't know if he'll come home with enough money to keep us going for another month...in hell! I'm exhausted all the time. Sam, I'm getting old too fast."

Sam did not respond. He didn't want to lie, nor did he want to tell the truth. Instead, he looked overhead, up through the gnarled, twisted branches of the ancient apple tree. Admiring the view, dappled sunlight splashed across his eyes. Sam studied its tender leaves, left behind once the blossoms had fallen. He could see the pips scattered throughout the branches as it began to bear its fruit for the season. Excited by the prospect, Sam hoped, in spite of his news, the family would still be there at harvest time.

"I wonder how they'll taste...probably Delicious...maybe Macintosh."

"With my luck, it'll be forbidden fruit." Carolyn was beyond discouraged. She did not see the beauty of the moment or appreciate her country place for what it had to offer besides the obvious; the summer of her discontent.

***

Roger returned home a few days later with better news, having established solid contact with a wealthy new client who owned a tourist-trappy business in Newport. He was not afraid to spend money even though the economy was in trouble and the season had been slower than usual that year. One customer lined Roger's pockets with cash; he took every bit of it, sending the salesman home with an empty trunk to show for the trip and his efforts. Spirits soaring; Roger was always like a kid at Christmas whenever success smiled upon him and always generous to a fault whenever it did.

"I sold half the load in Jersey. I don't know what made me think to run the coast on the way home. Before I knew it I'd crossed the bridge and parked in front of his store. It was hot so I stopped to get an ice cream cone. We started talking...I told him what I had. He bought all of it for his gift shop!"

"You could sell snow to the Eskimos, Roger." Carolyn's deadpan comment was delivered in monotone.

"He took *all* the gold. All the silver earrings. Chain. Rings. He paid cash!"

"Great. What do you want for dinner...there's nothing in the house."

"Let's go to **Rocky Point**!" (Someone wanted to ride the *Wildcat*.)

"Are you out of your mind? We can't afford to waste a dime of that money. God knows when we'll see more." Conditioned reaction; reflexive response.

"The **Shore Dinner Hall** is cheap enough. I'll get you a lobster. What will the **Arcade** cost...maybe ten bucks?" He could be so congenial.

"It's ten bucks too much and forty miles too far."

"Come on. We'll have a great time!" Roger's prompts did nothing to soften her stance in the least; not in the mood for an amusement park. Not amused.

"Then take the girls...I'll stay home." Growing more reclusive by the day, Carolyn had no interest in driving more than an hour for clam cakes destined to sit in her stomach like stones. Her lack of enthusiasm was apparent to the children as well, as their father suggested the outing to them in her presence: subversive, coercive, manipulative man; he *knew* they would convince their reluctant mother to come along, and they did…and they all had a wonderful time, though no one understood how dad would be willing to drive another mile after returning from his long trip. The *Wildcat* was quite the temptation: Best roller coaster in Rhode Island. (The *only* roller coaster in Rhode Island.) Carolyn actually smiled; she laughed again! That night it remained warm and breezy on the coastline. As tempestuous as a relationship had been in recent months, this night Roger and Carolyn shelved their differences then focused exclusively on their kids; what made it such a fondly memorable excursion. The girls heard **"yes"** so often they'd eventually stopped asking for anything, so as not to take unfair advantage of this generosity extended. Pure ocean air knocked everyone out cold. All the girls fell asleep on their long ride home. Their parents traveled in silence, allowing them to rest without interruption. It was welcome respite for all. Peace and quiet replaced sarcastic bickering. A cooling wind swept through open windows. Moonlight guiding the troupe, homeward bound along a lonesome path, country roads as dark as death; life had become a study in extremes. Finally arriving home…out went the Light.

Since Roger's arrival, the couple had managed to avoid discussed anything pertaining to what transpired in the house in his absence…or what occurred prior to his departure, for that matter. As they drove the front seat of their car became crowded by thoughts with no voice. When they returned to the farm, the light-hearted mood dissipated into stagnant, moist midnight summer air.

"This house smells like death!" Roger's demeanor changed so abruptly that it left everyone else speechless; bleary-eyed children stunned. As he opened the door, stepping across the threshold, the chilled stench of the house forced him back out onto the porch. It was loathsome; a vile, disgusting odor, as if a ten-day-old carcass was buried and rotting beneath the dwelling.

Both cellar doors were open wide. Pantry doors…open. In their absence, a haunting had occurred. When the cat is away…but their cat was well-hidden, huddled in a dark corner of the parlor behind the sofa. The dog was whining, cowering beneath the dining room table, too terrified to run to her own kids. Before Roger could spoil an otherwise perfect evening, Carolyn sent them to bed. After closing all the errant doors, she rejoined her husband on the porch. Sitting beside him, she began to speak in a somber, sedate tone reflecting the gravity of their situation. He never spoke a single word in response. Instead, he listened; really listened to his wife. She told him what the girls disclosed the night they shared their horror stories; nightmares...he could not imagine. She described Cindy's abject horror at having been approached by an entity, one with which Carolyn was all too familiar; a spirit hell-bent on taking their daughter away. He had seen the illustration but Cindy never did. Explain it? He could not. Recognizing this apparition from the *dream* she had while her mother was under attack...he just shook his head. Bestowing a kiss; contact had been made, whether or not he knew it at the time. His skin serrated while he was *asleep*...a clock stopping at exactly the time these incidents occurred. There could be no shadow of a doubt left in his mind.

When Carolyn finished recounting mournful tales, Roger leaned forward, propping elbows on his knees, head in hands. Several silent moments passed. The man felt defeated. He was overwhelmed in the same way his spouse had been, time and time again. He stood, walking into the house: No Comment. In the interim, the house had returned to *normal* and, noting the absence of a presence, part of the new paranormal, Roger promptly went to the bedroom. This night, there would be no rest for the weary...for wicked and good alike.

The following morning their bed was moved halfway across the room, then placed at a crooked angle. As the couple slept they were visited again though neither had any recollection of the incident. Roger's booming voice woke his wife just past six...dawn breaks on Mr. Marblehead.

"Jesus Christ! What the hell is going on here?" Both doors open behind it.

"I told you last night, Roger." Carolyn rolled over, indicating needed return to sleep. "Hell is happening here." Her muffled words came from the pillow.

"Get up…help me move it back in place!" Roger was obviously aggravated by his wife's lack of interest. Her husband was not home frequently enough to realize; this was something the woman dealt with all the time. Carolyn sat up in bed to survey her surroundings from an alternate perspective. Likewise, she was determined to address their situation head on. Still groggy, she spoke softly, in a firm tone, the message direct, so to be properly received.

"Roger, whatever power is present in this house is capable of manipulating objects, even a bed. When will you listen to me? Why move it back in place? What's the point? This will only happen again…and again." White flag up.

"This is crazy! Absolute fucking insanity!" He wanted to scream the words he'd whispered instead, remembering that children were sleeping overhead.

"Regardless of your opinion about this, *this* is life as we know it now… and Sam says we can't do a damn thing about it." Carolyn felt defeated.

"What does *that* mean?" Less a question…more a command.

"No disclosure laws. Not a legal leg to stand on. We are stuck here; unless we sell it and lie to a prospective buyer who asks why we're leaving so soon. I don't know if Mr. Kenyon deliberately withheld it from us or not but I can't believe he lived here for a lifetime without knowing this house was haunted. Nor do I believe the man would knowingly place this family in harm's way. I would certainly hope not. Maybe you're right; maybe he was questioning his own sanity, but birds in the chimney? A little hard to *swallow*! I don't know what to think about Mr. Kenyon but I do know you don't think it's dangerous here and I don't think you're right about that. Please, leave me alone now."

"Cup of coffee?" He rarely requested her companionship. She ignored him.

Closing the demon doors, Roger shoved the bed back to its former position while his wife huddled beneath the blankets. It was well past time for him to come to terms…on his own. He went into the kitchen to make a pot of coffee. Standing alone in the pantry, measuring out the grounds into a basket, he felt the steady, gentle stroke of a woman's hand across his shoulders then down, along his back; Carolyn had reconsidered joining him for a cup. Of course.

"Changed your mind?" Roger turned to discover he was entirely alone. The hair on his arms rose before the Sun. "Where'd you go?" No reply; she was not there. Peeking into the vacant bathroom, he'd returned to their bedroom where he found his wife sound asleep. There she was; and there it was again: behind his back, as strokes of midnight at dawn. Roger cringed, pulling away from perceived fingertips pressing into his skin. He felt the waves of nausea barrel through his stomach. It was not clam cakes or chowder *or* the *Wildcat* turning inside the shaken soul. Reality was sickening enough.

When Cynthia got up she found her parents hunkered down at the kitchen table, deeply engaged in a private discussion; she had to interrupt. Asking her mother to follow her into the bathroom, the child appeared grim; forlorn. As she closed the door Carolyn became alarmed. A mother recognized the face of fear on her girls, having seen it there before, but this was something else; a different expression, one she instantly associated with grieving a loss.

"Mom. I saw, I don't know what I saw, last night while Chris was asleep."

"What is it, honey? Tell me what you saw."

"Something happened to her. You know how our beds are...I woke up...I don't know when but it was still dark. The nightlight was on so I could see. I heard something...like the cat was growling. It woke me up. I rolled over. I thought Chrissy was sick or talking in her sleep. Oh, Mom... it was terrible!"

"Sweetheart." Carolyn was fighting demons of her own, hiding the anger.

"God. It was so terrible." Cindy wrung her trembling hands. "It was not my sister Christine. The eyes popped open and it stared at me. I couldn't scream. I tried. Mom. The eyes were black. It wasn't her eyes! They weren't human."

Carolyn listened intently as a frantic child described what she'd witnessed. Chrissy was no longer. Her face: twisted and distorted. Her features; gnarled and mangled. Cindy said it looked like snakes slithering underneath her skin, like something had crawled inside her and was trying to escape. It was not her sister's face at all. Cindy was terrified by what she saw...what she heard. Growling. Moaning. Pain. As two hollow, vacant orbs peered in her direction she'd covered her head then prayed, begging God to make it go away. It did. She cried herself to sleep, too afraid to lower the blanket, to look at the bed beside her own; too terrified to check on her sister's condition. Instead, she'd crept as deeply beneath the blankets as she could, making certain nothing of her was exposed beyond its border: an act of self-preservation. There she fell asleep. When she awoke, Cindy saw the edges of their blankets were singed; scorched all around: Burnt offerings. She could see a lump in Christine's bed but did not peek beneath the torched blanket. Carolyn opened the door.

"Roger. Go upstairs. Check on Chrissy. Go now." Responding to an urgent tone in her voice, the equally alarmed father bolted for the nearest staircase.

Returning to Cindy, Carolyn bathed her flushed and tear-streaked face with a warm washcloth. Getting her breathing under control, the child had come close to hyperventilating. A knock on the door was Nancy, just about ready to bust. Carolyn relinquished the bathroom, taking Cindy into the kitchen. A few minutes later Roger returned with Christine in tow. Relieved to see her, Cindy ran over for a hug. Chris appeared exhausted; older, as if she had aged a decade overnight. Carolyn studied her face; the youngster was puzzled by the shower of attention. It didn't make sense. She was interested in pursuing the hot pot of oatmeal prepared and waiting for them on the stove.

"What's going on here?" Roger was rightfully confused.

"I'll tell you later." Accepting this dismissal as necessary, what mattered at the moment was a hoard of hungry kids gathering in the kitchen. The family of seven had breakfast together, talking excitedly about their great outing by the seashore. As the warm summer breeze filtered through their screen doors, the fresh scents of sweet air (compared to what they'd walked into the night before), Carolyn wondered silently if what occurred since their arrival home the previous night had been some kind of retribution for having left the house en masse: punishment. Cindy sat quietly as Carolyn slipped off to inspect the bedrooms. Their blankets were burned as she had described; all five were the same, like a ring of fire surrounding each one of her children. Carolyn could barely breathe; touching the scorched edges of each blanket, she shuddered. The burn marks were identical, as if someone had taken a blow torch to satin binding. Yet another incendiary threat: torch and spark, rekindling her anger, enflaming a passionate hatred…reigniting a mother's fear of fire.

After breakfast the family went for a walk down by the river. The children ran on ahead as Carolyn informed Roger about what happened. He suggested it may have been a nightmare. She told him about the blankets. He suddenly stopped walking…dead in his tracks: Frozen in time on the knoll of a hill.

"Roger. Are you among the living? Roger! Didn't you see the edges of the blankets when you went to get Christine?"

"I wasn't looking at her blanket. I was looking for the kid underneath it!"

"Are you completely oblivious to what is happening here? Don't you *dare* try to tell me this isn't dangerous! Wait until you see it; all five are scorched! All of their electric blankets are burned and not one of them was plugged in. I checked. No power surge. There is no *logical* explanation for it. Don't you see? This is a threat to me! That bitch is playing with fire; trying to scare me to death!" As desperation dissolved into anger, he listened to his wife but he did not comprehend the fullest implications, as if a slab of granite kept this message from penetrating his thick skull. This time it was different; this time he felt it in his gut. It was a power surge of sorts. Roger felt overpowered.

"I was touched by something…or someone…on the shoulder and down my back. I thought it was you." Contact: taken by force.

"What are we going to do?" Carolyn actually sought her husband's advice.

"I don't know." His perplexed gaze found hers. It had been awhile since an at-odds couple felt like-minded, unified by a protective purpose: an intention. Roger had told her the truth. He did not know what to do...or what to think.

***

The days grew long and warm that summer. Hot. By August everyone was wrung out, wilting in the relentless heat. The house remained relatively cool; a place to escape the worst of it: Ironic. Carolyn felt certain dread of another winter, promising more of the same punishing cold. A Georgia girl preferred sweat to sweaters and spent her days with her children at the river's edge.

The couple discussed listing the house in an attempt to sell it during a year when property values were dropping by the month. They spoke with Sam. He suggested they wait to see when the market rebounds which was inevitable; it was only a matter of time. Ambivalent, Carolyn wondered what time spent in this house would hold; the constant anticipation of impending threat haunting her more than the looming winter. Breaking even didn't matter anymore.

Cathi returned on cool September breezes. She and Carolyn spent the entire day together, well into evening, an arrival coinciding with Roger's departure: perfect timing. All the "girls" enjoyed a fine reunion. They played and sang, danced and made a joyful noise created by so many females in one place, at one time. It was wonderful to see her again. Both women spoke at length on a variety of subjects. There was news on both fronts...Cathi met a man and fell in love. She left him behind in Nova Scotia. The ladies snuck off into the pantry like two giddy schoolgirls. Later in the afternoon there were sobering moments between them when Carolyn discreetly retrieved her notebook from its not-so-final resting place and they poured over it privately. She shuddered at seeing those images again. Cathi was far more fascinated than frightened; something with which to tease her facile mind. She wasn't intimidated by it except on behalf of the kids, concerned about the potential impact made on a bevy of impressionable youth. Curious by nature, Cathi asked thoughtful and erudite questions, most of which Carolyn remained unable to answer in full. She believed in the existence of supernatural phenomenon but did not believe the spirits were dangerous; more of a nuisance. Explaining multi-dimensional aspects of such theory, it precluded actual physical involvement; interaction between the living and the dead. Apparently well-informed, Carolyn listened carefully to her young but learned friend, wanting to believe this theory to be an accurate one... for the sake of her family.

"How do you know so much about the supernatural?"

"I don't know much. Reading...things I've heard from reliable sources."

"So you think the same way Sam does; there's really nothing here to fear."

"Well, I have not had to live with it. This is more of a cerebral exercise for me, but for you; I'm sure you've seen and felt things you'll never forget. I'm sorry to say...I wish it weren't so. I know how much you wanted this place."

"That's what I'm afraid of Cathi; images trapped in my mind for eternity."

"There are things we see in life we're not supposed to forget." A wise one.

Though invited, encouraged to spend the night at their farm, Cathi declined the invitation. It was nearly 10:00 p.m. by the time she left for home, calling her mother first to announce she was on the way. Elsie was anxious to spend some time with her daughter after such an extended absence. Cathi promised she'd be coming home and had to go. With hugs and kisses, Carolyn sent her off into the darkness. The ride was a long one back to her neck of the woods; Seekonk, Massachusetts. Plenty to occupy her mind, Cathi cheerfully cruised down Round Top Road. Nova Scotia had her by the heart. Rather than dwell on all Carolyn disclosed, she instead revisited the place where she longed to return...to the man waiting for her north of the border.

Suddenly Cathi smelled something foul in her car; she hadn't driven farther than a mile or so when a putrid stench permeated the vehicle.

Something was wrong. Gripped by unbearable cold, it felt as if her fingers had frozen to the steering wheel. Someone touched her long, flowing hair. Panic; pure dread consumed her being: petrified in place. She glanced into the rear view mirror and caught a glimpse of it; a fleeting image of something wicked turned her heart to stone. Jagged, yellow teeth: Death. She was in the presence of death. Her mind refused to absorb what she witnessed with her eyes. Cathi couldn't stop the car; flee the scene. Knowing she was not alone, she kept on driving, faster and faster, racing toward the safety of home...the arms of her mother. Though the apparition vanished almost as quickly as it appeared, its putrid stink lingered for the duration of the trip, trapped within her sinuses, perhaps trapped in her own memory forever... somewhat more to fear than fear itself. Calling Carolyn as soon as she finished debriefing her mother, there was no making light of it allowed... not yet...not ever; this was a too-close encounter of the bizarre kind and Cathi knew firsthand what a dear friend had endured.

Her spooky status report was equally disconcerting to Carolyn. She offered an awkward apology then went into her bedroom to look at it again, an image revealed in the open tablet. Furious, she slammed it shut and held it in the air.

"You bitch! If you cost me this friendship I'll hunt you to hell and back!" The irate woman issued a formal threat of her own. Though a confrontational approach was not in her best interest Carolyn felt compelled to state her case. Replacing the notebook in its hiding hole in the wall, to rest undisturbed for years to come, there it would remain until the day two strangers appeared on her threshold with a genuine offer of help. As a solid bridge of trust was built between them over time, Carolyn would eventually agree to relinquish this notebook, along with all of her research, with an explicit promise made for a timely return. All of it...placed into hands where it was laid to rest; out of her possession...never to return.

Autumn ushered in yet another brutal winter. Carolyn remained watchful; pensive. Though an extended period of time passed without a major incident, she was perpetually on guard. Electric bills continued to spike, rising steadily month after month, even though Roger had their original meter replaced that previous summer. As a constant source of consternation between the couple, the blame game got old. Carolyn became increasingly intolerant; resentful of her absentee husband. Snide comments, harsh accusations were taking a toll as their relationship deteriorated into a series of caustic remarks; arguments. They were unknowingly feeding a force within those walls...and it was quite likely returning the disfavor. Negative energy is powerful. Hostility is potent. The inimical approach toward one another bred contempt, neither willing to make amends. They felt no desire to reconcile issues as differences between them became too stark; the depth and breadth, a chasm too wide to traverse. Roger and Carolyn were two opposing forces...at war on uncommon ground. The occasional peace treaty drafted would then be mutually agreed upon but the truce never lasted very long; their once marital bliss had evolved into so many blisters: deep, festering wounds...so occurred the scarring of the heart. Over time, they would prove to be permanent, irreparable: wounds too deep to heal became infected...irreconcilable differences; deadly to a marriage.

Rumors spread, wildfire-style, through town; inflammatory and inaccurate. Though the girls remained relatively isolated over the course of the summer, socializing with just a few close friends and neighbors, when they returned to school the reception was distinctly different; as chilly as the raw autumn air. Teased and taunted on a regular basis, the five girls began withdrawing from those they'd perceived to be friendly the year before. They learned important lessons very quickly, including who their *real* friends really were, receiving quite an education about ignorance, intolerance and the roll of thrill-seekers in their young lives. During this time, all five children forged bonds based on sound protective instincts, defending one another against this onslaught on numerous occasions; unity which lasts a lifetime. They stopped blaming each other for such annoying anomalies as rearranged toys or missing objects and they soon discovered the intrinsic value of a sisterhood. What the girls faced was nothing less than blatant unabashed discrimination. Circling the wagons, warding off the evil spirits, living and dead, those who intended them harm; they found their way through it within loving arms. As their parents waged a civil war with uncivil discourse the children prayed for peace. Watching over one another, setting an example of civility, they practiced the presence: God.

***

Carolyn cursed at the spirits and husband alike while Roger played the role of Devil's Advocate. An abundance of evidence at his disposal; how much of it was required to convince him? How could it be that he did not recognize so many omens for precisely what they were? Why did he feel justified arguing the logic of an illogical situation? It was an argument he could not, would not win in reality and yet he persisted, sometimes amenable to Carolyn's point of view, sometimes staunchly opposed as if to taunt her, deliberately making an obvious spirit matter worse. Why was it so important for Roger to be right? Opposing forces: Perhaps what was called for was a happy medium. In time, she would appear at their door. Then he could begin not believing in her, too. At least Carolyn would no longer feel so desperately alone. She would listen to the terrified mother, pass no judgment; recognize the omens as harbingers of things to come and realize a danger; the true Nature of an imposing threat.

"In this unbelievable universe in which we live there are no absolutes. Even parallel lines, reaching into infinity, meet somewhere yonder."
Pearl Buck

from frying pan into the fire

Murphy's Law: "What can go wrong, will go wrong, and at the most inopportune time."

Sizzled and scorched, over-fried chicken clung to the bottom of a cast iron frying pan, cemented in place. It was so unlike Carolyn to lose concentration when cooking. A long-standing reputation for preparing the best Southern fried chicken, she was mortified by her own lapse of attention paid to dinner. It was ruined. Good food wasted. Thank God Roger was not home to see this happen then critique her skills accordingly. Bouncing down the stairs, Nancy emerged into the kitchen, inevitably prepared to state the obvious:

"Something's burning! I can smell it upstairs!" Smoke does tend to rise.

"No shit, Sherlock!" The cook's response was slightly defensive.

"Who's Sherlock?" Nancy's question met with some intolerant resistance.

"Never mind." Disgusted, Carolyn was in no mood to teach from a primer on English literature at the moment; she was much too busy learning her own lesson while trying to salvage what she could of their supper.

"Elementary, my dear sister. You should know it already. Doctor Watson? Sherlock Holmes? You should try going to the library once in a while." Quite snippy, Andrea's attitude toward her next of kin was sarcastic, dismissive at times. "Instead of the sand banks!" Ouch! Calling her sister a super-slacker, all Nancy had done was bring the aroma of charred grease to their attention. Out the door she went, ignoring the blatant insult, perhaps oblivious to it.

"I'm goin' fishin' down at the river." The great escape artist was gone.

"No problem, mom. I can scrape off the scorch. It's still good." Consoling her mother, Andrea took over the task at hand. Returning to the potato salad, Carolyn remained quiet, reflecting upon time lost; on her inadvertent lack of concentration when cooking on fire (albeit electrical heat) and knowing how dangerous it was to be anything but mindful when grease is boiling in a pan. Upset with herself, she mixed her salad, allowing the distracting thoughts to continue doing their work, pulling her further away from the mindless task, compared to the more serious one she'd relinquished to her eldest daughter.

It was a sense of dread consuming a soul, this watching and waiting, taking its toll. Nothing happened to provoke it; nothing seen or heard which would indicate the presence of a nefarious force. No apparitions; nothing unusual of late, so why was Carolyn so preoccupied? Why was her mind wandering into dark spaces? She'd felt an oppressive weight which she did not generate and could not shed. It occurred to her that this process was, in itself, a malignant blight; an omnipresent influence working its blackest magic on her thoughts, keeping her fearful, robbing her of time. This was not the first time. As hours passed at the sink, she'd stare out the back window and lose track of time; an afternoon gone as if it were an instant, reliving moments she longed to forget while knowing she never would. Time lost lingered with an evil spirit which was haunting her in absentia, or was it actually gone? Carolyn continued to sense an overwhelming presence and yet nothing had manifested in form; no one had issued any threats. Yet, was it not a threat unto itself if she had been unable to properly tend to a skillet which posed a hazard of its own? Maybe Roger was right. Perhaps her imagination was getting the best of her…maybe the memory was enough to do this damage on its own. Why sense impending doom when some sense of normalcy prevailed? Truth be told, it was fallacy; no such thing as normalcy in their house. "Normal" *was* the new paranormal. Their family had purchased a piece of surreal estate. Carolyn didn't dare trust her intuition, didn't dare believe she was alone, because on some level, she knew it was not true. A wounded woman in the midst of a transformation she could not fathom, her real sense of foreboding was omnipresent with purpose and reason, if for no other reason than to warn her to prepare for what was to come. What she sensed was not coming from beyond her; she sensed it from within… the most frightening sensation of all.

"Mom!" Apparently Andrea had splattered some grease on its burner while removing the seriously crispy chicken from a skillet. Flames shot up from the surface of the stove, around the outside of the cast iron frying pan.

Fire in the hole! Rushing into the pantry, Carolyn slapped a metal lid over the exposed oil while pulling her daughter away from a stove. Checking to be certain that burner was off, as she'd suspected, she had indeed turned it off when initially discovering the problem: what is done can be overdone! The heating element was totally cool to the touch. No grease had splattered after all; no fuel added to the fire. No fire! Message received.

Cutting the crusty skin away from the meat, it became dinner for the dogs. In spite of a mishap, it turned out to be, as Annie predicted, a delicious meal. Carolyn might have been more gratified by this outcome if not for a niggling sensation which continued to trouble her. Had the sense of foreboding been her intuition at work, as warning of a pending situation in the pantry? Or had the pantry provided another venue for yet another manifestation of the spirits playing with fire? She considered the scenario as metaphor: out of the frying pan…into the fire. Something told her a haunting was not over. Looming on a darkening horizon, ominous clouds were gathering, creating the solid wall of worry, shrouding her mind in despair. Carolyn could feel it all around her. She could feel it inside her. Omnipresent…like God. It could not possibly get worse…or could it? Of course it could…and would.

It was only a matter of time; this period of intense sensations of doom and gloom finally subsided. A heavy shroud of clouds lifted, no damage done by its darkness, or so she thought. Inexplicably, this gathering threat seemed to dissipate. She returned, escaping unscathed from its grasp; as energy robbed was naturally restored by warming breezes and bright blue skies. Regaining her sense of direction, soaking in the summer…things were looking up. She had forgotten about Schwartz's Law: Murphy was an optimist!

One need not see to believe and one need not believe what they see. A seer is one who is looking at life, observing its intricacies or revealing its secrets, at times, in equal measure. Carolyn paid attention. She was right to be wary. It would have been easy enough to dismiss these sensations as a brief bout of depression, yet she knew better. This was an omen: powerful and oppressive and greedy; the voracious, vociferous silence in her mind, forewarning her of things to come. This was a mental infestation as manifestation. Soon enough Carolyn understood what she'd been experiencing; the deep, despairing sense of dread, the vision of fire surrounding a skillet as the precursor to a circle of fire destined to surround the woman in her bed. Paying attention, monitoring one's own thoughts and emotions: of critical importance when dwelling in a house alive with death. What was invisible was equally powerful; fear of fire. Elemental, my dear Carolyn: Fear is the most powerful element of all. It was almost time to take the plunge, make a leap of faith out of the frying pan into the fire. Time to learn that faith alone can keep a soul all fired up safe in the midst of a crisis. It wasn't over. What can go wrong, will: Best pay attention.

―――――――――

"I have always thought the actions of men the best interpreters of their thoughts."
John Locke

blue light special

"Each separate dying ember wrought its ghost upon the floor."
Edgar Allan Poe

Though another spring had officially arrived its nights were still quite cool, chilly enough to warrant a fire. Burning low in its grate, embers needed some tending. Carolyn was distracted, in rapt involvement with characters of note from a beloved novel; revisiting a few old friends. The parlor was practically silent. She sat on their loveseat directly across from the fireplace. The ladies, poised on the floor, books scattered around them on the Oriental rug. Andrea required more space, so had spread out at the dining room table, materials for her current project turning its wooden surface paper white. Everyone present was engrossed in a project or assignment; homework time early one evening.

Andrea finished her work at the table. Heading into the parlor to inform her mother she was free to help with dinner, as Carolyn looked up from her book an incredible event occurred. A solid blue tubular beam of light shot down the chimney, snuffing out the flames. It turned at a hard right angle and came out across the room, landing directly in Carolyn's lap, impaling the book she was holding. A collective gasp filled the stilled air. A split second later this light retracted along precisely the route it had traveled, withdrawing up the chimney. It all occurred in about two or three seconds. No one could believe what they had just witnessed. Andrea was in shock but retained the presence of mind to assist her mother. Carolyn's facial expression appeared frozen in time, eyes fixed; wide and alert with her mouth partially open...aghast!

"Mom! Are you all right?" Andrea was frantic, afraid her mother had been injured. A light struck directly in the center of her torso and her daughter had no idea what damage this might have caused. The tube of light was perfectly cylindrical, solid blue, roughly the diameter of a walnut. A stunning thing to see: this event, defying the basic laws of physics. Light travels linearly. Light does not bend at right angles. Light does not snuff out the flames of a fire nor does its absence or retraction reignite the flames in a fireplace. Had it been a bolt of lightning? Carolyn seemed fine. The girls recovered momentarily and approached their mother en masse. She stood, examining the point of impact. There were no signs of any injury; no scorch or burning book; no pains at all. Reassuring her children, all was well, she suggested they *all* relocate…away from the front of the fireplace. Compliance was not an issue. Carolyn moved across the parlor toward the sofa, there to finish her chapter undisturbed.

This was the first of three times that phenomenon would occur within their house and each time it was as shocking as the initial encounter with this very special force; a blue light with a mind of its own. Though she was apparently uninjured by the event, Carolyn would speculate about the effects of the light for many years to come, especially with regard to their friends, two of whom would eventually have an exceedingly close encounter with the beam of light as it sought them out. When the Warrens became involved, Lorraine offered a detailed explanation of it as a presence. The ray was a beautiful and bizarre display of pure light. Its power defied natural law. Claiming familiarity with such phenomena, Mrs. Warren later described it as one form of supernatural plasma, manifesting as a beam of Cosmic Light traveling through space and time, then entering a specific portal; delivering a message received by mortal souls who have witnessed its affect yet remain unable to discern its meaning. Some see it as a blessing. Some see it as a curse.

The explanation seemed as implausible as the episode but Carolyn listened attentively, trying to make sense of it. Mrs. Warren assured her, it was not as uncommon as she might suspect, claiming it as another supernatural Light in manifestation; an *entity* in its own right. Though Carolyn was skeptical, she was Roger's polar opposite. He assumed he knew everything. His wife, sure she knew nothing. Lorraine, the happy medium, would try to convince both of them that this was another aspect of the paranormal activity in their home. The mistress of the house had no apparent residual effects from an encounter which could not be explained and could not be denied; too many witnesses for Roger to question these identical reports among his family.

However, the same could not be said for others touched by Light; one coming from above.

"The illuminable, silent, never-resting thing called Time, rolling, rushing on, swift, silent, like an all-embracing oceantide, on which we and all the universe swim like exhalations, like apparitions which are and then are not: this is forever very literally a miracle; a thing to strike us dumb, for we have no word to speak about it."
Thomas Carlyle

an old torch carries a flame

"The communication / Of the dead is tongued with fire beyond the language of the living."
T.S. Eliot

Winter had found its way to spring. Though it had been as cold as the first, it was made bearable by the existence of a fireplace, a major advantage over the previous year. Carolyn huddled on the hearthstone for the duration of the season. She'd discovered, given the opportunity, a house will not keep itself. It was obvious. Her energy continued to dissipate; evaporating into the ether. She appeared gaunt and frail. April started school in the fall so Carolyn used much of her time alone to read and sleep...all she had energy to do. Bless her heart and soul. It was only the beginning; the worst was yet to come. Do tell.

***

The Perron family enjoyed their first Christmas together in the farmhouse. Roger was a Santa unlike any other, doing everything in his power to lighten Carolyn's burdens. He'd done the shopping, even some cooking, spoiling the girls and his beloved wife. They had gone deep into the woods to cut the tree. Carolyn stayed behind at the house, preparing sugar cookies and hot cocoa. It was quite picturesque; a rare Norman Rockwell moment. Invoking the spirit of Charles Dickens might have been more appropriate to this scene, as ghosts of Christmas past were making their presence known.

An armistice was declared for the holidays. All bickering subsided; it came to an abrupt HALT! Words are weapons. In the spirit of the season, the milk of human kindness flowed with the eggnog on a Christmas Eve. Decorating the tree proved to be quite the festive event. Carols were sung as bells rang in the church steeple. Though their family didn't attend Mass often, on a sacred night they decided to attend at midnight so the morning would not be rushed as the children opened their gifts. Roger had excellent taste. He'd purchased a beautiful suit for Carolyn which he'd presented to her after dinner. She was excited and so grateful, anxious to try it on…then show it off. As she stepped through their bedroom door her expression revealed a sentiment expressed by all of them as a collective gasp, though not for the reason one might suspect. Knowing why everyone reacted, the elegant pantsuit hung like a sack on her withering torso. Roger tried to hide his alarm, though it was clearly evident. "We'll go to exchange it next week." Holding her in his arms, he whispered: "You need to call a doctor; make an appointment." She nodded then changed into something more fitting. They went to church.

Upon entering St. Patrick's, heads turned. Carolyn wondered if it was her dramatic weight loss drawing attention. Their parish was rather small and the Perrons nearly filled an empty pew by themselves, though quite noticeably, nobody joined them in the remaining seats as the crowd filed in for service. Once Mass began this scrutiny ceased. Everyone focused on the altar. It was fine until the priest uttered familiar words: "The Father, the Son and the Holy Ghost. Amen." As excited as she was uninhibited, April shouted a few words with such jubilance, from choir to altar boys to the priest, everybody heard.

"Mommy! Did you hear that? God has a ghost too, just like us!" She knew; mystery solved. It was an innocent statement from the child whose innocence was in jeopardy. Carolyn covered her baby's mouth in that moment of panic. Too late. They left as discreetly as possible within a few minutes; vibrations of disapproval driving them away from the House of the Holier than Thou. Merry Christmas to all…and to all a good night.

Roger and Carolyn tucked their children into bed then spent the rest of the night silently assembling toys and drinking coffee before a raging fireplace. Lights adorning their tree illuminated a parlor, bathing it in a glorious glow. A chorus of carols played softly on the stereo, so not to wake the youngsters, providing the home with peaceful notes to end on, a splendid soundtrack for another gift-wrapping session. It was past 2:00 a.m. when the tired but happy couple finally went off to bed, knowing their children would be up and out of bed by dawn. They'd remained silent about what happened in church, neither one of them willing to put a damper on an otherwise perfectly holy night.

~ warm but weary on a Christmas morning ~

Carolyn stood in front of the fire, her coffee cup on the mantel board, never far from her fingers. Roger sat across from her on the sofa. They watched the children shred wrapping paper and toss bows at one another. It was as joyful for them as it was for the kids. Carolyn received a pair of very fuzzy slippers from Santa, warm and soft and very pink. While opening a simple gift, Roger stoked the fire, placing a Yule log he saved for this special occasion directly on top of the pyre. Carolyn put them on her feet then resumed her position on the hearthstone. Igniting quickly, the log burned with a brilliance everybody noticed. Warm and cozy on that chilly Christmas morning, Carolyn, as usual, was standing too close to the flames.

Leaning down to see what Santa Claus brought to one of the girls, Carolyn stood abruptly then grabbed a hold of the mantel board. Collapsing onto the granite hearthstone, she hit it with such force, everyone froze except Roger. He sprung up from the sofa, leaping over the children so quickly, no one saw him go but there he was, pulling her feet out of the fire. He lifted his wife as if she were a rag doll and placed her on the long sofa at the front of the room, away from the flames. This fainting spell would have had dire consequences if not for his rapid response on a rescue mission. Carolyn came around as the children scrambled to her side. Insisting she was fine, just tired, their mother made light of the episode, encouraging everyone to return to the pleasant task at hand. It would be the first of a series of spells, threatening Carolyn in other ways as well. Her energy was being depleted; resources challenged...nothing left in reserve. As her strength continued to diminish, as if the life force was being drained from her body, no one knew why, not even the family doctor.

***

Weathering their second winter fairly well the family again looked forward to spring. The girls were thriving in school in spite of an occasional harassing comment from fellow students who didn't even know them or what they had endured. Their real friends remained their friends and some were even brave enough to visit the house from time to time which took wind from the sails of their harshest critics. Guess it wasn't so bad after all if so and so would go.

There was a long period of calm; several months during which nothing of consequence occurred; nothing noteworthy...so peaceful and quiet Carolyn's fears began to subside. She'd gained a few pounds, looking healthier than she had in quite awhile. The house became dormant. Its doors stayed closed. The telephone did not lift up or float away from the receiver; the refrigerator was sealed tightly. No perceptible footsteps on stairs. The temperatures remained fairly constant. Had whatever it was wreaking havoc simply given up? Given in? Had they accepted the presence of mortals in their farmhouse? Hardly.

Easter marked the last attempt made to be part of the congregation at Saint Patrick's Church; the morning they'd discovered the depths of discrimination within the parish. Slightly late for Mass, they assembled in a pew at the back of the church. Heads turned. A few people sneered. An elderly woman seated in front of them, sporting a fresh bottle of blue hair, turned around in her seat then stared at the family, shamelessly leering at Carolyn. Turning toward the altar this presumably Christian woman growled out the hateful words: "Satan worshippers." When service was over, the Perrons left their church, for good; an awkward priest made mention to Roger, suggesting he seek another place of worship. Treated as if they were pagans who'd crawled in from the woods; rather than offering help, he too shunned them, based on rumors. Indiscreet, instead of fulfilling the role of spiritual advisor he chose to be judge and jury, tacitly expelling them from a parish with a few thoughtless words. Obviously confused about that separation of church and state thing, a chronic condition in Rhode Island, he was clearly unsure of what century it was, but at least no one got drowned in the lake or burned at the stake. In a cloistered community ignorance often abounds. There are those who wear it as a badge of honor.

***

After Carolyn nearly went up in flames, she altered her hearthstone habits, keeping some distance because there's warm and then there's hot!

So few of the paranormal anomalies occurred, she nearly forgot about the threat, even though their dog still refused to cross in front of the cellar door, regardless of any enticement. Complacency is dangerous leaving one woefully unprepared.

June rolled around, as gorgeous as their first at the farm. Old gardens were resplendent with fragrant blooms; an old apple tree full to bursting with pips. They were still enjoying the succulent fruit from the previous year when new buds appeared. Days were warm; children excited about a pending vacation. Their mother; perplexed about but grateful for this stark absence of activity, as the once omnipresent problems seemed to vanish; not just invisible: Gone. Perhaps it was safe to stay at the farm after all.

Remnants of previous encounters still lurking in the recesses of her mind, she was able to exert more control over the impulses by banishing imagery at will...whenever it reared its ugly head. Carolyn found it ironic; the closer she felt to God the more she abandoned religion, as mutually exclusive concepts: revelation. Refusing to seek another church she chose instead to go within, to explore her own spiritual Nature from the center of a more welcoming place. Resentful of Catholicism, a religion she'd been forced to embrace in context of marriage, compelled to convert by a mother-in-law who would never have it any other way, Carolyn felt liberated by tacit dismissal from the church. It excused participation altogether. This mother's prayers were reserved for her grand garden spot while her children practiced the presence bedside or in the woods they worshipped by Nature. Roger turned the soil; rows were planned and planted. Carolyn worked countless hours in its rich, black earth, relishing each moment while teaching her children how to plant and tend the garden as the circle of life; engaging imaginations. She taught her young to worship the cosmic secrecy of seed... absorbing its treasures by *cosmosis*: a new theory.

Soon thereafter Carolyn experienced the most horrifying encounter she'd ever have in the house. Roger was there; the couple went to bed as usual after the news and slept peacefully through the night. Just before dawn disturbance erupted in the bedroom; Carolyn awoke to a distinctly violent vibration in her headboard. Their bed was moving. Disoriented in the darkness, she could not understand what was happening until the room became frigid; a foul, familiar stench flooding the space, filling the air with something toxic: un-breathable. The woman could barely move her body. Her boggled mind was fully alert.

Swoosh! The room was suddenly ablaze with light; an ominous fiery glow, illuminated by flames on top of torches carried by the dead. As unbearable as it was to watch, Carolyn could not look away; her gaze transfixed on objects which meant certain death to her family. She expected her heart to stop. This would be their end. So many of them! Perhaps eight or ten spirits standing in the bedroom, each holding a wooden torch with something atop it resembling brittle broom straw, each fully engulfed in a ball of fire. There was nowhere to hide. The house was humming with a reverberation Carolyn could feel in her sternum. It was deafening, loud enough to muffle a mother's screaming if she'd had a voice to use but the woman knew she'd been muted. She yanked on Roger's hair, shoving him repeatedly, jerking the covers from a cold, limp lifeless body. Again, his back had become serrated, scratched beyond mortal recognition by the claws of a demon. A precise cadence emerged, established by the perpetual pounding of torches striking a wooden floor. This primitive syncopation echoed throughout the house. Their rhythmic chant; a torch song incantation uttered in tandem by spirits who didn't seem to notice the victim cowering in her bed which had been dragged to the center of the room. There they stood, gathered together in front of both windows, encircling the bottom of the bed, a small child posted at each side of the footboard. Carolyn's rapt attention remained focused on the fires; she listened to their words, what they had come to warn, only as an afterthought, as flames leapt toward the ceiling. Fire was her enemy… her greatest fear.

"Beseech thee, leave! Afore ye go, beware the flame, the fiery glow.
Was mistress once afore ye came and mistress here will be again.
Will drive ye out with fiery broom.
Will drive ye mad with death and gloom."

Mesmerized, as if suspended in some type of post-hypnotic trance, Carolyn stared at this group of lost souls, appearing as a coven of witches engaged in a ritualistic initiation ceremony. Their language spoken grew louder, shaking the structure, rattling the glass in its windows. The apparitions included two children, a young girl and an even smaller boy. It was difficult to distinguish their features due to the intense glow of flames; a haze, obscuring her view. She saw a few of them grinning, as if attending some festive event. An entity emerged from the crowd and began her approach. Carolyn recognized her as the one who'd come before, the same spirit who petrified Cynthia in her own bedroom. She began slowly floating forward as many other spirits continued chanting the incantation, impaling words into memory. Her movements were tediously slow and deliberately threatening; Carolyn could never mistake this entity's evil intentions. It was reading her mind. She had time enough to run if only her body would allow her to escape. She could not. In complete panic, during the fraction of a second she'd spent considering flight over fight, the bedroom door slammed shut, effectively trapping her inside. Flames leapt up from straw on top of torches, yet there was no heat, no smoke in the room. It burned like wildfire, lapping toward the ceiling with every brutal blow, each strike of the floorboards resulting in the torches being raised once again, in preparation for the next heavy blow. The drumbeat was relentless, deafening as they stood beside her and still, the demon advanced. An emaciated figure: no hands or feet, snapped at the neck; death by hanging, or so she presumed. This time though, it had a face as hideous as anything she had ever seen. The eyes were black: hollow sockets peering into her soul. The nose appeared to be rotting off. What remained of that grotesque appendage was nothing but a few pieces of decaying flesh dangling loosely beneath a mesh of cobwebs. Its horrid sight and smell caused Carolyn to wretch. Its mouth, drawing closer to her with each passing moment, uttered these threatening words with pleasure. As this wicked creature smiled, reveling in the terror expressed on the face of it victim, it revealed a set of chipped and jagged yellow teeth protruding from beneath thin, shriveled lips. Carolyn was certain she would lose her mind before she lost her life. None of the others even acknowledged her presence. The spirit crept and conjured around her bed as light of dawn began to break, illuminating a gruesome scene in lurid detail. Leaning over then in toward its victim, the apparition issued the threat it had come to deliver; with purpose and reason, a message received…loud and clear:

"Was mistress once afore ye came and mistress here will be again.
Will drive ye mad with death and gloom. Will drive ye into Satan's tomb.
Thus has been spoken, thus has been read.
Take leave of this place or ye too will be dead."

Suddenly the bedroom became flooded with thick acrid smoke; an ominous haze surrounding the emerging beast. Carolyn's aversion to this dark demon was so intense violent tremors began to erupt throughout her trembling body, traveling uncontrollably through her frozen limbs, responding to the jolt as if being struck by a bolt of lightning. She lurched forward in bed, inexplicably drawn toward that which repulsed her. As Carolyn was about to receive the kiss of death, the apparition slowly withdrew from her then began to encircle the bed again, floating toward her husband. Arriving by his side, it hovered over him for a moment then glanced upward, those black vacant orbs staring through her. Grinning again, baring its evil along with its fangs, the creature leered at a paralyzed woman while leaning in toward her man. Roger was the one; the recipient of a kiss bestowed. Carolyn closed her eyes. She prayed, speaking words in mind which would save both of them. "Lord, be with me now." Whispering the 23rd Psalm: "I will fear no evil…for Thou art with me." No question. It wanted her to observe what it was about to do to her husband.

The identical sound announcing their arrival, the combustion of flames in the bedroom, occurred once again. Carolyn waited, certainly knowing fire would consume them all. She could not move her mouth but instead, prayed from her soul. "Bless me Father. Take me if you must but spare my children. Dear God, I beg of you…have mercy on us all." Her prayers had been more potent than any words the woman had ever uttered in her lifetime; silently or aloud. Moments passed; she dared to open her eyes. Roger turned over, groaning in pain. She peered through tear-drenched eyes to behold the vacant bedroom. Flames extinguished. It was over. They were gone.

The bed was in the center of the room. Soft, warm breezes filtered through open windows, fluttering lace curtains. Rancid odor and bone-numbing chill began to dissipate in thin morning air. Carolyn wept as she never had before, sobbing uncontrollably, thanking God redundantly for sparing all their lives. It took some time for her to gather herself enough to climb out from beneath the covers. Certainly still in shock, stumbling toward the parlor, arriving at the loveseat she glanced toward the clock. Roger recently tinkered with the old family heirloom and had gotten it running again. The pendulum was still. Again, it had stopped, precisely as it had at her first visitation; at 5:15 a.m.

Though immediate peril had passed, Carolyn could not dispel its imagery. Wandering the house, upstairs to check on their children, they were all asleep and seemed undisturbed. She came downstairs then went into the kitchen to brew a strong pot of coffee. While standing alone in the pantry Roger walked up behind her. His presence so startled the woman, she dropped the container of coffee on the floor, spilling it everywhere. She instantly fell to her knees, distraught, attempting to reclaim what she could. He did not realize she was crying, far too concerned with pressing issues of his own.

"The goddamned bed is sitting in the middle of the bedroom again and my back hurts like hell!" He watched as her torso lurched, heaving in sorrowful spasms. "What the hell is wrong with you?" He offered to clean up the mess. Carolyn stood then looked directly at her husband. Streaked with tears of her ordeal, the expression on her face frightened him. Roger grabbed her in his arms then held her there until sobbing subsided. He knew something terrible happened. He had never seen his wife so upset. It took time for Carolyn to be able to speak. When she did it was to ask him to escort her into the bathroom. He thought she was sick but when the door was closed she took the man over to the mirror, exposing deep, bloody abrasions to the cold light of dawn. He too felt panic. She might have described the man as "white as a ghost" except Carolyn knew for certain the ghosts were not white at all. Shaken and stirred, Roger trembled, asking if she knew what was happening. Yes. She did know. While cleansing the wounds she told him a tale still omnipresent in her mind, the details of which were destined to remain part of her life for the rest of her life. At this moment Carolyn can close her eyes and conjure the image again, as if the manifestation had occurred only a moment before. Once something so extraordinary is witnessed, there is no escaping the memory.

Though Carolyn had been angry with her husband after the first visitation, falsely accusing him (albeit privately) of abandoning her to the forces of evil, powers that be; it was not the case this time. She felt compassionate instead; sympathetically tending wounds as he cringed in pain. He too was its victim; unconscious and unwitting. Though she couldn't comprehend what occurred, she realized it was not his fault. Reserving her blame for the spirits, she knew instinctively he had somehow been placed in the bubble, a suspended state of being, rendering him virtually helpless, not helpful at all...as if he was dead.

"I don't know who she thinks she is...some old flame who literally carries a torch, but she wants you, Roger. A *very* old flame by the looks of her! And the smell! She wants *you*, she wants our children and she wants me dead and gone from this house. There is no doubt about it. I *know* her intentions now."

No making light of it...not then...not ever. No need to draw an illustration this time 'round; Roger got the picture. He'd seen a reflection of the damage done in a mirror, as if needles gouged the skin off his back. He saw the shock and horror of the ordeal reflected in his wife's eyes. They felt pure empathy for one another. There was no one to blame, save the spirits haunting them in the night at light of dawn. She took him into the parlor, there to examine the clock, repeating the incantation line by ominous line. No doubt about it. His only reply uncharacteristically muted, almost prayerful: "Jesus Christ."

During the month preceding this episode, their electric bill quadrupled. The following month it was reduced to a fraction of the amount required to run a household and feed a demon. It took some time for the proper connections to be drawn between manifestations and their power source but finally, Carolyn realized the expenses incurred had nothing to do with leaving their lights on. The house was being utilized, as was its inhabitants; its main energy supplies being routinely circumvented with reason, for nefarious purposes. After this, the most dramatic of manifestations, the energy drain on their house abruptly ceased. Spirit surge accomplished; they required respite and replenishment.

"The countenance is the portrait of the soul, and the eyes mark its intentions."
Marcus Tullius Cicero

fire and brimstone

There was a subtle vacancy, a longing in the child. She needed to believe in God, to feel some kind of spiritual connection; something more than prayers by moonlight: Contact. Andrea began seeking the truth about life and death from a young age and this deep craving for knowledge grew along with her. By fourteen she was attending church sporadically, whenever she could get a ride, she would go on her own. By fifteen, she was singing and playing guitar in the choir. Confirmation classes began. She had taken the plunge, attending several sessions just prior to being summarily dismissed from Saint Patrick's Church in Harrisville, Rhode Island. Thank God!

This youngster was a misfit from the start. She never felt any true sense of belonging but wanted to attend, to be wherever her two closest friends were, so she went where they worshipped; back to Saint Patrick's, there to receive formal instruction in creed, doctrine and dogma of the holy Roman Catholic Church. Confirmation classes were supposed to be a type of school of **higher** learning; ironically, held in the parish basement every Wednesday evening. She attended the sessions for three weeks; until her intellect interceded. Once her sense and sensibilities were offended, she returned the favor in kind.

Raymond Perreault and Timothy Robidoux were a tremendous influence in Andrea's life and remain so decades later. Both are brilliant. They met on her first day of school, as desks were reassigned to accommodate a new student. They met alphabetically; a perfect metaphor to describe their shared love of literature. Timothy sat directly behind, Raymond in front: wedged together as they were in room B-3 of Burrillville Junior-Senior High School. It was to be her greatest blessing; a gift. Their friendships generated spontaneously in the form of cerebral combustion. She has treasured that fire they set in her soul ever since. With so much in common, the three of them soon began spending a great deal of time together outside of their classroom.

Tim played trombone in the band; Andrea, flute. Raymond convinced her to become involved with him in Poetry Workshop. They attended nearly every class together and were often involved in projects as a team. The odd triptych of personalities proved a wonderful blend, providing quantum leaps in consciousness as they learned what they shared and shared what they learned. During the time of "The Mod Squad" they were the original Geek Squad, all but inseparable. Both young gentlemen were frequent visitors to the farm, though she'd spent time at their homes as well, and all three families integrated with a delightful ease. When the time came for two former altar boys to make their pledge to the church in Confirmation, she was cordially invited to join them on the spiritual journey; an ill-considered decision they would all soon come to regret.

As both had been spared any altercations with spirits, it was not a topic for conversation. They did not know her family had a strange reputation in town or, for that matter, within the church. Neither of them was prone to gossiping nor tolerant of those who did. They had accepted Andrea on her own merits, without prejudice. Timmy and Ray were mature, open-minded, well-adjusted individuals who came from loving homes. Their parents welcomed Andrea, embracing her as a member of their family; welcome respite for a young lady whose tumultuous life frequently required a discreet escape. Faith Perreault was a fabulous cook and Lorraine Robidoux had a concoction brewing in her glass ginger jar on the kitchen counter, known to all as Brandied Fruit Sauce; a delicacy when drizzled over a bowl of French vanilla ice cream. Access to it was based on threats made / promises kept; good, you get some…bad, you don't…how she'd kept her five rambunctious boys in check. Andrea realized how fortunate she was to know such remarkable people. Her extended family provided kindness and support, a sense of normalcy for a child whose home life was anything but… and nobody ever mentioned anything about what they might have heard around town. Even if they had known the reputation of the farmhouse and the family who dwelled within it they would never abandon a friend or pass a harsh judgment upon the Perrons. Heads turned when Andrea entered their church basement. There she sat, wedged between two altar boys whose families were prominent members of the church and their community. All three of the youngsters felt the scrutiny. Parents talk. Kids listen.

The first couple of sessions were designed as a refresher course, reiterating much of what Andrea already learned of the Catholic religion, including the structure of its hierarchy: Pope, cardinals, bishops, separate (though entirely unequal) priests and nuns, Mass, Immaculate Conception of Mother Mary, the saints, the Rosary and the Stations of the Cross. The third class began and presumably ended with the subject of **SIN**, concluding about an hour earlier than anticipated for Andrea. As the students entered the hall they saw a large reversible chalkboard boldly listing **The Ten Commandments**. On the other side, beginning with Original Sin, then listed a breakdown of **all** other sins, both mortal and venial, in order of significance. As this lesson progressed the students listened attentively, never questioning their ongoing indoctrination. The room became stiflingly hot, as if Satan himself was present; undoubtedly due to the fire and brimstone, a frequent mentioning of Hell and Damnation. Fear. Guilt. Sin. Shame and more shame. Andrea found herself becoming an increasingly uncomfortable participant, disapproving of the priest's treatment of subject matter. He, too, appeared to be uncomfortable, though not for the same reasons. It was as if he had drawn the short straw and had to be the one to impart information on issues he did not care to discuss. Yet there he was, up on the podium, stoically stiff, talking to a group of teens who longed to be anywhere other than where they were on a Wednesday evening. Even though the floor remained open to questions for the duration, not a single hand went in the air until the precocious young lady heard something she found utterly unacceptable. It was time to mount her challenge, which would culminate in confrontation. Up went the hand. Down went two friends low into their seats, undoubtedly wanting to crawl behind or hide beneath metal folding chairs.

Out of character for Andrea, the girl was not one to instigate or antagonize anybody, especially an elder or any authority figure. However, she believed this challenge was warranted. She asked for an explanation of "Solitary Sin". Ray and Tim were mortified. Crouching down on either side of the culprit, it was the only way to avoid detection…or guilt by association. A penetrating white hot glare: the eyes of a priest spoke to what he obviously considered an inappropriate comment. He refused to answer her question as posed. Andrea pressed onward, perched at the edge of her seat in anxious anticipation of an answer she already knew. Suddenly, the priest had the rapt attention of their entire classroom. His face began to redden and swell, as if he'd been hit with a flame-thrower; a voice steadily rising with his blood pressure. Throughout this altercation he refused to refer to the word "masturbation". Unimpressed, Andrea asked him why sex of any kind was such a taboo issue in the church; why married couples could not practice birth control and were only allowed to envision procreation while engaged in sexual activity. She wanted to know why he was reluctant to openly discuss it in a room filled with adolescents at a critical time in their physical and emotional development. He became angry and even more embarrassed while she continued her commentary unabated. Since sex seemed to be a topic by proxy, Andrea wanted to discuss abortion and homosexuality as well as celibacy and the ecclesiastical elevation of men as juxtaposed to their overt subjugation of women, dispossessed of any real authority or position in the Catholic Church, as if suffering some diminished capacity to spread the word of God; based not on heart or mind but genitalia. A flustered priest lost his temper, accusing Andrea of deliberately interfering with his lesson then insisted the tenacious teenager leave class immediately. She did so, never to return. It was a long walk home on a frigid spring night. She took every step wondering if friends would be as angry as their priest or forgiving of her; equally fearful of a reaction she'd receive from her parents. It was wasted worry…on both counts. Mom was upset because she had not been called for a ride home; distressed her eldest daughter had walked so far, alone in the dark. Carolyn did not consider the questions she had posed to be disrespectful. Instead, she found them thoughtful and erudite, as did her two Catholic friends. "Told you so" was her mother's frame of reference; having forewarned a youngster anxious to establish an association with the church, knowing she might not like what she heard.

About a week later a terse letter arrived from the bishop of the

Archdiocese of Providence: message well-received. Carolyn informed her eldest she was no longer welcomed to participate in Confirmation. Class dismissed! Andrea was not considered to be *a good fit*, finding fault with principle tenets of the church. Mother reassured daughter of her worth and place though she always privately doubted it would ultimately be inside an oak pew. The two spoke at length about faith and freedom of religion. Carolyn never did try to channel her children in any specific direction; she was not that kind of indoctrinating influence. Rather, she encouraged them to explore the world as they found it, as each intrepid spirit endeavored to find her own way along the path of life.

Though she perceived it as rejection, Andrea had no intention of returning to the church. She'd accepted the fact that she was a misfit, gratefully so. Her vision of a higher power, the concept of God she had already developed was far more expansive than any religion she knew which existed on the planet. A conscious decision made to learn more, to study God; thus began a lifelong fascination with philosophy. Andrea would soon discover immersing oneself in religious study does not necessarily bring one closer to God. Truth be told; it prompted more doubts, which is, in itself, an avenue toward faithfulness. It was then she found the metaphysical poets; transcendentalism was appealing. **Emerson's Essays**, Thoreau's **Walden** and Whitman's **Leaves of Grass** were three fine volumes commanding her attention. These thinkers seemed to find solace in concert with Nature. A reverence and respect they'd bestowed upon the natural world captivated the youngster, an element of their literature to which she could wholly relate; the worship of Nature as God. During this period of rapid growth, an occasional pause for reflection was called for as a Natural conversion began; transformation, turning her away from organized religion and into the woods. She came to consider religion incompatible with common sense and sensibilities. Seeking inspiration, she'd gone to the forest, looking down, then up. Locating a proper niche; perhaps she was a pagan.

The recovering Catholic was not offended by the dismissal, knowing in her heart and mind she did not belong there in the first place. Her concept of God was unrestricted; not based on the limitations imposed by doctrine or dogma. Essentially, it was bigger than they could imagine, continually evolving as a perception of power as being; God as infinite mind. Not harsh or judgmental in application of Natural law; not cruel or exclusive; no intolerance allowed. A not-so-subtle predisposition toward natural science was taking root in her consciousness. The notion of Original Sin was, in particular, pure absurdity: anathema to the young lady who knew the difference between good and evil, right and wrong; darkness and light. Self-righteously policing her behavior; recognizing it as a matter of personal responsibility, the idea of being *born* in sin was idiotic. Andrea did not rely upon a higher authority. She *was* a higher authority; a living manifestation of God-consciousness. Ultimately, she alone would determine how best to live her life. Neither Holy Ghost nor dastardly demon had the right to interfere or intervene in a supremely personal process.

The spirits were not culpable in any conceivable way; not even a rumor or innuendo of their existence appears to have factored into a decision made by a bishop to expel her from the Catholic Church. Innate intellectual curiosity was quite enough to do the trick. Hallelujah! Praise the Lord!

"Christian fundamentalism: the doctrine that there is an absolutely powerful, infinitely knowledgeable, universe spanning entity that is deeply and personally concerned about my sex life."
Andrew Lias

trial by fire

"The most powerful weapon on earth is the human soul on fire."
Ferdinand Foch

Curled up into a ball at the center of the loveseat, knees to chin, a wounded woman gazed pensively into the fireplace, studying the sights and sounds of flames. Fire: A beautiful, powerful force of Nature; an unparalleled source of fear. It had become a test of wills: trials and tribulations to the infinite power. Carolyn closed her eyes and she prayed, hoping faith alone would sustain her through an ordeal; intangible, invisible faith. It was all she had left to rely on, all she had to call upon in the dark of night; this...and her own restless spirit.

The clock above her head remained silent, its slender tendrils fixed in place at 5:15 a.m. The timepiece seemed destined only for display, hanging in their house as vintage artwork; a legacy piece, otherwise abandoned, as if a license to claim what it all but demanded was bestowed by right (or rite) of passage. An evil presence marking her moment, from then on it remained undisturbed, eerily absent its chiming; at rest, set at precisely the time it had **twice** chosen. (Or at an hour chosen for it; a timely reminder: **all of them** are always there.) Perhaps if this clock was left alone, unwound and unprovoked in its singular position, such a passive acknowledgement might insure the absence of future manifestations. A purely superstitious notion was enough to foster a renewed sense of hopelessness in the woman; she was lost in dark shadows of fear and despair; terror illuminated by the light of torches. She stared for some time at the face of the elegant timepiece, wondering...what if it were left untouched; left to keep the time it covets: in suspended animation...appearing to be dead.

Returning to the hearthstone of a fireplace, its imagery swirling in her mind as Carolyn gazed upon the feral flames, she became transfixed by its power. Lapping at sides of logs like a wild animal licking its lips after the kill; after a brutal slaughter of something smaller than itself, something helpless locked in its jaws, crackling sounds were like its bones being crushed alive by a grip precluding all struggle, haunting the air she breathed; those invisible currents on which sound travels. Piles of gray to ghostly ashes mounded into corners, flickering with sparks of light, embers eager to reignite, as would any life on the verge of extinction, anxious to survive. Its glow resembled melting gold, glistening in the light of its former existence, always able to be rekindled, as if at will, blown back to life with the wisp of one solitary breath. Fire finds a way to persevere, much like the Phoenix reborn from the ashes of itself. She closed her eyes and saw again the vision of torches fully engulfed in flames; no smoke. She saw the face of evil illuminated by an unholy light. She heard threatening words: "Was mistress once afore ye came and mistress here will be again." Carolyn prayed: "The Lord is my shepherd…I shall not want…He maketh me to lie down in green pastures… leadeth me beside still waters. He restoreth my soul. Yea, though I walk through the valley of the shadow of death, I will fear no evil for Thou art with me. Amen." Death's prayer in life.

Returning to the loveseat, she buried her face in the blanket. Suddenly, the heavy pendulum of their clock, a timepiece possessed, began to swing again. Its docile rocking restored, the lilting sound sang Carolyn to sleep, as it had done so many nights of her life. She did not twist around to inspect it nor did she seek an explanation for what she'd instantly perceived to be a benevolent gesture; a prayer acknowledged then answered. Carolyn crawled beneath the quilt and bowed her head in gratitude. On this night, her faith took a quantum leap, touched as she was by a force more powerful than anything manifesting in her home. She knew it was there; a holy protective influence always came when called, perhaps because it was always there, as well, as omnipresent as the spirits. Had the ghosts been the *real* gift? Was their presence a conduit to Carolyn's burgeoning faith? Would she have discovered her beliefs without them to guide her along a journey to spiritual enlightenment? She wondered.

In time, the antique clock would stop again, at precisely 5:15 a.m. The next hiatus would prove to be its final pause for reflection in an old farmhouse. The timepiece remained quiet from then on, for the duration of its tenure. Its silence was deafening to those so familiar with its song. As the years passed, Carolyn studied its peculiar face, wondering why it would not sing anymore. It was left alone, hardly touched, displayed only as vintage artwork on a wall. The finely-crafted timepiece was not dead, merely dormant. In time the clock would sing again, once relocated to another wall entirely, in another time and place. It would not chime again until it was dwelling in a land far, far away.

"Time is the substance from which I am made. Time is a river which carries me along, but I am the river; it is a tiger that devours me, but I am the tiger; it is a fire that consumes me, but I am the fire."
Jorge Luis Borges

~ **tick tock time stands still** ~

lady bug

"Let the fear of danger be a spur to prevent it;
he that fears not, gives advantage to the danger."
Francis Quarles

Mortal fear is visceral; a twisted gut wrenching clenched jawbone grinding sensation which consumes the soul from within. Fear has a life of its own. It lives vicariously through those who'll provide it safe passage; a harbor in any given storm. The spawn of evil, it lurks in consciousness, beyond the shadow of a doubt, ready to spring forth into action, to make its vile presence known at a moment's notice. It does not require a specific spark to reignite. Merely considering a concept in mind can rekindle it, as if on a whim, with a breath of fresh air blown beneath the grate of its unholy pyre.

So it was with Carolyn the day she drove into their village to do something as innocuous as buying two loaves of bread and a gallon of milk, all she had enough money on hand to purchase until Roger came home again. Perhaps it had been the trigger, what prompted a panic attack. Feast or Famine: a tough way to live, in perpetual fear of the unknown quantity of money available to properly care for her family. This was her constant burden; a permanent state of mind now known in the vernacular as a poverty consciousness. How many times she had rolled loose change, grateful she'd had it to roll, wedged as she was between the proverbial rock and a hard place to live. But why the sudden sense of dread? It was a beautiful morning, there was an ample supply of gas in her tank and a meager purchase had been made with change to spare; good omens all around: a favorable circumstance which would ordinarily be cause for celebration! So where was this terrible trepidation coming from and why?

On her way home, meandering along Round Top Road, Carolyn was quite startled; struck by the inexplicable urgency seemingly coming from nowhere and everywhere simultaneously. As she had done many times, she dismissed it from her thoughts: "Don't bug me!" A gut feeling persisted, in spite of her normally successful approach to resolving such problems.

Again, knocking at the door of her consciousness, attempting to make entry, Carolyn implored it to go far, far away…all the way back to the devil. The hellish image began to form. Thus began a quarrel raging inside her mind. Intuition sounding the alarm, the woman could feel her foot, as if it were unattached from the rest of her body, pressing pedal-to-the metal against the gas. This was that moment; a shadow of a doubt. It was when she least trusted her own instincts because of a fear so powerful it altered her behavior, forcing her to take action against her better judgment. Faster she went…at light speed…to get to her children.

A nursery rhyme traveling the ether had lodged in her brain. She'd listened:

"Lady bug, lady bug, fly away home.
Your house is on fire, your children all alone."

Where the hell did that come from? Hell, presumably. It was not as if one of those delicate creatures had been trapped on the dashboard, reminding her of the limerick. This poetry was potent. Best to fly away home. Better safe than sorry! The imagery haunting her was automatically suspect because its origin was likely spawned from the encounters she'd had with a spirit who enjoyed tormenting the woman with fire. Her children *were* home alone: Danger! Had she been able to truly trust adept protective instincts, they alone would have told her that the girls were fine and everything was as she left it when she left but it was not to be. Instead, she raced up the road; a calculated risk taken as she floored the pedal and pressed the engine into service. They had come too close to disaster too many times in that house already, and she was not going to relax and dismiss this persistent and perilous notion: better to risk feeling foolish when she arrived…a small price to pay for being wrong…being right was something wicked she simply could not tolerate in mind and so she sped up, revving her mental engine into high gear, along with her automobile: Try to avoid becoming nervous wreckage in the process! Invading thoughts were impairing her sense of direction; knowing the way, yet feeling confused by familiar surroundings, trying to gauge where she was along the rural route. In panic; mortal fear taking its toll on the road of life at an intersection of death. Critically important; imperative she get home as fast as possible…but what if this was a part of the plan? As a ploy to compel her to drive too fast? Charge! Paranoia strikes deep…it was creeping through her mind, in every cell of her being. "Fear is that little darkroom where negatives are developed." (Michael Pritchard) Carolyn's fears were being used against her, no matter the source, which was never actually established. Point of origin was not the point at all. When the niggling little voice speaks it's best to listen; *better safe than sorry* assuming an entirely new meaning. An urgent sense identified, it was always best to err on the safer side of self-doubt. That is what she told herself as she crested the top of the driveway to see all of her children playing in their yard, right where she left them. She had only been gone a few minutes yet returned to them feeling somehow altered by an absence. Having questioned her sense of direction along that intrepid journey, she looked up, getting her bearings and giving thanks to the over-riding power which got her there. Perronoid?

"I do not believe in a fate that falls on men however they act;
but I do believe in a fate that falls on man unless they act."
G. K. Chesterton

burnin' down the house

"Fate is nothing but the deeds committed in a prior state of existence."
Ralph Waldo Emerson

The inclusion of these mysterious episodes may not in fact, be warranted. It could be they were not supernatural in origin, but were instead several rather strange flukes of fate; bitter but random happenstance. It's impossible for the family to determine if the odd incidents were the result of a nefarious force at work or blessings in disguise. Perhaps both apply. Nobody in this life can be certain. However, in every case, something frightening occurred: Dangerous! Whether natural or supernatural at its source it certainly did appear as if there was someone benevolent in Nature intervening on their behalf to preserve an ancient farmhouse and protect the family living within its clapboard walls.

***

Their second winter proved to be as brutal as the first. *"Ya get used to it."* Not so. Everybody in the family heard the phrase somewhere in their travels on a consistent basis. It was always snowing; whether a lot or weather a little, its presence was *Omni* in Nature. Frozen ground never had a chance to thaw or get all filthy dirty before the next layer arrived, the pristine cover of winter whiteness obscuring previous blemishes. As the fireplace raged on in protest, the family gathered to absorb whatever warmth could be generated from that simple hole in the wall; its smoke stack doing double-duty, and then some. It seemed, at times, as if most of the precious heat was being swept up then out the chimney...carried by the winter wind to places and spaces far, far away.

During the previous autumn, after a full summer of nesting and perching no one noticed, the chimney had become littered with debris. One chilly night in September Roger decided it was time to fire her up! A few pieces of kindling were ablaze in moments. Suddenly, the lining of a chimney ignited in a flash. This powerful force, a rush of fire erupted into an inferno; a chimney fire so spectacular, it literally stopped passing traffic.

The chimney burst into flames with such fury it sounded like a distant, muffled explosion. "Whoosh!" Bird nests began falling onto the flames, each fully engaged with the furious burn. Engulfed, crackling and hissing; tiny, meticulously twisted fragments of dry timber sprinkled the landscape with flecks of fire. It was twilight. Roger flew outside to examine the extent of the damage occurring. Carolyn propped the screen in place then ran for the hose behind the house, shouting at everybody to *get out!* It was a frantic few minutes, everyone scrambling to evacuate the premises, children directed to follow their parents in one direction or another. The spitting, spewing ashes and embers were rapidly escaping their chimney, bouncing off the roof then scattering on the lawn, producing a vivid display: a frightfully cruel intermingling of darkness and light. Fire in the chimney!

Moments past sunset, lingering colors of daylight created a backdrop for an awful event. Wildfire: lapping at chimney walls like the flaming tongue of a trapped dragon, captive; fighting for release. A potential for disaster was real. Fire flailed through every orifice of a solid metal topper which was supposed to prevent such occurrences. Roger's lapse in judgment could have resulted in dire consequences for a family; his nearly tragic mistake was in neglecting to call a chimney sweep, logic based on time in service. It had not been long since the fireplace had last been in relatively constant use; not enough time having lapsed for the edifice to require such tending. He was wrong.

A thick smoke drew a gathering of neighbors from near and far, like Indian signals summoning the tribe together. Everyone watched as the fire raged on; curious onlookers were at once mesmerized and terrified, as was the family whose home was in jeopardy. By the time the trucks arrived from the village, it had nearly burned itself out. The chief said: "Let it burn." He'd said water would only damage the stone and the house. Though he didn't chastise Roger for this oversight, a gentleman farmer's agreement, he did mention how *very lucky* they were. The house had been in serious danger; an emergency posed by the sheer fact that it was a two hundred and fifty year old tinderbox.

***

That incident was not the only time their house was in jeopardy. Roger and Carolyn asked two friends of the family, a married couple, to come stay for a few days while they traveled to New York City, there to market their wares at a trade show. Though they did not mention anything to Lois and Joe about unusual *activity* in their house, not wanting to scare away these prospective babysitters, they were each spooked by this place in the country, nonetheless. However, nothing supernatural occurred over the course of a weeklong stay, unless of course one considers a miracle to be a paranormal event. There was only one anomaly...frightening enough to qualify as spiritually significant.

Joe was a city boy. He did not know much about building a fire but decided to set flames aglow in spite of his ignorance on the subject. He'd stacked the fireplace with several huge logs, placing them on top of an enormous pile of dried kindling. Ignition was virtually instantaneous. The blaze raged almost out-of-control, creating a white heat, far too intense to approach. Everyone remained silent. The snapping of crackling wood, a high-pitched hissing was an alarm: Danger. Andrea monitored from a safe distance in the dining room. She waited for more than an hour, watching it burn itself out, ever mindful of where her sisters were inside the house, an evacuation plan rumbling around in her mind, by necessity. When the wood finally simmered down, a palpable sense of panic at last subsided, replaced with relief. Fear and trepidation had been running rampant through the vulnerable old farmhouse. These children remembered well the terrible threat of watching a chimney fire burn.

Hours passed. Long after the flames were extinguished, the house began to quickly fill with dark, acrid smoke. Lois and Joe were mortified. He raced to the telephone. She ushered all the girls out their kitchen door. It had become bitterly frigid outside, below freezing; she'd sent them to wait inside the car. Sirens blared in the distance. All the girls fixed a frozen gaze on their house, observing through foggy glass steamed over with anxiety, as two fire trucks flew down the driveway, into their yard. They clung together, huddled in the car as each spoke of wishing mom and dad would come home…immediately. It was a frantic scene; firemen running in and out, smoke billowing through it as open doors and windows vented voluminous waves of smoke a brisk wind carried into the sky. When this crisis finally passed everyone involved with the rescue remarked about the great good fortune of salvaging the farmhouse. According to those in the know, regarding the true force of fire, it had been a miracle. As so much wind rushed through a structure from so many different directions, the fire chief was stymied that the flow had not actually caused its ruinous demise by fanning a few sparks into flames. He stated rather bluntly: "This house should have burned to the ground." The man shook his head.

Within minutes the source of the problem was located; threat extinguished. Apparently the earlier fire had become so hot, it fractured a stone beneath the grate, allowing ashes and embers to slip through a crack, igniting an exposed timber beneath it; an ancient beam smoldering in the cellar. It glowed; a red, ominous hue. When firemen finally reached it they knew the slightest breeze would have set it ablaze, erupting into a disaster: spontaneous combustion.

Those who came to help doused it just in time. Roger returned to discover the damage and had no choice but to replace the heavily compromised beam as well as the cracked stone inside the fireplace. There was nobody to blame. Everyone concerned considered this incident a blessing in disguise. The base of their fireplace was as old as the house and it was susceptible to cracking at any time. Had it happened during the night or while their family was outside, away from the house, perhaps off enjoying another winter sledding session, there would have been no way to salvage the house. The elemental power of fire is as frightening as it is comforting…both a blessing and a curse.

***

Andrea was home alone, working on a school project. All of her papers and materials were sprawled across their dining room table. She was about fifteen at the time. The rest of her family was off on a festive excursion, a trip to the local bakery down in the village; a favorite haunt. Far too devoted a student, she preferred the quiet (a rarity in such a crowded household) to a doughnut, especially since something special was bound to later come her way. While hovering over a muddled mass of notes begging to be organized, she detected an odd scent in the air. At first Andrea thought she might be about to receive a visitor as the air would often become damp and acrid just prior to a spectral show, something she'd accepted long before. *That* she was prepared for...

But it was not that type of odor. In fact, it was something more threatening. The metallic smell triggered her internal alarms. She knew it was something serious. The house began filling with a gauze-white smoke. She yanked open the windows in the room then ran into the kitchen. As she'd passed the cellar door, it was obvious from billowing smoke squeezing itself through cracks in the wood: the cellar hole was at its source. It was the most frightened she had ever been in her life. Seizing the telephone, placing the receiver to her ear as she dialed, Andrea was petrified to discover there was no dial tone present. Their phone line was dead. Dread instantly transformed into a panic-stricken attack. The telephone was not working and there was fire in the hole.

Plowing out the door, the youngster ran as hard as she'd ever run; knowing time was of the essence. It was critical she get to someone fast, someone with a phone. The house was secluded and the neighborhood was so in name only. At that time, there were a few neighbors particularly close by. Running to the closest house, nobody was there. God! She moved on, heart pounding out of her chest. Tears began pouring as she realized how far away the next house was; and what if no one was there? As she cried it became harder to breathe, harder to see. The aroma of rotting leaves was all she could detect in autumn. The earth was wet beneath her feet; she slid and fell on slick leaves. Moving into the middle of the road, Andrea focused all of her attention on the double yellow line, unable to bear thinking about what might be happening to their house. There was very little traffic on Round Top Road during those days; it was safe enough to race head down, for speed. She finally found her way to Mrs. Dublin's door. Collapsing in a distant neighbor's open arms, trembling and exhausted, she begged for help. Barely able to breathe, let alone speak, the woman placed the distraught child into a chair; a sip of cold water cleared her throat. She uttered only one word: Fire! Instantly on the telephone, Mrs. Dublin summoned assistance. She and her husband dashed to their car with the terrified teenager in tow. It required far less time to drive the mile than it had taken to sprint the same distance. Sirens were not far behind them.

The farmhouse was filled with white-to-yellow smoke. Mr. Dublin insisted the ladies remain outside while he went inside the perilous structure. Having identified the problem before the firemen arrived; he took them directly into the cellar, where he'd discovered the boiler had run dry. It took hours for the house to clear once the boiler was shut down. The fire chief shook his head, knowing how close this family had come to losing their house...again. Three times over three years. A pattern was emerging. It seemed the element of fire and this particular home were inextricably linked.

The rest of her family pulled into the driveway directly behind the red fire engine. One can only imagine how they must have reacted to the sight. Roger leapt from their car then ran to his eldest daughter, anxious to know what had occurred and if she was all right. Her brief explanation of events sent him in search of the fire chief, who had returned to the cellar. Roger caught up with him and saw for himself how close they had come to complete destruction of their property. It was chilling. The telephone wires were literally fused to the beam overhead, bonding together with the other electrical wires nearby. The intense heat emanating from a broken boiler system melted every wire in its wake, rendering useless the telephone in a house gone entirely dark, due to a piece of malfunctioning equipment on the verge of exploding. Roger stood paralyzed, staring at the scene; a potential disaster mercifully circumvented.

Though the crisis was averted, fallout was extensive; serious damage done. Roger would soon have his hands filled with bills though he didn't complain. There was nobody to blame. Roger knew how this could have gone, how the inflammatory scenario might have played out without the intervention of his daughter and their newest family friends. With sincerest thanks extended, the couple sent the neighbors home. Andrea remained in the back seat of the car, trying to regain her composure. Cynthia sidled up beside her, wiping tears from her biggest sister's eyes; she saw how upsetting the ordeal had been and offered to help with the distraction of a sweet treat, a kind gesture of support. Cindy placed her jelly doughnut in Andrea's hands, the damp napkin first.

"Here, Annie. I got the *best* one in the case! You can have it. It'll make you feel better. Daddy said you should be proud! He said *you* saved our house!" Ah, comfort food...the beginning of a dangerous trend. Andrea took a deep breath, accepting the tasty morsel, a special gift from an even sweeter sister. They shared the doughnut, though Andrea's portion did not have far to travel to reach its intended destination, as her stomach was still in her throat.

"Is it eradicating evil? Or are we like children, left alone in the house at night, who light candle after candle to keep away the darkness. We don't see that the darkness has a purpose – though we may not understand it – and so, in our terror, we end up burning down the house!"
Margaret Weis

feet to the fire

"A spark neglected makes a mighty fire."
Robert Herrick

Carolyn stood too close to the flames. It seemed as if she was begging for a disaster or perhaps secretly wishing the pink fuzzy slippers dead. Sometimes the smell of singed polyester, mixed with the distinct odor of melting rubber, would indicate a potential problem. In spite of the repeated warnings from a concerned family she would tempt fate unconsciously, coming within inches of white-hot embers. Had she been barefoot, it would have blistered delicate skin. Instead, fire shriveled the protective slippers, crinkling the only barrier between her toes and a blatant health hazard. On a few different occasions it posed a real danger. Her children wondered if she could feel the heat at all. It was obvious their mother was otherwise preoccupied; lost in thought of word or deed whenever these frighteningly close encounters occurred. Unaware of her surroundings, there was a vacancy in her stare, startled as someone pulled her away from the flames. In no way deliberate on her part, not a death wish, whenever it happened she was distant; not fully present. It happened several times…too close to the flames…too far away to notice.

How could it be, Carolyn had no sense of danger; no sensation at all while standing on the hearthstone, on the verge of combustion? What was it about a fireplace which produced this ethereal affect, soliciting then deflecting her attention away from what she should have been watching most attentively? There were times when she kept a safe distance, enjoying its glowing warmth along with the rest of her family. Then there were times when she'd virtually covet the flames, hovering above them; moments when she would claim to be cold to the bone; cold as death. Huddling up, feet to the fire, she could not get warm, no matter how close she'd draw her shivering torso to the inferno. Carolyn was not accountable for this behavior; she was a vehicle for it.

The fire was a life force, sending cryptic messages from within its flames. It smoked and spoke by hissing out its own language, never the same twice. Numerous manifestations occurred on the slab of cold granite beside a metal grate, logs lapped at by flames licking its lips to escape.

The hearthstone was a magnet: a special place, the specific portal where dimensions intermingled. Over the years in the house it proved to be the point of passage. Apparitions made an entrance there and its blue light bent the established laws of physics: visions and visitations...a point of grand entrance for the stars of the show.

The mistress of the house was tired and overwrought one night. It had been long, hard labor cutting wood all afternoon. Everyone was tired. Most of the family was in the parlor as Carolyn entered, fresh from the steaming shower. Emerging from her bedroom, she passed by her husband, feet dangling from the loveseat; her deliberately antagonistic gesture startling the dozing soul, a single swat from the belt of her robe. "It's your turn." Crossing directly to the fireplace, she dried her hair beside an open flame. After a few minutes, while leaning forward to rewrap her flowing locks in the towel, she suddenly lost consciousness and crumbled to the floor, landing in a pile on the hearthstone. The sound of impact was so alarming, the sleepy man sprung from his prone position before anyone else had a chance to react. He leapt over his children like a terrified gazelle evading a pursuer, running for its life on the Serengeti Plain. A stunning achievement: instantaneous, heroic rescue as an act of love. Carolyn's feet were on fire.

Defying gravity, he was beside her with a bounce from sofa to hearthstone. A single yank had pulled her feet from the slippers, fully engulfed in flames. Cradled in his arms, he carried her away from danger while Andrea ran for a cool washcloth to place on her forehead. The putrid odor of melting polyester fibers and rubber permeated the air. While the girls rapidly opened doors and windows, Roger closely examined his wife. She had escaped unscathed from an ordeal with a potential to claim her, had circumstances been different, had she been home alone. It was no time to chastise her for standing so close, too close to the fire. It was no time for any kind of reprisal. Instead, her children gathered around to welcome her back to them. Hearts raced. Hands trembled. A few fearful tears were shed that night...the fear of what could have been.

Remarkably, both her feet were uninjured, not burned at all. Roger's quick actions spared her the horrible pain of blistered skin. As Carolyn was able to speak again, she did so by gratefully acknowledging his efforts on her behalf. The girls described those few tense moments to their mother, explaining how daddy had sprung into action. Roger seemed embarrassed by all their praise, disguising it with the devilish grin he kept in reserve for awkward emotional interludes. Playfully accusing his wife of hating those damn Santa slippers enough to set them on fire, while she was wearing them…she finally smiled. A crisis averted…this time. She would have to be more careful.

Carolyn continued to suffer from the fainting spells. It was not an isolated incident. This persistent dilemma worsened over time. Within several weeks Roger would be, once again, plucking his wife from the jaws of a fiery death. They were home alone. She collapsed in a pile on the hearthstone and both of her legs folded into the open flames. A pair of heavy denim jeans bought her husband time enough to snuff out the fire; another disconcerting episode, to say the least. His fears coupled with frustrations; he had legitimate concerns. What if he had not been home that morning? But he was…and used this near tragic opportunity to confront the severity of the situation; time to address the issue…to acknowledge the inherent dangers to heart, hearth and home. It was time to resolve the dilemma. He had his wife's attention. He'd saved her life, and she knew it. Carolyn felt increasingly weak and vulnerable; frightened again by what might have been.

Roger insisted and Carolyn agreed to visit another doctor. There had to be an explanation, some remedy for a condition which became life threatening. In time they would discover the truth; a mystery more than medical in nature. The will of another was being exerted upon this mistress of the house, with malice and forethought...with deliberate intent: A bitch from hell.

Her light was being excised and extinguished. Carolyn began entering the realm she could not comprehend and was therefore unable to fight its entry. Flight was no longer an option, no fight left in her; there was nowhere to run, not a peaceful place to hide away from herself. The woman was beginning to experience an *oppression* imposed, inevitably leading her where she did not want to go, leading her to experience the terrifying presence of another in her consciousness. It was the presence of a spirit so cold she could not get warm. Ultimately, Carolyn would begin to see the world through the evil eyes of an intruding soul and come to know the unbearable darkness of being.

"If you follow reason far enough it always leads to conclusions that are contrary to reason."
Samuel Butler

bats!

There were thousands of them. Their property was littered with bats; in the barn and in the trees; amazing displays at twilight. Darting frantically across the yard, diving and flirting with the horizon as the sky turned shades of rose and lavender; they were a wonder to behold. Mosquitoes were never really a problem, even though they grew to approximately the size of these predators themselves, destined to be meals for hoards of brown bats dotting a skyline; flying across the landscape at light speed. Though relatively harmless, their number was intimidating. At first the children were terrified and their parents were overwhelmed by the sheer volume, but, as with all things at their farm, "Ya get used to it." Lining the rafters of the barn, hanging upside down like little vampires, they'd sleep all day and come to life only as the Sun began to wane at the strange time wedged between day and night. From dusk 'til dawn the nocturnal souls re-emerged: creatures of the night. Whenever moonlight illuminated their wild journey, it was pure spectacle.

It was late, sometime after eleven o'clock when an evil onslaught occurred. Roger and Carolyn were watching the news when the shrill, squeaking beasts made their presence known. During ten summers spent in a farmhouse prone to remain cold regardless of the weather, there were only a few stifling nights when it was too hot to sleep upstairs. The heat of the day would rise and get trapped; bedrooms would become intolerable if the wind died after sunset. It was one of those nights. There was a sleeper sofa out on the porch. Christine and Cindy asked if they could camp out there for the night. Roger pulled the heavy monstrosity open as Carolyn gathered sheets. The porch was spacious, even with the full-sized bed sprawled wide open. It was fully screened in and well-protected from the elements and insects. Andrea had intended to crash out there, too. Nancy and April braved their own bedroom with nothing but a box fan and wide-open windows but no one was asleep yet. The temperature topped one hundred that day. No one *could* sleep!

The night remained quiet; moist air was stagnant. Even the crickets seemed lethargic from steam heat. Suddenly, a screaming rush of bats flew down the chimney, filling the parlor with wings and things. Parents began bobbing and weaving to avoid impact. A farmhouse was instantly alive with exceedingly unpleasant activity. As the bats, five or six in total, realized the error of their *way,* a mistaken path taken directly into the house, they did of course become as panicked as their hosts and tried to promptly exit the premises. Both front doors were wide open onto the porch and they followed the scent of fresh air. Where did it lead them? Onto the front porch: Shrieking is never as loud as when it comes through the pinched vocal chords of an adolescent girl...times two. Christine and Cynthia were hysterical. Ducking beneath the sheets with each pass, they begged for deliverance from the wretched vermin. Roger sent Andrea running to the woodshed to retrieve the set of badminton rackets: Let the games begin! Had anyone been outside watching in the bright moonlight of the night they would have witnessed events at once comical and traumatic. With eyes closed, it would have sounded much worse than it actually looked. Upheaval reigned supreme. Nancy and April came running downstairs to see what huge disruption was happening on the ground level of their house, thus plowing into a pair of bats circling the dining room. Both girls had an ample head of hair in which to tangle, which naturally happened. Chaos! Bedlam! There are no words which adequately express a frenetic scene as it unfolded. Roger threw one racket to Nancy. She began flailing wildly through thick air, not really aiming, but relying instead on a lucky strike. Carolyn was on their porch trying to open the door, providing access to an exit, swatting at them with each pass; not to injure, but rather to usher them outside. Andrea joined her, weapon in hand. Roger covered the parlor. April hid up underneath the dining room table, making a bit of a racket. One down... at April's feet...only wounded. She instantly retreated from an insecure position. Roger bounced one off the wall, finishing the job with a single swat. Meanwhile, mother and eldest daughter were proving to be lousy doubles partners; a poor match for crafty critters. As formidable adversaries, these bats used uncanny evasive maneuvers, outwitting their opponents. Finally, at precisely the same time, both ladies made contact and each bat went flying into the bed: a grand slam. One fluttered furiously in protest at the center of Cynthia's lap and one was caught in the web of Christine's hair, wounded and fighting to extricate itself from an impenetrable blond mass. Chris still has nightmares about this brief but horrific event and has never recovered from her fear of bats. Nor has she forgiven her eldest sister for having such pathetically poor aim. Cindy cannot tolerate anything flying near her head; she's instantly transported back to that terrible night of her life whenever a bird or even a butterfly draws too close. Childhood trauma: the gift that keeps on giving.

Perhaps it was an innocent mistake as a single bat chasing something under cover of darkness could have been followed by others in search of a meal and then down the chimney they all came. Though it would happen several more times during their decade on the farm, there was nothing necessarily sinister or supernatural about these bizarre occurrences. It may well explain why the chimney had been sealed...perhaps mistaken as swallows? Yet, the bats did seem to gravitate to the structure and they were repeatedly found dead in the house; one thirsty creature drowned in their toilet! The first one up and out of bed that unfortunate morning let everyone else know about an intruder with a single high-pitched holler, vibrating the household, walls to foundation: poor Nancy. It was always a rather unsavory encounter. The odd and inexplicable occurrence cannot, in good faith, be attributed to anything other than the law of averages; with that many bats incessantly circling their property someone was bound to take a wrong turn from time to time. It was certainly a spooky but apparently natural phenomenon, or so they presumed. Mrs. Warren later claimed it was yet another manifestation of the resident demon attempting to possess the mistress of the house, though no one in the family subscribed to her lurid interpretation of its meaning as an evil threat or omen; harbingers of things to come. Like the flies; only bigger. It warrants inclusion because, for *some* members of the family, it is still a delightful tale to tell, though others are not quite so fondly amused. Carolyn steadfastly maintains her position on the subject of bats: of all the occurrences in the house over the years they lived there, natural or supernatural, her most horrifying memory is the sound of a bat flying over her face in the darkness of night. Nothing ever touched her core fears more profoundly than these creatures. No one could afford to forget an obvious connection made. The name Bathsheba begins with B-A-T.

"May you have warm words on a cool evening, a full moon on a dark night, and a smooth road all the way to your door."
An Irish Blessing

The Child in the House

Walter Pater (1839-1894)

"*For sitting one day in the garden below an open window, he heard people talking, and could not but listen, how, in a sleepless hour, a sick woman had seen one of the dead sitting beside her, come to call her hence; and from the broken talk evolved with much clearness the notion that not all those dead people had really departed to the churchyard, nor were quite so motionless as they looked, but led a secret, half-fugitive life in their old homes, quite free by night, though sometimes visible in the day, dodging from room to room, with no great goodwill towards those who shared the space with them. All night the figure sat beside him in the reveries of his broken sleep, and was not quite gone in the morning — an odd, irreconcilable new member of the household, making the sweet familiar chambers unfriendly and suspect by its uncertain presence. He could have hated the dead he had pitied so, for being thus. Afterwards he came to think of those poor, home-returning ghosts, which all men have fancied to themselves — the revenants --- pathetically, as crying, or beating with vain hands at the doors, as the wind came, their cries distinguishable in it as a wild inner note.*"

~ A figure gray and ghostly ~
Christine as a 19th Century maiden in a vintage fashion show

"In death, I am born."
American Indian Proverb

III.
WICKED WOMAN...EVIL WAYS

"Judge not according to the appearance but judge righteous judgment."
John VII v. 24

Once the worst of the shock subsided from the "*torches*" incident, Carolyn became hell bent and determined to identify the demon who wished her dead. As months passed she became increasingly sad and preoccupied with morose thoughts, all revolving around death. She began serious historical research. Carolyn became as a tortured soul; the one who did the haunting. From local graveyards to dusty record rooms, archives of libraries to tattered parchment of old family Bibles; whenever and wherever she could find a reference to the house and its history, she took detailed notes, compiling a story centuries past and personalities passed. Who were these spirits? Why do some remain when most move on? Would there be any salvation for their souls? She was compelled to resolve this dilemma; send them on their way to the other side. But weren't they already on the other side? So how could they be in two very different spaces simultaneously? In spite of numerous, sometimes horrifying encounters, it was the mystery she longed to absorb intellectually; the only thing she and her husband were in total agreement about: there had to be a logical, scientifically-based explanation for what was happening. There had to be some reason why the spirits had lingered after death; some way to usher them onward, to achieve a release from what she perceived to be a perpetual imprisonment. The woman *needed* to understand; a moral imperative on two fronts. First, she'd longed to spare her family and herself this gross intrusion. Likewise, she'd wondered if she had been called to this house to help these spirits escape it. Carolyn believed if she had the power and knowledge to do so, it was her ethical obligation to provide an escape hatch for them; a portal from which they could flee but one which could also be sealed shut; the door closed so tightly they could never return: Part of the plan...selfish by design.

Before Carolyn could be an usher in the grand theatre of life and death, she had to know far more about whom and what she was dealing with; it required educating herself on a taboo subject with which she was formerly unfamiliar. There were no tickets; no assigned seating for these patrons. How would she lead them down dark corridors to a proper place in the cosmos if she did not know where they belonged? And what if they belonged precisely where they were? And what does God have to do with any of it? Emotionally conflicted, she possessed little compassion for their plight. Beyond unsympathetic, she felt nothing but contempt for the wicked one who was known as Bathsheba. Feeling at once defeated and empowered by this process, she applied skills of a studious observer to a problem made manifest in her home.

Carolyn began to consider other aspects of their existence, spawning a holy host of questions mulling around in her mind. An intellectual evolution born of her natural curiosity quelled some of the intrinsic fear which had become a prominent aspect of her daily (and nightly) existence; never a time when she did not look and listen around the house and wonder what was coming next; never an hour when she slept peacefully even in the presence of her husband, as he was utterly incapable of protecting her, through no fault of his own. He too had become its unwitting victim and this could happen again, at virtually any moment. It could happen to her children again with her presence in their farmhouse, a few feet away, incapable of hearing them scream out for help; unable to intervene on their behalf…no means of protecting her young.

Not for an instant did she lose sight of Reality: the new paranormal. It was what perplexed her most; the love her children had for a place offering only a promise of pain and torment. Carolyn felt nothing more than self-righteous indignation for those who'd disturbed her lovely dream, converting it into a nightmare; ones who refused to relinquish their hold on a place she rightfully considered to be her own. It had called to her. It had tempted her and begged her to come. The farm all but beckoned the family to love it, to come and call it home. Then, in a home place they adored, the farmhouse did everything in its supernatural power to drive them out; after embrace came total rejection. It made no sense at all. This farmhouse had robbed her of so much, including motherhood. It was impossible to be the mother she had been prior to taking up residence. Her rapt attention had been drastically diverted. She'd become a fear-based mortal whereas once she had been carefree, happiest when with her children. Believing *all* she could do on their behalf was be watchful and listen; to do her best to protect them against this supernatural onslaught, she wondered: how could she possibly intercede? As long as the family remained in the house she believed her girls would remain continually subjected to the whims of the dead; one scary scenario after another. She had no conceivable way of defending them, short of abandoning the house altogether. According to all of her children and her husband, for entirely different reasons, this was simply not an option. Their complicit willingness to dwell in the midst of the constant fear of intrusion was unbelievable to her.

Questions persisted, magnified further by so many discoveries made within the dust-laden shelves of the town library. Writing for hours, the woman was well aware the books she was using could not be removed from the premises. They were simply too old and fragile, far too valuable; she had no choice but to read / write simultaneously, often recording pertinent entries in shorthand. Learning much about the folks of a town, time allotted for this task was brief, usually only two or three hours. The library kept odd hours so it was a matter of getting there when she could: reading and writing until the librarian began turning off the lights. A chore with its own reward: Uncommon knowledge.

The same held true for Burrillville Town Hall. Carolyn was free to browse through archives but there were only certain hours to do so. It took months to compile the historical docudrama of a region; only the beginning of a project which consumed a great deal of her time. Mindful she had to return home, there to decipher the details of scrawled and scribbled notes, writing again in more thorough language what had been transcribed then interpreted earlier, the work frequently continued late into the night. Carolyn did not notice her attention slipping away from the children...but they did.

From pure fact to folklore she dug through piles of books the way she'd dig through a mound of earth, in search of buried treasure. It was never tedious work but was instead the most fascinating endeavor, filled with the history and mystery of those long dead. It was in fact, a labor of love, in spite of the original reason she considered the chore to be a necessity. Cold winter days kept her inside for the duration of that mean season but once spring arrived, Carolyn was gone, off to some old building, sitting among volumes of even older pages; writing feverishly to chronicle extensive information at hand: a what-when-where-who-why and how; abridged version, as she summarized everything even remotely associated with her house and its history. Seeking stories of everyone who ever lived there, Carolyn believed the manifestations were people, albeit dead people, whose history within those walls left them with a reason to remain there. It was not happenstance. They were not some random spirits passing through; floating in on a lark. Of this, she was certain. They were a sudden chill in the air, recognizable figures; familiar characters by the time any attempt was made to identify them. Her children had given them names, as if they'd been pets: Manny. Oliver. As always, Carolyn held steadfastly to a belief which presumed a direct correlation between entities as former occupants. The task to prove it such was formidable.

While Carolyn worked diligently to establish the identities of many others, her own was undergoing a radical transformation as two disparate elements were combining in a conspiracy to create a woman nobody recognized. She'd shriveled up like fruit left out in the Sun. Her voice became hollow and shrill compared to the deeper, richer tones with which everybody was accustomed. Tastes and interests changed. Her language became peppered with archaic words and terms seldom heard in modern society. Presuming it was because of books in which she was immersed, her constant exposure to centuries-old terminology, no one thought much of it at first, passing it off as the result of repetition, the power of suggestion tucked within the pages of time. Carolyn assumed a variety of different traits, a collection of quirks and foibles which had not been present in her personality prior to living in the farmhouse. For a while it seemed as if death and darkness blocked all the light, shrouding her existence, bending her mind to its will beneath a blanket of utter despair. To a certain extent her identity was slipping away but it was being replaced with a more well-established understudy who brought a personality all her own to the stage. The children could see their mother changing though they'd never discussed what it was they saw happening. It was a gradual decline; the slow descent into hell for those who had to witness the metamorphosis, just as it was for the woman feeling the ravages of its effects. Though she had always been a thoughtful, self-aware woman Carolyn did not, could not comprehend the transition she was experiencing. In time she would relinquish her being, allowing the change to occur naturally; no idea of the difference perceived by others, family and friends alike. It seemed as if she simply gave up, stopped fighting it; acquiescing to the will of another. Sam had noticed within a few months of the move. His eyes did not lie. He witnessed how rapidly Carolyn was aging, how depleted she'd become. Her youthful glow extinguished, the vibrancy muted: Technicolor turning to shades of gray. Diminishing further with each passing day, deteriorating rapidly, her lust for life itself, a formerly insatiable appetite, appeared to be wasting away with her physical form.

Cathi, too, could not help but notice her friend being adversely impacted by experiences she'd endured, depriving her of something elemental, essentially altering a woman she knew well. It was distressing, especially for those who had not seen her in quite some time. When they returned to witness her state of being it was shocking, as if decades were compressed into a few months. Beyond startling, it was disheartening: Spooky. No one discussed it with her, afraid to bring up a difficult subject. Boo! Who the hell are you?

During this period, Carolyn's saving grace arrived. As if this presence was intended to counterbalance the malignant character tormenting her, no matter how wicked, this evil spirit was no match for someone so pure of heart. Fran Sederback was a loving soul, an ethereal entity held captive by the corporeal world. She did not belong here...too damn good for the place. Yet, she took full advantage of her pause on this planet to reflect upon the true Nature of existence...the gift of life. Enjoying a lifetime of adventure and discovery, when the time came, she would not willingly relinquish it.

Magic manifested when this friendship formed, as another confluence of events occurred.

Carolyn headed into Glocester, there to rummage through their archives at the town hall. Before the town of Burrillville was incorporated, it had been a part of its neighbor to the south. She was told by the clerk in Harrisville that some of the documents she was seeking could be found there. She had a very productive session in Chepachet, due primarily to unfettered access, having met a historian in the records room who'd been eager to assist in the effort.

Driving through beautiful downtown Chepachet was a sensual pleasure in any season; a sight to behold. There were no traffic lights and only one main drag through this village; don't blink! To do so meant missing the quaint old haven entirely. Anxious to return home before the bus arrived, Carolyn was rushing and nearly forgot what she had intended to purchase while there. She quickly looked around, locating a perfect parking spot. There were several. Chepachet was a sleepy little hollow. Most of its residents had no choice but to travel elsewhere for work, into the city to find gainful employment. At this time of day it was all but deserted; a veritable ghost town.

No need for a list. There was only one item Carolyn wanted...and just one place to buy it. She pulled into the space right in front of **Brown & Hopkins Country Store**, there to purchase a wedge of Vermont cheddar cheese. Any excuse was a great one to step across the dimly lit threshold of this charming business establishment: America's oldest, continuously operated retail shop. It was splendid; an antique lover's paradise: a destination. All of the display cases and fixtures were authentic, hundreds of years old. REAL penny candy in heavy glass jars lined their oak shelves, awaiting little fingers to pillage for favorites from red and black licorice to Squirrel nuts to Mary Jane bars...and everything else imaginable. Carolyn felt guilty coming without the girls but she had only enough money to purchase the cheese so it was best if she went alone. Glancing up at the clock bought her a few extra minutes to peruse the premises and still make it home on time. High up on a shelf, deliberately out of reach, she spotted the display of old bottles. One of them caught her eye. Admiring them from a distance, the clerk asked if she would like to look at anything more closely. Yes...that one, please. It was free blown, lopsided, with a beautiful apple-green tint. The word COCAINE was embossed across the front. While studying its raw pontil bottom, deeply inset at the base, an unusual woman approached her. Without any formal introduction, she began explaining how all free blown bottles were snapped off at the stem of the blow pipe. Thus began a lively conversation regarding the digging of bottles from centuries before their own, from abandoned dumps of households like their own: old. Each had discovered a treasure trove of bottles on their own property and each knew the intrinsic value of every one of them.

"Cocaine, huh? That'll cure what ails ya." The petite woman was joking; an equally diminutive giggle escaping her lips as she handed the bottle back to Carolyn. Bewitched by the charming demeanor of the little lady she would soon consider a cherished friend, in a matter of moments their bond began to form. As for Carolyn, a casual acquaintance proved to be her salvation.

"Never touch the stuff myself." Carolyn smiled at the woman, watching her pale green eyes through the round, wire-rimmed granny glasses which suited her face to perfection. "Can you even believe they used to sell cocaine for medicinal purposes at *ye olde apothecary shoppe*...cheap as dirt?"

"Ah, the good olden days!" The ladies laughed and soon lost track of time.

"Fran." Extending her hand, she juggled her few items so not to drop them.

"Carolyn. It's a pleasure to meet you." Returning the gesture in kind.

The price of the bottle they'd examined together was $6.00; more than fair. Carolyn knew she couldn't afford it, offering it to a newfound friend instead. Neither of the women could justify the expenditure with a bevy of children to feed. Handing it over to the clerk with their thanks, they wandered the store together, discussing 17th and 18th Century glassware, including old medicine bottles they had salvaged, snatched back from the jaws of time and depths of Earth. The chimes of a clock struck, startling both of them. It was 3:00 p.m. and Carolyn had yet to choose a block of cheese. Fran lived close enough to make it home on time, but Carolyn knew she could not do the same without breaking the speed limit or the sound barrier. Quickly exchanging telephone numbers, as Vermont cheddar happened to be on sale, there was money left over so Fran helped her choose several pieces of candy for the girls. Waning light cast shadows as they stepped from the curb. Each departed with a wave, smiling broadly, bubbling with enthusiasm. Carolyn raced the sunset home, arriving at the farm in record-breaking time, carrying the small brown paper bag as a token of her affection and apology. Her girls were all out in the yard, wondering where their mother had gone; no note left on the table. Once they saw the bag, they knew where she'd been…and all was forgiven.

Fran called early in the evening, anxious to make sure she had written the number down correctly in all their confusion and haste. She was lonely, too. The women spent an hour or more on the line. Thus began a friendship with Fran Sederback; one which would last the duration of her lifetime.

During their initial visits, Carolyn chose not to disclose anything about the "trouble" in her home, afraid to scare her away. Fran was a history buff. She fell madly in love with their old farmhouse. Carolyn was equally enamored with Fran's house, a magnificent Federal style built in the 1770's, as large as her own. It too was constructed on a splendid piece of property, about five acres, adjacent to the Smith and Sayles Reservoir on Chestnut Hill Road, just beyond the village of Chepachet. The two women began exploring what they had in common; neither of them especially anxious to discuss the one thing they each secretly feared might chase the other to a land far, far away.

One warm summer morning Carolyn loaded her brood into the car headed for Chepachet. Fran had big plans for their day. The women would tote eight children to the flea market in Foster. It was an out-of-doors outing, open only on weekends, (weather permitting); about twenty-five booths set up to please anyone interested in anything old. There they discovered one treasure after another, none of which they were able to afford, of course, but it was most certainly enjoyable to peruse: vintage clothing, antique glassware, tools that had been well used hundreds of years before. It was a fascinating trip back in time. Fran's three children were as well-behaved as five girls, so two mothers were free from worry as all their young ones scattered throughout the market, according to interests. Christine gravitated to anything in miniature and was found admiring hand-carved doll house furniture and tiny tea sets. Michael, Fran's eldest, was located within a vast array of fine china and collectibles. All in agreement: a balmy summer Saturday is a wonderful thing to waste.

Returning to her home, Fran began to brew a pot of chamomile tea as their children played together outside, all but Andrea, who was instantly drawn to Fran's lovely antique piano, located on an inside wall of the parlor beside an open window. From where she was sitting on its bench Annie could see Fran standing at her kitchen sink. Leaning over, she asked permission to play the ancient and elegant instrument. Permission granted.

"Help yourself! No one ever plays it...that poor old thing must be lonely!" Fran's kindhearted words were a premonition of sorts, as *someone* warmly welcomed the youngster's nimble fingers to its yellowed ivory keys.

While the women shared a hot spot of tea at the kitchen table Andrea began sight-reading from the fragile sheet music adorning the instrument, displayed before her eyes. "Simple Gifts" a traditional Shaker hymn. Approaching the end of the page, it turned by itself. Andrea stopped playing, a bit startled by the odd timing of the event, though she assumed the breeze from the nearby window must have been her unwitting assistant. Finishing the piece, Andrea went back to the beginning, a creature of habit. One thing she'd learned over years of music classes: repetition was her friend but apparently not her only friend. Practice *does* make perfect. When she again arrived at the end of the page, it turned. The tune abruptly ended. Andrea's fingers froze on the keys.

"Excuse me, Fran? Do you have a ghost?" A question: to the point, as blunt force trauma; the kitchen suddenly became as silent as a piano. Andrea rose from the bench, joining muted mothers at the table. Fran finally responded.

"Why do you ask?" Some trepidation detected in her quiet voice, Fran had no idea how familiar her guests were with such anomalies. Andrea explained what happened...twice. Fran went into the parlor. Sheet music left open had been folded shut, neatly placed at the center of its upright stand. Proof!

"You *do* have a ghost! We do, too…more than one. We even have a spirit who *plays* our piano!" Andrea was entirely forthcoming…nothing to hide.

Newsflash: Fran looked at Carolyn, who then nodded knowingly. A shared glance opened a whole new chapter of friendship as a mutual secret kept was instantly revealed; a subject on which to dwell and often commiserate during difficult ordeals: stories to relate, images to describe over tea. Fran returned to the kitchen; conversation began in earnest. Andrea had a tune stuck in her head, one she wanted to master. Remaining at the piano, she sat down beside a harmless, helpful new friend, someone who obviously appreciated hearing the beloved instrument played once again.

There was one particularly emotional story to tell. Carolyn found herself on the verge of tears as she told Fran about a wicked woman and her evil ways, recounting the life-altering events she had endured. Fran was astonished. She tried to comfort the tortured soul sitting across from her at the table; reaching out to someone she cared for but could not help in any way, except to listen. Her own situation was benign by comparison; the spirit in Fran's house was rather innocuous, appearing occasionally, no hint of malfeasance attached to her persona. She too had a woman wandering the halls of her house yet she never challenged Fran's status as mistress of the house. Instead, her behavior was consistently kind, seemingly grateful there was a caretaker in her home, one who loved the place as much as she had in life. Though Fran was unable to determine who this was, she identified her as a former occupant, perhaps the original mistress of the house, based in part on the clothing she had worn; 18th Century garb, always the same simple dress with wide, worn pockets.

Later in the afternoon, believing Carolyn could use the fresh air their walk would provide, Fran invited her to come along as she fed the birds. Andrea went as well, satisfied with her progress on the piano. Following Fran deep into the woods, after a brief pit stop at the back of the house where she filled her pockets with seed, both of her guests became mesmerized; inspired by the sight of something holy. The diminutive woman walked quietly into thick woods, silently motioning for her guests to lag behind. Wading through the thicket grown up beneath towering oaks, she stood in the center of a natural clearing, filling both palms with bird seed. Slowly raising her arms up to the heavens, they came...descending from branches above. A symphony of bird song erupted, filling mild air with nature's sweetest sounds, graciously and gratefully welcoming her into their home. Swooping down from their limbs overhead dozens of birds landed upon her outstretched arms waiting to be fed by hand, as gentle with her as she was with them. When her palms emptied, they hovered as if trained to do so, anticipating a refill they'd clearly come to expect; Fran kindly obliged. The birds, waiting patiently, perched upon her shoulders or head, anxious but polite, each ready for its fair share of the daily feast: holy to behold...a miraculous sight. The few precious moments spoke to Carolyn in heart. She'd been blessed to find this special soul, someone she could trust and confide in; someone close to God. Theirs was spiritual union, precisely what Carolyn required; so to restore her faith in humankind. Fran's daily ritual was as intimate as a prayer, as lovely a sight as Carolyn had ever seen in her lifetime. Her friend was truly an ethereal creature, in touch with Nature, in concert with the Universe: a poet. Fran had much to teach and in those moments, Carolyn saw she had much to learn from this extraordinary woman. They would have years together; each free to explore the recesses of the other's heart and mind; destined to become the dearest of friends.

Andrea watched in awe, silently observing a process, wondering how this kind of trust was born. She too had an affinity for birds, an innate ability to communicate with the delicate creatures, though she could not even imagine being able to entice them in such a manner. At the time, she felt the slightest twinge of envy seep into her thoughts, instantly dismissing it as shamefully inappropriate. As the birds gracefully ascended through dappled sunlight, she marveled at the variety of colors exposed beneath their extended wings. Like the spirits, the color is there all the time; one simply needs to know where to look and how to look up. Otherwise, their magic remains invisible to mortal eyes. Sated, returning to their nests, a child hoped someday to possess a spirit Light enough to attract birds from the heavens above.

It was a joyful day. Friends parted wishing it was dawn instead of dusk. In time there were many visits between the homes and several dumpsites to dig. Fran came into Carolyn's life as an act of God; as Divine Providence County residents who first met in an olde country store: Perfect. Neither could afford the six dollar medicine bottle: Typical. Both husbands, virtually in absentia: Irrelevant. So much in common; so little time. No doubt; Fran Sederback was the good witchy woman, in touch with The Mother...Nature. Her presence in Carolyn's life was indeed a Godsend; her saving grace. If not for Fran, her friend would not have made it through what was yet to come. Together they scoured the archives. In the village of Chepachet, they soon discovered the identity of Carolyn's arch rival and nemesis; one evil mistress of the house. Bathsheba Sherman. Based on what they learned of her life, she became the principle suspect in death; the likely culprit: The bad witch.

Power is power. It is how this is utilized, what is done with it which counts. What emotion and intention human beings possess is energy expended in an infinite variety of ways. Free will determines choices which shape a destiny; whether or not of divine design the future unfolds through the consciousness: (I am, therefore I think.) If mortals choose to use this power wisely, for good works and acts of kindness it leaves a mark; permanent imprints on a world which could use all the love it can get. Instead, when a dark heart exists, any soul void of good intentions, this too leaves a mark; a permanent scar. We make decisions in every moment of life. Internal conflict is often resolved in conscience, though most people struggle at one time or another with simply doing the right thing in a given situation. Those without conscience; void of Light, both mortal and immortal, are the scariest souls of all.

If what they discovered was correct, if the accusation was true, Bathsheba Sherman had no conscience. If the whispers were accurate she was the devil incarnate; a criminal who got off the hook. According to the town historian, her inquest was infamous, drawing hoards of interested spectators from many miles away. It stands to reason that the courts worked diligently to separate fact from fiction; such a young woman with her whole life ahead of her, with much to lose; there was a lot at stake and there were those who thought she should be burned at the stake, those at the time who proclaimed her a witch, accused of performing a satanic ritual, resulting in the sacrifice of an infant. It was all too gruesome; the mind-bending description of a baby convulsing then dying due to a needle impaled in its scull. They could find nothing in the records fixing the location of what she would plead was an accidental death but Bathsheba was an Arnold and she'd lived on the Arnold Estate at that age so there was every indication to believe the event occurred in Carolyn's own home. There would come several psychics who assured her of this over time. In the interim, these ladies could only speculate, in much the same way town folk had done so many years before. The mid 1800's seemed so long ago and far away, yet if indeed the woman had returned to claim what she perceived to be her rightful place as mistress of the house, Carolyn could do little else than jockey for position or relinquish it altogether. Her choices set in stone: Stay and fight or flee the scene of an alleged crime.

Who was this spirit appearing in the night? What motivation possessed her; for what ungodly purpose or reason does she manifest in form and threaten? What was her intention toward Carolyn and the rest of her family? Questions without answers became a burden on her consciousness while attempting to comprehend why some souls defy the Universal rule of law: Physics. Perhaps they adhere to established laws mortals have yet to recognize and interpret. Why do some return when most move on? Time does not always tell or heal.

Bathsheba either escaped the mortal rule of law in a courtroom or she was quite rightfully acquitted. If she was the one who came to haunt and taunt the occupants of the old Arnold Estate, she was capable of bending cosmic laws at will. Her presence, and that of the others, defied everything – from gravity to time and space – as mortals grasp the concepts. Perhaps the time had come to broaden narrow-minded precepts, to determine what forces were at play or how to circumvent their power. Two heads are better than one.

Fran did her utmost to become a resource of support, to offer guidance and encouragement to her friend. Pure of heart, this esoteric being was as close as Carolyn would ever come to an angel in the flesh. Her advice was invaluable; distraction she provided was welcome respite for this troubled woman who could only escape her circumstances when lost within the Earth…up to her elbows in dirt. So that is what the ladies did for fun: intense, focused efforts to detect and exhume lost treasures from shallow gravesites. Plowing through mounds, discovering relics buried beneath the surface so many years before, Carolyn and Fran salvaged rare and valuable fragments of history, someone's trash, assembling quite a collection of perfectly preserved glassware from centuries gone by. The tiring drudgery of the task at hand kept Carolyn from losing her mind. Fran was like a potent antidote, the remedy to counteract the effects of poison, as if God said: "Here, dear…this'll cure what ails ya." Fran was living proof that good triumphs over evil, as Bathsheba never once dared to rear her ugly head in the woman's holy presence. Fran's power was great: pure white Light, casting no shadows, disallowing of the darkness. Whoever or whatever she was, the wicked woman kept her evil ways at some distance for a time, incapable of penetrating the veritable fortress of love surrounding Carolyn. In the perpetual battle between good and evil, Fran Sederback was a formidable opponent, a queen of passive resistance. As a mighty force to be reckoned with, her purity was so intimidating, Bathsheba never attempted to infiltrate it. Friendship is a blessed gift of human Nature. Fran was evidence of a higher power, proof of the existence of God, destined to become one of the angels she emulated on Earth…as an everlasting Light in the firmament.

"Have you learned the lessons only of those who admired you, and were tender with you, and stood aside for you? Have you not learned great lessons from those who braced themselves against you, and disputed passage with you?"
Walt Whitman

demon doors

The farmhouse had a life of its own. Its doors were not simply wooden and hardware barriers between rooms. They were passages between dimensions; the form and function of time travel. Each door in the house was a portal to the past and future, as well as present, but they were also utilized as an overt method of communication; for the pronouncement of a presence. The spirits were all perfectly capable of coming and going without the benefit of doors and windows. They often walked right through them, especially the children. None requiring anything tangible to make a grand entrance; their presence alone was enough to capture the attention of any mortal and yet, the wrought iron latches would mysteriously lift, creaky doors would slowly open, as if for dramatic effect. Click. Thankfully there were no doorbells; based on how they misused the telephone, a doorbell would have been, at best, an incessant nuisance. They manipulated many objects with ease. It was rather unnerving, walking past their cellar door as something wicked pounded on it from the other side. Even more rattling: to be a child trapped inside a dark space with no escape due to a door which refused to open...because that's how the light gets in. Or, to be suddenly and inexplicably released during the course of the struggle, the violent thrashing; the begging and screaming with tears pouring from eyes which could not see in the darkness, knowing no one could hear it. Click. A vicious joke played time and time again; a hideous game of cat and mouse: the haunting and tauntingly common occurrence in their household. Click. It became an identifiable sound, an eerily familiar snap to attention for whoever was within hearing distance, prompting immediate notice. A trigger. A calling card. A warning. A threat. Click. Whoever heard it happen would instantly question: does someone want a sweater or is it the essence of death entering the room? Those few seconds were the most intolerable of all; fear of the unknown. The time to be scared; nobody knew what was coming from the other side: Next. Fear is born of the unknown; mortals are captivated by the darkest recesses of imagination. Boo! but who was holding them captive? To be locked inside a space where no lock exists on the door one is wrestling with…this is the definition of fear. The demon doors would not always allow access or escape. An incredibly powerful force could keep them closed, as if locked, when it came time to run for one's life. The series of pathways and portals throughout the house were completely benign one minute, malignant the next. Cellar doors, pantry doors, bedroom doors, borning room, chimney closets, every entrance to the eaves: all problematic at one time or another. Each was a potential prison, all twenty-four of them. No Exit. No Entrance.

Click.

Yet another definition of fear: being the sister on the other side of the door fighting to release her captive sibling; a story all its own. So many incidents happened, it would become redundant to tell every tale, but those of marked significance have been included. Of greatest importance to note is this fact: the farmhouse was alive with death. Those who'd passed, desiring to make a grand entrance, did so in terms mortals were capable of understanding. Click. It was a signal. A clue. An omen. A harbinger of *someone* to come, perhaps (but not necessarily) someone wicked. As a putrid odor and a pervasive chill frequently accompanied whatever spirit flipped the latch, it became easier to distinguish friend from foe relatively quickly. High alert was the paranormal reality of life. After awhile, everyone came to accept it as such. Just as every spirit had its own personality, every door made an original sound all its own, based upon its weight and depth, how warped the wrought iron had become over centuries of use. So many variables; never the same sensation twice: so many souls…prepared to make a grand entrance.

It was frightful. It was likewise a gift. Not everyone on the other side was so frightening. That's how the Light gets in; the crack of a door could often be quite illuminating. Click. Boo who knows? An intrepid journey continued.

In time, a conditioned response, a reflexive reaction became the norm with every member of the family as they learned it might *not* be a mortal entering the room. Heads up! Cynthia made this mistake only once. Lesson learned. Hide 'n seek was destined to be abandoned as a pastime. Roger would offend a friend and April would make one. Holly felt comforted, as someone was watching over her in the night. Carolyn would find herself comforted by an unlikely confidante; a spirit who had likely been in the same position at some point during her lifetime. To hear the sound or see the light from beneath the crack of a door opening was never a mundane event, not simply a promise of procession, of someone coming and going. It was often far more significant. There was a reason to take notice; reason enough to remain mindful of who was in the farmhouse and where they were located. Mommy's in the kitchen. Daddy's in the parlor. Few children grow up in such circumstances, though it does make them exceedingly self-aware, with purpose. When space is shared it is best to know who is languishing in the shadows and emerging from the light; best to be alert. Friend or foe…you never know.

Opening the fireplace was essentially an overt act of removing a door, thus exposing a portal. Once that dirty deed was done, open, everything changed. Ultimately it would prove to be a pathway to uncommon knowledge; another way for the Light to get in…creating a crack in the cosmos.

What prompts a five year old child to hear a *click* then look toward a door, pointing out the true nature of the problem? How could she know ***something bad happened in there***? Was its opening an invitation to discovery? No one knew. A declaration? Perhaps. It was intentional and it was a paranormal part of life: Familiar. This chapter of their story began when opening the fireplace as the pantry door in the parlor soon became a persistent dilemma. It had not "behaved" this way prior to the demolition process. As these two events had coincided, it followed logically. Some connection must exist between them, though no one has been able to determine the precise nature of this presumed attachment. April believes someone in there was trying to escape and did not succeed; she was the one who sensed a persona related to the space, insisting something awful happened to the spirit in the pantry. But why the delay? Had restoring a fireplace disrupted the Universe? Had it somehow created a ripple effect? Sent a shock wave through the space / time continuum? So it seems. One explanation seems as good as another when no one knows what they are talking about. Over time, one entirely dismisses the desire to know. Truth be told, there is no rational explanation for it. Period. A single event triggered something supernatural, unleashing an evil influence. A cosmic presence: A vital force of Nature as a wonder to behold. Something was already present when this family arrived at the farm, so it matters not, the reason why. It was there and it had always been there, long before they crossed the threshold. So why wonder? What difference does it make? Why does this insatiable thirst for knowledge persist when it serves no purpose? The spirits were not going anywhere and coming from everywhere? Why not accept defeat gracefully? Let the chips fall and the doors slam. Attitude is everything. Sam had said so.

It is said by those who claim to be *in the know* that when God closes a door He opens a window. But what happens when He opens a door? Who knows?

"If we wonder often, the gift of knowledge will come."
American Indian Proverb

~ click ~

knock knock knock

Stagnant air refused to move, refused to breathe a breeze through any open window: Oppositional. Defiant. August was brutal, an unforgiving month in the valley. Antagonistic. Belligerent. Relentless heat settled like squatters in pastures thick with fog, moist with morning dew as mist descending to Earth on a moonless night before attempted to rise and reunite with the Sun, but the air was heavy as honey and the day had just begun. A run down to their river would be the only respite. But first...Carolyn made her list. Destination: the A&P in Pascoag, there to do their shopping for the week. Under the guise of helping mom, the children went along in hopes of catching a refreshing wisp of air conditioning from the only place they could; the frozen food section of the blissfully cool business establishment. There was no point in buying ice cream. It would never survive the ride home. The delightful dairy treat would succumb to this heat; it could not endure the trunk and would surely liquefy by the time the carton made the trip, much like the kiddies crammed together in the back seat of the car. No harm in looking, though...or breathing it all in.

The vehicle was like a pressure cooker, wide open windows barely venting an unbearable steam heat. As the crowded car made its way back through the village onto a desolate Round Top Road, all but deserted of traffic during this time of day, air unfit to breathe was suffocating the lot of them, including the driver. Carolyn glanced in the rearview mirror. An artificial breeze feathering through their flowing manes, carefree kids stuck their heads out of windows, urging her to drive faster...faster...pink tongues flapping in feigned protest, wagging like a pack of wild dogs rounded up and out on a joyride. Everyone grabbed the brown paper bags from the trunk then dutifully folded them for reuse once groceries found their way onto pantry shelves, perishables into the fridge. In a few minutes, the task at hand complete, they made a break for it; downhill racing...escaping a hot house for a cool riverbed.

There was a special kind of freedom all the ladies enjoyed when Roger was away. They loved him dearly though could not help but frolic in his absence; no schedules, no expectations: Liberation! Whenever he was gone it afforded the six who remained behind an opportunity to relax, to abolish the routine; a luxury they did not have when he was home...unless it was *his* idea. Dinner was served around eight, maybe nine; whenever it was ready and everyone was good and hungry. It tastes better that way! Nothing too elaborate: simple soup and sandwiches as a main meal; something Roger would *never* tolerate: a meat-and-potatoes Frenchman. Its timing to the table was dependent on so many other activities...not the other way around. Their music was too loud, the laughter raucous; frolicking was encouraged. In fact, it was a compulsory program during the summer, if for no more purposeful reason than to create a counterbalance to the many chores and responsibilities the children assumed as occupants of the farm. During the dog days of summer it was a priority to play with the dog, romping through the river. She got hot, too. The water was safe; low and easy to navigate. The shoals were brimming with activity, alive with the excitement of discovery. **Scrabble** and **Parcheesi** were reserved for evening hours. While the Sun was still shining a day was not done; as long as there was sufficient light to see where they were stepping, the girls retained a blissfully unfettered access to the river. There was no such thing as boredom on the farm; for a variety of reasons...never a dull moment.

Returning several hours later, everyone agreed; the only thing missing, the only one who'd kept it from being a perfect day was Cathi, her stark absence duly noted. She had recently returned to Nova Scotia again and was missed. Other than this, all the ladies thoroughly enjoyed their outing into the woods. Tick inspection time. When the unsavory ritual was finished and the girls had picked each other's bodies like monkeys in the forest, they turned the parlor into a flop house: Crash...naps all around. The house was quiet. Carolyn was the first one off the sofa, heading for the kitchen; a pantry full of provisions giving her an array of ideas for a dinner plan congealing along the route. She decided on tuna sandwiches and tomato soup; a quick fix well-received by a drowsy crowd. Sated; time for a shower then early to bed. Early to rise: much earlier than anyone could have expected or predicted.

By 10:00 p.m. Carolyn was sloshing around in their king-sized waterbed, once all the girls were soundly asleep. Having recently renovated the summer kitchen so to escape the many perils of their unusually super/active bedroom, supernaturally speaking, Carolyn was in her new digs, minus one husband on this particular night. Exhausted by the heat, wrung out like a wet dishrag, she began falling off to sleep almost immediately. As she began to relax, a jolt of electricity passed through her, converting her body and mind instantly rigid with panic; fully alert. Danger! **What the hell was that!** The house shook. It rumbled and groaned from the impact. Jennifer was suddenly up on all four, as alarmed as her family, barking hysterically. Carolyn could not move. Her natural instinct was to rise up and investigate; to go protect her children and vanquish the intruder. Someone had pounded on the door with such force and fury it rattled a rib cage. A body oppressed by a power she couldn't discern, it held her in place. Struggling to free herself from a virtual stranglehold so intense she could barely breathe, Carolyn heard the footsteps of her children. They were running to their mother, terrified, certain someone was attempting entry under cover of darkness. At first Andrea, then Christine and Cynthia came thundering down their bedroom stairs. Nancy and April came from the far side of the house. They'd found her lying in bed, her eyes searching their faces in desperation. Andrea went to get the flashlight and began peering out windows, peeking onto the porch. It sounded as if it had come from the front door in the parlor, or possibly the other front door situated in the hallway to the kitchen. Nancy insisted it happened on her side of the house, nearer to the kitchen, though nobody knew for sure because the explosive, booming noise reverberated throughout their farmhouse. April hovered close to her mother. An apparent paralysis afflicting the woman began to subside. It was a frantic few minutes of girls scampering beneath the overlay of a frenetic soundtrack; an incessantly barking dog. The frontal assault sounded like a battering ram striking the structure – three heavy blows in perfect syncopation – blunt force trauma for all involved. Everyone wished dad was home. Freedom isn't free.

Carolyn rolled over the side of the waterbed. After a few minutes of feeling shaky and unstable, she regained her equilibrium then joined her eldest child in search of the culprit. Overcome with a sense of dread, she'd immediately suspected the event was of supernatural origin for several reasons. No mortal being could have generated that kind of power, nor its subsequent sounds. A preponderance of evidence lacking, there was no sign of any damage done to the structure; neither door. Inspecting the façade of the house the following morning, Carolyn found no indication anything had struck the surface of the clapboard. Based on the volume of sound it created, whatever made contact with the farmhouse would have surely left a mark… as it had on a family.

It was what happened to her body during this episode which solidified her belief in it as supernatural in Nature. There was no one at the door that night, certainly no one visible. As Cindy later described it, her mom had been put in the bubble; the type of force field with which they were all familiar had kept her from responding to a threat…and it was a threat. Carolyn believed it was an intentional act to immobilize and terrify her; to instill fear and render her helpless, unable to protect the girls. She was its target. Message received.

Carolyn did not sleep that night. Instead, she wandered the house, guarding her young, watching through windowpanes, a view increasingly obscured by low, dense fog enveloping the valley. Every light in their farmhouse was on. Finally she settled into the rocking chair, there to keep a constant vigil with a .22 as her companion, draped across her lap, just in case her initial conjecture was erroneous. There she sat, hour after hour, thinking about a tacit threat of invasion, considering it quite impossible to defend against something unseen. What choice did she have but to lay in wait? No keys, no locks, three knocks at the door and no husband at home to answer the call. It grated at her frayed nerves; ate away the lining of her stomach as she rocked, not to sleep, only to stay awake. A force to be reckoned with; so who is the boss in this house?

Carolyn felt decidedly out of control. Fighting sheer exhaustion, she began wondering what on Earth (or beyond) was powerful enough to cause a house to tremble from rafters to foundation; thought about the tale Mr. Kenyon told of two men who had crawled beneath the floorboards of a nearby blacksmith shop for shelter only to meet their bitterly cold end in the midst of a blizzard. Were they afraid? Could they see an old farmhouse off the road? Were these poor souls out there again, seeking sanctuary? Three deafening blows against a door in the dead of night…a shotgun in her hands…what a way to live.

***

Three times: This happened three times over the course of nearly a decade. The next episode was far more dramatic in nature, because Roger was home. He arrived late for dinner, having been detained by the various obstacles so often associated with a blanket of fresh fallen snow. Seated at the head of the table, dining alone, Roger voraciously devoured the contents of a platter, still hot from an oven where it laid in waiting while the family nervously awaited his long overdue arrival. He watched as the children, gathered together near the fireplace, became involved in a heated game of cards. Enjoying the scene playing out before his road-weary eyes, Roger was finally able to relax. He did not expect to be literally knocked from his chair by three extremely loud, heavy blows against the front door; invasion of a space he called home. As a flying chair was literally pulled out from beneath him, Roger leapt from his seat simultaneously, flying to the door. Alarm, anger and adrenaline: mighty forces converged to provide him super human strength and speed as he flung open the heavy door and raced out onto the porch. The strings of their piano were still buzzing; humming from the syncopated series of powerful strikes, causing the entire house to vibrate.

It was a disturbing sound; violent and threatening; the rage to rival Roger's own. The girls huddled near their mother as the protective father ran outside, surveying the property then rushed in through the front door, into the parlor. Jennifer was hysterical. So was her son, Pooh Bear…twice her size and twice as loud. Their dogs had no concept of "inside" voices; they were distressed, expressing alarm at the highest pitch and volume possible. Roger had to yell out in order to be heard over them: "Get my gun!"

"Why bother? There's nobody out there." Carolyn snapped the words like a wet towel against his ruddy cheeks. Leering at the woman as he galloped past her, making his way to the bedroom, he returned a few seconds later with his handgun then was instantly out the door. No one could recall ever seeing him move with such velocity. He was scared. He knew the truth. Roger knew in his gut where he'd viscerally *felt* three tremulous reverberations of perfectly timed blows; NO mortal could have made that kind of impact. He knew his chair had become an identified flying object and his speed out onto the porch precluded an escape by any human being; none quick enough to evade notice or capture. He knew Carolyn was right... and had been all along.

Searching their property thoroughly, a flashlight in one hand and a weapon in the other, Roger returned to his cold plate of food. There he sat, quiet and contemplative, as he finished his dinner. There was a vacant stare in his eyes, an odd expression on his face. No need to ask questions. The family knew. It was time for bed. Each child approached then kissed her father goodnight, grateful for his efforts on their behalf; grateful for his protection. They could sleep peacefully knowing he was home. Carolyn was in an unyielding frame of mind, grateful only because her husband finally heard what she'd tried to describe to him once before, something he'd dismissed as a falling limb or a barn owl striking the side of the house; as natural as the wind. Now he *knew*; his sternum still vibrating with the supernatural aftershock.

Their house remained quiet; Roger settled into his favorite chair to read the newspaper. Carolyn huddled near the fireplace with a book. He never said a word. For more than an hour only the sound of turning pages passed between them. Flipping then folding the paper in half loudly enough to capture her attention, he abandoned the sports section to address what was really on his mind. Roger had a tendency to hide behind the paper when he did not want to be disturbed: too late; he was disturbed. Emerging from crumpled newsprint, Carolyn looked up from the book.

"Do you suppose it might be those two men who froze to death underneath the blacksmith shop?" Carolyn could not believe her ears. He actually asked her opinion, literally suggesting a *supernatural* explanation! Shrugging her shoulders, a muted response, she considered his question, albeit speculative, a bold admission; an insightful and erudite sign of progress made. Roger then retreated, tucking himself behind the sports page again; untouchable. There he remained for the duration with no further mention of the event. It was the first time and the last time he ever discussed it; as close to a conversation as they would come on this subject. Still, Carolyn listened, absorbing his words into her mind as manna from heaven, intuiting some sense of him attempting to tell her she was right without actually breaking down and admitting same. She was as warmed by vindication as she was by that fire raging at her back. It was a long time coming; quite a wait for an appropriate acknowledgement of circumstances beyond mortal control. Carolyn had always been the one to introduce the concept, to initiate a necessary communication regarding spirit matters in their house. Roger had always been the one to dismiss anything his wife had to say, as if her intellect, her sensory perceptions were either faulty or irrelevant. With a single sentence he had effectively reversed that trend. It revealed a subtle shift in his thought process and qualified as a breakthrough. Validated by his willingness to accept her initial assessment of this intrusion, satisfied with the outcome, Carolyn left her husband alone to reflect upon the realization she had experienced well before he ever considered opening his eyes to behold the new paranormal: Reality.

Another incident of supernatural origin; the triple knocking, presumably at the door, would occur one more time during the family's tenure at their farm; the next proved far more traumatic. Everyone was present in the house; time to rock 'n roll: a pounding, shaking, trembling incident is detailed along with another phenomenon occurring simultaneously; one of the most horrifying, significant encounters they would experience together. Suffice to say, it was not bats or a barn owl or falling limb or even swallows in the chimney. It was not the wind…but they would all be blown away.

Mrs. Warren later described these specific incidents as *demonic* in nature, explaining this particular phenomenon has a history. It is often referred to as "*Mocking the Trinity*"; in her opinion as the devil's footwork. Once Carolyn told the Warrens about these and many other occurrences, the scenarios were repeatedly mentioned, details revealed during seminars and public speaking engagements, sparking the nefarious interests of those attending; those with dark hearts and warped minds. The information disseminated and subsequent knowledge gained resulted in an unimaginable consequence for their family, as it was eventually used against them in the most hideous conceivable way.

Fear the living…not the dead.

"Ask and it will be given to you; seek and you will find; knock and it will be opened to you."
Matthew 7: 7

blown away

"We rarely forget that which has made a deep impression on our minds."
Tryon Edwards

A Nor'easter is to be respected; a formidable force of Nature. New England is often the prime target of coastal storms, jutting out just far enough to bear the brunt of whatever barrels up the Eastern seaboard; land and sea monsters. When one is forecast it is best to prepare for the worst and then quite literally batten down the hatches. It was spring, officially, and it had been for several weeks, but one would never know it, stepping out into a bleak landscape and wild elements. Savage wind gusts had already begun doing damage; only the beginning. The calm before had passed; an impending storm looming on the horizon. The sturdy farmhouse weathered many a harsh gale during its time, including the most infamous of all; Hurricane of 1938. Cindy felt safe in the house but was worried about their horses, hoping her mother would get home soon enough to help her barn them. They were in the corral and needed to be put up in their stalls, secured as soon as possible. The rain had not yet arrived but it would soon begin whipping at them like some maniacal rider anxious for an increase in speed. Both boys were already nervously pacing, especially Pineridge. He was naturally skittish, hyperactive at best. Royal was infinitely more patient; more demure than his companion though he too was starting a protest, frantically prancing to and fro along the fence line of the corral. This threatening storm was practically on their doorstep. Gazing outside through kitchen windows, Cindy paced as nervously as her four-legged friends. Soon they would become too frenetic, too hard to handle alone. She needed help. It was obvious; a threat issued by the sky. She didn't have much longer to wait.

Roger was away; again. Carolyn had gone to town to stock up on groceries. Chrissy and April went with her to expedite the process. Nancy was at home, upstairs in her bedroom, sequestered in a reclusive huddle over her desk, in a valiant attempt to finish an overdue term paper. Ignoring Cynthia's pleas for assistance, abruptly slamming her door, Nancy did not wish to be disturbed: too late. Cindy knew all too well, she was on her own; abandoned, left to her own devices on a blustery afternoon. Preparing to go outside to deal with this dilemma alone, coat and gloves a must, a sharp crack split the howling wind. She ran toward the window, thinking a tree limb was about to come crashing to the ground. Instead, she saw the terrifying sight: one of the wide planks on the corral had blown off its post and was dangling by a single nail, creating a natural escape route for the horses. Cindy was seized by panic. She had only a few moments to avert a disaster.

The horses became increasingly agitated; highly vocal about their distress. Cindy raced into the woodshed, retrieving a hammer and nails. A brisk wind carried their voices across the valley; the high-pitched whinnying and hissing squeezed in between unmistakable snorts; they were both about to bolt. What began as the sensation of helplessness instantly transformed into frustration; Cynthia was furious with Nancy. The only one available refused to assist her sister in a crisis. No time to "Whoa! Nelly!" as she passed the bedroom stairs in a full gallop. Instead, Cindy yelled loud enough to muffle the raging wind, as she flew within earshot of Nancy's bedroom. It was useless; no movement at all from above. Slamming the kitchen door, she ran across the yard, yelling at the horses to get away from the fence, attempting to spook them to a safer side of the corral. They were preparing to jump and run. Cindy was left alone to handle this potentially disastrous dilemma…or so she thought.

Savage wind was her nemesis. It beat up on the plank; gusts from multiple directions, tugging at the two remaining nails intended to secure it from the other side. Had they held, it would have been a simple fix. As that eight inch wide slab of wood went flying off its post, Cindy turned, screaming toward the house for Nancy to come: Help! The board was heavy. She *couldn't* do it alone. Her sister would need to hold one end in place as she nailed the other back on the post. No response. The child literally could not abandon her post. Her presence there was all that kept two creatures from unfettered access and total liberation. Nancy never did emerge through their kitchen door. Cindy's anger began bubbling up in her eyes, spilling profusely forth with the curses.

Left to her own devices, with a heavy hammer and about half a dozen nails, a child not quite thirteen had a huge responsibility in hand as she attempted to stabilize a flying object, balancing the precarious plank in such a way that she'd be able pound a few nails into it before the next gust sent her reeling. The plank fell from its place over and over again; it was not a one person job. Poor Cindy; as frantic as their horses, she could feel the wind whipping and lashing at her tears, streaking drops across her cheeks. Her natural inclination was to pray in a crisis though she only did so during episodes of supernatural origin. It never occurred to her to request a divine intervention in this case, as Nature itself was the culprit. Instead, she cursed at her sister then cursed at the horses then cursed at the storm. In an instant, she would be blown away, not by the wind but by an intervening force; one there on her behalf.

The far side of the plank lifted up off the ground. Someone had come to her rescue. It rose several feet from the grass and was held in place, suspended in midair by someone invisible. Cindy stood up and still, shocked into silence, disbelieving her own saturated eyes, stinging tears evaporating in the wind. The heavy plank securely held in place and ready to receive ten pennyweight nails, she put her end of the board up against the post and began banging into the dense pine, anxious to finish the task quickly lest her assistant suddenly dissipate with another gust of wind; heart pounding as hard as her hand.

Amazed, stunned by this revelation, Cynthia walked cautiously toward the other post, pulling a few more nails from her pocket. When she arrived at the spot where the plank was obviously still being held off the ground, precisely where it needed to be nailed, she humbly uttered "Thank you" then resumed the chore. The heavy board never moved. It was held in a proper position for the duration of this task. When completed, Cindy did not know what more to say. The horses were safe. She was able to bring them into the barn, one at a time, before the brunt of the storm was upon them, all the while sensing she was not alone in the effort; someone was there to watch over her, to intercede if anything went wrong. The jittery horses were responding to something but it was impossible to interpret; it could have just been the inclement weather they were reacting to by acting up. It may have been an invisible companion; no way of knowing for certain. However, Cindy was able to get both of them fed then watered then blanketed without any further disruptions. On her way back to the house from the barn, Carolyn pulled into the yard. The next chore was a very quick offloading of paper bags before rain arrived in force. By the time this was accomplished, groceries safely stowed away on pantry shelves, Cindy sensed her helper had departed; services no longer required.

The other children scattered but Cindy remained behind in the kitchen with her mom. There must've been a rather odd expression on the child's face as it prompted Carolyn to ask: what's the matter? They sat together at the table. Cindy began to tell her story. When she arrived at the sentence regarding her sibling's unwillingness to help, Carolyn stopped her abruptly, yelling out the name of the offender, the one who'd shirked a critical responsibility. Uh-oh! Nancy knew *that* tone of voice; her desk chair scraped across the floorboards overhead and she sailed down the staircase. Time to be held accountable for her inaction: gross negligence in a time of crisis. It was strange, considering the severity of the infraction, yet Cynthia harbored no grudge against Nancy, having subsequently forgiven her sister, without so much as a well-deserved apology. Carolyn was not quite as forgiving. Confronting Nancy, Cindy tried to re-establish eye contact with an angry mother, a gaze focused elsewhere.

"Mom! Listen! I'm trying to tell you something important!"

"You *begged* for horses; then left your sister alone with them in a storm!" Carolyn was as disappointed as she was livid with Nancy. "How could you? Cindy needed your help. She would *never* have done that to you!"

"But *that's* what I'm trying to tell you, mommy! I *wasn't* alone!" Grasping her mother's full attention along with her forearm, Cynthia sat back down on her chair, prepared to continue telling a miraculous tale. "Someone *did* come to help me...someone held the plank for me while I nailed it in!"

"Who came to help you? No one else was home." Carolyn was confused.

"I don't know who it was!" There was a serene expression in Cindy's eyes.

Nancy was summarily dismissed. Suddenly, just as curious as their mother was, Nancy was clearly not invited to participate further in this conversation; her totally inexcusable behavior destined to be addressed at some other time. Meanwhile, Carolyn listened thoughtfully to her daughter's description of the event as it unfolded like blankets used to warm the cold horses, providing the equivalent sensation for her mother. Carolyn had not been there to help her, to intervene during a perilous situation, but someone else had done so in her absence. For the kindness Carolyn was deeply grateful but to what or whom? Acknowledging the episode occurred, never doubting for an instant the child was telling the truth, her mother marveled at the news, wondering aloud with Cindy about the source of such an inspiring intervention. Obviously someone was watching out for her...and watching over her.

"Maybe it was your Guardian Angel. How did you feel when it happened?"

"It felt all warm inside me even though I was freezing then all of a sudden I stopped being mad and I stopped crying. I was too shocked to cry anymore! It held the board in place for me, mom...*it did*...until I was done hammering. It held the board right where I needed it to be and it never let go!"

"I believe you, honey." Carolyn smiled, embracing her daughter.

"Mommy, I felt love...so much love it made me stop being mad at Nancy!"

"Oh, baby doll..." Carolyn winced. "That was one pitiful sentence but I *do* understand what you're ***trying*** to say."

As wind-driven rain pounded against their windowpanes, billowing clouds released a torrential flow of fluid from the sky. Carolyn made cocoa. Mother and daughter discussed the effects and importance of gratitude over mugs of heavenly hot chocolate. Cindy was grateful to have the horses secured in the barn. Above all else, she was truly thankful to her saving grace. Carolyn was grateful her daughter had not been injured in the process and was supremely appreciative of the supreme being who'd come to provide rescue in a time of need, no matter from whence it came...it was there when she needed it most.

"Do you think it was one of ***our*** spirits?" Cindy searched for an answer.

"I don't know, sweetheart. I really don't know how to answer that question. Whoever it was obviously cares for you and could see from *somewhere* that you were in trouble."

"But I didn't even pray for help this time! I just yelled at Nancy's windows from across the yard. I'll bet all the neighbors heard me way down the road, I was yelling *so* loud! I said some really bad words, too, mom. I'm sorry. I was *really* mad…and really scared the horses would get out. Sorry for swearing."

"Maybe the wind carried your voice all the way to Heaven and it *was* your Guardian Angel who came running to the rescue." No less plausible a theory.

"Maybe it was Mr. Kenyon." That thought had not yet occurred to Carolyn. Cynthia had an innately reliable sense of all things pertaining to the Cosmos. The mother had learned to listen closely to her daughter well before this day. He had not been gone long and perhaps he was not long gone. In her heart, Carolyn hoped Cynthia was right; perhaps her dear old friend had helped the hapless child. She hoped he had come back to this farm he loved so much in life…back where he belonged. Even though she would never wish upon him a presumed curse of remaining an Earth-bound spirit, she privately hoped he'd been dispatched from afar for the useful purpose served.

"It doesn't matter who it is as long as we say 'thanks' they get the message. I believe it was a good spirit; it's all that matters. You said you felt loved and protected. It's all we *can* know and sometimes, it's enough." Carolyn cradled sweet little Cindy in her arms then enlisted her as the little helper; assistance required in the kitchen. Pay it forward; an important lesson to instill in one so young. (Perhaps **pray it forward** was an equally important lesson to learn.)

Boo! Who in God's name was it? Cindy has since wondered often where a kind assistant from beyond originated; too many times to count. She remains as awestruck by a memory as she was by the event, that such powers exist; a force capable of manipulating objects at will or rescuing a damsel in distress. About the will; the intention behind an action: the child was in an untenable predicament. At precisely the moment she required another set of hands and a stronger back, it *appeared* as an invisible manifestation. It *knew* what she needed and did her bidding, in spite of the fact she had requested assistance only from a mortal soul; a corporeal problem causing her to seek an equally corporeal solution. A truly benevolent soul was watching over her; someone willing and able to help in a crisis. To this day, Cindy is as blown away when recalling that encounter as she was on the blustery day it occurred; the day a rogue plank from a horse corral went sailing with the wind: a pivotal moment in her spiritual development. She did not just rebuild the fence with a savior that fateful day; she built a bridge to a higher faith. Whoever it was, whatever altruistic spirit intervened on her behalf, whoever the metaphysical force was coming to her aid in a storm, it stunned away her tears and warmed her to the bone. Holding that heavy plank in place, it steadied the weight of the wood in spite of a gusty wind whipping against it. Cynthia made contact, the implicit messages clearly received in both directions. It was something miraculous; someone wonderful stepped through the portal of eternity. In return for effort extended, it received the eternal gratitude of a child as an everlasting Light.

"Will is to grace as the horse is to the rider."
Saint Augustine of Hippo

~ going for a joy ride ~

Bathsheba

"A wounded spirit who can bear?"
Proverbs xviii. 14

Could it be true? Was this the evil temptress so many proclaimed her to be in her own time and since? Was the young woman accused of impaling the skull of a baby with a needle the same old woman haunting and threatening and chanting incantations in the night? There is no written history of the life of Bathsheba Sherman, save what records remain of her inquest regarding the death of an infant. Folklore and fable, rumor and innuendo: all that remains of the one called Bathsheba; scary stories handed down over the generations as she became more a punch line than a persona. Anecdotal evidence alone does not make a spooky story true. There was something deeper to discover.

Carolyn had to know more about her. Fran became the sidekick, her partner in pursuit of the whole truth. On a raw November afternoon, Carolyn scoured through dusty archives at Glocester Town Hall. This time, though, Fran was there beside her. On their way through the front door they literally ran into a local treasure. Edna Kent was the woman who knew more than anybody else about the history of that region; a sauntering encyclopedia. She was quite the lady; stately and majestic, gracious and good-humored, willing to share what she knew with anybody interested and inclined to listen. The natural historian possessed a voracious appetite for knowledge, much like Carolyn. Edna Kent devoured every old book she could locate; anything pertaining to their area: Foster, Glocester and Burrillville; rural, remote northwest corner of the state. Most of the earliest homes had survived, many as farms, including her own; a spectacular Colonial specimen surrounded by rich, fertile lowlands on the outskirts of Chepachet. Fran's instinct dictated she detain her friend; keep her from whatever chore had brought her there by introducing Carolyn. The three women shivered as they stood beneath black, billowing clouds...an ominous promise of winter: an impending doom. It was really quite spooky; perfectly suited to their subject matter. There they huddled blocking the main entrance, outside in the cold damp air, chatting for the better part of an hour. Three fair maidens spoke of ancient graveyards and an assortment of obscure dumpsites they had discovered over the years; the earliest homes and names of original families in the area going back to the Colonial era. Lost in thought, distracted by the content of their conversation these ladies apparently forgot the three of them were free at any time to step back inside an almost too toasty town hall. It never occurred to any of them to do so.

Mrs. Kent asked Fran what and who they were researching. Fran divulged the mission. Carolyn was anxious to hear Fran's longtime friend expound on anything she knew though she knew little of Bathsheba. However, Edna did know Mr. McKeachern, deeming him a reliable source of information as well as a lovely companion. Her endorsement was in keeping with his sterling and gold reputation in Harrisville. This gentleman knew well his own neck of the woods and everyone dwelling within them, past and present. Explaining how well-acquainted she was with him, the man as kind and gentle as their mutual friend Mr. Kenyon, Carolyn told Edna how they first met.

"We were just out joyriding again...searching for cellar holes, graveyards, abandoned dumpsites; the usual." Carolyn remembered details of excursions. "Fran knows this local area better than I ever will. We drove past his house off Sherman Farm. I noticed all the outbuildings and wondered if he had any old tools for sale so I went back a few days later. We never did talk about his tools but we've discussed *everything* else ever since. He's a wonderful man."

Mr. McKeachern befriended Carolyn, passing on whatever he knew of the infamous Bathsheba Sherman. He'd found her eagerness refreshing and must certainly have enjoyed her fascination with all things historical, closely akin to interests of his own. Sometimes they would meet in passing at the village butcher shop or inside their local bakery, prompting a cordial chat. There was a genuine fondness between them, one transcending time. He was an elderly gentleman whose attempt at discretion caused him great consternation as he struggled to describe the Bathsheba *he* knew in terms he considered suitable for feminine ears; a most endearing part of his eccentric personality. She got the message. Euphemisms aside, Bathsheba was implied a bitch from hell.

Delighted to know of their association, Mrs. Kent graciously offered access to her library as these women delved deeper into local historical records. She had an extensive collection open for lending only to close friends; a generous offer Carolyn accepted as a compliment. Edna owned an enormous collection of vintage clothing, all carefully preserved in trunks, some dating back to the early 1600s. Her mind-boggling assortment became an invaluable resource as later, when Carolyn was enlisted to be a **Band Booster,** (parents coerced into fund-raising for the high school) she put her new contacts to good use. It was a more than worthy cause. Fran and Edna produced the clothing and Carolyn willingly produced and coordinated an *antique* fashion show. Along with the tireless help of a group of fine ladies, mothers of musicians, they put on quite a display. Word was out by that time. They may have whispered a bit behind her back but presented nothing but respect for her many talents and abilities. Mrs. Kent gave Carolyn unfettered access to an attic stuffed full of vintage clothing and their fashion show was a standing-room-only success, raising a huge chunk of the money required to purchase new band uniforms and send their troupe (including her eldest daughter) off to Florida to play at the grand opening of **Disney World** in February of 1974. As Fran's friend, Edna Kent embraced Carolyn by proxy, doing her utmost to assist in that effort any way she could. They supported one another sharing information, tossing reference materials around like so much penny candy. Each enjoyed their like-minded companions; an association beginning on frigid granite steps in Chepachet.

The three bolted for shelter when cold rain began as light showers. Carolyn said goodbye then raced for the car. Though her search through the archives proved fruitless on that day the greatest discovery had come from outside the building as she rummaged through the mind of a learned soul sister, gaining more insight than expected from this trip. Immersing herself in the history of local villages was exciting; meeting the grand dame of historians...inspiring. Finally, after so much time feeling isolated and alone, Carolyn made friends who understood her compulsion to know more, to learn as much as possible about the former inhabitants of her home. As if it was a given, as if everyone lived in a haunted house (as many in this area do) the ladies never discussed the ghostly manifestations in their homes. Research had a presumed purpose; to identify the characters with whom they had become familiar over time and space. No need for gossip about them, no point in divulging the details; what mattered was the answer to the questions: who was it and when did they live? How did they die? Where had they been buried and what did they do in life which might have compelled them to remain behind, Earth-bound in death? These were pertinent inquiries; all else qualified as peripheral to the process. A hunt for Bathsheba was on with a vengeance: Time to visit a friend again.

Mr. McKeachern happily welcomed the company, inviting Carolyn into his house. She told him about meeting Mrs. Edna Kent and he told her where to find the "old" Arnold cemetery, tombstones dating back to the 1600's. While sharing a cozy cup of tea, some warmth to ward off the chill of another harsh winter looming, he made a veiled reference to a longstanding rumor he could repeat but not substantiate; some question regarding the final resting place of Bathsheba. He was not at all certain she had been buried in hallowed ground, after all, even though her gravestone rested in the center of the quiet village. An intriguing notion, Carolyn wondered if she was buried somewhere on the Arnold Estate, perhaps beneath the unmarked bell stone out on her property near the old cellar hole. It became her fervent intention to investigate further, come spring. In the meantime, she asked what he remembered of Bathsheba. Bitter. Vindictive. Hateful and Unholy; only a few of the words he'd chosen to describe an evil woman. She was horrible to the help; he'd accused her of starving and beating the staff in her charge at Sherman Farm. Womenfolk of the village considered her a harlot; men folk leered the same way except they did so with rapacious eyes. Bathsheba was a ravishing beauty in youth but he claimed she sacrificed both due to choices she made in life. Mr. McKeachern never tired of discussing historical aspects of this area, apparently enjoying a little gossip on the side; a pleasant perk of the research. Carolyn marveled at his memory and a resplendent Christmas cactus displayed in his kitchen. He beamed with pride speaking of his prized plant: "It's more than one hundred years old; older than me...but not by much." As Carolyn departed, he waved, sending her along an intrepid historical journey with an old Scottish proverb: "Be happy while you're living...for you're a long time dead." His new friend got the message as prophetic advice.

***

Bathsheba: A God-forsaken Soul. By all accounts, her life had been tragic. It was easy for some to believe she was evil; to pass swift judgment and then suggest a harsher punishment. Harder still to listen to such a horror story and *not* believe there was at least some merit to an accusation leveled against her. In her time, there was not DNA evidence to exonerate her or, for that matter, conclusively pin that event upon her as a brutal crime committed. She'd said it was an accidental death. Some said she was a witch, exclaiming her actions those of an evil temptress, a child used as lamb in a sadistic ritual, a sacrifice made; a deal struck with the devil...in exchange for preserving her youth and beauty for eternity. Words are weapons...as sharp as any needle on Earth.

"When one tears away the veils and shows them naked,
people's souls give off a pungent smell of decay."
Octave Mirbeau

a stitch in time

"Absence of evidence is not evidence of absence."
Carl Sagan

The evening never did relinquish the heat of the day, coveting it instead. A refreshing breeze tickled the lace curtains as it feebly attempted to enter the house, causing the fabric to flutter, dancing gracefully inside window frames. Carolyn had no objection to the heat. She always warmly welcomed summer, embracing it as some long lost friend, inviting it in to stay as long as it liked; welcome home. It was quite late, perhaps 1:00 a.m. as Carolyn lay sprawled across their long leather sofa, belly down, taking full advantage of lamp light from the end table. Engrossed in a book, she felt nothing but a comfort zone of calm around her as familiar words she'd revisited many times in the past. Entire passages of it had been memorized long before, but she went back to it whenever sleep eluded her, using these words as a natural tranquilizer.

Dressed in a sleeveless blouse and white cotton shorts, quite comfortable in every regard, Carolyn's thoughts remained uncluttered. The house had been quiet for hours and she had nothing pressing to resolve. There had been no manifestations for months; such a prolonged absence of activity, duly noted. Of late, everyone had been feeling much more at ease. While laying in place, enjoying the solitude, relishing beautiful language unfolding page after page before her eyes, Carolyn was abruptly struck...attacked from behind.

She felt a sharp stabbing pain in her calf. Turning quickly around to see if a bee had stung her, Carolyn saw nothing on her leg except a mounding puddle of blood at the point of impact. The wound was deep, plunging well into the muscle. She leapt up from the sofa, certain a creature was loose in the parlor, preparing to strike again; perhaps a wasp or maybe a beetle. It did not occur to her this event was anything other than a *natural* phenomenon; to consider she was not alone. There had been none of the normally expected indications usually accompanying paranormal episodes; no sudden drop in temperature, no odors in the room; nothing which would compel her to believe otherwise. The pain was real; the blood was real. Her muscle went into spasm, hobbling the woman. As the "Charlie horse" subsided, she began looking around in the parlor, initiating a thorough search of their premises to determine where the culprit might be hiding. She checked the sofa over for sharp, foreign objects. The windows were clear of flying critters, as were the curtains, a cozy place to cling. The notion of a bee sting was remote; little chance a bee would have stung her at night. She pulled the sofa away from the wall, peering behind it. There were no insects or stray objects on the floor; no empirical evidence of anything unusual, nothing protruding from the cushion of the sofa on which she'd been laying, nothing on the coffee table: Nothing.

Carolyn finally abandoned her search. She went in the bathroom to cleanse the wound inflicted. It was still bleeding profusely. Once the point of impact became visible, she noticed the size of the puncture wound. It was distinctly round, quite deep, as if a large sewing needle had impaled her skin, leaving behind a perfectly concentric circle; a sudden stick doing more damage than merely scratching the surface. Her calf was very swollen, though not the way it would have been had some type of venom been injected into a tender area. Limping as she went along, Carolyn tried to walk off then rub out the spasm. Returning to the parlor, a perplexed woman investigated the immediate area around the point of contact, attempting to determine the nature of an injury sustained. Confounded, she gave up and revisited her book.

Dismissing this event as some sort of anomaly, several days passed before the wound healed, stiff muscle softened and a painful leg returned to normal. Life went on; time to prepare for the girls' return to school in September. She was a busy mother and simply forgot about the queer incident, shoving it into the back of her mind. It would be a couple of years before she recalled this episode, during a conversation she had with Ed and Lorraine Warren. While Carolyn was displaying her research to the couple, she told them the story of Bathsheba Sherman: The needle. Was it even possible? Could it be true? Had the woman taken a weapon with her into the afterlife? Could she use it from beyond this world...beyond the grave? Lorraine posited a theory of her own: demons are indeed capable of inflicting pain upon mortals; capable of doing harm across dimensions, defying *time* as we perceive it. Their conversation triggered her memory of this strangely disquieting incident and so it remains; a painful consideration. Intuition revealed a likely suspect; a logical lead to a culprit. Divulging the tale of a woman supposedly wielding a weapon in life, from that point forward this psychic presumed it was *her* needlework doing the devil's footwork; a needle and the damage it had done in life and perhaps in the afterlife. From then on Mrs. Warren referred to the God-forsaken spirit as the lone demonic presence in their house, calling her by name: Bathsheba.

"Since we fear most that which is unknown to us, defining moments of change occur when we choose to know our fear."
Lee J. Cohen

from insult to injury

"Think twice before you speak, and then you may be able to say something more insulting than if you spoke right out at once."
Evan Esar

Roger would never believe this! What would be the point in telling him? A needle or some other long, thin, sharp object had been plunged into her leg. It drew a substantial amount of blood then caused her calf to cramp into a knot; a striking sensation in every conceivable sense of the word. It was a can-of-worms moment. Pandora wanted in on it. No ugly bugs lurking in the parlor. Nothing had flown into the room to bite or sting her that evening. Instead, the woman had been blatantly attacked from beyond the grave: physical damage done. Extrapolating out, it meant the spirits were capable of inflicting injury. It *felt* like an evil intention to deliberately harm another, albeit from another dimension! If it was indeed crossing over which culminated in an aggressive encounter, it posed a physical threat: Punishment. The weapon of choice was an interesting pick; jamming into her skin with some force and real velocity. It was no accident, not a coincidence. Not a beetle or a bee; the depth of this wound precluding any insect from a list of usual suspects. In fact, the suspect in this case was quite unusual and she had a history: Bathsheba.

Was she capable of reaching through time and space to draw blood? If so, was it a clue to her identity? As an omen: as the harbinger of things to come? Carolyn was learning much of her sordid history, accusation levied; details of a crime she had supposedly committed in life which some said claimed her in death. If she was the culprit, one suspected of using a needle to get her point across, the only evidence left behind at the scene of the crime was blood.

However, it was a corresponding lack of evidence which caused Carolyn's investigation to continue. The parlor had been thoroughly searched after this assault occurred. There was no explanation for it in the natural world and, as strange as it may seem, a supernatural explanation was the most likely and *logical* regarding the recondite event; a viable option, after all. Over time and with a concerted effort, research revealed Bathsheba Sherman's personality. Mr. McKeachern did much to advance the cause. He'd described her as being prone to violence; a spiteful, vindictive woman capable of inflicting physical harm on another as she'd been known to do with her servants or farm hands; loathed and feared, in equal measure. If she had shown someone compassion in life, it was later kept as a well-guarded secret in death and was certainly in conflict with her reputation. She was considered diabolical by many souls.

Considering the possibilities as well as the improbabilities in earnest, it was incumbent upon Carolyn to piece this puzzle together. If she wanted to solve the riddle it would require her rapt attention. As spiritual enigma, Bathsheba worked on Carolyn, consuming her mental and physical energy. The insult: Get out of *my* house. The injury: self-evident. A mortal soul felt increasingly imposed upon, clearly unwelcome in *her* home. She'd had wanted to inform her husband about it, needed to trust him enough to impart a message which might not be well-received. There was always a risk he would say the wrong thing but this time she thought it was worth the risk and one she should take. If only he would listen...

To tell or not to tell Roger: From injury to insult, he expressed himself in a way which would offend almost anyone except for someone who was just as obtuse. Thick-headed was not just for hair anymore. Beneath that ample load of locks on his head was a thicker skull. He just didn't get it. He did not hear her. He did not listen. He did not know how, preoccupied by formulating his next argument against whatever position she had taken on any given matter. Make matters worse...she finally told her husband...well after the fact.

"That attack happened while you were away...a couple of summers ago. I told Lorraine. She says it is a significant encounter; a demonic manifestation.

"So, now you're both assuming it is the spirit of Bathsheba Sherman."

"It seems rather obvious to me. Yes. That's my conclusion; hers too."

"Want to hear my conclusion? I think you're *both* out of your minds!" His response knocked the wind out of her. Wounded again; his tongue as sharp as any knife. No reason to go any further with a combative conversation. It had been snapped off at the point of impact: this time...her heart.

According to the wise Confucius, "Ignorance is the night of the mind, but a night without moon and star." If the shoe fits, Roger, then see if it fits in your mouth, along with your foot! Conflict: "Against logic there is no armor like ignorance." (Laurence J. Peter) He had insulted her intelligence and integrity; she considered her words as pearls before swine and would not cast another. The conclusion logically drawn; them was fightin' words... and this was war.

Breaking the icy tingle between them, a husband approached his wife.

"What could you possibly want from me, Roger?" The sincere woman was a little sarcastic, but that predisposition came quite naturally by this time.

"I want you to tell me what happened again." Roger, equally sincere.

"Why? What's the point? Other than a sharp implement at the end of your tongue, always ready to strike out at me. I mean, other than unleashing a host of false accusations, another one of your venomous tirades, tell me, Roger, what sense would there be in telling you what happened to me, again, when you didn't believe me the first time; a waste of breath. I'm supposed to try to convince you? I have much better things to do." Made her point! With that, Carolyn turned her back on her husband and walked away, abruptly ending the uncivil discourse. He had done the same to her for years. How insulting.

"He who wishes to exert a useful influence must be careful to insult nothing. Let him not be troubled by what seems absurd, but concentrate his energies to the creation of what is good. He must not demolish, but build."
Johann Wolfgang von Goethe

is this the party to whom I am speaking?

"There are no guarantees. From the viewpoint of fear, none are
strong enough. From the viewpoint of love, none are necessary."
Emmanuel Teney

No one dared presume the spirits were gone. Even though there had
been a long period of relative peace in the farmhouse, this had been the
case before. Something always shattered their silence. In fact, there were
frequent periods of tranquility; respite from a disruptive influence everyone
came to expect. A return to normalcy was always welcome…never taken
for granted. The mood was lighthearted this night. Everyone had settled
in front of the tube to enjoy another raucous, hysterically funny episode of
Laugh-In; the family favorite.

Apparently, it was sock-it-to-me time…again.

The telephone had been an issue in the past. Those incidents seemed rather
mischievous in nature, as the tampering committed by an invisible force with
too much time and outer space on its hands, capable of manipulating objects;
lifting it, dropping it, pulling it from human hands at inopportune moments,
but this was different. It was around 3:30 a.m. when their telephone began
to ring. Roger and Carolyn instantly arose from bed, each sprinting to a
separate part of the house. Carolyn went straight to the parlor, Roger into
the kitchen. Any call coming at that time of night is usually not very good
news. Each of them alarmed, both jolted from sleep, they were equally
anxious to silence an intrusive presence of noise before it woke their entire
family. Arriving at her destination quickly, Carolyn expectantly answered
the telephone. "Hello?" It continued to ring in her hand. Roger arrived in the
kitchen and answered the phone, not realizing his wife had already done so.
His receiver continued ringing as well. It seemed so loud; perhaps because
the house was quiet. The normal sound of it became magnified. "Hello?"
Husband and wife met in the dining room, each aggravated by a disturbance.
"Mine's not working!" then "Neither is mine!" "Try tapping the receiver!"
and then "I did that already!" Both telephones continued ringing unabated
with both receivers off of their respective cradles. Roger walked back into

the kitchen and hung it up twice, trying over and over again to make a connection stick. Carolyn did the same, answering it again with certain trepidation in her voice. It kept ringing. Roger slammed the receiver down, unplugging it from the wall unit. It kept ringing. Carolyn disengaged the jack in the parlor. The telephones continued chiming. Roger pulled its wires from the wall, effectively disabling it; under *ordinary* circumstances. Not so. It became a mind-numbing alarm signal, torturous to mortal ears. Roger found his wife in the parlor, attempting to comfort their confused children. They had made their way downstairs, awaking with all the commotion as that monotonous ring tone continued to expand, reverberating within the walls of the old farmhouse, burgeoning with each passing minute. Children were nervous; their parents annoyed by an obnoxious and relentless middle-of-the-night wake-up call: Contact. Roger cupped his hands around Carolyn's ear, virtually the only way she'd be able to receive this message: *"Someone or something is trying to reach us!"* She nodded with its receipt. The frustrated man went into the center of their dining room, a spot where he could and would be heard throughout the dwelling. Forewarning his family in advance to cover their ears, Roger then deliberately unleashed a fast-rising temper, shouting an objection in his deepest, burliest voice...for *all* to hear. *"Stop it! Leave us the hell alone!"* His caustic demand instantly snuffed out the sound. Dead silence. Roger had effectively scared away the ghost.

Sending their children back up to bed, the couple sat together in the parlor discussing what had just happened. There was no sense to make of it at all. The intention of the call seemed obvious; to disrupt the peaceful, quiet home. A restless night after such an unnerving incident, they both stayed up until dawn, waiting for it to happen again. Waiting and watching, listening as one, they sat in silence as deafening as sound which preceded it: keeping vigil.

***

So far removed from those troubling times, it is now much easier to make Light of such spirit matters. Carolyn recalls the irritating episode with clarity; quipping in jest about something which struck her years later, a notion she still finds amusing. "It's too bad we didn't have an answering machine. Had it even been invented yet? That would have been one *hell* of a message!" A sense of humor can be quite a valuable asset when reconciling incidents such as these; encounters which would otherwise plunge a somewhat less pliable mind into a black hole: the pit of depression. Ah! Levity! In homage to Lily Tomlin: either laughing in or crying out loud, mortals found a way to cope.

one ringy-dingy…two ringy-dingy…

"Reality is that which, when you stop believing in it, doesn't go away."
Philip K. Dick

~ **Can you hear me now?** ~

a pain in the neck

*"I reached for sleep and drew it round me like a blanket
muffling pain and thought together in the merciful dark."*
Mary Stewart

Carolyn had taken a sudden turn for the worse. The pain she'd endured was more than distracting. It was relentless. There was no time of the day or night when her neck did not throb. Sometimes sharp and stabbing; at other times, a low, dull ache, but always...always, it hurt. It was not something attributable to any injury she'd sustained. To her knowledge she had not done anything to disturb the bones and muscles of her neck, but she had disturbed the Cosmos.

***

A theme was emerging; there had to be a direct connection to an apparition whose neck appeared snapped, a head hanging off to one side. Why Carolyn? Why had she been repeatedly attacked on the neck? First, it was the scythe in the barn and then the coat hanger wielded as a weapon in the warm room and now the sensation of her neck being literally broken. As she had never before experienced such severity of pain, not even during childbirth, it was beyond a mortal imagination. Ice packs, hot compresses... nothing provided any relief. She could not turn her head without turning her entire body along with it. As a serious predicament worsened with the pain, Carolyn sought the assistance of the doctor in town. He ordered x-rays and blood tests then kindly provided the prescription for an equally serious pain killer. It made her face itch like a sonofabitch; a small price to pay for a break from the pain of a broken neck. No rest for the weary...Carolyn was exhausted beyond mortal measure.

Certain these films would reveal the true nature of her problem, as it turned out, the Nature of the problem was invisible to modern medicine. There were no signs of arthritis or any obstruction; no swelling or attributable causes for the excruciating discomfort. The doctor was as stymied as his patient. When the results came in and the conversation altered, it was enough to plunge this dispirited woman into hopelessness. No exit. No way out. Perhaps over time it would heal: the only suggestion he'd offered; Darvon, the lone remedy. For Carolyn, it was like putting a bandage on cancer, in the hope it would heal by benign neglect. Huddled in front of the fireplace, she wondered if she would ever sleep soundly again; wondered if there was a legitimate affiliation to be drawn between the way she had been targeted and this chronic pain. Was it an outcome of assaults she'd sustained at the hands of a demon? Why was no physical sign of this kind of agony evident? What had a hold on her? If there was no logical explanation, should she consider an illogical cause? The root of it had to be supernatural in origin, yet she refused to accept the notion of the affliction occurring to her physical form as a psychic attack. It seemed so implausible. It was actually one element of her transition: Transformation.

In retrospect, Carolyn now believes that period of time was reflective of an assault on her person and her personality. She has listened to her children and knows what they witnessed was real; including her metamorphosis endured a few decades before at the hands of a presence which was literally attempting to usurp her being. Looking back, it makes more sense as a manifestation of the apparition who appeared to her. Which one was it? Boo! Who was it that came to her and then her children? So many women have died there; Arnold, Richardson and Baker: only a few of the family names she would discover associated with the property. Records indicated multiple deaths had occurred there and relatively few of these documents were complete with any details. In fact, some certificates seemed to be deliberately vague and non-descript, especially regarding the cause of death. Was there something to hide?

However, Carolyn had yet to learn of the long, rich and infamous history of the Arnold family at their homestead. Mrs. Arnold hung herself in their barn. There was no way to determine if she'd been the one appearing in the night; no way to know for certain who this entity had been in life. Mrs. Arnold was into her nineties at the time she committed suicide. The form and substance it assumed appeared young and well-preserved. As for Bathsheba, she lived to be an old woman as well, so who could it be?

According to Mr. McKeachern she was well into her eighties when he was just a boy. What about the young woman who appeared in the kitchen? Who was it that died inside the pantry?

So many questions...so many souls.

Essentially, the entire story is one gigantic puzzle and, in some cases, it has literally required decades for these pieces to come together, to come into play as this tale unfolds. Yet, this is destined to be a story without an end, a puzzle left incomplete; no means or desires to reconcile the disparate elements or to attain coherence, no matter how rigorously Carolyn had done so in the past. Left unsatisfied, in certain corners, it might be considered a futile effort made from the beginning, unless it doesn't matter who or what caused these events to occur. That they happened at all is miraculous. These missing pieces have much to do with what is unknowable and it is incumbent upon those involved to acknowledge it is so. This story is not an investigation. It is a memoir. The investigation supposedly happened some thirty-five years ago and it was then determined by Mrs. Warren, concluding that the entity with the broken neck was Bathsheba Sherman, but nobody on the planet knows for sure if it is true. Speculation, intelligent guessing is all mortal souls have at their disposal and to claim otherwise is utterly disingenuous. To a certain extent, belief factors into this equation. Anyone present at the time would attest to this fact; based upon interpersonal communications, Mrs. Warren was acting and speaking in good faith because there is no doubt she believed what she was claiming and was certain she felt psychic vibrations of an evil spirit, a demon in the home. One piece of the puzzle at the center of the bigger picture: something wicked was intervening in Carolyn's personality and was adversely affecting her in a multitude of ways: physically, mentally, emotionally, psychically: spiritually.

There was no defeating this enemy, not with conventional weaponry. If this was indeed Bathsheba's doing, she had become a real pain in the neck on too many levels to count. Carolyn had to take an alternate route around an enemy position; the road less traveled. In time, she accepted the presence of the pain as something supernatural in Nature. In the interim, she found her tolerance for pain increasing with her intolerance for the cause of it, each expanding in equal measure. Turning away from the bottle of pills in a medicine cabinet, it was only a matter of time before she'd find a path to peace. The doctors tried but could not help her. Instead, she sought respite where she'd found it in the past, in times of crisis, during trial and tribulation. Ultimately, Carolyn was a victorious combatant in a brutal battle waged against her invisible adversary. She turned to something far more powerful than the pain then prayed it away.

"History, despite its wrenching pain, cannot be unlived, however, if faced with courage, need not be lived again."
Maya Angelou

message received

*"The only way to discover the limits of the possible
is by going beyond them into the impossible."*
Arthur C. Clarke

Whenever Roger arrived home in a good mood from a successful road trip it usually meant a happy family outing was in the offing. **Janet's Ice Cream** in North Smithfield was a frequent haunt; a tolerable drive after days on open highway. The black raspberry was addictive; Carolyn preferred the pistachio, though Roger would occasionally indulge them with banana splits all around. It was always quite a pleasant excursion with the exception of one evening. The car became exceptionally crowded. Seems someone had hitched a ride.

Throughout dinner Carolyn talked about Bathsheba Sherman, recounting what she had learned from Mr. McKeachern just the day before. Perhaps she should not have been so forthcoming in front of the children, unaware she'd been frightening one of them. The folklore he shared with her was gruesome, not the kind of visions one wants planted into a child's gray matter, there to reside forever; the stuff of nightmares. Cindy was being particularly affected, sensitive as she was to the other side of twilight. Carolyn thought of it more as a history lesson and spared no details retelling the tale she'd heard from an old man who knew it well; someone who knew Bathsheba Sherman as a boy. Cynthia finally put the name to a repulsive face she knew all too well.

Roger arrived home to spaghetti dinner, one of his favorites. The meatballs were luscious. He was in a delightful mood. Night air cooling nicely after the very warm day, everyone was instantly amenable to his bright idea. Once ice cream was mentioned, Roger thought Carolyn would drop the sordid subject and move on to another but she continued to further inform him all about Mr. McKeachern's visit; how she created a divining rod with his instructions and what he said about the legendary and infamous figure…Bathsheba Sherman. She told him about the crime of which she'd been accused, about the inquest which followed and how she got off the hook: Insufficient evidence. Free at last…but not really, because what she was accused of doing haunted her for a lifetime. A bad reputation was further tarnished: a witch who sold her soul to the devil for eternal youth and beauty…a plan which apparently backfired as she grew old and haggard well before her time.

Finished with dinner, the children began squirming in their seats, anxious to go on their promised ride to the ice cream stand. Expediting things, Roger declared dishes could wait and the kids loaded into his car. All the way down Round Top Road, through Harrisville onto Victory Highway, all the way into North Smithfield, Carolyn kept telling her husband and anyone else who was listening, the lurid details of a gory story. She found it fascinating; believing what she'd discovered would answer some questions regarding the house and its history. As a compelling exploration, this was a privileged excursion into the past through the words of a man whose eyes beheld what he spoke of; she considered the elder gentleman a piece of living history, contributing a rarity: firsthand knowledge of events. He was only a boy when Bathsheba Sherman had grown old but he knew a great deal about her life (because children listen to the adults around them) and he'd apparently retained all that information. Carolyn became transfixed by the subject, a point obvious to all.

Though the girls managed to escape a rather lopsided conversation between their parents while seated some distance away at the picnic table, they would soon reunite, traveling together again. Carolyn was engrossed. She seemed to be unaware of this discomfort level, rising steadily. Cynthia had enough of it. Though she was known as the most demure among that bunch, a soft spoken, temperate young lady, her intolerance piqued; a temper reared its ugly head.

"Mom! Stop this! I can't stand it! I don't care about Bathsheba Sherman!" Everyone fell silent as she took a deep breath then continued. "You've been talking about her all night long! I'm sick to death of hearing it!" Cynthia's shrill voice grew much louder, magnified by the quiet of her rapt audience. "As far as I'm concerned that old witch can go straight to hell! Right back to where she came from!" The child's outburst was angry and uninhibited.

She did not consider the impossible consequences of such a harsh indictment or a judgment call made at the top of her lungs. An order issued: Cindy was still too young to be mindful of the concept…what gets put out in the Universe is important and may come back to haunt the one sending a message received.

Fire in the hole! At the precise moment Cynthia shouted her condemnation, Roger threw a cigarette out the front window. The evening air cooled quickly after sunset. Windows were sealed shut all except for Roger's window which was open a crack because he'd been smoking. As he flicked the butt from his fingertips, (away from the car, as was part of this habit) the object defied all physical law. It flew alongside the car, abruptly stopping outside the window. Then it flew through the glass, landing directly in Cynthia's lap. Legitimately awestruck, she could not believe her eyes. Shorts were scorched. Her eldest sister was frantically trying to douse the fire and expel the offending object. Tirade over: the eruption ending as Cindy was rendered virtually speechless.

"Get it! There! Knock it onto the floor!" Carolyn was leaning over the seat, attempting to help. Roger drove erratically, trying to observe the commotion created behind him from the narrow mirror. Having logically assumed he had been at fault, the one to blame for this incident, he felt responsible and guilty about it in equal measure. "There it is! Step on it! Put it out on the mat."

No one got burned. Cindy's favorite shorts were history. A recurring theme emerged: Punishment time. Sassing an elder…disrespecting the dead.

"Everyone all right back there?" Roger waited for an affirmative reply then said: "*That's* what you get for talking to your mother that way!" He winked at Cindy, catching her frantic eyes in the rearview mirror; letting her know in an instant with one sly gesture how sorry he was for his perceived infraction. She was off the hook for saying aloud what everyone else had been thinking.

"Dad, it *didn't* come in through your window. It came in through the glass, back here." Andrea stomped out the offending flame on the floorboard as she said something no one understood, except for Cindy. She saw it, too.

"What? That's impossible." A grimace pinching his lips tugged at the sides of Roger's nose. "If yours is shut then it came back in through mine."

"I'm telling you, dad...I saw it happen! The windows are closed. It came in right through the glass! I can't explain what I saw but that's what happened."

"Sorry, mom." Cindy's voice trembled; not the boisterous tone she'd had a few moments before while chastising her enthusiastic mother then dismissing a vindictive spirit, effectively banishing her from the center of conversation.

"The car *does* feel crowded tonight; either you guys are growing up too fast or a witch came along for the ride!" Roger tried to make light of their hectic situation without realizing he may have inadvertently spoken truth to power. "Hey Cin, maybe you're apologizing to the wrong woman!" Making Light.

"It's *crowded* because we're growing *out* too fast! Ate too much ice cream! Thanks, daddy!" Patting her belly, Nancy smiled and waved in the mirror.

"Mom...I saw it happen." Cynthia gazed pleadingly into her mother's eyes. "I think I made Bathsheba Sherman mad."

"I think she was *mad* way before you came along!" Andrea made her point.

"Don't worry, sweetie. It's over." Trying to assuage a daughter's concerns, Carolyn wondered if Bathsheba had taken offense, if this incident was some form of retribution, as Cindy's punishment for name-calling: Consequences. According to Mr. McKeachern, Bathsheba Sherman enjoyed being the center of attention. Perhaps she did not *want* the subject changed...

"I swear to God."

"No swearing...that's what got you into trouble in the first place!" Tapping number four on the nose, her mother's playful posturing was called for in the moment but Cindy would have none of it. She wanted to explain exactly how it happened and clearly needed to be believed.

"I swear to God! I saw a cigarette flying out the crack of dad's window and start to pass by my window about half way down when it stopped! It stopped outside! Then it shot like a bullet! It shot straight through the glass right here, right in front of my eyes! The window is closed all the way! Look! I haven't touched it!" Desperate to be understood, Cindy cried tears of frustration.

"I believe you, honey. I can see it's closed...all the way up." Carolyn tried to calm the distraught child. "Just relax...we're almost home."

"It landed in my lap! Sparks jumped all over the place! It landed in *my* lap! *I'm* the one who made her mad! Look what she did to my favorite shorts!"

"Maybe she didn't like the way you were yelling at mom." Christine finally had use of her tongue, probably frozen stiff by the ice cream. It had thawed.

"Well, you *did* call her a witch!" Nancy justified this perceived retaliation. "You hurt her feelings. That oughta teach ya!" Test comes first; lesson later.

Never ditch a witch...they have great aim and are usually on target.

History lessons learned: Cindy refused to speak ill of the woman ever again and has never said a single word against her since; a sign of fear and respect. Bathsheba Sherman's power *is* formidable and it should be acknowledged as such; as two children witnessed the overt manipulation of a dangerous object, likely meant to frighten then to silence one youngster. Mission accomplished. Message received...by all. Perhaps their discourse had divulged her identity.

***

"I shut my mouth after that!" Cindy recalls details of this incident; a vision she'll never forget. However, over several decades of reflection she has come to an understanding and has realized how the experience specifically altered her conceptualization of the spirits in fundamental ways. She now asserts the most significant element of this manifestation was invisible: the evolution of thought. Cindy no longer cares who believes her because she knows what she saw; likewise, she knows what it means. Cynthia changed her mind about the spirits during that evening. She saw them in a different light because of this encounter and realized they are no different than we are…they have feelings, too. Attitudes. Responses. Reactions. No matter what or who it was there, it *was* there: a stowaway had accompanied the family on an outing; someone in (or just outside) a moving vehicle heard the offensive words of the teenager, sparking a consequence. Cindy believes she was **supposed** to see it happen, insisting there was a deeper message imparted, intended as an integral part of her ongoing spiritual development. Her natural reserve made Cynthia nearly dormant in comparison to her sisters, yet on the evening in question, hostility she could not control had suddenly consumed a child, unleashing an entirely foreign, out-of-character spontaneous combustion of negative energy, further charging an atmosphere already enflamed by emotion. The blatantly targeted negative response Cindy received was as immediate as it gets. Her attention was deliberately diverted, drawn to the event as it transpired; her gaze fixed on the cigarette as it flew from her father's fingers then out his open window. She witnessed its momentum as the wind caught the object. Then, watching it stop in midair saw it catapulting back inside the car with a force she could hardly imagine; its fire flying in her direction, passing through a solid piece of tempered glass. It occurred with purpose and reason. It was a Revelation. No one should even attempt to convince her otherwise. Cindy's recollection of those few seconds now run through her mind as if in slow motion, much the same way it appeared to her that night, during one of the rides of her life. The youngster learned a series of valuable lessons in the context of a singular event, primary among them, certain knowledge that spirits are not tethered to the homes in which they dwell. They are free to be. Bathsheba is free to pass judgment in death in much the same manner it was passed on her in life, free to reply to her harshest critic by whatever means she chooses, free to express her feelings and make her presence known, perhaps as an act of retribution. There was no escaping the spirits unscathed. As Cindy so often bluntly states regarding their existence: "No matter where you go…

there they are." Death looms larger than life at light speed and they are the source of enlightenment.

"As far as we can discern, the sole purpose of human existence is to kindle a light in the darkness of mere being."
Carl Gustav Jung

twisted sister

Christine had the face of an angel. This child, with enormous blue eyes and platinum blonde hair accentuating the smile which could melt human hearts; the middle sister shared a sweet disposition with everybody she met. So often a large family has one who gets lost in the fray, but this was not the case with Chris. Her sisters gravitated toward her; they felt the desire to include her in everything they did. Because of her reliable sense of humor, well developed, they were bound to share some laughter with the one always ready to crack a quick joke. Christine was somewhat shy around strangers though her buoyant personality was fully unleashed around her siblings. Generous to a fault, her very best toys were routinely and graciously loaned. Meticulous about their bedroom and her belongings, incessantly cleaning up behind those who often used her space for play, she did so without complaint, counting the trolls and puppets while she replaced them into compartments of a case she kept neatly beside the bed. Her sense of order, an innate ability to organize things came quite naturally to the child, though it clearly failed to rub off on her siblings. They frequently took advantage of her exceedingly good nature because she made it very easy for them to do so; Christine's temperate ways were tolerant and forgiving; this predisposition disguising her secret, most heartfelt desire to have a place for everything... and everything in its right and proper place.

Her softness and innocence nicely balanced against an edgy pragmatism, a sardonic sense of humor much like that of Mr. Kenyon; bordering on British, Christine was observant and understated. Nancy, as polar opposite, regularly got on her nerves. Born only eleven months apart (that Catholic thing again) they could not have been more different. If a harsh word or a cold demeanor ever escaped the child, it was, without question, directed at Nancy. However, her kind and gentle spirit would resurface within moments as she'd sincerely apologize for something she had every right to say! Perhaps this is why the rest of the family took it so hard when Christine was hurt or subjected to any offense. This was why, in spite of the ordeal Cynthia was enduring, she was so upset by what happened to her darling sister while she slept. Cindy adored Christine, with whom she shared a bedroom. They had always been close and were highly compatible, sharing many of the same toys, tastes and habits, so it really was a perfect fit for both. One fateful night it came to be that Cindy witnessed one of the most disturbing episodes to ever occur in the house, one she vividly recalls with incredible detail. It is one story, so many years later, still capable of producing mournful tears. What Cindy witnessed in midnight moonlight profoundly affected her for life. To see it happen to her cherished, beloved sister was more than one young mind could absorb. To observe this event with her own eyes as the face of an angel became a refuge for a demon, was something she will never forget; imagery she will never escape.

Chrissy's lovely face was the picture of serenity as she slept. Cindy saw the flawless, delicate features of that face become infiltrated and then distorted beyond recognition by a demonic presence. Cindy could not move, could not breathe throughout the manifestation. It happened slowly and deliberately, as if whatever it was in their bedroom *wanted* Cynthia to see the face of evil. It woke her just before it went after Chris, the one most pure of heart. Perhaps it was this essential purity, the sheer beauty and innocence of the child which initially attracted something wicked...a demon this way comes.

It began as odd, indistinguishable sounds. Because the girls so often spoke during the night, if one sensed the other was awake, she responded, as Cindy did: "Chris, is that you? Are you awake?" With her back turned, Cindy relied on an answer; it never came so she rolled over beneath the blanket. She could hear the sound of growling and thought it was the cat stalking her shadow in the night, an all too frequent habit she had developed since moving into the house. The sound persisted, growing in volume as Cindy searched their room for the presumed suspect. An ominous, unusual sound deepened in intensity. It began reverberating throughout the bedroom, noticeable enough to awaken her other siblings within adjacent rooms. The distinct sound did not resemble any kind of animal sound with which she was familiar. It was a low, guttural, menacing tone, alarming to the child. Propping herself up in bed, searching the darkness for an intruder, Cindy soon realized the awful noise was coming from beneath the blankets in the bed beside her own. Only a few feet apart, that slight distance provided an excellent vantage point from which to view a horrible sight. With benefit of the nightlight and the natural moonlight shed, spilling through their narrow window, Cynthia watched and listened intently. In the darkest heart of night the house was so quiet it made the menace all the more disturbing. She could not remotely identify those sinister sounds which were, quite literally, something she had never heard before.

The child lying beside her began to moan. Her sister was obviously in pain. "Chrissy? Are you all right?" Only her placid face visible, in peaceful repose, it was an expression about to be drastically altered. Christine had a tendency to bundle up like a papoose even on warm nights. Distinctly foreboding noise emanating from her bed signaled the threatening presence as something wild: utterly untamed. Just as fear and curiosity ushered Cynthia into a completely conscious state of awareness, Christine's face began to tremble, as if erupting from within. Startled, Cindy sat bolt upright, frightened out of her mind as an utterly helpless sister's features began to bubble up and boil like the cone of an active volcano. Watching in horror as Christine's skin began warping and twisting in muted shades of light, if Cindy could wake her, perhaps it would stop, but she couldn't force herself to crawl out of the bed. Paralyzed by the shock of it, she was rendered motionless by this gruesome image. Breathless, unable to intervene, Cindy watched in abject terror as her sister transformed. What movements appeared beneath the girl's supple skin became even more pronounced. It looked like fingertips protruding, trapped inside; attempting to escape by rupturing the surface. Cindy would later describe it like snakes slithering inside of a pit. Contorting her face, inflicting pain, Cindy remained frozen in place. It got worse. Christine's mouth quickly became gnarled and mangled. The tender skin of her lips seemed to disappear, as if being sucked inside her body and then her features began moving, scrambling and shifting out of place. A pitiful cry for help oozed from strained, pained vocal chords. Cynthia's heart was pounding. She could feel the rapid pulse throbbing in her temples; hear it rushing through her ears as tremors passed through her body. Whatever was gouging at the skin beneath the surface of Christine's face was attempting to puncture it from within, tearing through it like a creature caged, seeking release; escape. What was only moments felt like torturous hours as Cindy begged it to stop in her mind; no words would come. It was a struggle just to breathe but nothing like the fight her precious sister was engaged in right before her tear-filled eyes. Wanting to scream for help, wake the house, Andrea was sleeping in the next room. Nancy and April *must* have heard this horrendous commotion. Surely *someone* would come…but no one ever did. Cindy was alone as the sole witness to this hideous disfigurement, incapable of saving her sister from a demon. The tormentor continued; just as it seemed Christine would succumb, her once beautiful eyes exploded open, revealing the demon within. That was not her face and those were not her eyes. Black, glistening orbs peered directly through Cynthia's soul, challenging her sanity as it taunted the helpless child in moonlight. Chris became completely still as it stared, penetrating the only one who could identify the evil lurking within. Cindy distinctly recalls hearing herself screaming and gasping for air as the demon slowly, deliberately smiled at her, displaying the remnants of chipped and jagged yellow teeth, resembling the fangs of a beast about to pounce its prey for the pleasure of the kill. Gloating, it shot the stench of its hot breath across the room as steam, into the thick, icy air surrounding the corpse-like body it had chosen to inhabit. A spasm of terror gave Cynthia the strength to pull the blanket up over her head. She wept, begging God to spare them both, her sister and herself, from the grasp of something purely evil; there was no question of its intentions. It had crawled up from the bowels of existence to stake its claim. Cindy could feel a hot, putrid breath at her throat. She prayed. Then at the back of her neck; she pleaded for help, retaining the presence of mind to invoke the presence of God. She could feel evil all around her, intent on consuming them both. Swirling through a bedroom delivering its message with a nauseating stench and petrifying cold, it was hell bent and determined to scare her to death...Cindy prayed. Dear God: Deliver us from evil. Amen.

Evil does exist. It seeks out the innocent to expose itself within. It stretches and taunts to taint all it touches. It covets pure and fertile ground to penetrate and poison. It permeates to mortify its victims; in disbelief. Huddled beneath her blankets, Cynthia waited and prayed. Too terrified to look, afraid of what she might see, she sat perfectly still until the sound had subsided, then lay her body down, hoping it was over. Sobbing uncontrollably, eventually she cried herself to sleep, still praying for her sister. Cindy awoke sickened, unsure if Chrissy had survived the night, ashamed she had not intervened; but she had. Chris was safe; very tired but otherwise fine. Her prayers had been powerful.

"God pours life into death and death into life without spilling a drop."
Author Unknown

solitary confinement

*"We can easily forgive a child who is afraid of the dark;
the real tragedy of life, is when men are afraid of the light."*
Plato

Cathi had mustered the courage required to return to the farm; she'd missed the girls and her dearest friend, Carolyn. Her serious concerns for their well being outweighed a certain reticence which weighed heavily on her mind. The horrendous ride home from her previous visit still vividly in memory; an image she could barely tolerate to recall, Cathi felt compelled to take the risk and make the drive again, on behalf of those living souls she loved so well.

It was one glorious late summer day laden with a golden glow of abundant sunshine. The breeze was bound to carry its summer song along. Andrea had all but mastered the guitar she received the previous Christmas and everyone gathered on the front porch, anxious to share a celebratory tune. Music was a normal part of life in the farmhouse and everyone sang as frequently as they spoke, or so it seemed; simply another form of communication. Cathi was as musically inclined. She played bass guitar in a local band and had real talent. Andrea's repertoire had grown over the months. One song after another rang out like bells through the rafters. Sweet tea kept throats moistened as a tray of cookies mysteriously disappeared...and no one dared blame the ghosts. It was as festive an event as a formal holiday... but there was someone missing. Cathi was the first to notice her absence from their formerly crowded porch. "Where's Chrissy?" Everybody looked around. Perhaps she'd gone off to the bathroom or maybe upstairs to snag the tambourine. Cathi called out through an open window but there was no response. The house was huge so it wasn't surprising if Christine could not yet hear her. She went into their parlor then hollered up the bedroom stairwell with a voluminous voice as big as the solar system. Still nothing; no reply from above...very strange.

Having arrived at the farm by mid-morning Cathi left herself plenty of time for romp and play. It'd already been quite a long day when afternoon rolled around, hours spent down at the river and in the dense woods. Everyone was a trifle drowsy after lunch, yet most fought the fatigue and kept on frolicking. Cathi suspected Chris snuck off to take a nap which turned out to be the case. She initiated the thorough search. At first she went quietly upstairs, so as not to startle the child, assuming she must be in her own bed. If, after the earlier bellowing, (which could have caused the dead to rise) there were no signs of life, then her darling girl must be deeply asleep. Cathi and Christine had the most endearing of relationships. Chris adored her and the feeling was mutual; thick as thieves. Cathi did not have favorites, per se. She loved all of the girls equally, much as a mother would. She'd been a significant part of their lives, a magically powerful influence on all of them for many years. Though, if she had a *secret* favorite, it was Christine.

Room by room, she searched for her then ten-year-old cherub. Everyone in the family knew she regularly slept **beneath** her bed, especially if she did not want to be disturbed...or found. It was a quirky habit. No one ever teased her about it. Privacy was a hard thing to come by in their house; a quiet, peaceful resting place, feeling safe when asleep, a more rare and precious commodity. Peeking into every bedroom, reaching under each bed, there was still no sign of Christine. Cathi called out to Carolyn as she descended the center staircase into the front hallway. She was in the kitchen pantry, up to her bony elbows in soapsuds, humming a happy tune they had sung together earlier.

"I can't find Chrissy." Cathi's somber tone indicated some worry. Scraping the lather from her arms in preparation; it was time to join in the search.

"Did you check *all* of the bedrooms?" Carolyn read Cathi's expression as a cause for concern.

"Even yours." Cathi thought she might stay downstairs where it was cooler. She was right; a proper assumption to make.

"That's strange; Chris was just out on the porch with us a few minutes ago. Where did she go after lunch?"

"I never saw her leave the porch."

"Me either." Carolyn was perplexed. "Did anyone else see her leave?"

"No." Cathi tried to reassure her mother. "She's here...just hiding."

"She usually tells me if she's going off somewhere. We'll find her. Chris disappears sometimes...when she doesn't want to be found."

"I know it. I checked underneath all the beds...in the closets, too." Cathi had been thorough.

"How about the eaves?" Cathi nodded. Carolyn began to share her concern. Chrissy was officially missing from the farmhouse.

"I'll go and check again." Heading back through for a second sweep, Cathi took off...a woman on a mission. Carolyn sent the others out to look inside the barn and around the property. They all scattered on command, anxious to complete the task of relocating the soprano then return to their sing-along on the porch. Cathi yelled across the yard from the parlor window.

"Check out at the rabbit hutch." Christine loved her bunnies dearly. Cathi assumed they would find her playing with her fuzzy little friends. The child often slipped away to attend to their needs without being asked. It was never a chore. She thought of it as a pleasure and a privilege.

Cathi realized she had not looked underneath the bed in Carolyn's room so stepped back inside for another glance. While four siblings were searching outside, Carolyn went upstairs so the house was silent. Leaning down to look beneath the frame of the bed, Cathi heard something strange. It sounded like whimpering; the soft shallow cry of a child. Pulling the quilt away she found nothing under the bed, though she could still hear the sound distinctly. Panic pulsed throughout her body, the startling alarm; fear. The mournful, muffled sounds were coming from the floorboards. Something was dreadfully wrong. Chrissy was in terrible trouble. Cathi could feel it.

Closing the bedroom door so she could hear it more clearly, Cathi listened intently to the distant voice. Desperate to locate the source of a pitiful sound, "Mother of God!" came suddenly, breathlessly, drawn inversely through her lips; she realized the sound she heard was coming from within the bedroom, from an old trunk tucked into the corner. Latched tightly, it was inescapable from inside. Cathi leapt across the bedroom, nearly ripping the door from its hinges. "Carolyn!" Frantically fidgeting with a rusty iron latch she called out. "Christine? Is that you? Are you in there?" The hardware was ancient; she could not get it to budge. Facing the door, summoning a voice to full volume, Cathi yelled again: "Carolyn! Come help me! I found her!" Returning to the trunk, she was struggling to open it as Carolyn burst into the bedroom. It was a terrible sight, a heartbreaking image to witness as they lifted the heavy lid.

Christine was curled up like an injured cat, a wad of human flesh contorted into a knot of unspeakable fear. The child was hyperventilating, barely able to breathe. Her face appeared to be scarred; delicate porcelain skin streaked, saturated with tears, hair plastered to it with sweat, eyes wide with disbelief. There, hovering above her was the savior she had begged and prayed would come. Cathi reached into the trunk, lifting the petrified child with one hoist, cradling her securely, releasing her from a virtual death trap, Cathi placed her gently on the bed. Carolyn held the lid steady then let it slam, rushing over to Christine. Quickly grabbing tissues from the night stand, Carolyn leaned in to swab her child's soiled face. Chris pulled away from her mother, lurching backward, as if somehow threatened by the nurturing act; the look in her eyes describable only as an abject terror. Wrapping herself tightly in Cathi's arms, seeking asylum, protection from a perpetrator, the confused and disoriented little girl had been traumatized, profoundly affected by the nearly disastrous event. She appeared to be in shock. The child could barely speak but when she did so, the words were stunning...enough to bring a mother to her knees.

"Mommy, why did you do that to me?" Christine was continuously gasping for air, her quivering voice, a mere whisper. Trembling uncontrollably within Cathi's firm and steady grip, the stinging accusation was breathtaking to both of the women. Searching for the answer on her daughter's tear-stained face, there was no explanation for the question...only fear. "Why would you do it? How could you lock me inside the box?" There was anger and distrust in her voice. The deeply wounded woman handed the tissues over to Cathi instead, so to wipe away the residual effects of a daughter's entrapment: that horrible state of solitary confinement...left alone to perish in the dark.

"Get her nose...there." Carolyn quietly uttered the directive. Cathi obliged.

"I thought I was going to die in there...I was afraid no one would find me!" Pleading words impaled a mother's heart like daggers. It was utterly surreal; mind-numbing statements had been declared with such sincere intensity, so much belief in the words; there was no point in questioning Christine about the obvious misunderstanding which somehow occurred. During the first few critical moments *all* that mattered was making sure she was safe. She could see. She could breathe. She was alive. Nothing else mattered at the moment.

Convinced her mother was the culprit, the one who had deliberately locked her into the casket-like enclosure, a daughter kept her distance. The place she had gone was dark and deep, she could not see or breathe; suffocating in that heat, a youngster had feared for her life. Carolyn did not know what to say or how to react to this charge. All the girls came into the house then found them in the bedroom. Naturally, everybody wanted to know what was happening. Cathi suggested Andrea bring a moist cloth and a large glass of water for her sister. Meanwhile, she asked Carolyn to escort the others from the room. She needed to understand what occurred; Cathi wanted to speak privately with an overwhelmed little girl in order to grasp the essential truth of the situation.

Gulping the water then wiping the beads of perspiration from her forehead, Chris took a few more minutes to gather her thoughts. Cathi sat beside her on the bed, patiently waiting for some sign of recovery. When Chris was finally ready and able to speak, she stuck like a steel trap to her story.

"I came in here to take a nap. I was real tired from playing at the river and I think I ate too much for lunch. My stomach felt funny and my head hurt so I wanted to go lay down for awhile. I came in here...it's too hot upstairs."

"Then what happened?"

"I fell asleep. I don't know how long I was asleep before Mom came in and told me to go get in the box; she told me over and over again to get inside of it. I don't know how I got in there because I can't open the lid. I think mom carried me. I don't remember how I got there but I **know** it was mom. I didn't see her...but I **heard** her...and she told me to go sleep inside the box!"

"Christine. You never actually saw your mother?"

"No. But I **know** it was mom!" Adamant, Christine insisted she recognized her own mother's voice, even if she was asleep.

"Honey, it wasn't mom. She was with me the entire time you were missing. It must've been a bad dream, sweetie. Your mother was with me and so were your sisters. We were all out on the porch together. Remember? Then we all went to the kitchen. That's when we missed you then came to find you, baby, and thank God we did." Cathi embraced her little one. Chris would not yield. She was hurt; highly suspicious. She did not accept this version of the truth.

Cathi became increasingly concerned. This was quite unlike the Christine she knew, entirely out of character for her to become so staunchly defensive, completely unwilling to listen to reason. It was as if something had a hold on her. A consistently amiable youngster, Chrissy was the peacemaker, loathing any kind of discord. She would address it diligently in others; repairing rifts, smoothing ruffled feathers; a referee between her occasionally argumentative sisters. Cathi thought it very strange; Chris could not and would not defer on such an obvious misunderstanding. Most troubling of all was her outright refusal to take Cathi's word. It seemed belligerent; as if Christine was trying to pick a fight with her, attempting to force an admission that her mother had maliciously trapped her own daughter inside an antique trunk; hot and dark, frightening and dangerous. An accusation levied, as if the mother of five had deliberately intended to kill one of her own offspring. It was disconcerting to hear or to believe Chris could even imagine such a thing, let alone presume it possible. Cathi began to suspect some nefarious forces were hard at work; an otherwise trusting child's obstinate reaction as evidence. She had repeatedly assured Christine the position was indefensible; promising her the accusation made was unfounded...absolutely false.

After a few more minutes, Chrissy calmed down then Cathi suggested they return to the group. She remained quiet, far more reserved than usual; sisters asked her what happened but Chris refused to discuss the ordeal.

Somber, she kept her distance from everyone then went out to the rabbit hutch with a cold pitcher of water for her pets. It was at least an hour before she came back to the house. Carolyn instructed her eldest to keep an eye on her sad little sister. Cathi requested to speak with Carolyn privately.

"What the hell happened in there? What did Chris say to you?" Carolyn's distress was evident. A frantic woman, keenly aware of the nature of a threat issued, an obviously life-threatening situation could have easily resulted in a tragedy of unspeakable proportion, altering a family forever. Sickened by the mere thought of it, she sat down, placing her head between her legs.

"Breathe, Carolyn...breathe in as deeply as you can then hold it..then out." Cathi knew what to do; her friend was about to faint dead away.

"I can't...I can't breathe...oh, my God...she could have died in there!"

"Carolyn. I don't know what happened. I only know what Chrissy believes happened...her mother was capable of closing her inside a trunk then leaving her in there to die. This is disturbing. I don't think I was talking to Christine; certainly *not* the Christine I know."

"What do you mean?" Carolyn pressed for some explanation while gasping for air; suddenly she was the one who required a cool rag and glass of water but there would be no recovery from this kind of shock.

"I mean some subversive force is involved with this incident. I'm certain of it. She didn't believe me, Carolyn. She *didn't believe me* when I told her you had been with me, with all of us out on the porch. Chris all but accused me of lying to her to cover for you. She told me over and over again...it was *you* who ordered her to go lie down inside the "box" and you've never referred to it as anything but what it is; a trunk, so where did that come from? She can't remember how she got there and claims she never saw you, only heard your voice, but she is certain it was you. I couldn't convince her otherwise. I tried. Thank God I heard her when I did." Thank God, indeed.

"Cathi, my children are in danger. This was a threat; don't you see this was a warning to me? That bitch! If she wasn't already dead I would find a way to kill her myself, I swear I would, with my bare hands if need be...*no one* goes into that room anymore. It's not safe. No place is safe in this house."

***

357

In time, Christine warmed to her mother again but she has never been able to reconcile the terrible, almost tragic events of that day. Her recollection of this traumatic incident in childhood haunts the woman still, a testament to the profound nature of an impact it had on an impressionable youngster: the gift that keeps on giving. Now, fast approaching fifty years of age, tears well up in her deep blue eyes whenever she dares to think about it: the brutal heat, an absence of air, darkness all around…the abject fear of her impending death.

"No passion so effectively robs the mind of all its powers of acting and reasoning as fear."
Edmund Burke

~ a favorite gathering place in the country ~

as the crow flies

Though Cumberland had more than its fair share of birds, marshlands filled with pussy willows and cattails, wild creatures on the wing, it was a veritable wasteland in comparison to their farm. Perhaps it was the stunning silence, a sublime absence of humanity which afforded this family the ability to listen more intently, undistracted, as Nature abounded around them. To be outside was to be fulfilled; in touch with sand and stone, wind and rain. Nature filled a void no one knew existed until they moved to the country. The land was so remote, left untouched; most of it unclaimed by human hands. Aged trees of every indigenous variety grew to become giants of the woods, keepers of the forest; their sprawling limbs providing all the comforts of home for countless creatures. Their property was a parcel left free to flourish; to soak up the Sun and drink in the rain. Birds of every conceivable shape, size, color and call took full advantage of the welcoming environment. This vast array of aviary wonders had free reign to live an unencumbered life. Many migrated when the weather was no longer hospitable but always came back and many stayed year round. Cardinals were abundant as were those mean-spirited blue jays. Robins returned with the spring. Nesting bluebirds were bountiful and very beautiful. Hummingbirds graced every summer. Bobwhite and whippoorwill alike would serenade them at sunset, the gift of their music lingering in the moist evening air: twilight tunes. Love songs sung at dusk. The cooing calls of mourning doves; as mated pairs in discussion, perhaps potential partners engaged in their own end stage negotiations. A lyrical debate was sometimes symphonic, at other times a cacophony of dissonant demands and invitations traversing the curvature of a deep green valley as a haunting series of echoes: birdsong. Whimsical and mystical; these were magical creatures from above, none more so than the stark black crows who came as omens...magicians on a mission...harbingers making their appointed rounds.

Carolyn was often in her garden when the ladies arrived home from school. Whether planting, pruning or weeding, it remained a constant chore. Always something to do next, preparing the ground was as important as tending to its seedlings. Crows would frequent the opulent eatery, fine dining at its best; a virtual cornucopia they treated as a smorgasbord. Brazen thieves, scoundrels, they were; no manners and no regard: rude to each other and inconsiderate of their hostess. A prolonged period of pilfering prompted Carolyn to place an ugly scarecrow in the center of the corn stalks. The culprits would land on it and laugh, stretching out their long lean necks, cackling at the woman as they used it for a perch...the better to see you, my dear: Bastards. Their disgusted gardener would grab her rake and chase them away to the clouds, to no avail. As soon as her back was turned they'd quickly return to rob her blind; help themselves to whatever they presumed had been planted exclusively for their benefit. The crows were pushy and petulant; a self-absorbed lot, to be sure. It was more toil and trouble than she had anticipated, keeping a garden pristine and safe from intruders. And it wasn't just the crows; there were bunnies and deer in abundance. Their family had moved to a place where the wild things are...and the wild things were hungry! It soon became apparent to Carolyn; it was a war she would never win, so a truce was declared. The white flag went up as one generous woman graciously acquiesced, making peace with Nature by planting a larger plot the following season. Problem solved. Much like the house, the land was shared space; the fruits and vegetables of Carolyn's labor of love providing a horn o' plenty for anyone and everyone depending upon the bountiful spot of Earth for sustenance.

Andrea was fascinated by these crows. Once her books were stashed inside the house she would go outside and sit on the retaining wall overlooking the garden; the perfect vantage point from which to study their gawky, awkward movements. Observing their antics was thoroughly entertaining. Andrea went there to converse with her mother and together, they enjoyed the show. There they were, usually fewer than ten of them at any given moment. Occasionally the crows would appear as a full-fledged flock, particularly at harvest time; loose kernels of corn plucked by the scavengers from the surface of scarred soil. They would hunt and peck, hop and flinch, posture, argue and compete for the grand prize, resembling adolescents released into an open playground. Though she had no way of knowing for certain, Andrea was quite sure all of them *must* have been of the male persuasion...like an unruly gang of youths.

As winter set in, their garden was abandoned for the season. This was best for bird-watching because crows prefer the spoils. Rummaging like dumpster divers, experts at gleaning the remains of any landscape, leaving stick-figure footprints in the moist, cool dirt, Andrea admired them. She had an affinity for the sleek, stark feathered friends who clustered around her. Though they never came too close there was a unique form of communication between the birds and their winsome child. Whenever she perched alone on the stone they began the carrying on, squawking an infamous "caw" so loudly others would come to call. Silently, patiently waiting for them to gather in assembly along the granite wall, she'd talk to them; not with words but in thought. The crows responded in kind. They would cock their heads and look knowingly into her eyes. There was no fear; no reluctance with anyone involved in the exchange. It's impossible to succinctly describe the level of trust they attained; the rapt sensation of connectedness she felt with the crows. They knew what she was thinking; she knew why they were there: Birds of a feather flocking together.

December had arrived. The wind was gusting; birds riding the stiff breeze. As her crows flocked in the garden, Andrea remained poised on a stone wall, lost in thoughts of the day. She wasn't watching too closely, but rather, was communing with creatures, writing about them and about herself; perceptions of time in continuum. As words came they were soon committed to memory, as if ordered to stick in her mind. They were meant to mean something. Over time she would comprehend the significance of a few solemn words written as wild wind tore at the sheets of her consciousness. Within weeks she would be confronted by an ugly, agonizing reality of life: Death.

"Either I am losing my mind or finding my way. I am here, now perched upon the precipice; on the verge of flying elsewhere. I am almost home."

Papers began to scatter from her tablet. The wind was wailing and her cheeks were freezing…time to go back in the house. Rising from the great wall, she turned away from the flock without any acknowledgment of moments spent together. Those crows had other plans and would not let her leave until their message was received. Andrea's melancholy mood was utterly inexplicable.

It had been such a good day. There was no reason to feel so dispirited yet it swept over her like the abrupt gust lifting birds into the ether. They swarmed like bees from a hive disturbed, circling the house with purpose and reason. Their patterns were distinct and intricate by design, the intention deliberate; dozens of dark-winged souls displayed perfect unison, following precisely, exposing their glossy black feathers, attracting her eyes to the sky. She stood quite still near the kitchen door, marveling at the structure of birds in flight, though there seemed to be some urgency in their sharp cries, as if they were attempting to tell her something. This flitting, fluttering bevy of birds were communicating; trying to tell her. She could not comprehend their message. It was beyond her capacity to grasp. The crows were spirits alive in the sky, an omen; harbingers of things to come…the Angels of Death come upon her.

***

Nancy was the rebellious child but she was also kindhearted and generous to a fault, especially with her belongings and sometimes those of her siblings. Always anxious to do the right thing whenever a need presented itself, it was no surprise when she befriended a sweet young girl named Lenora, someone fragile and delicate; so vulnerable to attack. She too was one of five children, something these ladies had in common, though Lenora had four big brothers. Nancy could not tolerate the way other children picked on her, shaming the girl for the second hand clothing she wore and snickering about her less than privileged circumstances in life. The unkind whispers offended Nancy to her soul. Having been herself a victim of such cruelty, she well understood how it felt to be shunned by one's peers. Nancy decided to do everything in her power to protect and fiercely defend her little friend; to be the *someone* to watch over her. It was a unique friendship born of pure sympathy. Initially, Nancy took pity on the tiny girl but quickly grew to love and admire Lenora. Carolyn used to tell the child that she was as bright as a new copper penny. Lenora would blush, as proof of the assertion. All the girls were fond of her. They welcomed her into the fold. As petite as a baby bird, the child appeared frail but could eat like a horse and appreciated Carolyn's skills in the kitchen. She spent several overnights with the family, enjoying her time with a group of sisters, a sensation she had never known...pajama parties and pillow fights were foreign to her but she happily adapted, flourishing from all the attention she received at the farm.

Her first overnight visit came unexpectedly on a school night; one hard and fast rule broken: an exception made. It was during late winter or early spring of the previous year. Nancy came home from school with a series of rather odd questions for her mother. Though Carolyn knew about the girl, they had yet to meet. Nancy was determined to rescue her foundling on a dark night.

"Mom? Do you know how far it is to get to my friend Lenora's house?" It was a rather subtle, sneaking-in-the-back-door request.

"Doesn't she live down the road that's just past the high school?"

Nancy nodded. "Across from the dump."

"That's right. I remember now...as the crow flies? It's about six miles."

"What does that mean, 'as the crow flies'?"

"It means...if you were traveling in a straight line, that's how far it would be without all of the twists and turns you'd have to make in a car to get to the same place." Carolyn tried to explain a linear concept to her confused kid.

"How far is it as the car drives?"

"Why do you ask?" A mother's intuition hard at work, she suspected what was coming next.

"Do you think she could come for dinner? We'd have to go get her…"

"I don't know, honey. I just started cooking and your father's coming home later tonight. I want to be sure we have enough left over for him to eat, too."

"We always have enough to share! I'll give her mine. Please?"

"Why is it so important to invite her over tonight? Couldn't this wait a few days?" Her mother was perplexed. She preferred to plan ahead.

"No, it **needs** to be tonight." Carolyn could hear the angst steadily rising in her daughter's thinning voice.

"We could pick her up Saturday morning, instead. She could spend the day with you. Better yet, you could invite her to spend the night." Working the logistics, Carolyn's suggestion seemed a more sensible option.

"I want her to sleep over **tonight**." Nancy was not whining…but remained steadfast in her approach.

"Nance, you said dinner; nothing about sleeping over. You know the rules. It's a school night." Her mother stirred the stew as they spoke.

"Please…" Nancy's eyes began to moisten; dewy brown orbs graced with fawnlike lashes tugged at a mother, breaking her heart. Something happened. Something was wrong. All the girls knew the rules. "She had a really bad day in school. Do you think…just this once…she could come and stay over, even if it **is** on a school night? She can ride on our bus in the morning."

"I see you've thought this through." Considering the plea, Carolyn listened.

"I don't know if her mother will even let her come but at least I want us to try…will **you** ask her?" Nancy felt a sense of urgency. "Can I call her?"

"**May** I call her…first, tell me what happened." Probing a situation further, Carolyn wanted to know what had prompted this sudden outcry for support.

"Some girls were **really** mean to her in gym class today. I really don't want to talk about it right now. I'll get mad all over again."

"Did you get suspended for defending Lenora's honor?" Carolyn was only half-teasing. It was entirely conceivable. "Expelled?"

"I wasn't *there*...*that's* why it happened! If I had been there...*may* I call her now? Will you talk to her mother?"

It then occurred to Carolyn, this kind of compassion was precisely the type of good character trait she wanted to instill then reinforce in all her children. Nancy dialed the number. Carolyn called her eldest to come downstairs and watch over dinner while she was away. Within minutes mother and daughter were on the road; on a rescue mission.

The town dump was one nasty bit of business. As the ladies drove past it a big fat rat ran directly across the street in front of the car, startling both of its occupants. Nancy had the address, pointing out the house to her mother; just around the corner...on the left. Lenora was waiting on the front porch swing, her knobby knees protruding from beneath a cotton dress; this and a sweater, too sparse an outfit for the season, but likely the nicest outfit she owned. The child was excited; she leapt from the steps and ran to the car to say hello. Her mother waved from the window. They were off; an excursion into the woods.

It was obvious why the child was teased and taunted at school. Everyone in town used the local dump. Whenever they did, they drove through the shabby neighborhood beside it; a series of row houses, neglected at best; at worst, ramshackle: "the other side of the tracks" in a town that didn't have a train. Carolyn knew why "Poor Lenora" had become a target of the cruelest among her peers; even the appearance of poverty was enough to provide them with ample ammunition...required to inflict mortal wounds. Words are powerful. Humiliation is weaponry. Lenora finally spoke up.

"You live far away!" She was amazed by the length of Round Top Road.

"It's only about six miles...as the crow flies." Carolyn smiled, listened and laughed as her young daughter responded to the question posed by her friend: "What's that mean?" Nancy recounted an earlier explanation of the phrase. It was a hoot any owl would envy. Lenora was adorable; two girls giggled as their trip home was a delight. To see them together, one would never suspect Lenora had been bullied, enduring the merciless wrath of her often hateful classmates. This child seemed happy and carefree; a blithe spirit. She felt an authentic acceptance from Nancy, allowing her personality to burst into full bloom. The charming cherub was sweet; a bit shy, smart and very funny.

Arriving home, Carolyn checked on dinner. Andrea had taken the initiative to add some vegetables, stretching the stew. The meal smelled sumptuous as it cooked, filling the home with tempting aromas. Nancy made introductions all around. Lenora noticed. "Something smells *so* good!" It was the first time most of them had ever seen her though everyone knew all about her. Carolyn was taken by how much she resembled Nancy…same long mousy brownish / blondish hair, petite-in-miniature; even smaller than the pint-sized version of her daughter. Though both girls were twelve, Lenora appeared no older than eight; nine at most, like a failure-to-thrive child, though she seemed healthy enough. Based on her buoyant laughter and equally hearty appetite, there was nothing wrong with the precious little girl. Carolyn wondered how anyone could be so unkind to her. Andrea stayed in the kitchen; all the other children went upstairs to play *dress up*; everything that fit her went home with Lenora the following day. Carolyn voiced no objections. Nancy was right. They had plenty to share and it *was* the right thing to do. As the first of her visits was a rousing success, Lenora was invited back again. It lifted her spirits to be out on the farm with friends. Truth be told, it did all of them good to share space.

***

Nine months later bad news hit as blunt force trauma. Word of the tragedy spread like the raging wildfire which consumed Lenora's home in a matter of minutes. The parents barely made it out alive. Standing in the front yard, they were forced to witness the demise of their own family; helpless to rescue the children as they begged for help at the bedroom windows. There would be no saving them. Each quickly succumbed to smoke; a tender mercy. Their house was incinerated before fire trucks even arrived; burned to the ground. It was transformed: cinders and embers, ashes and dust; inconceivable devastation.

The road remained closed to the public for weeks afterward, too gruesome a sight to behold. It was later determined an electrical short, a spark from the lights on their Christmas tree had ignited the blaze. Not two weeks before the blessed holiday, a hush fell over the town. No one could breathe. Their mind-bending loss colored black every private thought and muted utterance. Joy was dead. The Spirit of Christmas went up in flames along with its sacrificial lambs. When needed most, a holy, sacred day went unobserved, save the vast outpouring of parishioners who prayed for this family; the churches were full to overflowing, as was the church on the day of their funeral. Five caskets; five lives lost...all, gone too soon. Hundreds, perhaps as many as a thousand people stood outside, braving bitter cold air for the duration of their service, trembling with emotion as tears froze to cheeks. Nancy wept uncontrollably. She had hoped some of the mourners there to pay their respects in death were those who'd treated her friend disrespectfully in life; hoped this apocalyptic event would touch hardened hearts with shame and regret and would change their minds and lives. Do unto others...For Nancy, the loss was inconsolable.

Carolyn had been profoundly moved, haunted by this tragedy. It lingered in her mind for months, as pallor of death on the palette of life. She could not shed the image of coffins from consciousness; she could not bear to know how these five children died; tears erupting spontaneously at the thought of it. Meanwhile, as mother, her role was to comfort her own grieving daughter, to no avail. They mourned together; a painful and prolonged ordeal. To have had it happen at all was shattering enough, but to have known and lost such an exceptional child, as the victim of merciless fire, was more than she could tolerate. Knowledge of it forced her into the darkest corners of her troubled mind, compelling her to revisit painful memories of her own. Carolyn could not comprehend what the parents were going through: it had to be Hell; proof of the existence of Hell on Earth. It *had* to be an excruciating burden to bear; the vision of those final moments seared into their memories forever.

During her time at the farm, Carolyn had known fear. She'd witnessed fire lapping at the walls, tickling lace curtains with the flick of a flame in a room filled with smoke. She'd known the torment of the vile, haunting vision; one which lingered…known the sensation of paralyzed panic, an expectation that her five children were about to burn to death. In those moments it was as real as reality gets; as real to her as the flames which claimed Lenora; that vivid recollection of pure, unadulterated terror. In those moments she'd prayed to God, begging for His mercy, begging to die with her children, knowing she'd never recover, never survive their loss. This too had been a reality, branding her memory with a searing series of images for eternity. She understood. Her children survived an ordeal their mother endured; she had been saved and her girls were spared. No one could save Lenora. No one rescued a little damsel in distress. No fairy tale ending this time. No happy endings at all.

Carolyn's vision was intended to intimidate, provoke a response; to elicit visceral fear. It was a hoax; one perpetrated upon her in the night, appearing to be as real as anything she had ever encountered in life. Lenora and her brothers perished in a way mortals fear to the core of their being. Fire is wild; elemental. It has no agenda; no alliances or ulterior motives. It possesses the ultimate power to create and to destroy. It is, at once, a threat and promise: a blessing and a curse. It does not discriminate. It does not pick and choose. It is and it will, once raging beyond control, claim anything and everyone in its path until extinguished. Carolyn understood the nature of the threat as well as she understood the true Nature of Fire. An acute awareness of its pure power instantly transported her from sympathy to empathy, pressing her to feel in full measure entirely bereft by the tragic loss of a family. During her darkest hours she considered this loss as an evil omen: as a harbinger and a warning: five children…gone too soon. They could have been her own. Such thoughts possessed the woman, casting a spell ignited by pain of grief. Wildfire raging beyond control within her troubled mind; consuming her present, rekindling memories of past experiences she longed to forget, it required several months before Carolyn could extricate herself from a chronic mindset of abject terror and utter despair borne of the intimate knowledge of Fire. Sweet Lenora had broken the surly bonds of Earth and like the tiny bird she resembled, was free to fly away home; to touch the face of God. Lord, have mercy on their souls.

***

The following spring found Carolyn once again out in her garden preparing sacred ground. It was still frozen stiff in spots the rising Sun avoided along a daily star trek across the sky; icy patches left behind, tucked along the granite wall as plaques to remind an anxious gardener: full exposure was not making an appearance before mid-May. In the interim, places softened by the shining warmth gave her a point of reference from which to proceed for the season.

The school bus loud and clearly required some immediate attention: brake repair; a disquieting thought as Carolyn heard it squeaking and screeching to a halt in front of the farmhouse. A beautiful day though still a bit chilly, she had been outside for hours and was ready to take a break. The girls rounded the hill into the back yard in search of mother, knowing precisely where she would be. Carolyn stowed her hoe against the stone wall. Andrea joined her there. As soon as the woman vacated her own garden spot, the crows came to see what she might have stirred up for them. Crafty little devils, they'd been lurking in the nearby trees, watching and waiting for The Early Bird Special.

"Mom, where do birds go to die?" A morbid question right out of the blue.

"What made you think of something like that?"

"Look at them." Dozens of crows had come to call. "Look up." She did.

There overhead was a pair of spiraling red tail hawks drenched in sunlight, spinning gracefully in circles with the wind. Pointing toward the garden spot, she exclaimed: "Look at the huge one over there!" Staring at the magnificent specimen, hunting and pecking his way through organic debris, she noticed: "His feathers look purple in the light…he's the biggest crow I've ever seen! I didn't know they got this big...probably from eating out of our garden!"

"That's a raven...he's a close cousin of the crow." Carolyn knew her birds on sight, even from a considerable distance.

Andrea considered the circle of life. "There are so many birds in the world. How long do they live and where do they go to die?"

"I'm not sure, honey. I never really thought about it before...I enjoy them in the moment." In this respect, Carolyn was an existentialist at heart.

"Lenora was like a little bird." Her somber tone: evidence of a youngster's reflective, melancholy mood.

"That's what this is about?" Carolyn achieved clarity on this dark subject.

"On the bus ride home I was going through my notebook and I found this; something I wrote sitting right there on the wall...not long before she died." Andrea handed a torn piece of paper to her mother.

Carolyn recited the lines of a poem: "Either I am losing my mind or finding my way. I am here, now perched upon the precipice; on the verge of flying elsewhere. I am almost home." Handing it back to the woeful child, Andrea again presented it to her in return, a gift of remembrance; in memoriam.

"You can keep it. I memorized it as soon as I wrote it down."

"Those are poignant words, sweetheart. Thank you."

"I was with the crows when I wrote it. Something strange happened to me."

"What happened?" A natural element of concern joined the pair for a three-way chat...a cosmic conference call commenced.

"I really can't explain it but I think they spoke to me. All of a sudden they stopped stomping on the corn stalks then started hopping straight toward me. They got quiet and didn't squawk or bicker like they usually do. They just sat with me and watched me like they *knew* I was feeling sad and came to cheer me up. I came outside to watch them but they were watching me instead."

"You had a bird in the hand?" Relieved it was nothing too serious; Carolyn found the image amusing, smiling while she counted crows.

"They never got that close to me; they just hopped on the wall, cocked their heads and looked at me right in the eyes. Then I wrote this down but I didn't know where it came from or what it meant. Now I think I know."

"When did it happen?" Carolyn was growing more curious by the moment.

"Last December, a couple of weeks before Lenora died. That day the wind kept tearing the pages out of my notebook so I gave up and got up to go back inside the house. When I left they all stayed behind on the wall. Just before I reached the kitchen porch I heard them calling so I turned around and there they were…flying in circles right over my head! They were flying *for* me! I felt it inside, I swear it! They were trying to tell me something important!"

"No swearing." Mother gently teased her sometimes-too-serious daughter.

"It was beautiful! All of them were making the most perfect patterns in the sky…what's the word…when they all fly together?"

"In formation." Carolyn's brain functioned as an instant-recall thesaurus.

"Yes! Flying in formation! I *know* this must sound weird. It's why I didn't tell you before. When I found my poem again today it made me think; *that's* what they said to me. They were giving me information! At first I thought it was about me, but it wasn't…and it wasn't about them either… it was about Lenora. They were trying to tell me something bad was going to happen."

"Do you think it was a message…or maybe a premonition? You might have the gift, like Fran." Carolyn was no longer teasing; she was entirely sincere, admiring her friend's affinity for all things winged. Fran was known to dwell among angels, doing their bidding on Earth. Her eldest seemed to share the proclivity…if she could only decipher the messages she received.

"I don't *want* this gift! What good does it do? If it *was* a premonition then why didn't I know it sooner? Why didn't I *know* so I could have… what's the point if the answers to the most important questions come too late to help?"

"You cannot, ***must not*** blame yourself for what happened to Lenora. It's a tragedy, but under no circumstances was it in any way your fault." Carolyn's comment arrived in the form of a command. "You are ***not*** responsible for it. There is nothing you or anyone else could have done to save that sweet child or her brothers. You had no conceivable way of knowing what would happen to them…you could not have known. Annie. Do not blame yourself."

"And now Lenora is home…with God." A pause for reflection in the midst of painful thought, Andrea was still struggling with a loss; bewildered by it.

"You can't give it back, you know…the gift." With pure compassion in her heart and words, Carolyn peered deeply into her daughter's tearful eyes.

"I know. I have always known." Andrea wiped away droplets pooled at the rim of her wire glasses.

"So, about your morbid question…why isn't the floor of the forest littered with the bodies of dead birds? I do not know why. We walk these woods all the time. I've never seen the body of a bird. Have you?"

"No. They ***can't*** live forever…or do they? Are they really the spirits of our ancestors? Do they watch over us…from above? Are they like our Guardian Angels? Some say whenever a person dies, a bird carries the soul to Heaven. Is that really true?" A substantive philosophical question requiring an equally metaphysical approach to the response, Carolyn paused; ethereal or corporeal in nature…what is the essential Nature of these delicate winged creatures? A thoughtful mother had to admit having no definitive answers to any questions in this realm though she offered some suggested reading on the subject.

"I've been reading from **Ovid**. He wrote: 'All things are always changing, / But nothing dies. The spirit comes and goes, / Is housed wherever it wills, shifts residence / From beasts to men, from men to beasts, but always / It keeps on living.' I find his theory of life and death fascinating. Comforting."

"Me too. Thanks. You ***do*** believe me about my poem…and the crows?"

"Of course I believe you…that's one question you never have to ask me!"

Embracing her daughter, Carolyn suddenly realized their discussion was the beginning of a healing...for both of them. "Look at those scavengers!"

"Red tail hawks approaching...warp factor six!" Andrea pointed upward.

"You've been watching too much **Star Trek** lately." Carolyn laughed then noticed the creatures had indeed decided to *drop in* for an afternoon snack, at the speed of light suggested. Both ladies stood quietly beside the stone wall, marveling at the precision technique of two miraculous birds of prey, gasping as they swooped down into the garden. One snagged a field mouse. The other took flight behind its companion, talons empty; along for the ride, no doubt. Their presence, though fleeting, was quite enough to draw vehement protest from the crows...rather selfish creatures...not prone to sharing the spoils.

"Look at their wings, mom. They look like angels."

"How do you know? Have you ever seen an angel?" Carolyn, cajoling her eldest, never expected an answer to her rhetorical question.

"Yes, I have." Andrea's prompt response prompted an "Oh, my God" from her mother. "Mom, do you think Lenora is already up in Heaven?"

"I don't know. But if there really is a Heaven I believe she is there."

"If Heaven is a real place in outer space how far away is it from the Earth? How long does it take to get there after we die?"

"As the crow flies? Who knows...but I suspect it's not far. Not far at all."

***

It has been scribed in the folklore of civilizations, described throughout the ages: the raven as an omen of death, harbinger of things to come; its ominous presence portends impending doom. In many cultures there remain common beliefs in birds as sacred messengers of the spirit world whose obligation it is to transport the dead: the souls of those who pass on. Foretold is forewarned. It is cruel to cage a bird; to rob it of its essence, its divine purpose and reason for being. These splendid creatures are born with wings so to be free to fly; to fulfill their destiny. As sacred symbols, they are to be worshipped as holy. Therefore, it is a moral imperative to admire the Angels of Death from afar.

"'Prophet!' said I, 'thing of evil! - prophet still, if bird or devil!
By that Heaven that bends above us - by that God we both adore —
Tell this souls with sorrow laden if, within the distant Aidenn,
It shall clasp a sainted maiden whom the angels name Lenore -
Clasp a rare and radiant maiden whom the angels name Lenore.'
Quoth the Raven 'Nevermore.'"
Edgar Allan Poe The Raven

~ as the crows fly ~

off the hook

"You can't run from trouble. There ain't no place that far."
Uncle Remus

Bathsheba Sherman may have been able to evade a conviction but not the blame game in life; then was apparently held accountable on some level after death. At least this was the assumption made by many, at that time and since. Town elders still spoke of her with contemptuous condemnation; a blight on the spirit of the village. Mr. McKeachern would often lower his voice and his eyes when he'd mention her name, not with reverence or respect, but disdain. Humanity abhors the vacuum created when a crime goes unsolved or worse, unpunished. According to many, past and present, Bathsheba Sherman was the guilty party who walked away from a heinous accusation free of charge; free as a bird. Some would argue the point. She was imprisoned in her home, shunned by her peers; enough to make any innocent woman angry, perhaps vindictive. Those who know the history suspect she suffered through life and paid the ultimate price in the end, as it was only the beginning for this Earth-bound spirit. In the grand scheme of things, she may not be so free after all.

***

"I didn't do it!" Most often this was true. The claim staked, an assertion of this kind was usually delivered in a defensive posture most closely associated with self-righteous indignation. "It wasn't me!" had a "how dare you" tacitly attached to its gruff tone. During the first few months in the house, a problem emerged which had not existed among the siblings. Personal belongings and precious treasures were missing, disappearing at an alarming rate. **Someone** needed to be blamed. "I did not go near your bedroom!" Arguments suddenly began to erupt where they had never been present before; false accusations became commonplace events and hurt feelings were a matter of course. None of the girls owned much but what they had, they cherished. When these items were missing it was usually cause enough for serious dissention in the ranks. Things would vanish then miraculously re-appear days or weeks later, often found in precisely the same place from which they were taken originally, like magic, as if there all along and merely invisible; the girls became suspicious. Occasionally things would vanish, never to be seen again. Borrowers became keepers. Sometimes objects would be relocated to especially strange places; a troll found inside the refrigerator, a treasured story book discovered within a dark stairwell in their woodshed. It was odd how frequently, how routinely possessions went missing, as if someone were deliberately misplacing them, to solicit a negative response, thus prompting rather suspicious, contentious, sarcastically terse inquiries among this paranormally close group of five soul sisters: "Well, I *finally* found *my* gray sweater…in *your* room!" In response: "Well, I didn't *take* it! I never even *liked* it and it doesn't fit me anyway!" Inquiry: "And what were *you* doing in *my* bedroom?" In response: "Finding my missing sweater…*stuffed down behind the headboard of your bed*!" The children were sensing encroachment; shared space within a house three times the size of the one they had left behind. Appearing ungrateful at times during such petty discourse; this pervasive, negative energy began pulsing through their veins; an electrical vibration which had never been present before, not in this family, not among these siblings. The blame game didn't persist much longer as the true Nature of the problem soon became apparent to all of them.

No one to hold accountable: No mortal being, the culprit. Boo who? Roger was the only one who refused to accept the fact that there were mischievous spirits in their house. He preferred to blame anyone *visible*; guilty or not. His frustration with these antics sputtered and brewed as in a sealed cauldron, an unstable pressure cooker; the smallest infraction would pop his lid, spewing the contents at a heavenly host of innocent children who did not understand why their father was so upset, again. It was a double-barrel effect: an assault so disconcerting no one was capable of verbalizing it as fear of the unknown. Not only were they forced to contend with a house riddled with an arsenal of invisible weaponry but their father had a hair-trigger and perfect aim. No one ever knew what was coming next or from which direction; a situation which called for courage; uncommon valor in the face of a perceived enemy who'd again become the target of yet another childish prank...victims, one and all.

One late spring afternoon several of the girls were gathered in the kitchen, chatting about events of the day at school. The sky was bright and beautiful. They were packing up snacks and making plans to escape into the woods: the land of the free! It was warm enough to play in the river or at the cascading waterfall beside the pond. While they busily prepared for an excursion their father quietly entered the kitchen. No one took much notice of him; they had greeted him already and were decidedly distracted at that particular moment, which was probably why nobody noticed him placing his precious fingernail clippers on the corner of the sideboard. He had come strolling through on his way to the bathroom. Emerging moments later, Roger walked back toward the sideboard to retrieve his clippers; the object he insisted had been placed there only minutes before. Suddenly a farmhouse became home of the brave.

"Where are they?" Everyone snapped to attention, hearing the harsh tone of his voice, the familiar sound of an implicit accusation levied. Chatter ceased; the kitchen fell silent except for his booming words. "Where'd my fingernail clippers go? I laid them down right here a minute ago...*right here*...so who took them?" The furrowed expression on his face raised heart rates all around the room. High anxiety reigned. Nancy unwittingly entered the room, coming through the front hallway behind him. Roger leapt at her like a wild beast.

"Did *you* take them?" Caught completely off guard, Nancy did not know how to respond to his stunning demand.

"Take what, daddy?" The child's voice collapsed into a faint whisper. She immediately moved back, away from him, repelled by the sinister discharge of dark energy. Cynthia hovered nearer her big sister, in fear of the unknown. How loud would he get? How angry might he become? What next?

No one understood how he could stare into the innocent eyes of these girls and think ill of them; maintaining a presumption of guilt. How could he bear witness to their fright then ignore the effects his temper was having on them? How could he fail to recognize this? Their faces told the truth. It should have been obvious to the man. How could he not instantly absolve them of a crime they obviously didn't commit? Roger *had* to know his false accusations were creating a toxic atmosphere of intimidation and yet he indulged it unabated, apparently comfortable with his own outburst. Nancy was not afraid of him. She was perturbed; disgusted by his melodramatic reactions. She found him obtuse, as dense as a slab of stone regarding an issue with which they had all come to terms. He was spoiling everything! She looked at her sisters' distress then leered resentfully in his direction; challenging him to make amends for this cruel and unusual punishment. He had taken their smiles away, again. In one moment they were happily hanging out together and then suddenly it's a major crisis, the end of civilization as we know it; paranoia striking deeply in his heart. Roger was feeding the beast…and it was returning the favor.

"I want to know *who* took my clippers! NOW! WHO! Was it *you*? *You*?" Little bodies began to tremble, shaking heads indicating a uniform response. Everyone went mute. Thrusting his hands deeply down into the bottom of his pockets, he must have at least considered the possibility he'd been mistaken, but the search came up empty as would a bucket dipped into a dry well, so an irate interrogation continued: Inquest. Nobody knew what was coming next, including Roger; quite volatile when enraged, he'd often shock himself. This could screw up everything; possessing the potential to cancel an excursion as the highly probable penance. Nancy intervened. She'd had quite enough of it; of him. Displaying an uncommon valor worthy of a medal, Nancy confronted her father on a variety of issues, disarming her adversary in the process.

"Dad! None of us took your clippers! We have our own in the bathroom. I wasn't even in here! And no one else took them either so stop blaming us for something we didn't do!" Her tone was equally abrasive.

Roger was momentarily startled by his daughter's equally fervent outburst.

"Then *someone* is playing a dirty trick on me! Which one of you is it?"

"You're right! Someone *is* playing a trick on you, and it's no joke! But it's *not* us and it *never* has been us! Which *one* is it? *We* don't know…ask *them*! We have lived here for more than three years now, and what happens to you, happens to all of us, too, *all the time* and we don't blame *you* when *our* stuff is missing!" Nancy was not finished. "Maybe you're the one who misplaced your clippers! Or maybe you're just the one *they* decided to pick on today!"

"They were right here!" Roger slammed his fist down on the sideboard.

"Well, they are *not* there anymore…and none of *us* took them!" Nancy was taking one hell of a risk; she could end up grounded until she was thirty!

"Daddy? We could all help you find them." There was a distinct tremor in Cindy's sheepish voice. She was scared but so anxious to make things right.

Jaw grinding, veins bulging, temples throbbing; Roger looked directly into his daughter's pleading eyes: Epiphany. He'd been living in the darkness of denial. Dawn breaks on Marblehead. Let there be Light. No one was lying to him. If there were not human beings to blame, he would *have* to admit it was something or someone else responsible. Glancing around their kitchen at this cluster of mortified mortals, Roger realized what he had done; overreacting in a way which can only be described as Classic Roger. So he got upset about getting upset, as if what he had put them through wasn't punishment enough.

"I hate this goddamned house!" Arms flailing, huffing and puffing, he blew out of the room, blazing through the place he hated…on a scavenger hunt.

Relief: it was palpable. It was over, or so they thought. Everyone escaping Roger's wrath unscathed, it was time to congratulate Nancy. Hers was an act of bravery unparalleled in their collective experience. No one had ever stood up to him like that before; none ever dared. It was a moment of triumph for all: Vindication. Validation. Victory! Grins cautiously returning along with a glint in their eyes; no one had forgotten it was gorgeous outside. They could hear the woods calling in a full-throated song of spring. Ladies-in-waiting quickly loaded up their backpacks and were ready to waltz on out the kitchen door, to make their great escape, just as their father re-entered the kitchen. There he stood, inside the threshold, staring silently at his girls as if he had something to say but it had gotten stuck in his throat; perhaps his pride? All movement stopped. All eyes fell upon him. It was not over yet.

"Sorry." Their father's voice, indicative of emotions hovering somewhere between humility and shame, had suddenly dropped with his guard. This was difficult to identify because no one had ever heard it before. His expression, his demeanor was suddenly foreign to them: A milestone moment. This man had more to say in his own defense. "I'm sick to death of it; every time I lay something down around here it disappears." It was his flimsy excuse, lacking sincerity and substance with the qualifier as a tag. Absolving himself of any blame for his behavior; simply not good enough. Do unto others...

"Yes. We know the feeling." Andrea finally spoke up, unimpressed by his act of contrition. In his words she heard some attempt to disguise the truth of it, sensing some effort on his part to justify this inexcusable behavior. During his previous altercation with Nancy, Andrea had remained silent and felt like a coward for doing so; it was an opportunity to address several longstanding grievances, to make a few points of her own. "They *like* to get us in trouble, dad, and *they like it* when you get mad! You should think about that the next time you're tempted to blame us for taking something you can't find. That is *not* the only explanation. If you accuse *us* then you don't have to admit what the *real* problem is...it's not fair to us! We are all used to it; most of the time our stuff shows up again, usually in some strange place we'd never expect to find it. You should think about the times you flipped out for *no good reason* then found what you were missing when they decided to give it back to you!"

A pause for reflection.

Andrea decided to breathe. Roger was shocked. He never expected to be held accountable for his actions, especially to such an extent, but to his credit, he took it like a man. She was right and he knew it. She was firm and serious, as stern with her father as he'd been with them; unwilling to absolve him of the perceived crimes and misdemeanors: to let him off the hook based solely on a single word apology, especially one so long overdue. They lived together in the house of the spirits. It meant every member of the family had to rightfully acknowledge their existence. This mischief was *their* doing and it was about time he recognized the truth of it, the realities of a space shared. There was in fact at least one spirit who enjoyed this upheaval and Roger had always been quick to oblige; to answer the clarion call-to-arms flailing in the wind created by a blow hard; at-the-ready to feed on its negativity while it fed off his own. Andrea intended to become a catalyst, to catapult his consciousness into their presumed realization of oneness; into the *"we're all in this together"* mindset which had been sorely missing from him, like so many *lost* objects over the years. How she longed to prompt a series of flashbacks in his mind; wanting her father to explore complex concepts, needing him to remember and revisit these incidents, every time he'd lost his temper, every time he prejudged then punished his children based on insufficient evidence, because something he wanted was missing. Inviting him to examine his own aggressive tendencies with those who'd been watching all along, she wondered aloud if their house was changing him in fundamental ways. Then she insisted his outbursts stop; come to an abrupt halt. It was not a suggestion. It was an order. He complied. Presenting as a solid line, the united front was formed. An all-hands-on-deck approach was effectively emboldened by those most outspoken among them. Words used as weaponry, Roger saw the tactic turned against him. Disarmed and outnumbered, he surrendered. His eldest was not inclined to forgive then forget the sins of the father. Her accusations were not false but well-founded. As far as she was concerned he'd gotten what he deserved. As a former altar boy he should have known with confession comes a corresponding penance.

It was the last time Roger ever accused his daughters of anything, falsely or not, having learned his lesson well. They weren't perfect but they were good girls and he knew it. As the epitome of grace under fire Nancy then issued an open invitation, one designed to make peace. Of course, there was an ulterior motive attached, intended to insure their planned outing occur on schedule. Nancy was no fool. "Dad, do you wanna to come down to the river with us?" He gratefully accepted. There they spent the afternoon chasing crayfish along the shoals. There, he reclaimed his right and proper attitude. It was a start.

***

Everyone in the family still swears the spirits did it just to annoy hell out of Roger. Empirical evidence sited: this *only* happened when he was home. The telephone rang off the hook. Sure, all the girls had friends and the phone got plenty of use but it would frequently ring and no one was there; nothing but fuzzy static on the line. Sometimes the line would be dead. More frequently there would be an unnerving noise, a crackling rather convoluted sound, as if someone was calling from far beyond the realm of possibility; from long ago and far away, but their calls could not properly connect. It would ring to the point of distraction. The line was repeatedly checked. It was fine, according to the phone company. Boo! Who is it? Who's there? Can you hear me now?

"Take that goddamned phone off the hook!" Message received. The call of the wild one usually came from the parlor, behind a newspaper; their father's reverberating voice echoing throughout a massive house, as if attached to an equally massive megaphone. Indeed, it *was* a "mega" phone by design as was the innocuous unit hanging on the kitchen wall...the one driving him mad! In fact, their telephone could take itself off the hook; an ingenious invention: a trick and a treat. Judging by appearances, the party line was being utilized by *everyone* in the dwelling, some by rather surreptitious means; manipulating a common object in uncommon ways, circumventing the current, redirecting energy at will. It was a freaky physics lesson. Interacting with the telephone was always challenging, its form and function far exceeding any purposes originally intended for its usage. Mr. Bell would have surely been amazed! As a common method of communication from a distance it worked perfectly well. Nancy called Katy. Holly called April. The uncommon characteristics it possessed are what made it noteworthy. No one understood cryptic messages they received from the other end of the line; they seemed to come from the other side of the Universe, from somewhere beyond the grave or just beyond the speed of light and sound: testing the patience of mortal souls as well as the outer limits of technology. There is, of course, an implicit question posed by the ringtone of any telephone. "Is someone there? — Is anybody home?" The logical response: answer the call. "Hello?" Perhaps those calls from long ago and far away came through, after all. It could be they all had the proper connection with these intended callers…especially when the line was dead.

"Hope begins in the dark; the stubborn hope that if you just show up and try to do the right thing, the dawn will come."
Anne Lamott

no rest for the wicked

*"What I give form to in daylight is only one percent
of what I have seen in darkness."*
M. C. Escher

Bathsheba. If it is indeed she who haunts the farmhouse, in the truest sense of the word, the one who conjures spells and utters threats as enchanted rhymes before dawn then she is haunted still by what she bartered in life and by that which claimed her in death. Perhaps there is a penance meant to punish those in the afterlife...perhaps the penance is in achieving what mortals often seek: an everlasting life. Be careful what you wish for...for surely you will have it.

***

No rest. A wounded spirit who can bear; a wounded soul is she: a woman who covets children not her own, one who presumes to claim another life for herself in death. These clues come from a former lifetime: scandalous rumors and innuendo intermingling with folklore and lies spread over the passage of time and space like so much manure in the garden; see how it grows? Smoke and mirrors obscuring the view of most, Mr. McKeachern knew the truth. He had been the one to establish her identity, remembering much about this old woman he'd known as a child, though they were not very pleasant memories. According to the elderly gentleman, she was a mean-spirited soul, angry and resentful, closed off to the world. Bathsheba Sherman had quite a reputation to uphold. Whether because of it, or in spite of it, she was hated and hateful. A wicked woman's torturous life was openly judged on the streets: tried and convicted in the court of public opinion within the village square, well before her final judgment day actually arrived. Reflecting upon history as a whole, it seems many mortal souls are comfortable in the leading role...playing God.

By all accounts hers was a tragic life. Bathsheba was a young and beautiful woman when an infant died quite mysteriously in her care. A mortal wound, presumably inflicted with a needle which was discovered impaled at the base of its skull, the baby went into convulsions and then died. An inquest ensued; the heinous charge, vehemently denied. Judgment rendered, the court found for the defendant, the judge's ruling based not upon suspicious activity but rather, insufficient evidence: no proof of malfeasance. Case dismissed. Yet, the accusation haunted her for life. People *believed* she killed that baby, as an innocent sacrificial lamb. People believed a criminal, a wretched murderess, a wicked witch escaped unscathed. As Queen of Denial, Bathsheba could not defend herself against the onslaught of something as powerful as belief.

Whether true or not, and who besides herself could know for certain, much speculation circulated within the void created by a dismissal, suspicions that she had ritualistically sacrificed the infant, many at that time and since who claimed Bathsheba sold her soul to the devil for eternal youth and beauty; a dark heart in a pretty package. Many perceived her as evil incarnate and were not surprised when she seemed to age so rapidly afterward, once she was let off the hook for some alleged crime. Word spread as wildfire rumors swirled about this wicked woman and her evil ways: Witchcraft and devil worship. Someone prone to beating and starving her servants; an unflattering portrait painted of the woman considered to be a bit *too* beautiful: yet another charge leveled against her; it *must* have been because of a secret pact with the devil! The womenfolk were as threatened as the yeomen were attracted. Bathsheba had a following; a bevy of secret admirers as well as detractors, but there was no indication she'd paid much attention to any of her suitors. In spite of it she was persecuted; prosecuted out-of-court. She was labeled and libeled, treated as an evil temptress, a murderess and a harlot; looked down upon as nothing more than a whore: an unholy seductress who had been first seduced by the devil, so to do his bidding with promises made but never kept. The town folk quickly dismissed the notion of her innocence, faster than the court dismissed the charge. They had apparently forgotten about her *presumed* innocence, the law of the land, neglecting to consider even the remote possibility she might have been a victim of circumstance. It was a tale of life and death; enough to leave any spirit restless, wicked or not.

Mr. McKeachern imparted his vast knowledge as pearls of wisdom without ever mentioning the *afterlife*. Carolyn was unable to determine if he was an actual "believer" or not, as this concept was never discussed between them. He spoke of Bathsheba only in terms of her tormented life, describing a bitter old woman; someone filled with rage and contempt. He came to the farm one day, a place he knew well, to instruct Carolyn in how to create a divining rod from the limb of an alder bush. They'd walked the land, talking for hours; he kindly answered every question he could, telling Carolyn all he knew of the woman who once dwelled in her home: a fascinating tale. As the presumed mistress of the house, Carolyn had much to learn and much to gain from this knowledge, assembling an intricate puzzle one obscure piece at a time, until she had a picture in her mind of the woman called Bathsheba. Her temptation to know more had a root ball buried in a dark place. The more she discovered the more she wanted and needed to know. It became as much an obsession as Roger's compulsion to murder the flies; an imperative. A current of negative energy charged a desire to know a woman she was surreptitiously becoming; a woman fulfilling her destiny through the living soul of another. Carolyn's yearning for knowledge deprived her of sleep and deprived her children of a mother's undivided attention for a time. A cosmic confluence was beginning to occur; a convergence of souls: an intermingling of the living and the dead. No one dared speak of it. None among them could fathom the depths of this transition. Essentially, her family could not believe their eyes. Carolyn could not close her eyes to rest. She remained awake, keeping constant vigil, laying in wait, watching over her young for an intruder who may come again under cover of darkness, one already present. No rest...for good and evil alike.

"Time! where didst thou those years inter
Which I have seene decease?"
William Habington

~ A restless spirit who can bear? ~

sink or swim

"Live in the sunshine, swim the sea, drink the wild air."
Ralph Waldo Emerson

Carolyn was essentially on her own. As she attempted to unravel a mystery and put the pieces of a puzzle together, she felt isolated and alone; no support from a skeptical husband. Thoughtfully considering all she had learned of the woman named Bathsheba, it occurred to her that she'd been accused of being a witch at a time in history when she could actually survive such an insidious accusation. Not long before her birth, women accused of witchcraft were all presumed guilty until proven innocent, methodology employed to determine their status often resulting in a horrific death. Draconian measures utilized, superstitious at its ignorant core, women were routinely being burned alive at the stake or thrown into the lake. Those who held these poor souls beneath a pool of water would draw their ultimate conclusions based upon whether or not the body floated or sunk: either way, she was dead. Victims, one and all.

Flagrant abuses occurred during this time in history, including those who'd perished just up the road. Salem was not so far away; on a road to hell paved with *good* intentions: to rid the world of powerfully evil women, accustomed to taking matters into their own hands. In moments of contemplation, she had decided to take her children there, to show them the stocks, to expose them to the barbaric history associated with a town where intolerance was the norm. A history lesson learned: men are often threatened by women. Witchcraft as a manifestation is predominately a religion. Wiccan is the worship of Nature as God. Practical magic is essentially creative, the oldest and most potent form of magic in existence. The casting of its spells and gathering of covens in celebration was condemned by those fearful of the inherent power of such practices. Fear…the foundation of actions more evil than anything a woman could cook up in any cauldron. If Bathsheba had indeed been falsely accused of practicing witchcraft, little wonder she spent her life resentful of those who wished her dead. Had she not been punished enough in life? That alone would be enough to keep any spirit Earth-bound, if for no other reason, than to clear her name in the chronicles of history.

Field trip! Carolyn convinced Roger that it was time; and a crime to live in the lap of history in a region of the country filled with such fascinations and not avail oneself of the lessons history is supposed to teach. Since their girls knew about Bathsheba she thought they should know the true history of New England...the land of their birth. He agreed. It was October during the season of the witch when they loaded up the car and made the drive up the coast to a place with homes older than their own. Andrea was thrilled by *The House of Seven Gables*; a big fan of Nathaniel Hawthorne. The museum was awesome and the tour was grand. On the way home daddy took a huge detour through Cambridge heading west into Lexington and Concord, all the while telling a tale their kids were learning in school. How cool! To see places they studied, visiting Walden Pond, Thoreau's old stomping grounds; to see the house that Emerson built was astounding. They were amazed by how much he retained from his own childhood lessons in Catholic school; Sacred Heart Academy. To apply that knowledge where appropriate was incumbent upon them all.

"You can swim all day in the Sea of Knowledge
and still come out completely dry. Most people do."
Author Unknown

a rude awakening

"A Fear that in the deep night starts awake / Perpetually, to find its senses stained / Against the taut strings of the quivering air, / Awaiting the return of some dread chord?"
Edna St. Vincent Millay

Lorraine Warren had a sense and a vision of a spirit she called Bathsheba, proclaiming her a purely evil entity, portraying her as one of those doing the devil's footwork on Earth; one who deliberately killed an infant in the house, in the very bedroom where Roger and Carolyn slept. She likewise claimed to psychically intuit this spirit, sensing her presence within two specific rooms; assuring Carolyn she was demonic in nature: Satan's foot soldier, at war with a living soul, attempting to capture what she coveted. Mrs. Warren identified Bathsheba as a nefarious and malignant force, feeding off the energy in their house, with an especially voracious appetite for husbands. Insisting this beast dwells in the cellar, near the well, directly beneath their bedroom, it was Mrs. Warren's fervent hope the room be sealed and permanently abandoned. Then another suggestion: Stay the hell away from the well and out of that cellar!

***

Christine had literally reached the point of **no return**. Unwilling to tolerate the middle bedroom alone any longer, she decided instead to stake a claim on the bedroom her parents had formerly occupied then deserted for a renovated summer kitchen. Even though Carolyn tried convincing her otherwise, it was vacant and Christine insisted...she could not remain in the bedroom upstairs, directly above the one she'd chosen as a replacement. Cindy recently moved, claiming Andrea's space as her own when their big sister went off to college. Though the girls always left the doors open between their bedrooms it proved insufficient to quell the fear. Within a few weeks of Cindy's departure Chris began moving her belongings into an available space downstairs. Though she has never shared what scared the hell out of her, what scared her out of there, something happened...something wicked...

prompting a rather sudden move; a necessary relocation. Convinced she would feel safer, being in much closer proximity to her parents, it made the child feel more secure to be on the first floor with them but no one understood why, not even Carolyn. *That* bedroom had been forsaken for a legitimate reason, as the space where all of the major manifestations occurred. Unaffected by the warnings, Christine reassured her mother she'd be just fine. Nancy then claimed the middle room as her own, leaving April behind in the room above the kitchen: musical bedrooms. None of them realized the truth of it yet…no matter where *you* go, there *they* are. No point in wasting time and energy on ineffective evasive maneuvers; there would be no escaping a savage beast when, once again, she decided to return and rear her ugly head.

Placing the bed precisely where her parents once had their own, Christine centered the headboard up against the side-by-side doors opening into their dining room, leaving plenty of space for all of her other belongings. Lying in bed she faced a set of windows overlooking the garden; an exquisite pastoral view revealing expansive pastures, far better than a portal provided overhead. By the time Chrissy completed her own renovation project, the bedroom had a whole new personality; her own. Transformed into a feminine oasis, though not overdone, it was elegant. No frills…Classic Christine. With her presence the room became inviting again. She'd soon receive an unexpected guest.

It had been several years since any manifestations occurred in the bedroom. Though spooky episodes and corresponding apparitions involved continued unabated, the room in question remained eerily quiet. A decidedly false sense of security set in, albeit superficially. They developed an "out of sight…out of mind" mentality; a natural defense mechanism: a coping skill. No one ever assumed their spirits were history, per se. Though they had been *gone* a long time they were by no means long gone; perhaps dormant… at last? If they'd only lost interest and then moved on; no such luck. Theirs was an invisible existence most of the time but that did not mean they weren't there, watching and waiting: the Light of the World lurking within its shadows. Christine had always been as fascinated as she was frightened

391

by what she saw and heard in the house. The child frequently exhibited admirable fearlessness regarding the spirits but something upstairs spooked her enough to abandon that space. At fifteen, Chrissy wanted and deserved a quiet bedroom of her own; a room with a view. It was the only other one available, so, a calculated risk taken.

Throughout fall and winter the house remained relatively docile; no acting up or acting out. During the following spring several incidents occurred but each was benign; no explicit threats issued or insinuated… then it happened. Christine had spent several months in a room with a history and yet, she slept peacefully; unafraid and undisturbed. They **knew** when defenses were down; Bathsheba knew it was time to make her presence known…again.

Yanked from the depths of sleep, Christine was awakened by the presence. Her eyes opened suddenly. Chrissy felt herself being watched and there *she* was, hovering over the child, moving closer and closer, as if leaning down to make contact, perhaps to kiss one she covets. This mind-altering experience: the making of a memory; that image as vivid now as the moment it occurred. Christine could not move…could not breathe. As she tells it, still with such reluctance after so many years have passed, her face flushes, her heart races simply remembering an entirely too close encounter which proved pivotal in her life. Trauma changes human beings. It shocks them into a new reality and nothing is ever the same. This event caused a psychological shift to occur in the child who'd been confident, unshakable in her pragmatic approach to the new paranormal; a visitation transforming her into a mass of quivering flesh.

The spirit moved quite slowly, deliberately toward the girl who could not squirm away. Her body jolting taut, it was all but frozen in place. Reporting an inability to breathe the frigid air in the room, Chris distinctly recalls many details of the entity as her eyes remained fixated on this apparition the entire time. Its manifestation occurred precisely the same way it had with her mom years earlier, in the same location, right beside the bed. There she was again, though Christine insists she sensed no overt threat, unlike Carolyn. Instead, she felt as if she was being lovingly attended to by something so repugnant it literally took her breath away. During the moments which followed, Chrissy recalls hearing herself scream; a frantic, shrill, wholly audible shrieking-out-loud holler for help. She distinctly remembers yelling until her lungs hurt and her nostrils burned. In actuality, Christine was redundantly uttering a single word in monotone: "mom...mom...mom..." Her cry was *heard* by several members of the family. Her mother came running, as did Nancy and Cynthia, both asleep upstairs, far beyond earshot of the plea. They heard her in heart and felt her fear; that mysterious connection again...as if sharing one mind.

This entity steadily approached until they were quite literally face-to-face. Christine closed her eyes. The next thing she remembered of the incident was her mother bursting into the room; vacant upon arrival, save a terrified child.

Even after Carolyn had grabbed tightly a hold of her daughter, Chrissy kept on chanting, "mom...mom...mom" as the monotone mantra drew more help from above with this consistent repetition. The child appeared to be in shock. It was obvious to Carolyn. Something wicked had rudely awakened Christine in the middle of the night. She found her bundled beneath the covers. Gently rocking the youngster, reassuring her that it was over, assuming she was still in the midst of a nightmare, a mother knew it was a wide-awake nightmare.

Nancy and Cindy arrived seconds later. They took Chrissy out of bed then held on, guiding her trembling body into the parlor where they all huddled together. What Chris described instantly informed everyone of the situation; it was a visitation: manifestation. Her voice was hoarse...the tears flowing.

"Its head was leaning off to one side. It was round and it was gray all over it. I couldn't see anything underneath it...no eyes or mouth...it looked like the cobwebs hanging in the corners of the cellar." Christine gasped for air.

Carolyn suddenly felt sick. She knew precisely what it looked like and who it was; Bathsheba had come to call on her daughter...an uninvited guest.

"I smelled it but then I couldn't breathe anymore. I couldn't move at all! It kept coming closer and closer and I just kept screaming! I could hear myself! I could taste it in my throat! The arms were up like it was reaching out to me but it didn't have any hands! Oh mom, it was floating over me, right next to me...right next to the bed!" Christine was overwhelmed. Her throat was raw. Cindy got up and closed the bedroom door then returned to her sister's side.

"It's all over. Come and sleep with me." Carolyn was firm. Her girl needed to feel safe. Roger was away; plenty of room left in the king-sized waterbed. Encouraging her to come along, Christine followed her mother, as did Nancy and Cynthia. Reassuring all of them, a mother tucked three of her own into one bed then crawled in beside them. All cuddled together, Carolyn stroked Christine's hair. A comfort zone established, she began falling asleep almost immediately. Poor thing, she'd been exhausted by the harrowing ordeal; such a rude awakening in the dark of night; a monster's reach had again grasped the consciousness of a kid. There was an off chance if she didn't dream about it, Chris might escape the vision of this apparition. Perhaps she would forget it while immersed in deep sleep, as so many dreams effectively dissipate this way, evaporating from the conscious mind once fully awake. A mother could only hope for such an outcome. The final conscious words she murmured to her family before slipping away proved to be supremely thought-provoking: "Mom, she didn't mean to scare me...she wasn't trying to hurt me." Gone: Rest in peace, sweet girl, for at least a few hours. It was as if she'd collapsed into a coma. Chris had endured an episode of unmitigated terror; unspeakable fear. Carolyn pondered her words, the last to come regarding this visitation for almost thirty years. It was the first time she had referred to the entity by gender, identifying it as a female. Prior to that point, she had referenced the specter only as "it" throughout her breathless description. Astounded that she did not perceive it to be sinister in nature, Carolyn would later question her daughter about the statement made regarding the apparition. It was too late. Christine had shut down...internalizing the disturbing event: Friend or foe?

***

Many months into writing this manuscript Christine finally divulged what she had witnessed that night. As she sat quietly on the sofa, stroking her dog Libby, the words finally came, beginning with one blunt rhetorical question: "Why me? Why did Bathsheba come to me?" There are no answers in this realm. Anyone present would have witnessed Christine conjuring images she had long ago repressed; relegated to the far recesses of her mind. The look on her face spoke of the pain a memory provoked. And there it was, instantly, as if it happened last night or only a moment before…as if no time had passed at all…manifestation in the form of a revisitation to the past.

"Her head is hanging off to one side from the neck. The face is round but it has no features. It resembles a fencing mask; a gray webbed mesh cover. She is wearing a gray dress, like a smock, with large square pockets open at the waistline. It has a wide squared off bodice with a boat neck collar. It looks handmade to me." Christine paused, as if gazing at a photograph, attempting to describe every detail. "She's a normal size I suppose…not too tall, not too thin…average. The dress is long but I'm in bed so I cannot see if there are feet beneath it. She floats…she doesn't need feet. That's all I see. That's all I remember about her."

It was just the beginning. A few questions prompted submerged memories of that dark night, flooding her mind, releasing a deluge of pent up emotions regarding the event. Chris lowered her voice, staring at a fixed point within the room. "I thought they all came because they heard me screaming. I never saw mom come into the room. Nancy and Cindy came too. My lungs burned. My throat was on fire. They said I was calling mom over and over again; not screaming. I don't understand how they heard me at all from upstairs. It was my one and only encounter with her; Bathsheba. For a long time afterward I wondered about it but then, when we moved away, I tried to leave it behind. It's been…how long? I suppose it's an image that's with me for life. Maybe my fear colored it…when it was happening I didn't feel at all threatened by her…was she there to hurt me or to protect me? I wonder if *I'm* the one who made it into a negative experience. It was all too disturbing…I was just a kid, scared out of my mind. She was the ugliest thing I have ever seen. Her head was repulsive! That's what kept me from…oh; I don't know…that's enough reminiscing for tonight. I've got a good book going." Escape. Christine was gone, retiring to her bedroom for the duration of the evening; Libby in tow. Sweet dreams, dear sister…what one always wishes for another, especially when growing up together in a house alive with death.

***

Much like the beloved dogs in our lives, human healing often involves the licking of wounds; properly attending to inevitable injuries sustained in life. However, to identify the wound inflicted is paramount. It cannot be dressed until it is addressed. Truth be told, some wounds never heal. Exposing them to the air, to the light of day can be as painful a process as rubbing salt into them but it ultimately proves beneficial, as it too promotes healing. Lorraine Warren said *stay out of that room*. Chris said: ***that's my room now***, refusing to relinquish the claim she had staked. Suppressing fear, she'd courageously claimed this space as her own and defiantly refused to share it. End of story.

"Nothing fixes a thing so intensely in memory as the wish to forget it."
Michel de Montaigne

a fate worse than death

*"In our nature, however, there is a provision, alike marvelous and merciful,
that the sufferer should never know the intensity of what he endures
by its present torture, but chiefly by the pang that rankles after it."*
Nathaniel Hawthorne The Scarlet Letter

To be suspended in the ether, timeless in being: to be immortal.
That is the blessing. That is the curse.

***

Humanity has belabored the notion of immortality for millennium; time to re-examine the concept. The existence of the Soul has been in dispute since the beginning of **argument** as a linguistic high art form, when people began hypothesizing about themselves and their reason for being human. Once the mind was freed from the constraints of mere survival, once humankind could think about something beyond imperative food and shelter, mental evolution occurred. The human race began to consider itself. To know the significance (or insignificance) of one's place in the infinite Universe is important enough to consider. At least it seems so, based on the existence of numerous volumes written on a topic throughout the course of history. It became the imperative. Mortals began by worshipping what we can see with our own eyes: Sun and Moon, Earth and Stars: The Cosmos. Much later, only recently, in fact, that focus shifted to the molecules which hold it all together, as an intermingling of science and faith began to evolve.

Some of the earliest formal religions were based upon the conflict between good and evil; darkness and light. In the heart of the Fertile Crescent a belief system was developed by the Achaemenids and emerged hundreds of years before the birth of Jesus Christ. The Zoroastrian Religion based all worship upon two opposing forces; two dueling deities. Ahuramazda, Spirit of Light was constantly "at war" with Ahriman, Spirit of Darkness. Its emphasis was placed on Light and Truth in perpetual conflict with Darkness and "The Lie". This religion stressed personal responsibility as relating to proper conduct. Simplistic perhaps, compared with the intricate, multilateral diatribe of, for example, Catholicism yet basic tenets remain intact, standing the test of time.

Most of the major philosophers have weighed in on this complex concept, ever since someone originally sensed or conceptualized possessing a Soul, as humans became self-aware. Saint Thomas Aquinas wrote extensively on the subject. Much of the historical literature available on the Soul is found within religious text worldwide. Though it is often considered to be coveted by and exclusive to the framework of religious doctrine, philosophers consider the existence of the Soul theoretical in Nature; as a point of view to be argued or referenced, either for or against, in challenge of assumption. William Paley derived his conclusions based solely upon logic; deductive reasoning, posited by his theory of the Watch and the Watchmaker. Paley's argument for the existence of God, simply stated, is that God *must* exist because the Universe is far too complicated a place to preclude the existence of a divine creator. Logic dictates that it is too intricate and interconnected to have been created by chance. Much like the multitude of delicate mechanisms encased within a watch, it does not follow logically that these mechanisms would have come together accidentally in the formation of a device to measure time; his argument presumes deliberate intention and vision. In the stark absence of a watchmaker it does not stand to reason that a watch could even exist. If there is no one to create the device, a watch is utterly incapable of creating itself. Thus, crossing into the realm of mathematics, probability and statistics, Paley believed it entirely implausible, in fact impossible that the watch could create itself either by chance or happenstance. Intelligence is a necessary ingredient, a prerequisite, as an invisible component of the time piece. Essentially, he'd suggested: God creates man + man creates watch = God creates watch. An equation: the stuff of science: Imagine that.

The concept of God has been inextricably linked to the concept of Soul, the presupposition being that a soul cannot exist without a god to bestow it upon humankind. But what if the two concepts are mutually exclusive? What if the soul is a vehicle, an energy source which we arrive with and take along the journey through Infinity? God could conceivably exist without imbuing soul upon humankind and Soul could exist as separate and distinct from a Creator. One does not necessarily presuppose or require the existence of the other. It *is* conceivable these two concepts have been inappropriately intermingled as humankind developed a sense of self and began craving an understanding of the cosmos and our position therein. It is as if human beings, while grappling with notions regarding the origin of the species, came to require something more, something beyond ourselves, to praise and to blame; a parental figure of whom we are made in the image and likeness of; preserved by passing on recognizable characteristics, like a mother's eyes or a father's temperament. Or what if, as Mary Daly suggests, "It is the creative potential itself in human beings that is the image of God." Perhaps the Soul is the God-Consciousness within us; an invisible image and likeness we cannot see but sense by other means. William Paley passed away long ago but went where? On his journey through the cosmos, he may have found the answers to his most urgent and pressing questions in life, but if he knows something which would end all the speculation, he and other curious, like-minded souls should relieve us of the burden of conjecture and return to tell humanity the truth; unless, of course, it is supposed to remain inherently a secret.

Truth be told; we have no earthly idea regarding the origin of the species or the Universe so how can so many speak with such authority on a subject they know nothing about? Why is this subject treated as a matter of faith when it is as much a matter of science? Humankind may never resolve the dilemma of this thing called "life" but it will not be for lack of trying; our attempt to unravel the threads of an infinite tapestry. The greatest minds on the planet, past and present, have kept constant vigil with the concept as a central theme, a proposition of the thought-process, whether the catalyst be spiritual longing or scientific inquiry…whether the point of reference and persuasion begins in the study of faith or physics matters not. They are the same. They seek same. When science and religion merge as one the true enlightenment will begin.

What is *Spirit*: Some remote, esoteric being? An ephemeral state of mind? Real or ethereal? Physical or metaphysical? Natural or supernatural? Normal or paranormal? Or is it something beyond humanity, the touchstone between this and all other dimensions? As ageless sage or symbiotic symbol, Spirit is ghostly and mostly a feeling. Perhaps it is instinct or intuition, the sixth *sense* humans possess; intrinsic knowledge of something beyond ourselves as well as something within ourselves; an attachment to something we perceive to be greater than ourselves which manifests AS ourselves. Certain cultures have integrated this convoluted sensory perception, sense-of-self, with the concept of Soul, sharing mystical attributes assigned to both throughout time. Debate continues. Call it God-Consciousness. Identify and label it a dozen different ways. It may be just another delusion manufactured to create a comfort zone; not necessarily divine providence; rather, a realization of our own life force. In vast numbers, humanity *believes* in the existence of Spirit, if not the spirit world, as long as it remains invisible; an intangible, elusive idea. Yet, while willing to embrace the concept of Spirit on faith alone, once spirits manifest as substantive form it becomes suspect, no longer retaining any credibility in the eyes of those who would otherwise argue for its existence, some of whom stand and preach from gilded pulpits. Once they *can* see it they don't believe in it anymore: Ironic. Specifically regarding Roman Catholic doctrine, High Mass and The Liturgy virtually requires a suspension of disbelief, including a presumption of the existence of the Holy Ghost...Spirit.

What if humanity is a manifestation; energy taking form on plane of action; Earth, its current domain? We are all residents, in one form or another. Does a ghost feel any less "real" than we do in our own skin? When they appear do they *feel* anything? Do they sense any pleasure or pain, sorrow or joy, or are these sensations merely a distant recollection; a vague, non-descript memory they attempt to recapture or dispel? Are they present with a purpose beyond our ability to reason? Why would a presumably benevolent, omnipotent God allow any human beings access (or exposure) to supernatural entities if their existence was supposed to be kept a secret, unless of course, they *are* a gift? When revealing themselves to mortals in form and substance, is it a decision, their intention to do so? Do these beings control their own destiny? Does free will exist after death or is God willing it so as a message to be received from beyond the grave? Is there a predetermined outcome: to frighten or inform? This is a determination which can only be drawn by witnesses, if at all. Only through the Third Eye of the beholder can one discern what meaning, if any, should be assigned and attributed to close encounters of the bizarre kind; odd only because they are so unusual. What if all of the conjecture was no longer necessary? What if *everyone knew* beyond the shadows of doubt in which *they* lurk, awaiting acknowledgement; if mortals knew spirits dwelled among them, within their own homes, this would soon become an entirely accepted idea; commonplace...like having pets. As for their farmhouse in Harrisville, some "in house" spirits *were* pets; cats and dogs, to be precise.

Then why do some places seem particularly prone to supernatural activity? They all seem to share a common theme: history. For instance, the majority of people in England believe in spirits because they dwell within centuries old houses where many events have shaped the history, apparently affecting the energy of the places and spaces. As a society, they are far more accepting of the phenomena because it *is* commonplace: the older the home place, the greater the chance someone who once lived within its walls was either unable or unwilling to part with it in the end, to leave it behind in mind. Its ghosts may well be nothing more than consciousness manifesting in form; memory as hologram. The ongoing speculation regarding what holds and keeps spirits Earth-bound generally includes a theory pertaining to sudden or tragic death. It is a common belief that those who meet their end abruptly or savagely may become incapable of leaving this realm with unresolved issues, unable to go: move onward; to where, we do not know. Their transition may have occurred so quickly or traumatically, they either weren't prepared to die or do not yet realize they're dead. Likewise, there is an equally common hypothesis which suggests these souls suffer a morbid existence; struggling through eternity in miserable, depraved circumstances: purgatory. These timeless beings spend infinity wandering aimlessly through space, returning to the only home they recall, to the only place they know to go. In quiet desperation, lingering in eternal expiating darkness, they seek solace, grace and guidance to the other side, unable to follow or even see the

Light. An alternative hypothesis: They *are* the Light…the source of all enlightenment…but to please or provoke?

Based upon the numerous observations made over the course of time at the Harrisville house, the Perron family refutes some of these claims. They have both witnessed and interacted with spirits who did not seem to be the least bit uncomfortable in their current circumstances. They have witnessed a variety of apparitions seemingly present with no purpose or reason at all, certainly never intending to scare or harm anyone. The spirits were often oblivious to the mortals sharing space with them at any given moment, as if the mortals were the invisible ghosts sharing *their* space. Several members of the family encountered the spirit they refer to as Bathsheba, one who apparently loathed Carolyn but adored and coveted her children. Each of the ghosts arrived from the netherworld with personality intact. The same apparition would manifest at different times wearing different outfits, appearing at different ages and stages of *life*: old…then young again…amazing. Immortal beings recognized and acknowledged over time, relationships, bonds of trust formed between individuals based on this familiarity. As an awareness of the spirits gradually increased, acceptance accompanied knowledge and a certain comfort level was naturally attained as these non-threatening entities repeatedly made their presence known within the house. The Perrons perceived them as being quite like "us" in many respects: they retain moods and emotions. From peaceful, loving souls to antagonistic and hateful; sometimes placidly observant and sometimes bemused and mischievous; other times vindictive and belligerent, jealous and cruel. The mix of characters could, at times, seem like a cast of thousands. Bathsheba, mean-spirited in the extreme, is the only troublemaker in the lot of them. However, it was not so unusual for an otherwise benign presence to become equally intrusive, especially when they were receiving company. Some do have a tendency to show off, seemingly relishing *shock value* associated with their presence. Surprisingly, they *do* take **NO** for an answer…even Bathsheba. "**Get out!** Just say it like you *mean* it and they'll go, usually pretty fast! Begging God works, too!" Some advice, according to Cynthia: a reliable source from an experienced perspective. Precisely what are they responding to as they depart so abruptly...as quickly as they came? Are they respecting a request or fearful of divine intervention? Does it hurt their feelings? Do they leave feeling satisfied by the overt acknowledgement received or offended by the dismissal? A mesmerizing, illusory intermingling of dead and living alike; encounters ranged from provocative to disinterested, malignant to benign, imaginable to inconceivable. Encounters occurred quite frequently; sightings so repetitious, they lost a certain "supernatural" quality and became a rather natural part of life to a family forced to adapt to the new paranormal. It is within this context they consider the ghosts as individuals; each one had a hidden agenda...every spirit intrinsically motivated by some incomprehensible desire **to be**. Therefore, assigning any particular meaning to the afterlife is absurd; it is to presume and articulate knowledge mortals simply do not possess. The significance of Spirit lies in its existence instead of its reason for being.

Doesn't the presence of spirit indicate or presuppose the existence of God? Should they be classified as same with the Order of Angels, whether risen or fallen, or are they separate and distinct entities? Does it not presume this *state of being* as a form of divine retribution: punishment; the result of a life ill-lived? Purgatory thus dooms those who occupy it, according to religious doctrine and dogma. It represents a perpetual penance, an infinite reflection upon a lifetime which did not quite measure up to divine expectations...no entrance to heaven but at least it is an escape from hell...or is it? There is no divine presence, no Oracle obvious to humanity at this time; no one available for the purpose of clarification. No one wise Soul to dispense the enigmatic, allegorical predictions we seek; no one to consult as a holy prophetic deity. Messages may come instead from the many who return. Most likely it will be science, not religion which ultimately resolves this ongoing dilemma, settling an age old-dispute while deciphering the ambiguous, revealing the dictates and parameters of our human comprehension of the Universe and this unique role we play within it. Perhaps philosophers and theologians, those scientists and scholars most interested in the subject over the course of time *should be* the ones to return, to reveal exactly what's going on out there in the Cosmos; revisit to answer those relevant questions posed during their mortal lifetimes. Perhaps they have returned over time and we have seen and heard them but did not listen because we did not know how…we could not believe our eyes.

Who knows? Is it a fate worse than death to pass on from this world only to linger eternally in the netherworld? Are spiritual beings plagued by desires of and for Earth? When they visit are they really homeward bound? Are they the haunted or the haunting? Everlasting life may be a quandary; immortality may be both a blessing and a curse. Spirits who currently inhabit the house at the farm do not appear to be particularly miserable, save one. Bathsheba was tormented in life and now torments her successors in death; of this the family is certain. Whether by association with or *as* the demon, she is still serving a sentence self-imposed upon her in life. No. She was not convicted; no jury of her peers convened. No judgment rendered in a court of law: case dismissed. Yet, during her lifetime Bathsheba remained perpetually haunted by a charge and the jury of her peers came in the form of suspicious villagers, assuming she was guilty of a horrendous crime; the murder of a baby as the sacrificial lamb. Perceived lifelong as one wicked witch of a woman, presumed guilty, Bathsheba's exoneration was meaningless to most. As this grave reputation preceding her, known to others far and wide as the infamous evil temptress in life, Bathsheba remains an enigma in death. There were whispers…that she hung herself in the barn to punish a family she loathed; rumors…that she is not actually buried beneath her tombstone because the church would not allow her internment in consecrated ground. There is still speculation; some who believe she lies in the well beneath the bell stone. As with her spirit, the mystery lives on for eternity.

As for the Perron family, they no longer seek details of her tortured life and death. It matters not. If she does indeed remain suspended in the ether of the netherworld, unable to move on to another existence in another realm it may not necessarily be as punishment or by her own doing, in agreement with and decreed by the devil. Satan may be the fall guy of the tale. Carolyn turned all of her notes and sketches over to the Warrens during an investigation of the house more than thirty-five years ago. Even though she would like all these materials returned as keepsakes for her children, she does not wish to pursue the historical element of this research any further. Her presumption that spirit exists, based upon her consciousness-altering encounters, is to know enough: knowledge integral to faith. Unlike those rooted in **faith** as an occupation, those who claim to believe in what they cannot see yet balk at the concept of Spirit as tangible force in reality, Carolyn knows better. When she witnessed a multitude of manifestations of spirit, in every conceivable shape, size and form, it was with a reliance upon keen senses, (the ones human beings trust), which she based her interpretations of what was there before her eyes...well, they don't call them *visions* for nothing! When sight, smell, taste and touch impact a consciousness it leaves a mark: a memory. A distinct sound can be retained in mind forever. Click. Though she remains curious about Bathsheba Sherman, her origin as well as her ultimate fate, this research ended long ago, well before the family left their place in the country behind; obsession over. It is now with reticence she invokes the name. As decades pass, as time and distance serve to ease and clarify consciousness the burden of this knowledge has lightened. Carolyn now refers to her spirit in terms of mild bemusement; usually whenever *disaster* strikes: the dog got out of the yard...Bathsheba's Curse. The handle on the hoe broke off...the Curse of Bathsheba. It is best to make light of the darkness.

A natural conversion, this integration of science and religion has begun to reveal a kinship between what was once perceived as two opposing forces. As ethereal concepts such as Soul, Spirit, God and Immortality endure such corporeal scrutiny, as scientific inquiry delves more deeply into the notions once relegated to worship in the pews of churches new beliefs have emerged; relative and relevant discoveries are now coming to Light. Quantum physics is taking another leap forward into the past. "If it can be imagined it already exists" is being revisited in relation to a cosmic consciousness; awareness of self in conjunction with a creator, as the creator of another esoteric concept: Destiny. Oh my God! Perhaps it is our destiny to discover ourselves through the spirits who return. If we overcome our fears we will receive the message.

At some point in the future, when human beings use half a brain, those quaint ghost stories of yore; tales told in the dark to spook kids around the campfire will have perfectly viable scientific explanations. In the interim, supernatural sightings will likely continue to be attributed to a variety of factors ranging from "live" historical drama to hysterical delusion. In the meantime, human beings continue to step across the threshold of churches and worship a power we simply cannot comprehend. We beg for immortality, pray to ascend to the heavens, there to be received and enlightened by God the Father; enmeshed with the Holy Spirit forever. In this respect, it seems we diminish God while engaged in the feeble attempt to define and envision a Creator. The old adage applies…be careful what you wish for…consider the ramifications of such an unenlightened request. Imagine such a fate; imagine being lost, suspended in the ether for eternity…it seems a fate worse than death. The ancient Chinese proverb "may you live forever" is imparted as a curse rather than a blessing. To some, death is a mercy; reprieve: life itself can be a fate worse than death.

―――――――――――――――
"To be — or not to be. That is the question."
William Shakespeare

Where Souls Dwell

"For most of my life I have wondered where souls dwell. Over and over, I have asked, 'Where is the other side? Where is the in-between?' What if some or many disincarnates are stuck between here and there and where is 'there'? I have come to a conclusion and the answer is simple: just beyond the speed of light. I believe this is where souls dwell. It is past our human senses, of sight or sound, but for those of us with the ability to tune in or to connect, it is as real as it gets. We can then vibrate and resonate with them.

There is no legitimate separation between science and spirit. We cannot separate science from soul. Each originates with a Creator and is therefore eternally, inextricably linked. The souls of spirits who dwell on the other side or the in-between state of being need and want to be acknowledged, to be understood by mortals as much as we need and want to acknowledge them; to comprehend their existence, so to illuminate our own.

I have made a promise, a pact to do whatever possible to keep in touch with two souls who have passed before me. Most contact occurs in dream state. Some happens by synchronicity; synergy during waking hours. When more of us make an effort to remain connected to those who pass on to the other side, perhaps the understanding we gain will cause our fear of them to dissipate; a fear of what we cannot always see or hear, but can feel to the depths of being."

Margie Mersky

~ where spirits dwell ~

"Science is not only compatible with spirituality;
it is a profound source of spirituality."
Carl Sagan

IV.
SPOOKED

"Absent in body, be present in spirit."
Corinthians iii. 6

There were many mortals beyond their immediate family who were *visited* when they visited at the farm. Some simply came to expect it, others came in spite of it and some came once, never to return again. There were those who arrived with great anticipation, hoping *something* would happen to them and then, if nothing did, felt disappointed, desperate to come back and try again. Friendships were frequently tested. However, there was one friend who felt no fear at all. In spite of numerous encounters she had during years spent at the farm one frequent overnight guest came and stayed in peace and comfort. Nothing spooked her. Holly was that rare exception to the rule, the one who blended perfectly into the landscape of a farm and the fabric of a family. She belonged with them. The child of Light became tightly woven into a colorful, elaborate tapestry of characters. Her thread remains unraveled to this day.

April met Holly in detention. Destiny, they presume, confirmed by the fact that Holly spent only *one* period there during the course of her school years, whereas April revisited this corporal penance from time to time; relegated to parochial purgatory: in atonement for one perceived sin or another. The girls were devotional from the beginning. No question; Holly's secure placement within her adoptive family transcended bloodline. She occupies the position of sixth sister, rightfully so. Purity and sweetness drew her naturally to April, as she'd recognized these traits in another soul, one of her own kind. Initially welcomed into the fold as April's great find of a friend, a treasure to behold, she quickly shared her discovery...then everyone fell in love with Holly; an instantaneous absorption. Her laughter is contagious. Her demeanor meshes flawlessly with everyone in their family; even Roger is crazy about her. He never got close to any of his children's friends. Again, the exception made. She was more than just another kid hanging around the house. He found her delightful and included her by invitation on many family outings because she belonged: **# 6**. Holly became so close with them over time, when they finally moved to Georgia, she followed; logically. Within several months they were all together again, as nearby in miles as in heart; as the fates allowed. She'd deliberately altered the path of her life to remain in close proximity to family she adored and did so willingly; the sacrifice of losing all of them at once too much to bear. Holly felt abandoned. When Carolyn celebrated her sixty-ninth birthday in August of 2008 there she was standing right behind her Cherokee Mother, framed within the borders of the family portrait. Preserving precious moments for posterity, *click* went the shutter of a camera; the familiar sound reminding everyone present of the bond which will never be broken, even in death. This kinship has endured the trials and tribulations of a super/natural family based upon a super/natural love: something sacred.

Decades pass as decades do, yet some memories remain contemporaneous. Though Holly had not been for a visit in awhile, nor had she spoken of these specific incidents in several years, not even with April, this family gathering was time for celebration and revelation, prompting a spontaneous sharing of reflections and recollections. The subject did come up. Holly was quick to contribute from her personal memory bank. Life at the farm was vibrant with endless adventures. She remembers it quite fondly. Encircling a dining room table, the "girls" began speaking with exuberance about a time in life when everything was new; the element of surprise when seeing something they had never seen before, whether it was a lady slipper on the floor of the pine grove or a pronounced shadow in silhouette leaning against a doorway. Confessing that she *always* felt completely safe and protected at the farm, Holly went on to describe in detail an episode which occurred about one week prior to their family's departure for Georgia. She had come to stay for the weekend, there to help them pack...make a few more memories before they left her behind.

Having grabbed the vacant spot in the middle bedroom upstairs, the young woman fell hard into sleep after a long, hot day of relentless work. As Holly vividly recalls, she was abruptly awakened by the sound of "rummaging" in the chimney closet. The light had been turned on. There was a thin streak of pure white light cast across the darkened room from beneath the closet door. Rolling over in bed, she distinctly recalls the bright reddish background and glowing numbers on a new-fangled contraption called a digital alarm clock, illuminating 3:33 a.m. Drowsy and bleary-eyed, Holly leaned over to check it again, wondering why anybody would be up and about at this hour of night. Eddy spent the night as well, dutiful helper that he was, primarily due to the very late hour they finished working, followed by a heavy dinner. Everyone crashed and burned in the heat of a house baked in the oven of a sunny June day; broiled from above. Maybe Eddy was already up, getting ready for work but why would he be inside the chimney closet? It had been packed; empty. Click. The latch lifted. As its creaky door began slowly swinging open, Holly saw the silhouette of a man standing in the doorway.

He did not move. "Eddy?" He did not speak. "Is that you?" The figure was as tall and lanky as Eddy but Holly had an immediate sense it was someone else; the same man she had seen before, over all the years of slumber parties. A familiar figure, he was; someone checking in, watching over the children of the house, of which she was one. To her knowledge, Holly had never seen Manny though he had been described to her on numerous occasions. She did not think it was him, even though he too was prone to standing in doorways, usually in the front hallway downstairs. No. This was someone else, someone a good bit older. She wondered if this was dear old Mr. Kenyon, come to say goodbye. Though she never met the man in life, he too had been described to her and spoken of with an abiding affection, often in her presence. Perhaps he had returned home, to the children he loved. Holly propped her body up in bed and stared at the figure; mesmerized... and wholly unafraid.

As Holly remembers it, he stood there for what seemed an eternity, a single light bulb behind him illuminating a deeply dark night. Glancing at the clock again, it still read 3:33, as if it was stuck. Holly wanted to speak with him but could not muster the energy to voice or body, to rise from bed and approach the stoic figure. She insists it wasn't a sensation of fright prohibiting contact; she was simply unable to move. Truth be told, Holly expressed the desire to go to him, enveloped as she was with a sense of compassion and tenderness, the kind of feeling one might have toward a father figure. She knew him. She knew he loved her. Holly felt a certain kinship with the apparition standing in the doorway of that bedroom. He'd suspended time itself to visit her.

Then, after several moments, in precisely the same way it opened, the closet door began to close again: slowly, deliberately, with forethought; no malice. What Holly found astounding was the fact that this door *could not* close the same way in which it had opened; what she had witnessed defied the laws of physics. After so many years of coming and going through the rooms of that old farmhouse, she knew each one of those doors had its own personality; its own quirks and foibles. *That* door, once unlatched, would slowly sway open, much the same way it had when the apparition arrived. However, because of the slant of a house built long and lean, it required some assistance to close it and latch it again. That door always gravitated toward the pitch of the place. There the figure stood. He did not move or speak as the door closed. Its latch engaged. Lights out...and then he was gone... darkness prevailed once again.

Though Holly knew the answer before asking the provocative question, she felt compelled to check with the only likely mortal suspect before revealing her phenomenal experience to anyone. The next morning over steaming cups of coffee, she rather nonchalantly inquired of Eddy...had he awakened and wandered around during the middle of the night? Nope. He had slept like the dead, so to speak; as she'd suspected. One of many sightings Holly had over the years this was destined to be her last. Within the week their family would be on the road again, caravan-style, out of harm's way, as far as the mother of the clan was concerned. While quietly listening to their odd conversation, Carolyn made no further inquiry...she did not want to know. It was obvious to the outgoing mistress of the house; Holly had encountered a supernatural *someone* in the night. From her perspective, she did not want to hear any of the details. Carolyn had endured the most ghostly of encounters and was the one least likely to return, having no desire to revisit this place in the country she once loved but by this time, loathed; a house held in contempt of cosmic court and spark. As her mind was already half way to Georgia, the vision of yet another country place firmly planted as a promising seed in her brain, she turned and walked away from any suggestion of another manifestation, out the kitchen door, off to inspect the loading of a truck. Holly understood her lack of interest and kept the story to herself...for the next thirty years.

2008: There was cause for celebration. With the lighting of candles came a warmth and glow of a song in the voices and the hearts of everyone present: "Happy birthday to you!" A stark reminder of the dark days before; Carolyn had just returned from the hospital. As her daughters signed a birthday card intended for the cardiologist who saved their mother's life, a man responsible for insuring Carolyn would see another birthday, tears of joy were spilling as heartfelt messages of gratitude were scribed across the paper. Grandchildren signed then passed the pen to friends. Holly's turn came with little space left on a card crammed to its edges yet she found a spot to acknowledge the good doctor with a simple statement: "Thank you for saving my Mom." After cake and ice cream was served, Carolyn went to rest as a crowd began to disperse, mindful of her condition. Essentially, the entire family was recovering from her massive heart attack. Holly remained; *sisters* sat around the table telling tales of their shared childhood...noteworthy stories; the writer in the family taking copious notes.

"Remember the old song, 'Someone to Watch Over Me'?" That is just how it felt; like he knew me and loved me...like he was only there to protect me, from what I guess I'll never know." Recalling every detail of their encounter, Holly continued. "Never once did I feel unsafe in your house. Whenever I'd sleep over, I always stayed with April in her bedroom but not because I was afraid of **anything**. I just liked being with her. You never did tell me what it was going on in the chimney closet, though; this is the first I'm hearing of it. Why didn't you ever tell me?"

"I never told anyone...no, that's not true. I did tell Cathi about it... after we moved to Georgia. I think I told her when she came down for my high school graduation." April strained to remember precisely when she'd disclosed the great secret of her childhood. "It's not that I didn't trust you...I didn't want anyone to know because it was the only way I could protect him...from the Warrens. You know; they wanted to send them away, and he was my friend." Everyone nodded. Everyone understood. The Perron girls were emotionally attached to their holy spirits; not so spooked after all, it seems. Stories kept on surfacing as the clan revisited their past; page after page, until their scribe required a wrist guard in support of the process. Yes, there was an element of fear at first...though it didn't last. Holly smiled recalling those ethereal years as some of the best of her life. It seems the spooks had touched her heart, too.

"If you don't like something change it; if you can't change it, change the way you think about it."
Mary Engelbreit

going for a ride

"If you surrender to the wind, you can ride it."
Toni Morrison

As a regular visitor to the farm Holly learned to make herself quite at home. It was a second home to her. She was around so frequently, from the age of ten or so, she soon became familiar with every nook and cranny of the old house. She blended so successfully into the family she was welcomed not as a guest, but simply as one of the girls. Carolyn delighted in her presence. Everyone did. No one served; she got her own. It happened naturally. Many weekends were spent bunking in with April, crammed into a twin bed, giggling until all hours of the night; a perpetual play date lasting for years.

Relieved April had made such a wonderful friend, Holly's presence was a welcome respite from worry, alleviating some of Carolyn's concerns about a reclusive daughter. April was more isolated, less social than her other girls. She spent far too much time alone, something she did by choice. When Holly arrived in April's life she appeared as the fresh face of hope, a promise April would not be so lonely or withdrawn anymore. Born only a few weeks apart; the girls had much in common. Holly was a buoyant, happy child with a huge smile, who laughed from her heart; sparkling bright blue eyes with a devilish spirit the angel inside her kept contained. A truly good girl by any standard, she had staying out of trouble down to an art form. As a positive influence on everyone she knew, Holly was a virtual role model; a pillar of conscience in a crowd of adolescent mischief-makers: Nancy, as the case in point: Holly, saving her sorry butt from mortal mischief more than once! Upon reflection, it was Kate's fault; everyone else went along for the ride with the wild child.

It was winter again; much too frigid to play outside so the children were all making the most of the gigantic house. Hide 'n seek qualified as an extreme sport; so many spooky cubbyholes in which to tuck away. Holly's turn came to hide and she was seeking a place to go. Upon entering Andrea's bedroom above the parlor, Holly looked around, deciding that choice was too obvious. No. The woodshed instead; cold, but way more secluded. No one would find her out there; nobody would brave the cold to go look! The egg timer would expire and she'd win the game! This decision required sneaking downstairs and out through the summer kitchen. To do so and remain undetected would be a win by any standard; accomplishment in its own right. Gaining access to their woodshed the *other* way meant cutting through the window from inside the borning room. Having the reputation as an evil place to avoid at all cost, Holly thought better of it. Nancy had warned everyone not to go in there.

Standing at the top of the landing, peering into the dark narrow stairwell as it went winding down and around to the far corner of the parlor; Holly had to wonder if anyone was waiting at the bottom. Boo! The staircase posed some hazards by design. Guardrails installed with good reason, as a necessity for navigating the treacherous set of stairs in safety, Holly was about to discover one of the spirits…one with a good sense of humor; an introduction made by way of a rather unusual version of the twelve-step-program. Before she could even reach down and grasp the guardrail, Holly was suddenly flying, literally swept off her feet into midair, lifted up and carried by someone or something which gave her one hell of a ride…all the way to the bottom of the staircase. According to the still-startled soul, it happened so quickly, there was no time to reach for the rail; no time to react at all. In mere seconds she felt her body being *placed* at the bottom of the stairs, the first and only time her bottom touched any of them on the way down. She had not fallen. Of this, Holly was certain. The rest remains a mystery. She was not bumped or bruised, scraped or injured in any way. Boo! Who? Had someone just *stopped* her from going into that woodshed? Had it been some sort of divine intervention? Was it an act of God to keep her from falling (or being pushed) down that staircase? The excursion felt benevolent in Nature. Though, in retrospect, she questions the motivation, she did not do so at the time; mischief or mayhem…it felt as if someone had done her a really big favor. She remains grateful to this day.

What Holly found most bizarre about this event was, as quickly as the child went into flight, as swift the motion which carried her, she did not impact the facing wall of the stairwell. Instead, she rounded a sharp corner with ease, as if gliding down the slide on a playground. Whatever had control of her had *complete* control for those few seconds as Holly went for one soft spill of a ride, bypassing the hard right angle turn with room to spare. If the girl had accidentally tripped or fallen on the staircase, there would have been no way to avoid striking the far wall in the bottom corner. According to basic laws of physics, some contact would have been necessary to halt the momentum; she would have been thumped and tumbled; guaranteed. Insisting she had been gently placed upon the bottom stair, Holly found herself there sitting upright, facing the adjacent door into the summer kitchen. Carolyn opened the door. She stood there with an armload of wood, studying the child's face, so full of wide-eyed wonder; knowing for certain something odd had just happened to their houseguest. In that house, on that day, it was not just the living at play.

All these many years later Holly fondly reminisces about the old farmhouse she dearly loved: a home place offering high adventure, warmth and comfort (only metaphorically), extended family and a rather wide variety of *friends*. Having witnessed innumerable incidents, she reflects upon these episodes as tertiary moments, not the primary source of her memories. The relationships she established are in the forefront of the recollections she has cherished for her lifetime. Though she rarely speaks of her supernatural encounters, Holly insists she never felt frightened in the farmhouse and always had a sense of being *looked after* and *safe* at all times; not threatened in any way. Truth be told, Nancy scared hell out of her...not the ghosts!

When Holly speaks of this now, some memories are vague and nondescript while others remain sharp and fresh in her mind. Even if she was not actually present for an encounter she knew of it by proxy, almost immediately, as one of the privileged few to hear about any significant experience; one of the few trusted and trustworthy souls; one who was visited whenever she visited the farmhouse. As manifestations began occurring in her presence, nonchalance about it was impressive, especially for one so young: No Big Deal. Even as a child her maturity and composure was evident. Her complete acceptance of the circumstances made them somehow less disturbing to her friends, far less intimidating to those forced to live in this environment full-time. By her own admission, Holly has chosen not to reveal these events from her childhood as an adult. She passed no judgment then nor does she now seek validation from uninformed, unenlightened individuals who wouldn't understand. Holly does not care what others think...she *knows*. Though she and April have remained very close they hardly ever discuss these extraordinary episodes of their past; what happened in their presence so long ago at a farmhouse in a land far, far away. As Holly says, "It's just a part of our family history."

***

Cathi had come for a long overdue visit, her pug-nosed pup in tow; a pretty Pekinese named Cinnamon. They pulled in the yard driving a mail truck she bought at an auction. Cathi was always ahead of her time; recycling before it was hip. This unique vehicle with a steering wheel on the wrong side (on the right) was destined for use in the commission of a felony, aiding and abetting in the *rescue* of an old black stove; a crime which would require two intrepid trips. Bathsheba went along for the second ride. The smell was nauseating, even in an open air truck. Maybe she hated being house-bound. God knows she hated being Earth-bound! That witch hitched a ride on something other than the more conventional broomstick. Nobody saw her this day. Felt her? Yes. Smelled her? Oh, certainly so. It was to be a cool adventure in the heat of the summer. There would be junk food involved. Cathi delivered, toting a truckload of goodies; sustenance for a long journey ahead. They all crammed into the funky truck and headed into the woods of Foster, there to explore an old ramshackle estate, abandoned long ago. Carolyn had been there the day before with Fran, picking blueberries. From the moment she laid eyes on *her* stove, the mission was set in stone; cast in iron. She was certain the old place would burn to the ground. (It did, during that summer, roughly a month after their well-timed excursion.) The grand old estate was repeatedly vandalized; a tragic sight: the scene of the crime. Left exposed to the harsh elements, the windows had been shattered; its solid oak doors had been savagely fractured; splintered into kindling. All that survived these vicious attacks on a structure was something thugs and hoodlums could not destroy…it was stronger than the evil. The black stove, a **1909 Home Crawford**, stood alone in the debris, begging to be rescued; salvaged from the site. Carolyn was intent on saving it. All the men traveled together in the van; all the ladies gathered inside the mail truck. It was a bumpy, uncomfortable ride but spirits were high and the laughter, as pure as their purpose, sang along…even if their intention was to *retrieve* a valuable item from private property: Emancipation proclamation!

It was all Fran's fault. She was constantly dragging Carolyn off to *new* old places to explore, providing an exciting journey, to be sure; Fran as a virtual tour guide…one fascinating historical trek after another. The morning before the heist, Fran popped her head in the kitchen door: "Want to go for a ride?" There was a devilish glint in the eyes of an angel.

"Famous last words…so where to *this* time?" Carolyn giggled with delight. "Don't even bother telling me you just happened to be in the neighborhood and want some company; you want a co-conspirator!"

"To pick blueberries? I'm hurt! What could be more innocent?" Fran soon had her convinced. Carolyn abandoned her chores…again. They shared a cup of coffee before hitting the happy trail.

"Where are we going?" The hostess served her friend at the kitchen table.

"Out to the old Stanton Estate in Foster; there are hundreds of blueberry bushes there dripping with ripe fruit."

"Private property?" Based on Fran's history, a legitimate question she had to ask, though a response in the affirmative had never stopped them before.

"Well, technically speaking…don't you know the story? It's a famous one in these parts."

"More folklore? Do tell!" Carolyn claimed a seat. Fran could hardly wait to tell her another tragic tale of yore…days gone by…a personal predisposition.

"The Stanton family built the house in the early 1800's. After both parents died, the brother and sister kept the place and lived there together for the next sixty-five years. He used to do the shopping in the village but she never left their property; reclusive, I guess. Anyway, they were both into their eighties when it came to the attention of some villagers that Mr. Stanton was missing. He hadn't been seen for weeks. So the sheriff went out to their house and the old lady started shooting at him! Wouldn't let him anywhere near the place! Dementia; they had to take the poor woman by force...very sad. They found her brother's rancid, decomposing body in the bed where he died. She would not part with him and put up one hell of a fight; the state police got involved. It was in all the papers. They placed her in a nursing home where she died a short time later. The house has been deserted ever since, for years...all those berries...going to waste. Come on! I'll show you! Bring some big buckets!" Gulping her coffee, Fran headed for the kitchen door. Carolyn was intrigued and dutifully followed her friend. The girls had plans of their own, though a couple went along for the ride. Arriving home later in the day, Carolyn froze the blueberries then called Cathi, in search of another willing co-conspirator! Fran had been quick to introduce her cohort to the old black stove, endorsing the grand rescue plan though she did not participate in its liberation. Truth be told, she never thought Carolyn would actually do it!

Getting an early start was paramount. At first light the contingent headed to Foster, both get-away vehicles on the road by 6:00 a.m., before the promise of another hot day had a chance to manifest in form. When the group arrived at the site there was no time to waste, no chance to explore...quick: let's go! The work was hard and heavy. Everyone pitched in, stripping a stove of each detachable piece of cast iron, leaving only a vacant shell behind. And then they were off...just that fast...thick as the thieves they were. Stove pipe had been carefully dismantled and removed from a chimney flue; it went with the first load. Within half an hour the deed was half done. Their trip home was a long one but not long enough to recover from all the exertion. An enormous amount of energy expended during the morning, the worst of this chore was still ahead of them. Her mail truck practically dragging bottom, Cathi was vigilant in her attempt to avoid the potholes rural Rhode Island is infamous for, hoping to return to the farm with her prized truck intact. Everyone was a nervous Wreck of the Hesperus; sweaty, dirty, skin smeared, hair streaked with the rusty residual debris of unkempt iron. Escaping unscathed bolstered their confidence even though Cathi kept glancing into the rear view mirror all the way home, watching for the blue light special squad car, **the stove police** laying-in-wait, ready to bring their adventures to an abrupt and unfortunate conclusion: Gotcha! Pulses raced and faces flushed. Riding shotgun, the kids kept eager eyes focused **out**, scanning the luscious landscape for the fuzz! A thrill ride: the rush of an imaginary low-speed chase. How absolutely brazen they'd been: sheer audacity at dawn. With the first round of blatant pilfering behind them, everyone felt a real sense of satisfaction. Pulling into the yard, having pulled off the devilish heist with a heavenly host, in their light hearts and aching muscles they all knew that to finish the task meant a more painful return for the second, even heavier load. The girls were excited and ready to go. Adults were feeling it by this time; their enthusiasm waning. At least the trip back to the farm had been, though cramped, more comfortable: ballast. It made for a much smoother ride; this classic chase topping out at just about twenty-five miles per hour all the way from the backwoods of Foster to the backwoods of Harrisville. Rather than being nabbed for speeding through a town, fugitives from justice were far *more* likely to be stopped for driving so suspiciously slowly! No need to get busted by the fuzz for rescuing a stove. Best to pick up the pace!

Sustenance being served on the porch: all hands on deck! Chicken and tuna sandwiches prepared the night before, at Cathi's direction, the kids grabbed lunch then went to sit on the lawn. There Carolyn was not likely to notice all the *garbage* bags; assorted chips and cookies hidden among the gangly mix of arms and legs; another felonious act. Cathi had pulled three bags from her secret hiding spot underneath the transom of the truck: her stash. Completely surrounded, hands up, discreetly passing contraband within a tight circle of sisters; their devious criminal minds co-conspired to hide a bright yellow bag of Lay's Potato Chips because it's true what they say; you *can't* eat just one!

All fat and happy, everybody returned to their respective vehicles; time to unload the *other* stash. Once all the pieces of the stove were heaved into the barn, exhaustion began setting in but there was no turning back; the deed was only half done. It had to be finished; time for a second round, a second wind required in lieu of a nap. Cathi had a clandestine cooler hidden in the truck: Coca-Cola…the real thing! She'd held it in reserve, suspecting the beverage would become a necessary evil; a component of the workday. Divulging her secret to Carolyn, a covert cooler stocked with caffeine, the mother grinned. Brilliant! It was hot. They were tired. What better drug to ply the hordes with in regards to increased productivity? Artificial stimulation: Yes! The perfect solution for lethargy; Carolyn requested her portion be infused intravenously. Nectar of the gods, it was; not the devil's brew their mother often made it out to be, especially for these five children who'd rarely tasted the sweet treat on their lips. Each one of them downed an entire can. Laughter erupted with the bowels of somebody unaccustomed to digesting such waste products, so they presumed. Let the blame games begin! Who was to blame for this fragrant, flagrant offense? As the little *ladies* loaded into the back of a wide-open mail truck a rancid stench became overpowering. Something inside had died, gone to hell…and it had come back to haunt them.

"Okay, which one of you cut the Cheetos?" (A tendency toward bluntness; Cathi retains this propensity.) It was an odor pungent enough to bring tears to the eyes of its victims, which is what happened…from laughing so hard.

"Cheetos?" An inquiring mind, Carolyn had to know; Cathi holding out on her? "Any left for me?" Handing over a brightly-colored bag, Cathi stared as Carolyn shoveled junk in her mouth while stating the obvious: "You're a bad influence on these brats!" Her sarcasm instantly retrieved an admonishment, one feigned in the first place. They had a unique way of teasing one another.

"Terrible. I know. And you are quite a role model, destroying the evidence! By the way, your face is orange. Remind me who called last night for help to steal a stove." The cheese that goes crunch all over her chin: bless this mess.

"…to *rescue* a stove…" Carolyn: adamant about semantics, a proper usage in proper context with an unusually nuanced rationalization.

"Oh, yes, that's right, and who was it suggesting the kids come along to do the heavy lifting?" Be damned the Inquisition! Mom, mounting her defense:

"They're *really* strong!" A mother's pride: beaming through playful eyes.

"Yes! They certainly are!" Cathi waved a hand to her nose, indicating that God-awful odor had yet to dissipate. "So tell me, whose idea was this?"

"It was Roger's idea." Carolyn chuckled then choked on her Cheetos. Cathi had to laugh, the ripple effect like dropping a boulder into a pond. "Have you got any Fritos? They're my favorite!" Carolyn, waiting as expectantly as any child would; Cathi reached into the stash: half the bag of salty-flavored treats remained. Eureka! She'd struck gold-colored corn chips!

Yelling into the rearview mirror, Cathi declared: "***Whoever*** it is polluting the air back there, please step away from the vehicle!"

Nobody claimed responsibility, girls pretending protest; yet each insisting *she* was *not* the culprit. Andrea felt her first; they weren't alone. As crowded as it was, apparently there *was* room for one more. Sitting in the square metal box beneath a merciless mid-summer Sun, she got cold...chilled to the bone. Glancing over toward Cindy the eldest knew her younger sibling was equally aware of the drastic temperature change and what it meant. Cathi decided the only way to clear the air was to hit the road; to create some wind of her own. As they pulled out of the yard, Andrea leaned forward to whisper something sacred to her mother; the tattler had told the tale, ratting out their stowaway. Turning around in her seat, Carolyn caught a whiff of the foul, familiar odor. She caught the chill identified as Bathsheba. Not wanting to unnerve anyone, Carolyn closed her eyes then mouthed the words: "Get out of here." Within a few hundred yards of the house her *aroma* was gone, along with the intruder. Cathi, none the wiser; she had already endured one wild ride with the wicked witch of Round Top Road and did *not* need to know that bitch hitched a ride in her truck. Relieved it was over, Carolyn turned to comfort food for solace; hoarding the Fritos, she consumed all the chips left in the bag, washing them down the hatch with another full can of caffeine. Zoom zoom. They were off.

Heave Ho! It required brute strength to hoist the empty shell of a stove into the back of the truck. By the time it was secured there was no room left at the inn so the children rode home with a father and friends in the van while Cathi and Carolyn carefully navigated back roads…as discreetly as possible. Along the way, Cathi had to maneuver cautiously, keeping both hands on the wheel at all times, though her mind was free to wander. After a pause for reflection she uttered a statement so obvious, it was hard to believe it had been earlier overlooked: "You realize we're *Foster*-ing bad behavior in the children."

"I do now! Why didn't *I* think of that? Look! More blueberry bushes!"

"We're both a corruptive influence, but you're worse…a rotten mother."

"Awful." Carolyn shook her head disdainfully as a sign of self-loathing.

"We're setting another bad example for impressionable youths."

"They're tough enough to take it. They all live with ghosts." Mom: fooling around in fractions…by half…as the remark was inherently true.

"*I'm* an impressionable youth, too! So I'm actually corrupting myself!"

"How tragically convoluted!" Resist an urge to tease a willing accomplice? Never. All joking aside, Carolyn felt compelled to tell Cathi why she became so enchanted by the stove and *had* to bring it home. It reminded her of home.

"I remember being born, on the floor, in front of a black stove just like it."

"What?" Unprepared for an abrupt change of course: "Are you serious?"

"I dream about it all the time. It was the first thing I ever saw, as soon as I opened my eyes; a cast iron stove just as big and beautiful." Smiling serenely at her cohort-in-crime, Carolyn's gratitude was purely sincere. "Thank you." She considered the gesture of help a gift given. It was…from a dear friend.

Fugitives from justice, thieves escaped unscathed; they arrived at the farm about an hour later. Cathi had to crawl along the road, the weight of the stove causing the truck to scrape bottom entering the driveway. Off it came, out of the truck with one more strenuous Heave Ho! Carried in the kitchen literally a foot at a time, an old molded piece of iron took up residence. It was home; there to share space…to keep their family and a distant memory warm.

Carolyn's vision of and ensuing rationalization for pilferage on this grand scale had finally come to fruition: Mission accomplished. She would bask in its glowing heat for many years to come. It had worked! A rather ingenious, well-planned, pre-conceived notion of a heist had been a success, in spite of being a rather hastily arranged field trip. It was meant to be; astounding that she was able to convince her reluctant husband to participate then gather up his biggest, strongest men friends on such short notice. Efficiently executed: maximizing the time and space allotted for the task. Children: none the worse for wear; dirty perhaps, but otherwise, not a scratch. Contrary to the popular mindset, none of them went on to pursue a life of crime based on exposure; an excursion made into the woods to rescue a stove. Fostering felons was not an accusation which would stick; though they were free to plead entrapment and coercion courtesy of their mother's criminal mind, all of them will freely admit they all went along for the ride. Nobody suspected a thing. Nobody got caught red-handed, yet the telltale signs of their involvement were revealed when they spoke: evidence. The blue-tongued, finger-stained thieves pilfered berries, too. An inspired concept: Blue Girl Group…a great name for a gang. They had gotten away with it! A good thing, too! That summer the old house burned to the ground. Arson: the *real* crime committed at the Stanton Estate. The magnificent specimen rescued; the antique piece of sculpture cast in iron would have been transformed into a mass of molten metal, rendered useless, irretrievable; lost to the world forever. Theirs had been an act of perfect evil executed with good at heart…a scheme which saved a stove, after all.

Looking back on that bright summer day, Carolyn still harbors some regret, expressing it with a wince of shame when she speaks of the grand adventure. However, from the perspective of her accomplices, their rescue mission was necessary, still considered a triumph over evil; not an evil act. Truth be told, it was one of their best family outings ever…stowaway spirits aside.

***

Share and share alike: it was their motto. The Perron girls were growing up and a common childhood theme was apparently being carried into adulthood. Nancy was in the back of their Chevy van with Fred. It didn't much matter to her that he had been Andrea's first boyfriend only two years before; he had shown some interest in her **next** of kin; all that mattered at the moment. As a firm believer in sharing with her sisters, Nancy decided to entertain Freddy's sly dog suggestion that they take a walk together. Andrea was off in a land far, far away; she would *never* know. Had Fred been given the opportunity, he would have happily taken Nancy for the ride of her life. Having come to the house with his sister Katy, his options were rather limited. Fred's car was broken down. The keys to the van were inaccessible, tucked deeply inside of Roger's pocket while he slept on the sofa. Nancy knew they'd have to travel locally, on foot, but there were plenty of places available on the property to sneak off and hide in the darkness where they wouldn't be discovered, or so she thought. No one noticed when a lusty couple disappeared from the crowd gathered in the kitchen. Katy and company were highly distracted. With one *"come hither"* glance from across the table, Nancy enticed Freddy outside. There were no street lights, nothing to illuminate their whereabouts and yet she was capable of locating his voluptuous set of lips with ease…a miracle! Eyes like that of a cat, Nancy could see in the dark; another natural talent. It occurred to her the vacant van parked in their driveway would be the perfect choice for some privacy, offering a way to stay warm at the onset of winter. With a few suggestions of her own Nancy convinced him to follow her there. They crawled inside the open cargo space in the back. Freddy was just about to make his smoothest move when he turned white enough to light a path all the way back into the house. He followed it, opening the door and exiting the van without saying a word. Nancy was offended, having no idea why she had just been dumped. The young man leapt from a prone position and was out of the vehicle in seconds. She too jumped out, running after him; she *had* to run as he was moving fast. It was unlike Freddy to be so abrupt. Nancy found his behavior curious and equally impolite. Obviously *something* had happened!

Though it took some time to pry the tough truth from his tender lips

Freddy confessed he had been spooked. All he said: "We were not alone in that van." Apparently he'd detected a presence; a *someone* undoubtedly there to watch over Nancy (like it or not); so to preserve, protect and defend her honor, no matter how willing she was to relinquish it. Though she did not *feel* anything other than his hands at the time, Nancy believed him... the young man had no reason to lie. Whoever it was made his skin crawl; whoever it was made him run away like a scared little child, leaving behind a hot tamale teenager ripe for the picking. Fred never did divulge any details of the encounter. Instead, he took another path, slipping away from a family and friends in the process. He never returned to the farmhouse again. Over the course of the next year or so, Fred became involved with a group of unsavory characters who'd led him astray. The bright and beautiful boy was transformed by the substance known as Angel Dust; a powerful, often deadly hallucinogen. A sudden influx of the scourge struck like a dagger at the heart of Harrisville during the summer of 1977, changing everything; a sudden turn for the worse. Their sleepy village became a toxic waste dump, virtually overnight. Kids were getting *dusted* all over town, dosing and overdosing themselves; parents in a panic. Intoxicated teenagers were dropping like flies because a pusher was doing his footwork.

There are losses sustained in a lifetime; significant losses from which those who remain behind never fully recover. Freddy's death was one of them. No one could believe he was gone. Nancy called Andrea in Pittsburgh, sobbing hysterically; she could not speak. Carolyn had to take the phone to break the tragic news. His body was found in the village cemetery near his car, parked beside Bathsheba Sherman's gravestone. Andrea grieved for her dear friend. She was not as shocked as some; they'd met in passing the previous summer. During this brief interlude she had seen the startling vacancy in his eyes. His light had turned to darkness. He was already gone... across the Universe.

Freddy had to get high; he had to fly higher and higher until one dark night, while traveling at the speed of light, on devil dust disguised as angel wing, a little birdie whispered in his ear, showing him the way. He wanted to fly high enough to escape his demons on Earth. He did not escape unscathed. Sweet friend, rest in peace. Heaven isn't far. On the wings of angels fly away home.

"The desire to fly is an idea handed down to us by our ancestors who, in their grueling travels across trackless lands in prehistoric times, looked enviously on the birds soaring freely through space, at full speed, above all obstacles, on the infinite highway of the air."
Wilbur Wright

bed knobs

"We turn to God for help when our foundations are shaking,
only to learn that it is God who is shaking them."
Charles C. West

What if everything is *one* thing? What if God is *one* thing and everything? What if the Universe expands with our consciousness? These are some of the questions young children pondered as they tried to fall asleep in a house alive with death; not free to have sweet dreams of David Cassidy or Davey Jones. Their minds were otherwise preoccupied: a blessing and a curse. Each night was a challenge; fear, the obstacle to overcome. Cindy went for a ride almost every night. Her bed would shudder and vibrate, as a matter of course. It did not begin to levitate until she was thirteen. Cindy had reason to want another bedroom but she did not want to abandon Christine. As five sisters, watching and listening throughout the nights spent waiting for what was next to come, doors remained open between bedrooms; theirs was a supernatural existence. Whenever the veils thinned, shredding between the dimensions, moonstruck shadows revealing a translucent presence; space and time became irrelevant. All that mattered in the moment *was* the moment; certain knowing they were not alone; knowing, for as long as they lived there, never would be again.

***

September ~ 1976: From the minute the car left the driveway for a journey to Pittsburgh, Cynthia began making moving plans of her own, her intention, to stake a claim: Andrea's vacant bedroom. It was the perfect solution to her perpetual dilemma. Christine could have the middle room all to herself but Cindy would be right next door. If they each placed their beds back-to-back against the adjoining wall then, technically, they would be sleeping closer together than ever. Problem solved. Cindy's guilt alleviated, her official plan was hatched. While Roger was away, taking his eldest to college, the fourth of five was single-handedly rearranging the entire room. On a warm, sunny afternoon, while everyone else was busy outside, Cynthia moved her dresser and all of her stuff into unshared space, forgetting that, no matter where you go, there they are. At the age of thirteen she *finally* had a room of her own.

It proved to be a task and a half; a real feat for one so young but Cindy was reluctant to ask for help. She did not have permission and presumed if she did the job alone no one would have a chance to protest. There was a desk, a full-sized bed and a vanity at her disposal, each of which she arranged to her liking. Then came the arduous and incessant back-and-forth motion: toting assorted toys and trinkets, filling an empty closet with clothing. Cindy swept and dusted, polished and primped the bedroom for hours, lending her unique style to the surroundings. She washed windows then hung the set of curtains which matched her quilt. Andrea had been forced to leave a lot behind, as the dormitory room was miniscule by comparison. Consequently, Cindy felt rich in the same way a pauper suddenly endowed feels like a princess. The bed, a four-poster pineapple spinet, was one lovely and familiar space to inhabit. It was like a cushion, a cloud of delightful sensations, luxurious in every way. She had no regrets leaving her old twin-sized bed behind in the middle room. She'd spent many nights cuddled up with Andrea in a bed she had covetously longed for and loved for years... and now it was hers! Placing her quilt across the mattress, Cindy stood back to admire the room, results of an effort made; a wonder to behold. It was beautiful. It looked *so* different. It looked like *her* bedroom; a vision she'd held in reserve, in the back of her mind for years.

It felt so peaceful to her; calm and quiet. Having always desired a bedroom of her own, more importantly, the child wanted to get away from **whatever** it was in the middle bedroom seeming to seek her out...to haunt and taunt her, especially in the night. Children have a tendency to think literally: linearly. It did not occur to her at the time; there was no escaping the sights and sounds surrounding her in the darkness. This change of location a few feet away was highly unlikely to alter the inevitable outcome; merely a change of scenery. The grass is not always greener on the other side of a shared wall; inevitably, it was the same grass planted somewhere else. No matter where you go, there they are; lessons learned over time are, at times, of no service in the moment. Cynthia's desperate craving for a different bedroom was equally misguided and ill-conceived; the rebellious act of a child would soon be duly noted by disgruntled spirits Earth-bound to display some rebellion of their own. She'd be punished accordingly. How dare she reject them! Going somewhere, little girl? Attempting to leave us behind? No such thing! As if she had left a trail of crumbs through the woods, they followed her...with a vengeance.

This youngster attracted supernatural activity unlike any of her siblings. Perhaps it was due to the fact that she'd come so close to death herself. From the first night the family moved into the farmhouse, the room where she slept became the place where spirits gravitated. Smells and shapes moved through the shadows of spaces so dark it was difficult to see, even with the lights on. There was something about this room...something wicked. Her bed vibrated almost every night. It was moved in the morning. At times it would lurch and scrape across the floor, even though its metal feet never scarred the wood: no telltale signs; no evidence. When approached, she'd frequently hide beneath the covers begging God to make it stop. Cindy saw things in the middle room she will never forget so when the opportunity presented, when she perceived an escape route had cleared, a way out, she literally *took* it.

"Mom, please don't get mad at me." Apprehensively, the child approached her mother in the pantry after dinner.

"Mad about what?" Carolyn was perplexed. She never did anything wrong.

"Come see." Mother dutifully followed her daughter up the staircase.

"So *this* is what you have been doing all day! Why didn't you tell me so? I could have come to help you."

"I was afraid you would tell me I couldn't have the room and I just *had* to get out of...there!" Pointing toward the room next door, Carolyn understood. "I'm sorry I didn't ask first." Confession is good for the soul, so they say, and Cindy was relieved her mother was not upset by the slight deception. On the contrary, Carolyn appeared delighted by the initiative taken; hard at work on such a beautiful day when her sisters were hard at play. Impressed by the results of an obvious effort made and muscle extended, Cindy received only high praise; no harsh judgment against her. Carolyn looked around the room.

"No point in a good room going to waste, I say…and a good thing you've snagged it before Nancy did…then it would be a wasteland! Of course, when Annie comes home from school you'll have to share it…does she *know* you took her bedroom?"

"She knows I wanted it but I didn't ask her, either. But I know it will be all right with her…she's like that…she shares everything!"

"I know it will, too. Good job! What does Chrissy think about this move?"

"She's okay with it I guess…she's putting her bed up against the same wall as mine. I'll help her move it so we can still hear each other at night. I don't want her to feel all alone in there. It was scary enough with the two of us."

For a few nights Cynthia slept like an angel; utterly undisturbed: Reprieve! It could not have been more blissful. And then it began. Within several days of occupancy she noticed the bed ajar whenever she entered the room. This bedroom had always been quite active as well. Soon other pieces of furniture followed suit…rearranging the suite in her absence. She'd return from school to find the room completely altered; a desk shoved to the center of the floor, her bed, cockeyed, pulled out of place; stuffed toys thrown off the bed into the corner. Cindy had worked hard to set it up the way she preferred it to be; to find it repeatedly tampered with, left disheveled; such disrespect angered this urchin. Frustrated, she cursed whoever it was doing it as she struggled to return everything to its original position, in its right and proper place, all the while chastising the spirits interfering with her life. Cindy threatened them, rather harshly, to get the hell out; leave her new bedroom alone: Big mistake.

Andrea had numerous encounters during her tenure. For the six years it had been exclusively her own, she witnessed a multitude of manifestations but

HOUSE OF DARKNESS HOUSE OF LIGHT

has no recollection of the bed ever moving while she was awake. However, she often awakened in the morning to find herself clear across the room, the bed having been relocated by several feet during the night. This was a rather common occurrence in the farmhouse, one of those lesser evils; venial sins: space invasion...a violation no one paid much attention. Cindy spent many nights curled up with her big sister in the big bed but it wasn't until she slept in it alone that she fully appreciated its innate power to petrify. Shaken like a kernel of corn in a package of Jiffy Pop, Cynthia was forced to endure the raging of the spirits or a demon intent upon keeping the child sleep-deprived; Cindy had to rock and roll with the punches in order to retain possession of a bedroom she was unwilling to relinquish...to anyone.

Andrea has vivid recollections of her quilt rising and falling, as if someone was sharing space in the bed beside her, visibly breathing beneath the sheets. Whenever this happened, the youngster would sternly demand, "Go Away!" Now *that's* an order! Firm. Decisive. Unambiguous. Obeyed. It always did resolve the problem perceived. Intervention was unnecessary; she never felt compelled to request assistance from God or anyone else, for that matter. She meant what she said when she spoke it; as the voice of authority, it proved adequate to dispel any intruder. Cynthia had a far different approach to this particular problem. She was willing to beg God for help whenever necessary. Once she'd moved into Andrea's bedroom, to her great surprise, it became a far more frequent necessity. No shame attached or pride allowed in the midst of a crisis; not above requesting help from above, Cynthia often called upon the Great Spirit to rescue her from a malicious spirit routinely harassing the innocent girl. Andrea's experiences had been similar though relatively minor in comparison with her little sister's encounters, which lead everyone in the family to believe that she had indeed been followed. Though the eldest had a tendency to observe then react based on the severity of the infraction, Andrea found their antics annoying or at worst, distracting...but otherwise harmless. However, Cindy had close encounters which appeared to be life-threatening in nature as they occurred. Andrea spoke with omnipotence to clear the space and reclaim it as her own. Cindy did as she was told. Repeatedly uttering the words

Mrs. Warren had instructed them to use when approached, she found the phrase useless, resorting instead to pleading as a heartfelt form of prayer. It worked. That's what cleared the bedroom for the child intent on claiming it and keeping it as her own: adamant and unyielding, she would *not* be chased away...to go where? Beginning to see the light, Cynthia realized the truth: no matter where you go...there they are. In time, an alternative approach was successfully adopted and beings would adapt, providing ease from dis/ease, a comfort to all involved. Initially, she was terrified out of her mind.

It had nothing to do with the choice of bedroom per se, but rather pertained to **the child** whose attention was solely demanded. As surroundings changed so did the nature of various manifestations she was subjected to; paranormal activity increasing overall. Cynthia had escaped **nothing**; in fact, her level of exposure was magnified by a lateral move. It only served to aggravate spirits apparently satisfied with habitually visiting her in a very specific location. A unique phenomenon occurred: Cindy had entered another realm of the house, another dimension, just a few feet away from a space she formerly occupied, thereby introducing her to entities with whom she was unfamiliar; those she had yet to encounter apparently relegated to this bedroom. Apparitions she'd never seen before began manifesting with such frequency; it seemed she was still sharing space against her will. Likewise, those she'd attempted to leave behind in their middle bedroom stepped audaciously, belligerently across its threshold into another. The massive relocation project spawned a realization: Cindy discovered the source of the haunting chant she'd endured nightly for six long years. It became louder, more succinct, less muffled, as if coming from inside the wall directly beside her bed. Acquiring Andrea's bedroom came with a series of characters and complications, lending further credence to the phrase, "Be careful what you wish for..." She knew this was one battle she had to win. In a vast theater of operations, a sudden repositioning is risky business. According to Cindy it was like moving from one stage onto another and taking the entire cast, only to discover another complete cast ready and waiting to play their parts as well; the making of an epic...with understudies!

She began hearing voices she had never heard before; strangers. Familiar voices came rippling through the ether with clarity she was unaccustomed to, yet these new sights and sounds were only the beginning. Within two weeks of taking over the bedroom, her peaceful repose became a thing of the past.

One evening Cindy went upstairs to get her homework then decided to stay and enjoy her privacy rather than joining her sisters in the kitchen. Settling in on the center of the bed, she'd worked quietly for several minutes before the onslaught began. It was dark outside but the room was bright. The last thing she ever expected happened. As if a gigantic hand reached into a dollhouse, retrieving the bed along with its occupant, it suddenly lifted off the floor. As she screamed it began shaking violently: naughty it was not nor mischievous; not like a kid trying to knock a doll from a piece of toy furniture. Instead, it was a vicious and relentless attack. While the bed hovered off the floor it was jerked and lurched so intensely, Cindy was certain she would be thrown from the mattress. Yelling; a shrill, piercing scream ensued at the top of her voice. Bumped and bothered, throttled and thrashed, Cindy hung onto the bedpost, pleading for safe release. "In the name of Jesus Christ, go back to where you came from!" Tears pouring from her eyes; there was so much fluid leaking from her face she could not see what was happening around her but she felt it, making the wild ride all the more terrifying. Jostled and tossed across the surface of the bed, an unprovoked attack continued unabated. The bed came alive. It vibrated furiously, tipping side to side. Then it began banging down onto the floor with such a force, it shook the entire structure; one strike after another. Steam escaped from Cynthia's mouth with each panicked shriek; the room became unbearably frigid. Books were bouncing off the walls as papers and pens flew imprecise patterns, trapped within a spiraling shaft of stench; a whirlwind as circling projectiles crashed into this child, over and over again; punishment time! She knew her family was downstairs. They *had* to hear it, what was happening to her...someone would surely come running!

"God help me! *Please* make it stop! Somebody please come and help me!" Cynthia begged. "Dear Lord! Jesus! Make it go away! Mom! Come help me!

Mom! Please God, send *someone* to help me!" Frantic, she was traumatized; in shock. Her memory of it is still quite vivid; emotionally compelling these many years later. Cynthia recalls this episode as lasting *a long time*, at least a couple of minutes, though she'd be the first to admit the inherent difficulty in establishing an accurate time frame for these episodes, as time itself seemed virtually suspended whenever they occurred. The aftermath of this episode is equally confusing. Just like Dorothy landing in Oz with a jolt, a sudden drop ending with a *bang* finally silenced her screaming and stilled the bed. As the air cleared, the room instantly warmed. It was over. Cynthia was clinging to the headboard, eyes wide open; saturated. The bed was centered in the room and those many objects which had defied gravity were all scattered across the floor. She dared not move a muscle. Barely breathing, once sufficient time to recover passed and Cindy regained her equilibrium, she leapt from the bed, running so fast, she tripped and fell down the stairs. Racing into the kitchen, she promptly confronted her mother, along with the rest of the clan. No one expected such an explosion of hostility...none were prepared.

"How could you **NOT** hear me screaming?" Hollering, crying hysterically, her voice completely hoarse from the strenuous workout it received upstairs: "Mom! Why didn't you come? You *had* to hear me! *All* of you *had* to hear me! Why didn't anyone come? How could you leave me all alone up there?" Everyone was stunned by the outburst. Nobody understood what happened; siblings sitting speechless in front of homework assignments were confused, unable to respond. Visibly trembling with rage or fear, perhaps both, Cynthia threw a spontaneous temper tantrum; a rant and rave unlike anything anyone had ever seen from her before; the youngster was out of her mind with terror. Carolyn went directly to her daughter. She pulled away from her mother, still furious with her and everyone else in the kitchen, accusing them of willfully, deliberately ignoring her pleas, abandoning her in the midst of a crisis.

"I swear to God, Cin...we didn't hear you." As meek as Cindy was usually, Nancy suddenly assumed this persona. She tried to reassure her little sister, still in one hell of a panic, but Cindy would have none of it.

"You all left me there! You left me alone! I was screaming! No one came!"

Nancy's face appeared pale and drawn. She understood precisely how it felt to be so frightened, left to her own devices. "Cindy, honest to God, we didn't hear anything. What were we supposed to hear? What happened to you?"

"You *had* to hear me!" Cindy persisted, incapable of believing the sound of the attack escaped the attention of anyone in the house, let alone shrill cries in the night. She simply could not accept it; they weren't telling her the truth.

"Sweetheart, tell me what happened." Carolyn sat her daughter at the table while everyone promptly put their work aside. Christine grabbed tissues and bandages from the bathroom as her elbows had been scuffed from her fall on the stairs. April stared at her sister in silence with wide-eyed wonder.

It was as if she had absorbed the rage with which she was assaulted, as if a transfer of emotion between assailant and victim occurred during the ordeal. Cindy could not calm down. She could barely speak. It took some time for an unnerved sisterhood to recover, everyone distressed by her upset. It took time for Cindy to come to terms and tell them the whole story…about thirty years. Carolyn went upstairs with her to inspect the damage done. It was as she had described it; *stuff* everywhere. They straightened out the bedroom, gathering up her homework; assignments destined to be completed at the kitchen table with her mother by her side. Sullen and withdrawn, Cynthia said very little to anyone. Carolyn was sickened by the sight of the room. It was obvious that a child had been terrorized, brutalized by something evil in their midst. This time there was evidence, and plenty of it. The bedroom was in shambles and the child was in shock. Though Carolyn suggested she take her to a hospital, Cynthia declined, insisting she was all right. A good thing…what would she have said to the charge nurse…they would have admitted both to the psyche unit! Involuntary commitment. Theirs was a secretive existence, by design.

Later in the evening, once they all retired to the parlor, things settled down; the house, a quiet place again. Time for bed. Before Carolyn could extend an invitation for Cindy to bunk in with her, the girl began to climb her bedroom stairs as her mother bolted across the parlor, stopping Cindy in her tracks.

"Honey, wait a minute! You **don't** have to go up there. You can sleep with me or any one of your sisters...or down here on the sofa if you'd like."

"It's all right, mom. I **want** to sleep in my own bed...in my own bedroom." Cynthia's passive / aggressive tendencies were operating at full force in spite of her exhaustion. It seemed as if she thought relinquishing the room for one night would mean relinquishing it forever; a white flag of surrender. No way.

"Are you sure? I wouldn't mind." Carolyn found her own pleading voice.

Cindy returned to her mother, backtracking down the stairwell. "Yes...I'm sure." Leaning her head out to speak directly to a mom and **anyone else** who happened to be listening, Cindy bluntly stated her position. "Nothing and no one is going to scare me away from **my** room. I waited a long time to have it and I won't give it up for anything...or **to anyone**...not even for **one** night." There's a fine line between brave and stupid. Her defiance was not so passive after all; Cindy had drawn her own line then courageously stepped across it, stupid or not. Steadfast, she refused to be intimidated. Up the stairs she went.

Lying in bed, her thoughts wandering back to that horrific encounter only a few hours earlier, Cynthia became angry all over again, this time at a rather unlikely subject; Mrs. Warren. She had assured the children they could dispel a spirit or even a demon by repeating a single phrase which had proved to be faulty: *"In the name of Jesus Christ, go back to where you came from."* Her tired mind reeling, she considered the chant and its implications. What if they are already where they came from...what if *we* are the intruders? Heady concepts for one so young but notions begging her consideration in much the same way she had begged to be rescued. She'd begged for mercy.

The same scenario played out again and again over the course of the next four years but Cynthia held her ground then held onto her bed knobs for dear life. Every time the bed levitated it would shake violently. She would cling to the headboard or grab onto its spindles; something sturdy enough to keep her from being flung off the mattress. Every time she'd say her prayers, begging God, believing a guardian angel or *someone* benevolent would be dispatched from above to halt a malfeasant force; someone to protect and defend her in the midst of madness. Cindy insists her prayers were always answered. "Dear God, please make it stop!" It did. It always did finally stop, if abruptly so, whether by divine intervention or because the offending spirit became weary of tormenting the child. Receding back into the mist of the Netherworld, this powerful evil would hover, waiting to strike again. Eventually she came to an inevitable conclusion. It had been a futile effort to move on and take another bedroom. There was no point in attempting to evade or to avoid these spirits. They were everywhere, omnipresent; like God. They knew where and how to find her; no escape from the persistent haunting and taunting she'd endured. Once this child realized there would be no release from her cosmic captivity, Cindy accepted it as fate. As for spirits invading her space; perhaps it was the other way around. It was ludicrous to think they would ever leave her alone for long. Instead, she prayed for them...then prayed them away.

In time, everyone in the family learned to acknowledge the presence. It was the beginning of a truce, of mutual acceptance: a path to peace. On one point, Cindy would simply not relent; refusing to compromise. It was *her* bedroom, at least most of the time. She would tolerate voices, hollow indentations on the mattress, breathing blankets; she endured what she must, yet still enjoyed having her own space and time to herself; a real luxury in such a big family. Dwelling in a farmhouse riddled with uninvited guests, though she remained wary whenever she entered her room, it was much like it had been with the space she had formerly occupied. "Ya get used to it." Besides, Cynthia had a plan; a strategy. No surrender. Before she would make peace...it was war.

"Enjoy when you can, and endure when you must."
Johann Wolfgang von Goethe

broomsticks

Witch way did she go? Their broom was not relegated merely to a fictitious mode of transportation for spirits; modus operandi, as the object has so often been portrayed in scary fairy tales. The straw broom in the Perron household served a dual purpose, one of which, as a signal from beyond; an overt form of communication, frequently moving from its safe designated storage space. Andrea *knew* none of her sisters were using it. So, boo who moved it again? In the alcove shared by the bathroom and second kitchen pantry doors, there was a rack discreetly tucked away in the corner, mounted on the wall. It held the mop, dust pan and brush and a straw broom. When not in use *this* was the space where these items were to be properly stored and kept out of the way. Carolyn repeatedly requested that these few objects *not* be floated all over an expansive residence; but instead, used and replaced where they came from so each use did not first require an extensive, exhaustive and unnecessary search of the premises. The kids were generally compliant with the mother's orders, as so few of them were ever issued. They did as they were told; *not* the ones being uncooperative. Whenever the broom was found out of place, becoming a chronic problem, the kids copped the blame. Boo! Who moved the broom?

Cindy walked into the kitchen through the front hallway, the spooky cellar door, something to avoid. Looking straight ahead as she made her brisk little move, she nearly missed what was going on to her left side as she entered the kitchen. The broom was sweeping the floor. It did not appear to be attached to anybody, but someone *had* to be manipulating the object! Right? The first time it occurred in her presence Cynthia was about nine. The girl was aghast; her mouth dropping open as she watched it in silence. With flair and rhythm, the broom swished and sashayed around the room, as if dancing in the arms of another, then abruptly fell onto the floor. Swept away by the sight, she did not know what or who she had witnessed…a housekeeper in residence?

As example and description of the method by which children adapt to their circumstances, Cynthia had precisely the same encounter again, several years later, though her reaction to it was decidedly different. In the interim, she had experienced so many inexplicable, beyond implausible episodes in the house, by means of overexposure she'd become somewhat jaded, even desensitized to their supernatural environment. She just was not that impressed anymore. Guess they were right; ya get used to it: following vignette as a case in point:

Keep on truckin' baby! Cindy was late: pedal-to-the-metal-put-the-hammer down: late. All of her sisters were waiting in the car as the child was hauling ashes through the house, a wholly polite euphemism the girls used to indicate someone moving their ass! Running through the kitchen, there it was again; that solitary broom, briskly whisking its way across the floor. Glancing over toward it along her trek to the door, Cindy barely gave it a second look, but said: "Good! *You* do it! *I'm* late for school!" Snidely whiplashing the kitchen witch with her flapping tongue, Cynthia opened the door and as she did, the broomstick went flying across the expansive room, clearly flung in disgust, instantly becoming wedged between the black stove and the chimney. Aha! *That's* who keeps putting it there! Whoever *that* is! Epiphany: Running up to the car, Cindy disclosed to her sisters what she'd just seen in the house. They weren't surprised but they were tardy for school, late slips from the principle tardy, all the fault of that damned kitchen witch, no doubt…the blame game.

Carolyn knew about her. She had seen her or seen the absence of her many times. Whether as a fleeting glimpse or long, hardened stare, she was always there and yet not there. Like some stoic romantic figure lost on the moors of history, it was difficult to discern her presence based solely upon appearance because she so frequently disappeared…yet remained. She had to be sensed, and sensed she was, by those whose paths she crossed like a cat lost in space. Actually, this spirit was cross! Though Carolyn expressed her frustrations at times, especially before realizing who the *real* culprit was, angst was minor in comparison to exasperation displayed by this perturbed, disgruntled ghost; one who obviously required her kitchen be kept a certain way…at *all* times. Unrealistic expectations: thereby setting her up for an existence mired in the muck of perpetual obstructionism…like dwelling in Congress! Hell on Earth!

Once the black stove arrived, she became more visible. When invisible, she became more active, often demonstrating her disapproval by leaving a pile of debris in the center of the kitchen floor with the dustpan beside it. There was nothing subtle about her approach. Wooden floor: each plank lined with deep grooves; crevices craving dirt from the bottom of work boots were magnets for whatever got tracked in. It was a farm! Short of sweeping incessantly, to the exclusion of virtually every other chore, there was no way to keep those floors spotlessly clean. The traffic was too steady; the other chores, too dirty. When particularly annoyed, she would *switch* the broom, twitching it rapidly back and forth; covering about a square foot. Indicating extreme agitation, she'd then toss it onto the floor. Irk and ire; it was easy to arouse her wrath: making a mess will make a temper manifest. Spill some coffee grounds in the pantry or drop a few woodchips at the base of the stove. It drove her crazy! This irascible spirit must have become infuriated during harvest time as their kitchen was always a wreck! Of all the spirits-in-residence, she was the one expressing her sentiment effectively; radiating gamma waves of resentment; her most righteous indignation regarding a perceived neglect of the premises. Essentially, she'd begun impacting *their* environment rather than visiting one formerly her own from another time. The spirit was not sweeping a floor two hundred years prior…she was *present* in the moment and made her presence known; disdain seething from every invisible pore: Obsessive-Compulsive: This level of irritation evidenced by her reaction; the shocking immediacy of her response to Cynthia's terse comment. It was no coincidence. She'd flung the broom across the room with malice, targeting the precise spot, the place it had been found many times before, *misplaced* beside the stove. There was no mistaking her intention. Everyone suffered her shrew-like symptoms, part of her disturbed complicated persona. This aspect of the spirit altered over time. A contempt borne of familiarity, she appeared to evolve beyond it.

The longer the family remained in the home, the less she acted out, finally exhibiting characteristics more subdued; reactions muted, as if with maturity, as if *she* was growing up...*with* them. This young woman, presumed to be an earlier occupant of the house, rarely revealed herself to mortals. Andrea saw her only once, a brief sighting; just a glimpse. Slender and slight, this entity appeared in the alcove, standing inside the dark corner beyond the threshold of the second pantry. Her auburn hair, washed out by the Sun. Body stooped forward; Andrea could not see her face, focusing instead on the curves of her shoulders, the outline of bones protruding from beneath the fabric of a rather drab full-length dress. In life, she'd gone hungry. There she stood, emaciated, a hollow figure, just inside the storage pantry...where all their food was kept. Slowly the door began to close. Its latch clicked. Andrea walked away, as she was unwilling to reopen it; to take another peek into another dimension. An opportunity for contact missed, it was simply too painful to watch.

Something else clicked during that encounter. Andrea felt sympathy for the fragile creature, this pitiful sighting of her revealing the truly sad realization. The spirit had suffered in life; she'd known abject deprivation and God only knows how she died. It appeared to be from starvation. After describing the sighting to her family, Andrea encouraged everyone to cease and desist with name-calling; from then on the spirit was no longer referred to as the kitchen witch. It was cruel and disrespectful; a mean-spirited approach to a lost soul. With one suggestion, a thoughtless practice instantly fell from favor.

An instant emotional attachment occurred; a connection established with a weakness exposed even if it was destined to be a rather lopsided relationship. The entity never offered any indication she saw the youngster standing there. She'd appeared lost in thought; elsewhere. Her position remained unchanged. A head bowed as if in solemn prayer, long hair obscuring her facial features, Andrea knew the spirit would appear weary, should she look into her eyes. It would be too intense; misery painful to watch…even at a distance.

She *was* someone: a Spirit and Soul dwelling in the Cosmos, someone who had lived and died upon the Earth. No matter who she was, she mattered. She felt defeated. A broom functioned as a reflection of her moods and emotions; its use spoke of what she'd endured. This once vital, feisty spirit of a woman manipulating a coveted object began to appear depressed; the broom slightly swishing their floor, an entirely lethargic effort. Mundane: another Sisyphean task. Perhaps they'd read her wrong all along. Could it be that the animosity an agitated spirit exhibited was intended for someone else; a wrath misplaced in time and space? Maybe messy mortals should not have taken a criticism so personally. After all, they had not walked in her aged, well-worn shoes.

Lesson learned: "Do unto others as though you were the others."

As girls grew older, everyone made more of an effort to keep their kitchen tidy, to become more sensitive to her feelings and needs, just in case it *was* them distressing her no end. Carolyn let all of them off the hook long before, realizing they were not responsible, not to blame for jamming the dry, brittle broom straw up against a burning stove; all well aware of their mother's fear of fire. Instead, Carolyn assumed it is where the broom had been kept during the time an impoverished woman hovered near a fireplace while cleaning the kitchen of her home. Boo! Who was she and why was she there and how had she died? When Carolyn scoured the records pertaining to former occupants of the town she found the name Harmonie Arnold listed among those who'd lived and died in the farmhouse, though no official cause of death was listed beside her name. Only the innocuous, non-descript word "accidental" was on her death certificate. More undisclosed details: this seemed to happen quite a bit back in the good olden days.

The young spirit remained vexed to be sure…but why? If she did not know Andrea was observing her then why had the pantry door closed on a figment who apparently wanted to be seen? What was the source of her torment? Was she the only spirit who closely monitored a kitchen of the future while busily revisiting the past? Her absence and simultaneous presence was remarkable, easy to discern but difficult to describe. When the broom was misplaced they all knew she was there. The kitchen seemed to be the place she was relegated to, but was this by choice? Clearly she wanted it kept a certain way. It never met with her approval; never swept to her satisfaction. Was she the one who turned on the dishwasher? *Someone* **learned** how to do it! Several times the machine began running all by itself, or so it seemed; buttons pushed with no assistance from any mortal on the premises. And boo who was it that kept on opening the refrigerator, deliberately spilling its contents on the floor. Was it punishment time? Was it her "I'll force you to clean the floor!" bad attitude?

Was she the spirit who preferred old bottles to be arranged by height rather than lined along the sideboard? When she lived in the house she must have stored her broom beside what was then an open, functional fireplace, so to sweep away the ashes from the hearthstone...and this was where she wanted it to stay: Period. Whenever this spirit manifested, it made everyone wonder about her depraved circumstances. Could she see Manny? Could he see her? Were they from the same time, perhaps the same family? Which one was the kitchen instigator, the mischief-maker who antagonized the kids? Who was it repeatedly opening the refrigerator door, flinging it violently back and forth, spilling its contents all over the floor? Cindy's frantic fears had nothing to do with an unruly spirit causing mayhem. As that door jerked and swayed, she'd beg it to stop, as it almost always occurred just prior to Roger's return home. Kids would be blamed for a mess they did not make; receiving a punishment they did not deserve. But then, *they* knew that. They knew everything! It was all a part of their plan. Timing is everything in life...and death. Scurrying to quickly clean it up, innocent children had resentments of their own. For some reason, Cindy was the one most frequently subjected to the cruel and unusual behavior, a particular stunt occurring in her presence on a fairly regular basis. It seemed to be a deliberate act, initiated with some forethought and malice. If it was meant to be a joke, it wasn't funny! Caught up in a situation not her own making, Cindy would curse the culprit, inviting further scrutiny: target!

***

Funny, the things one remembers from childhood. It was not all doom and gloom. As an aside, this vignette remains appropriate to the "subject" matter, intended to make a point; to make light. House of Darkness House of Light: it was both. In such an otherwise morbid setting there was light and laughter and love in abundance. Nancy had a nickname. Andrea was studying French and Nancy insisted on knowing what her name was in that foreign language, pressing her eldest sister for an answer. Andrea already knew it was *Nadine* though, during a rather quick-witted moment, dubbed her sibling *Nancois*. Nancy was so gullible she believed it; everyone in their family played along. The name stuck...for life. When Nancy entered a French class the following year, telling the teacher her name...*in* **French**... Mr. Beausejour was delighted! The man's hearty laughter rang through the hallways. Nancy was mortified; humiliated. She confronted her eldest sibling when she arrived home and the laughter throughout the family was undoubtedly heard all the way back to the school. Nancy has yet to forgive her big sister. Now, for the rest of the story:

Memory is a gift. For better or worse, a blessing and a curse, it is likewise a gift. One might presume, given the circumstances, only tortured or traumatic memories would remain, retained as visions of nightmares; as recollections from a lifetime ago dwelling in a house alive with death. Not so. Nancy now insists the following story be included in this tale of two houses, believing it captures then encapsulates the essence of a spirit: her own. It reflects the true Nature of enduring relationships between five sisters who adore one another, in spite of their differences, regardless of circumstances.

Christine was born just eleven and a half months after Nancy's birth. (It's a Catholic thing.) Anyway, because of their closeness in age and the structure of the curriculum in the middle school, the girls shared an English class. One day they had a test to take. They had studied hard together. Each did well on the exam; neither had a clue about the extra-credit question. They both got it wrong and their mutual failure was a point of contention all the way home; a long bus ride providing ample time to resolve the dilemma. They could not. Their assignment: Name the cliché. Each running the phrase so repetitiously through her mind, both had it memorized for life by the time they got home.

> *"The woman works tirelessly into the night, sweeping*
> *away her woes, wielding her mighty broom as a sword."*

So name the damned cliché! How hard could it be? Chrissy's test answer was admittedly the lamest one. "There is no broom like a new broom." Whatever! She wanted to be finished with the test and didn't care about the extra credit. Nancy gave it more thought. She'd relied upon the media to provide her with an extra-credit guess; one equally wrong. "O'Cedar makes your life easier!" It was so wrong. Both girls felt like imbeciles; the answer should be obvious to them and yet there it lingered, right on the tips of their tongues, flapping all the way home. Neither one came up with it. Distracted by other important issues upon arrival, snacks, they both forgot about it and moved on with life.

At thirty-nine, Nancy was engaged in a rather mundane task; sweeping her kitchen floor: Sisyphus lives on! Her mind free to wander, Nancy suddenly dropped the broom, running to the telephone. She called Christine.

"I've got it! I know the answer to the cliché question!" Epiphany: tendency to hyperbole. Chrissy remains a supremely patient person. However, Nancy's impulsive nature *still* drives her to distraction. Preparing for what came next:

"*What* question? *What* answer? What the hell are you babbling on about?" Suspecting her sibling may have lost a tenuous grasp on reality, she indulged a convoluted chat with great good humor. "Nance...deep breath. Tell it."

"Remember Mrs. Dacey's English class? Eighth grade; we took it together; that damn test we took and both flubbed the extra-credit question? She never would give us the answer...said she wanted *us* to figure it out for ourselves! Remember?" Christine's curiosity piqued. She *did* have a vague recollection of this specific event...come to think of it. "That broom thing!

Remember?" Nancy recited the quotation; from memory…the results of a mind left free to wander through time. Naming the cliché: *'A woman's work is never done!'* Chrissy began to giggle like a school girl huddled up with her sister on a bus; a hysterical message received, over the phone, no less! Memories…light the corners of her mind…of the way they were.

"I cannot believe you thought of that! We were…what…twelve? Thirteen? What is *wrong* with you?" Christine had to tease Nancy; it was compulsory, not an option. "What made you think of *that*?"

"I was sweeping and remembered the ghost who used to sweep our kitchen floor; how *her* work is *never* done!" (Christine remembered… everything.)

"All right. You get the extra credit, even after all this time; at least a gold star for having a *really* good memory! **A+**! Way to go…Nancois!"

***

The drudgery of it all; this miserable spirit could only hope for some basic improvements in the housekeeping skills. For the most part these mortals had better things to do. The girls would frequently pass her by and keep on going, noticing her presence less and less over time; non-threatening and innocuous; her only bad habit was placing the broom too close to the stove. The threat of fire kept Carolyn mindful; watchful of her. As one of the most active rooms in the house, the kitchen attracted someone, maybe more than one spirit. The telephone was frequently tampered with, as were several appliances. Antique bottles were routinely arranged then rearranged, moved from open shelves to windowsills then back again; *someone* had a flair for interior design! A pile of dirt left on the floor, the broom propped beside it, leaning against a chair; a message received then ignored. Household provisions spilled and splashed about the premises, chairs pulled out from beneath children; hair pulling was always a less-than-gentle reminder of their omnipresence. And the flies!

Is there no balm in Gilead? No salve to soothe these savage beasts? Is there nothing to be done on their behalf? Healing wounds in life may be preferable to suffering them after death. The concept of **Eternity** is virtually impossible to wrap a mortal mind around: Imagine that. We cannot envision the realm in which we live in the midst; we simply cannot fathom *forever*. Human beings, finite creatures by design, exist within an infinite Universe. Spirits defy logic as well as the law of gravity. Rather than being those subject to and governed by Universal Law some suspect they are a part of a grand plan; an immutable law unto themselves, revealing and expressing itself in ways we're incapable of comprehending. Is there an ephemeral spirit dwelling within all corporeal manifestations, released into the Cosmos upon death? What remains of us as we transform, when this vessel has perished? Can we have a strictly physical experience in a metaphysical sphere? By what laws are they governed if they defy natural law; supernaturally shattering a one-dimensional, preconceived notion of existence. According to existentialist John Paul Sartre, "Life begins on the other side of despair." If this is true, then where does death begin?

"The miserable have no other medicine
But only hope."
William Shakespeare

boo! who?

Boo! Who the hell was it? Who were these people! Carolyn had to identify the culprits. In spite of Sam's encouraging words, something still told her to be afraid...be very afraid. Fire was elemental to the threat perceived. She had to take necessary steps to create fundamental reforms in their living situation. Truth be told, she was not the only one impacted by fear. Roger knew it well.

He blew his chance. In retrospect, it is one of the regrets he now harbors, an opportunity missed to understand the circumstances in which he dwelled. He too was subject to the desires of a spirit seeking acknowledgement. When it finally presented itself, he blew the chance sky high...into the Cosmos and beyond. He now admits it was Bathsheba who approached him one evening when he was home alone, a rare opportunity for some privacy, as far as she was concerned. Sitting at their kitchen table with the newspaper and a fresh batch of steamers, it was a blissful few moments for a man who worked hard and deserved some down time all to himself, but someone knew he was there and available for a formal introduction. He heard her footsteps on the cellar stairs, dismissing it at first as his imagination. Click. When that door opened in the front hallway, there was no dismissing his fear. Overcome by a sudden sense of dread, he froze stiff. Though he had encountered this spirit before, he had never been confronted by this presence so overtly, her approach, quiet and subdued; frightening nonetheless. The hallway filled with a dark vapor, swirling in the air it consumed. The form in which she manifested seemed to change, assuming a solid form. He was too afraid to gaze at her, too startled to look away. After a few moments, he made a fateful, if fear-based decision. Roger denied Bathsheba her ritualistic **right** of passage. It was her home, too.

Guess who's coming to dinner? The man panicked. He spoke to her in the harshest terms, in a way generally reserved for loved ones, as a manifestation of his own terror. In so doing, he alienated the spirit wanting to befriend him.

"If you are not going to come in and sit down and talk to me...then get the hell out of here, you witch!" A very fine how do you do. She most certainly took offense. The swirling, translucent mist instantly evaporated. The cellar door slammed with such force, it rocked the dwelling to its foundation. The vibration was stunning; he felt it in his chest. Roger just sat there, trembling in his chair, believing it was time to accept Reality. He felt ashamed.

Bathsheba would not approach him again for many months afterward and the one opportunity he had was lost forever. There was a decided chill in the air and to this day, he admittedly regrets the snap decision made on the spur of the terrifying moment. He had been so rude to an unexpected guest. Roger could have been kind. He could have been welcoming but for fear of the unknown. He could have invited her to join him and could have learned so much in the process. Yet, as the cloud filled the hallway, the abject fear had clouded his judgment. Boo! Who? No question who this was; in his mind, it was the mistress of the house. It had been his one and only chance to verify her true identity; the one and only time she opened the door on a relationship and he slammed it in her face, so she returned his disfavor. Sometimes when opportunity knocks one must have the courage to answer the door and then invite even an unexpected guest to cross a threshold of the heart. Bathsheba wanted to befriend the man whose attention she coveted. Though he had on numerous occasions perceived her as such, in a moment of pure terror he had shamefully dismissed her, banishing a lonely old spirit from her own home. Sticks and stones...but words are weapons, too. Would he never learn?

"Seize the moment of excited curiosity on any subject to solve your doubts; for if you let it pass, the desire may never return and you may remain in ignorance."
William Wirt

kindred spirits

"Happiness can be found, even in the darkest of times,
if only one remembers to turn on the light."
Steven Kloves

They all stood together as a clan or a coven; vacant emotionless apparitions staring into nothing, oblivious, unaware they were frightening Carolyn out of her mind. Flames from their torches crept toward the ceiling as the mother of five envisioned her family burning to death. What her eyes could behold told her that they did not have long to live. Crouched up against a headboard, she screamed aloud in mind, begging for mercy, crying out in desperation: God! Kindred spirits, related in life and in death; children resembling the women standing behind them. One resembled a child of her own. Each recognizable as a solitary entity seen wandering their house at one time or another, within one space or another, this cluster of souls appeared to belong together...like a family photograph...they appeared, as portraiture, at the bottom of her bed.

***

During moments when she least expected it, while otherwise preoccupied, Carolyn's thoughts would often wander into a mine field of memories...there to pause and reflect. Spawning an emotional charge of dread coupled with an instant rage, a sudden surge occurred; a physiological reaction to a vision she struggled to extricate herself from as darkest of nightmares in broad daylight.

For years, she'd habitually expelled this scene from the minute it crept into her consciousness, beginning the arduous process of dismissing the intruders. Nothing less than something wicked; to dispel a memory required more than a modicum of mental discipline. A good brain-washing was called for; spirits are tenacious, even when they are absent from sight. One lovely midsummer day while cutting roses from her garden, Carolyn was inexplicably catapulted back in time to the night when pure fear pulsed through her veins. Lingering with the image, the woman was struck by a realization: a picture in her mind, so vivid and vibrant, it seemed almost alive; a vision of spirits resembling a family. My God! They all looked alike! Years removed from an exceedingly close encounter, she wondered, why had she not remembered this before?

Kinfolk: Was it her imagination? No. Carolyn determined it was far more likely they were actually related, as so few families ever lived in the house, chief among them, the Arnolds. Most of the recorded deaths which occurred on the farm were in that family: Mrs. John Arnold, Harmonie, Johnny and Prudence…even Bathsheba was an Arnold. It was like viewing their family portrait, studying the symmetry; adults in the back, children in the forefront: all were silent except for the syncopated rhythmic beating of brooms against the surface of wooden boards. Vibrating with each strike, the house trembled all around her. As if hypnotized, under some exotic spell cast, these spirits participated willingly. Those who had never posed any threat before were all involved…a gang mentality…or were they there against their will? Had they been beckoned, coerced into submission then issued instructions? Directed? So it appeared: Vacant; indifferent. No emotions expressed, no contact made. They were there to play their role whereas Bathsheba seemed more invested, speaking with purpose and reason while the others had merely mimicked her. The deafening noise had come from her and she alone; though it reverberated throughout the structure…as Carolyn remained focused on the fire.

Formerly, these spirits had been entirely benign. Manny and the children, the broomeister from their kitchen, the farmer and his son; none of them had ever displayed any type of threatening behavior before, yet there they stood, aiding and abetting a wicked woman; one who knew how to hold a grudge. Their reaction to Bathsheba, or lack thereof, indicated no malfeasance. There was no apparent interest or any attachment in their facial expressions. Blank slates…one and all. They'd functioned as automatons; robotic movements so precise it appeared to be programmed into their beings.

As if in some trance herself, Carolyn stood beside the roses, silent and still. This was revelation: awakening an understanding which did not exist before a discovery of this Nature. Other questions logically followed: do we remain with our families in death? Would she be capable of tolerating Roger's flaws and foibles for eternity? No answers forthcoming, she'd cancelled this image and focused on flowers instead. Pricking one of her fingers on a particularly sharp thorn, it drew brood, drawing her back to the present while watching in amazement as a crimson bead of blood trickled down the side of her finger. It resembled a teardrop; as water on an icy glass: Needle and the damage done.

***

One need not be related to relate; feel a real sense of kinship with another soul. Each of the girls developed a *real* emotional attachment to the spirits in the house while bonding between dimensions. Nancy frequently encountered Manny. She believes it's because he watched over her, a constant vigil, often keeping her safe from herself. Divine intervention or just enough *spook* to scare someone away? It was a thankless task. His work was never done.

Christine attracted the one who coveted her. Over time, developing feelings of sympathy and empathy for this spirit, Chrissy wondered why she had been approached, considering whether or not the apparition was there to harm her or protect her from something or someone else. She remains haunted to this day by intense sensations regarding this powerful manifestation even decades after its occurrence. She knows what Cindy saw in the night, as the face of an angel was captured by a demon. Though Chris has no memory of the event, it haunts her still. Or being trapped in a trunk; something she'll never forget. A mortally wounded soul is she, having seen too much in life regarding death.

April had a secret; an emotional attachment to a spirit, protective in nature. A profound friendship formed; a bond which ultimately resulted in the tragic breaking of hearts; regrets all around. It has haunted her for a lifetime. As for her long lost friend...perhaps for an eternity. There are some losses sustained from which beings never recover...mortal and immortal alike.

Andrea was fascinated by the holy spirits in their house and had several of them close by to her at all times. Compassion: elemental to her relationships, especially for the one who kept the kitchen, making her displeasure known to all who had tracked anything through her time and space. The misery of such drudgery, self-evident, Andrea so pitied the one whose hunger showed on her burdened shoulders; whose Sisyphean task required broom instead of stone: a spirit whose work was never done. A single sighting of her broke the child's heart; an image which lingers and, like the spirits, will not ever go away.

Cynthia: For better or worse, in sickness and in health; they ALL gravitated to the girl with the gift. She always felt a special fondness for and remarkable sadness about the little girl with whom she was, at once, disheartened by and intrigued with; the one who wandered around a house crying for her mother. Cindy cried with her at times, touched as she was by the poignant and pitiful request of a child lost, suspended in the ether. Whether predisposed to acts of goodness or attracting an evil presence as darkness gravitating to the Light in her soul, the child remained haunted by that which she sensed all around her in every room of the house; haunted by voices and imagery she would retain for a lifetime. Cindy often speaks of how closely the little girl resembled her eldest sister as a vision of her as a younger child. Was it possible? Alchemy: Could it be? What drew the family to the farm? Were they *all* from one clan, reuniting in common purpose in an uncommon place and time? Was theirs a reunion between dimensions, at the point of convergence where darkness and light merge as one: at dawn and in twilight? Was the intrepid journey into the woods a family affair: Kismet in the Cosmos? Time itself would tell the tale.

"To confine our attention to terrestrial matters
would be to limit the human spirit."
Stephen Hawking

clarion call

A distant music: a thundering, dissonant tone; no melody or syncopation, no drums or whistles. There was no accompaniment; only the lone, shrill cry of an archaic horn, its sound muffled by some invisible barrier. Andrea heard the clarion call. It had a rather harsh, militaristic twinge to it; a brassy, high-pitched urgency which seemed strangely familiar. Initially being perceived as the wind playing tricks with the wooden frame of an old farmhouse, rushing through hollow eaves on its way to nowhere, bending beams at will, she soon acknowledged having been mistaken. There was something deliberate about it; an intention behind it. Night after night, she heard a horn in the distance. Always consistently the same: as if the same instrument was being played by the same solitary musician; its ethereal qualities defied any concept of it in reality. As fluctuating winds of winter carried its tune throughout the valley, she listened attentively. After several weeks spent in still unfamiliar territory, Andrea began to wonder who it was for and why it rang out in the night.

"Can you hear that?" Cindy entered her bedroom, requesting a sister sleep-over. This night was colder than most and the eldest welcomed her company. "Listen. Do you hear it?" The siblings sat very quietly, side-by-side, bundled up beneath a cozy cotton quilt. There it was again. They whispered and then wondered about it together. What could it be? Cindy could hear it, too.

"Why don't I hear it in my room?" Cindy was more curious than fearful.

"Maybe it's just too far away." Attempting to conjure up a viable answer to a question posed, she had no explanation for the mysterious music from afar.

Cindy considered it for a moment and developed a good theory of her own.

"It sounds like that music they play in parades when all the men line up and they walk funny and they all dress the same…with heavy coats and big hats."

Andrea listened thoughtfully; perhaps it *was* a point of familiarity from her frame of reference. "You mean the bugler…he's the one who calls soldiers together to come and march; the ones wearing the fancy uniforms."

"That's what it sounds like to me."

They agreed. That was *exactly* what it sounded like…a call to arms. Then the music went silent for the night. It was late. Both girls were tired, so they snuggled in and fell peacefully asleep. Though perplexed, neither was afraid of what she'd heard. There was nothing threatening about it, nothing which posed any hazard or triggered any alarm. In fact, this sound seemed to come from such a distance, some nights it was barely audible. Initially, a serene, oddly comforting lullaby, its tone and tenor would later be altered; urgent.

As time passed and manifestations began occurring with drastic frequency, the sound took on a more ominous tone; a disconcerting note creeping closer. There were nights when she found it disturbing; an incessant and compelling call ringing in her ears and mind as she tried to rest. Then it began recurring in the middle of the night, seeping into consciousness, extricating her from sleep. The horn seemed magnified by silence in the house. It stymied Andrea as it never woke anybody else. Though she found it bizarre, this child fought the fear, reassuring herself, it could do no harm. So many other episodes of significance occupied her increasingly curious mind; she simply dismissed it, until Cindy told her of the voices; what *they* repeat in the night. Her younger sibling heard chanting in her room; several voices speaking together as one, telling her about seven dead soldiers buried in the wall. Sadly, it made sense. The horn was a call to battle, a clarion call to arms in the dark of night. These children had no choice but to conquer their fears, to be victorious over those who haunted their dreams. Imagine the fear of a soldier marching off to war, calling all of those within earshot to join him in the righteous cause. Some of those warriors were children, themselves; had they become separated from their elders? How frightened they must have been! So many perished on the battlefields; so many families fractured forever: Agony….no ecstasy in sight.

Decades later, Andrea attended the reenactment of a Revolutionary War battle on an expansive field in Lincoln, R.I. Just passing by, the window of her car was open enough to hear the call; music from a distance. She had to stop and listen. Instantly transporting her back in time, she heard the distant horn; a lone bugler standing on a nearby hillside calling his soldiers to arms. It was identical, disturbing her peace of mind. The woman remembered this distinct sound from childhood, the same music which rode the wind across a valley at the farm. There was no mistaking what she heard. No question what it was or what it was intended to achieve; the gathering together of soldiers who would be the ones to fight their mighty battles and die to win their wars. She wondered about the spirits she left behind in her childhood home; if their battles waged were still raging on, trapped as they seemed to be, caught up in an eternal conflict, held captive on Earth by a mission left unaccomplished: an imprisonment which must surely qualify as cruel and unusual punishment.

"It is better to conquer yourself than to win a thousand battles. Then the victory is yours. It cannot be taken from you, not by angels or demons, heaven or hell."
Buddha

things that go bump in the day

"Not only is the universe stranger than we imagine,
it is stranger than we can imagine."
Sir Arthur Eddington

The three eldest girls took the same bus, as all three were simultaneously attending Burrillville Junior-Senior High School. A marching band practice was scheduled after school which had kept Andrea and Christine on campus, stomping around in the vacant parking lot, dressed in their uniforms like two soldiers on the march. Nancy went home alone. (Of course, no one was really ever home alone.) A bright and beautiful spring afternoon, she ran toward the house, peeling off a sweater on her way to the door. Entering the kitchen, she distinctly heard footsteps from someone overhead, loud noises reverberating throughout her bedroom; sounds coming from the kitchen ceiling. Something heavy: the maple dresser or maybe her bed frame being dragged, oak against pine planks, across the bedroom floor directly above. Presuming it was her mother suffering a bout of spring-cleaning mania; Nancy ditched her books and hollered a greeting up the stairwell. The sounds continued. She must not have heard her daughter: "Mom?" Nancy had quite a set of lungs for a young lady so diminutive in stature. No answer: "MOM!" Scratching and scraping persisted unabated. If she didn't stop it the floor would be scarred for life!

Suddenly aware it was *her* bedroom being rearranged, the teenager pressed into action. Oh! No! She had things hidden from a mother's eyes, discovery of which would mean certain upheaval. God forbid! Even worse, it meant her mother was potentially organizing the familiar chaos, bedlam with which she was accustomed and perfectly comfortable *as is*; Nancy leapt the stairs two at a time. Approaching the landing, she recalls hearing the same footsteps again and the chimney closet door closing with a grand slam. Someone was pissed! Fearlessly throwing open the door, (as there were no perceived threats other than the prying eyes of a thoroughly disgusted mother) Nancy fully expected to find her room tidy and uncluttered; her mother engrossed in a diary…some not-so-light reading, yet destined to be illuminating.

Everything was precisely as she'd left it earlier in the day; like the game of fifty-two pick up. Snatching her precious diary from beneath a fat mattress, mad-dash-stashing what qualified as contraband securely in an undisclosed location for safe-keeping, Nancy walked back downstairs and out to the yard, locating her diligent mother alone behind the house, at work in the garden.

"Mom!" An outburst startled the woman. "Were you just up in my room?"

"Hi! No, babe…I've been out here for hours…want to come help?"

"Not really…" Nancy joined her in a row destined to grow string beans.

Carolyn swept the sweat from her brow and the hair from her eyes with an equally sweaty forearm then handed her daughter the spade.

"Work the ground there…this bed next. Go down about three inches deep, four inches apart. I'll plant today if the weather holds. You can help!"

"Great." Nancy was distracted.

"You used to *love* to help me in the garden. Has it lost all of its glamour?" Carolyn was in fine spirits; clearly enjoying playfully teasing her daughter. There was no response forthcoming. She turned to the youngster, an easy kid to read, prompting a quizzical expression on her face. Something happened.

"Mom…have you been reading my diary?"

"No! I didn't even know you *had* a diary. And even if I *did* know, I would *never* take it and read it! Not that I would ever be able to find it in that room of yours: Shame." Plunging her hoe into the soft dirt, Carolyn stood upright.

"You're sure." Nancy had her doubts and no good reason to question mom further; *her* word, as good as gold…and Nancy knew it: Miss Perronoid!

"Why do you ask? Is there something in there I *shouldn't* see? Or should?"

"NO! It's not that. (Yes; actually, it was precisely that,) When I came home from school I heard someone up in my bedroom and my diary wasn't *exactly* where I left it last night. So I thought, well, maybe..." Carolyn reassured her; there was nobody in the house. No cause for alarm.

"Mom, *someone's always* in the house...*someone* was just up in my room, moving all the furniture around...and probably reading my diary!"

"What happened?" Carolyn leaned against a stone wall to listen: "When?"

"I'm telling you, *someone* was dragging furniture across the floor and then slammed the chimney door. I went upstairs but nothing was moved, nothing was different in my bedroom."

"Too bad; I sure could use some extra help with the spring cleaning around here. You'd think if they were going through the motions and making such an effort, they'd actually get something done!"

"I thought it was you...but now I'm glad it was just a ghost!"

"I wouldn't worry about it honey...your handwriting is illegible, anyway."

"It's not funny, mom!" Nancy's wrinkled up, crinkly face: as evidence.

"Yes, it is. Paranoia strikes deep...into your heart it will creep! I'll get you, my pretty!" Flashing dirty fingernails: "Now, let's see what's in that diary!" Carolyn let go of her hoe then raced toward the house, Nancy in hot pursuit, both buckling over with laughter; breathless. Carolyn beat her to the kitchen door. Nancy gave up the ghost, gasping for air while shouting after her mom: "Go 'head! You'll never find it!" From a distance she heard her mom holler out an equally smartass reply: "I KNOW! But there's no harm in looking!"

***

One pleasant afternoon Carolyn greeted her girls at the bus stop. She had a surprise waiting for them inside. Mom had baked! Her chocolate chip cake! Everyone was gathering around the kitchen table enjoying their afterschool snack, still warm from the oven. Their chattering was as raucous as usual, but not quite loud enough to muffle a thundering lump landing overhead. THUD! Everyone jumped, startled by the jolt. It sounded like a body hitting the floor. As was her habit, Carolyn did a quick head count.

All present and accounted for: no one upstairs. It annoyed Nancy no end; it **always** seemed to happen in **her** room. (Perhaps the spirit had tripped and fallen over her junk!) Eyes met as glances were exchanged but no one said a word. Chrissy, the bravest soul among them shook her head, placing her fork beside the plate. "I'll go see." As there were no other volunteers willing to go in her place, Chris climbed the staircase, opening the door to a bedroom appearing to be ransacked. She stood on the landing for a moment, surveying the damage done. Then closing the door, she came back downstairs, returning to the kitchen table, prepared to deliver a brief but accurate, if rather unusual report. Timing is everything in life...and death. Chris had her comic timing down to a science. She waited for just the right moment, Carolyn providing just the right questions:

"So, what hit the floor?" Carolyn was curious. Whatever it was, the impact had shaken the house to its foundation, rattling china in the cupboards. It had to have been **something** very large and quite heavy to create such a racket!

"It's nothing." Christine shook her head again, this time in feigned disgust. She then resumed eating her mother's homemade chocolate chip pound cake while standing beside Nancy, glancing disdainfully at her slob of a sister.

"Are you **sure** nothing fell on the floor?" Perplexed by the sound all of her kids seemed to be taking in stride, Carolyn persisted; inadvertently setting up Christine to respond with a nonchalance for which she has become infamous in the family, adding insult to injury...a perfect George and Gracie moment:

"Mom. It's **Nancy's** room. Everything is on the floor!" The kitchen erupted with laughter, again at a sloppy sister's expense. Chrissy's line delivery was absolutely flawless. Little wonder she was destined for the stage. Nancy was the only one who didn't chuckle; did not yuck it up with the rest of them: the only one perturbed by the tale; not amused in the least. Buzz kill. Spoil sport.

"In struggling against anguish one never produces serenity;
the struggle against anguish only produces new forms of anguish."
Simone Weil

things that go bump in the night

One steamy evening Nancy invited a few friends over for a game of cards. During the summer of 1979 she socialized quite a bit. Seriously dating Eddy Richardson at the time, Nancy was certain he was *the one*. A casual game: an easy-going round of six; an enjoyable way to spend a date night in one's own home, unless, of course, there are those intent upon *crashing* the party! Boo!

No one remembers where their parents went that night but the girls had the house all to themselves for a few hours. The gathering came with permission and a verifiable head count. At the height of the sweet season, balmy breezes circulating throughout the room provided some comfort after a long, hot day in the garden. A kitchen; littered with colanders brimming with Swiss chard, tomatoes, green beans and cucumbers...destined to be pickled the following morning. However, for the time being all the work was done: Time to play.

While standing just inside the pantry door pouring a tray-load of lemonade-all-around, Nancy heard something scraping overhead. To her knowledge no one had gone upstairs. Instinct told her to listen. It stopped. Hoisting the tray, as she was approaching the table abrasive sounds became more pronounced. Without saying a word about it to anyone Nancy glared up toward the ceiling and *told* them to **stop it**...in mind. No one present noticed but Nancy; a room rocking and rolling with music and laughter, effectively drowning it out. A good thing she didn't say what she was thinking; her language was atrocious! Suffice to say, Nancy told a disruptive someone upstairs to *cease and desist.*

As there had been no mention of the noise from anyone seated at the table, drinks were served and the card game commenced. Katy was flirting with her dewy fawn eyes again. As if nectar of the gods Jerry drank her stare in faster than the lemonade placed to his luscious lips; soft, round, full lips begging to be kissed, so Katy thought. Kate had it bad, having already arrived at an age to do something about it. She had a plan for later; a detour on the drive home. Too bad it would not work out that way. Bathsheba had plans of her own.

Halfway through their third hand a sudden disturbance abruptly interrupted the game, calling everyone's full attention *upward*! The young folks looked like a nest full of chicks, necks outstretched, mouths propped open, waiting for a meal from mommy. Nancy hung her head, disgraced; certainly agitated by someone too rude to live! An inconvenient truth she had hoped to avoid, having been forewarned, her wishes were ignored by an uninvited guest.

The sounds became more intense with each passing moment, reverberating through the thick floor boards. Something overhead in Nancy's bedroom was being dragged across the floor; heavy: wood scraping against wood, perhaps a chest of drawers or an oak bed frame. The sound was distinct and familiar, a common sound occurring in an all too uncommon way. For Jerry, it was an unusually curious anomaly, based on the fact that all living souls in the house were seated snugly around the table at the time.

Nancy had no desire to identify their intruder and would have preferred to ignore it; the same way previous marching orders issued had been dismissed as irrelevant. Events such as these were all-too-frequent, embarrassing to her. After years of explaining them away, she'd grown weary of the practice. Her friends knew what to expect. Though Jerry, as a new addition to their group, had been to the house several times prior to this incident, it was his first bona fide supernatural experience. The young man had been forewarned as well, but he laughed it off, expressing his disbelief in ghosts and spirits, angels and demons. It was a rude awakening when the chivalrous skeptic volunteered to go up and "check it out" for the damsel in distress. Bounding up the stairwell before anyone could either accept or reject his offer, Nancy was mortified! She did not want him to see her disaster of a bedroom, nor did she want him to run into the stranger-than-fiction resident of the dwelling within its shared space. What she *had* wanted was simple enough, but apparently too much to ask; she'd wanted *them* to behave themselves whenever there was company, goddamn it to hell! Reassuring her haunted houseguests it was *nothing at all*, Nancy quickly followed Jerry upstairs. Cindy knew better…she knew these episodes often occurred with purpose and reason, a deliberate intention; not as accidental tourists. She remained seated at the table awaiting his reaction. Sipping the sweet tart lemonade, she crinkled her lips to disguise *told you so*, hidden within the wicked grin peeking out from the corners of her mouth.

Determined to prove his hypothesis, Jerry rapidly flung the bedroom door wide open. He was right…nothing there. The almost deafening noise stopped instantly, the moment he touched the iron latch; that awful grinding, gouging sound ceased. Not a single piece of furniture was out of place. There was no one visibly present in the bedroom…not a scratch on the floor…no evidence of any commotion. Jerry's hands began to tremble as blood drained from his face. Astonished, he turned on the landing then stared at Nancy, begging the question without saying a word. She found it to be a rather ironic twist. Jerry appeared to be more ghostly than any apparition she had ever witnessed over all her years in the house. He'd slowly passed her and went back downstairs, returning to his seat at the table…reserving comment.

"So? What was it? What did you see?" His equal as a skeptic, Katy asked him to describe the scene in detail.

"Nothing…like I said." Nancy responded for him as she walked back into the kitchen, leering at her closest friend, the inflection in her voice telling everyone present to hush!

"You're *so* brave!" Kate couldn't leave it alone. Nancy found her fluttering eyelashes nauseating; seemingly unaware she often emulated the practice.

"Kate! Shut up!" Gritting that caustic statement through her clenched jaw, Katy did as she was told you so; Nancy's glare, an expression she could read with relative ease, even if she was oblivious to Jerry's sudden shade of pale. The game resumed but Jerry was too distracted to play. After a few minutes he excused himself, asking Eddy to give Kate a ride home. Suddenly she was the pale face in the crowd, devastated he'd leave her behind. He hit the road; the only bump and grind that night came from floorboards above.

Petulantly pouting, Katy threw her hand of cards in the center of the table. Game over. Eddy had hoped to continue but Katy was hot and bothered; pissed off by the commotion culminating in cancellation of her plans. Her date night had been spoiled…nobody gettin' any nookie *that* night. She wanted to go home.

"I hate this damn house!" Regressing by the second, Katy threw a tantrum.

"Well you don't have to come back!" Nancy, noting how self-absorbed and immature her friend could be at times, Katy had her center-stage moments as the drama queen of arrested development. M' lady: ascending to her throne. Nancy, her lady-in-waiting: Birds of a feather always flocking together! The situation was quickly becoming all flocked up!

"Fine! Then I *won't* come back! This is a *creepy* old place anyway! I won't *ever* come back here again!" That was a lie and everyone knew it.

Nancy and Katy were tight; thick as thieves. Secretly wishing what Katy said *was* true, Cindy knew better. Truth be told, she'd be back. Grimacing at the thought of it, Cindy watched the scene unfold with some amusement.

Eddy promptly took Kate home, a mere mile away. He then returned to the farm to spend time with his girlfriend. This young man had long been aware of a presence in the house. He'd likewise understood *his* presence triggered supernatural activity. As a conduit Eddy Richardson was a distant ancestor of the original family, those who had settled this property and built the house in which he'd become a welcome guest. His ancestral connection, a presumed factor in the reception he often sensed whenever he crossed the threshold, the place had always felt like home to him…because it *was* home: Inviting him.

Not long thereafter, Jerry confessed what happened to him, telling Nancy and Eddy why he had become upset by what he heard but did *not* see in the bedroom that night; the stunning absence of life. He was reluctant to express himself further; ashamed to reveal the details of an encounter he'd had *after* he left the house. Eventually sharing, shocking his friends in the process, the macho man whispered as he spoke. As it turned out, Jerry had not gone home alone, after all. While driving the dark, long and winding

Round Top Road, he'd detected a presence with him in the car. It began with a sudden chill. On a hot August night he could see his breath, feel his heart beginning to pound. His car became unbearably frigid in a matter of seconds; whitening knuckles clenching the steering wheel. According to him it was impossible to describe. Jerry seemed shaken by simply retelling the tale; an abbreviated version.

"It was a real *different* kind of cold, nothing like *I* ever felt before: Death. The car stunk like hell! A smell so bad it made me almost puke my guts up!" How festive. A man of few words, Jerry always did have a way with them.

Averting his eyes, as if embarrassed by the disclosure, Jerry struggled with his emotions as he spoke; he choked up, blushing because of it, admitting he had been *touched* several times and could feel an icy cold breath on the back of his neck and shoulders; the hair on his body stood rigid, at attention, with contact. There was no dismissing it, no denying the fact: he was not traveling alone. Sensing himself the subject of some scrutiny, Jerry forced himself to glance into the rearview mirror. He saw her through the steam, a mouth full of jagged yellow teeth. Full disclosure: "I almost pissed my pants!"

Jerking the car off the road during his moment of panic, he'd leapt from the vehicle without turning it off. He'd had to gather his wits. It was obvious. No one was in the back seat, certainly nobody he could see. Pacing around in a circle, staring inside it from every conceivable angle, several minutes passed. Jerry conceded feeling ridiculous. He wanted to go home and forget all about it but could not bring himself to re-enter a car possessed. Terrified, the young man finally mustered the courage to drive home, blasting the radio, providing a diversion for a terrifying ride. Though an odor and ungodly chill dissipated, Jerry remained profoundly affected by the incident. Eddy tried to make light of it, knowing his friend had been deeply disturbed and seriously spooked.

"So, was she the *Ghoul of your Dreams?*"

"Eddy, go have a cup of shut the fuck up!" Jerry was not the least amused, having suffered the ensuing nightmares. Eddy, suffering the bout of nervous laughter, was unable to control his equally serious case of the giggles. Nancy suggested he try to be more understanding of a friend's obvious distress; kids can be cruel and insensitive, even into adulthood, and some never outgrow it. That night had become the ultimate date night from hell. Too bad Jerry went home with the wrong girl…the ghoul of his nightmares.

In time, this humbled soul would return to their farm again, requiring some uncommon courage to do so; a valiant effort by Katy's Prince Charming. His belief system had been formally challenged. He'd questioned his own sanity. When Jerry did return, months later, it was as a *believer*. He would never again volunteer to go "check it out" whenever a sudden noise erupted in the house. Instead, he'd take the opportunity to escape; inviting Kate to go for a walk in the woods. Due to the Nature of their walks, her attitude improved as well. Soon Kate was praying for the holy ghosts to appear at will: how ironic.

---

*"Look in the mirror. The face that pins you with
its double gaze reveals a chastening secret."*
Diane Ackerman

reality

It is said that thoughts are things; to be careful what you wish for, as surely you will get it. It is said: what is spoken into the Universe comes back to help or to haunt, depending on the intention of the desires. If thoughts are indeed things, they are intangible, invisible things until they are made manifest in form. When thoughts appear as *something* substantive, such as a manuscript, first written inside the mind then transposed onto paper, the object is defined; assigned its identity. Prior to the existence of the actual book, is the story it tells any less real? No. It was merely invisible, an intangible, out there in the ether of the Universe. Mortals function primarily within the confines of five senses, with all of their inherent flaws and limitations. These senses integrate with and compensate for one another, frequently working in tandem as five complementary co-conspirators. Defining the parameters of what's perceived as reality, humans predominately use the five senses to firmly establish what actually exists, to the exclusion of this vital sixth sense, with which we have been so generously gifted. Essentially, we do believe our eyes. We should. There is no legitimate reason to dismiss these otherwise consistently reliable senses. As trustworthy as the senses prove to be they are woefully inadequate if one's intention is to see with the Third Eye. They do not tell all, and thus, should not be relied upon as the sole litmus test of Reality; the determining factor of whatever is ultimately deemed real or unreal. Disregarding reality in the context of what is seen and unseen discounts the vastness of an intelligent Universe as well as the incomprehensible mysteries it harbors, establishing sensual boundaries where none actually exist. It is ludicrous for mortals to believe we know anything about the ways of the Cosmos; too presumptuous to assume we have any answers when we have yet to ask the right questions.

Reality ~ n. 1. The quality or state of being actual or true.

2. One, such as a person or an event, that is actual.

3. The totality of all things possessing actuality, existence or essence.
4. That which exists objectively and in fact.
(The American Heritage Dictionary)

It requires a certain expansion of consciousness to accept as "real" what is unseen, intangible; to perceive the absence of reality *as* reality requires a leap of faith. The Perron family was forced to leap from this precarious precipice in order to comprehend the essential Nature of Reality. By definition, these spirits are real as their essence manifests in form and function. The night they *all* appeared around her bed Carolyn was abruptly challenged to reassess her perceptions. One element of it was certain: her fear was real. During those moments, all else remained in question. She did *not* believe her eyes. She could smell the putrid air and taste the rancid stench in the hard palate of her mouth; she could see the flames and smell the smoke. The urgency she felt, the need for an explanation of this encounter was real. The terror consuming her being was all too real. It pulsed through her veins, as pure as the blood it swam with during those moments of crisis. Worst of all, it was the perception that she (and her entire family) were about to perish, to burn to death in their own beds, which gripped the woman's mind and shook her to the core of her consciousness. It was not just a visceral reaction but cerebral transformation which she endured in the darkness of night, at the break of dawn. Under such extreme duress an individual naturally questions the origin and interpretation of sights, smells and sounds which cannot be rationally explained otherwise. Little wonder Carolyn had questioned her own sanity, her own belief system; everything this woman thought she understood about the world underwent a seismic, cosmic shift once she and her family stepped across their threshold, into the house alive with death. There was nothing logical, nothing tangible in their altered frame of reference anymore. The mysteries of life and death, revealed to disbelieving eyes, ruptured Pandora's Box. There was no point in confronting them; best to give them their space and time to travel.

Her natural curiosity became a supernatural quest for knowledge. Her fear became a catalyst to questions destined to remain unanswered, as if by divine decree. Five senses were formally challenged as her sixth sense came to life; focusing its gaze upon death. In time, Carolyn came to rely upon perceptions having nothing to do with innate ability to see, touch, taste, smell and hear. In time, the eye of the beholder would see all: behold! She'd wonder why she had been the privileged one; as if chosen to receive these messages imparted. It felt as if she'd been targeted; likewise one entrusted with an awareness few perceive in life. This assaultive spirit certainly got her attention; an encounter she interpreted as a curse, literally and figuratively. Decades pass, as decades do. In time, Carolyn has come to *realize* a blessing: Uncommon Knowledge.

"The important thing is not to stop questioning. Curiosity has its own reason for existing. One cannot help but be in awe when he contemplates the mysteries of eternity, of life, of the marvelous structure of reality. It is enough if one tries merely to comprehend a little of this mystery every day. Never lose a holy curiosity."
Albert Einstein

Baker boys

*"The clouds that gather round the setting sun
Do take a sober coloring from an eye,
That hath kept watch o'er man's mortality."*
William Wordsworth

They all stood together on the landing of Andrea's bedroom stairs. She had seen them there several times before over their years in the farmhouse: as the father, the son and their holy ghost of a dog. They'd appeared as a Trinity of Souls, gazing through the bedroom wall, overlooking a familiar landscape, a place in the country they had all loved, as if surveying their property in death which claimed them in life. Their eyes remained locked; fixed and focused, a steadfast stare never to be broken by the intrusion of a mere mortal. Andrea looked directly into their eyes but they did not return her gaze. Elsewhere, they were, in a time long ago and far away, in a country place resembling the home she knew, unavailable for question or comment... no contact. Too bad.

During Carolyn's extensive research project regarding the history of the house, an interesting couple of stories surfaced. She learned of the tragic loss of two members from one family; a father and son, both of whom reportedly drowned on this property, some ten years apart. Town records indicated the father died during a weather event, out on the secluded pond, set deeply back on their property. April insists both of them died a horrible, frightening death in the same place; both lives claimed by the raging torrents, lost beneath the surface of the wild Nipmuc River. In either case they've remained together in death, inexorably tied to the home they shared in life, retaining a bond which will never be broken; the faithful family dog by their side.

***

There was something on her desk Andrea needed desperately. Racing home from school in the '69 Pontiac she inherited from her Uncle Donald when he bought his new car, the low rider had an uncanny ability to hug the pavement at high rates of speed, the fact she did not divulge to her mother as she sped through the house on her way to some critically important materials she had inadvertently left behind in her bedroom; materials required for the yearbook meeting…a meeting she was missing! Frantic to locate what was forgotten in the morning, aware a roomful of people were gathered, awaiting her return, the editor-in-chief of the yearbook knew she'd screwed up in a big way. Her mind was on one thing only as she flew up the stairwell head down, watching the twelve steps as she went, so not to trip while moving at the speed of light.

Raising her eyes to begin the process of searching her desk before the rest of her body actually arrived on the scene; it was a startling and unexpected sight to see: three partially translucent yet clearly defined entities standing on the landing of her stairs. There they were; a family: a man, a boy and his dog, standing side-by-side, peering through the wall of her bedroom. She'd nearly run right through them! About face! Down the stairs; rapid descent. "Mom!" Carolyn came running. Freaked and frustrated, late for an important date, this was the last thing she needed! By then, she should have known to expect the unexpected, but timing is everything in life and death; they were manifesting, interfering at the worst possible time. Needing what was on the other side of them, it was not a path she wanted to cross. They were literally blocking her way. She would have to pass *through* them to retrieve her belongings. There was no time to waste with spirit matters at the moment.

"Mom! They're on my stairs again! Please make them go away!" Andrea was harried and nearly in tears. Carolyn knew precisely who she meant. Her daughter had seen them there before, sharing details of those encounters with her mother in the past. They appeared to be exactly the same. The father was rather short and stout with a jovial smile on his face. He had a wide-brimmed straw hat, the kind used to keep the Sun off a farmer's back while he worked his land. He wore handmade clothing, the square bib of fabric covering his bulbous chest. His skin appeared to be as weathered as the boots on his feet; ragged leather, worn to a frazzle. The boy stood beside him; a young child to be sure, perhaps ten years of age, according to his height and weight. He too wore a pair of boots in much better condition than those of his elder. The boy had work pants; a gunny sack cotton shirt like his father, apparently from the same bolt of fabric, as the light gold color matched. Perhaps Mrs. Baker was the seamstress. No mistaking the family resemblance…they were kinfolk.

On this particular afternoon Andrea was in no mood to tolerate a perceived intrusion, though they were a decidedly unobtrusive lot. She often wondered about the three of them; had they all died together, including the dog? Or had they been reunited in death…after death? On the day in question, she was too preoccupied with more pressing matters. They were an obstacle impeding her forward momentum. At times when her mind was free to revisit the past, she considered their circumstances more humanely. However, on this especially stressful day she had no patience for *or* curiosity about them; Andrea simply wanted them to leave so she could retrieve her belongings upstairs and do the same thing; leave! Places to go…people to see…things to do that afternoon.

Carolyn climbed quietly, cautiously up a dark stairwell, secretly hoping to see the Light. Her approach was such not because she was frightened of this trio; she did not want to scare them away. Carolyn wanted to see them, too. Obviously they were harmless; entirely benign. Neither entity had ever even acknowledged the little miss mortal whose space they shared. Whenever they manifested it was in precisely the same place. No one else had seen them yet, unlike some other spirits who'd move freely throughout their house, at will. These three always stood together, stares apparently fixed on a single point in time or space. The father had the palest blue eyes, much like Mr. Kenyon: tired eyes. His son's were a brighter blue; watery, quite similar to this elder gentleman. They resembled each other in a variety of ways; clearly they were kin. Because Carolyn had seen so many spirits in her bedroom on the night she was threatened with blazing torches, she *was* curious. Had these spirits been involved? Had they been a part of the crowd? The only way to know for certain was to observe them; the eye of the beholder, anxious to bear witness, to see if the spirits were familiar to her, perhaps a part of the coven of spirits in her bedroom on that night in question. Alas, they were gone. She did not catch them in time; the vision lost...not even a glimpse. They'd all vanished. The "all clear" was sounded. Relieved, then grateful for her mother's divine intervention, Andrea went back upstairs and gathered her missing materials from the desk in her room with a heartfelt: "Thanks, mom. Be home later." A kiss on the cheek on her way out the door...her spirited daughter was gone.

"God brings men into deep waters, not to drown them, but to cleanse them."
John Aughey

go away little girls

*"Let tears flow of their own accord: their flowing is
not inconsistent with inward peace and harmony."*
Seneca

Time for bed: this obsequious child did as she was told. Cynthia followed directions well. She was the first to head upstairs, putting her flannel pajamas on while the rest of her siblings remained downstairs, stalling for time. Chris was still doing her homework at the kitchen table, which is why Cynthia was in their shared space all alone, or so the child thought. Sitting on the side of her bed, she leaned down, pulling her slippers from beneath it, sliding them onto chilly little feet. Suddenly sensing the presence of another, she assumed it was only her sister, assignments complete, coming to join her for the night. She didn't bother to look up from the task until she heard the mournful sound of an unfamiliar voice; certainly not Christine.

The family had just moved into their new old home, having been there only a few weeks; far too soon for such a rude awakening, especially just before bed. There she was, passing through the bedroom, on her way to somewhere else. She was crying for her mommy. Cindy's breath drew hard in her chest. She could not believe her eyes...or ears. It was pitiful: Heartbreaking. This voice was as petite as the child. Dressed in clothing from another time, the little girl was wearing a neatly pressed gray cotton shift covered with a pretty white apron; pint-sized, just like her. The entity appeared to be about five, or maybe six years of age. She was short but seemed to be a healthy, substantial girl; though she would not always appear so robust. A head full of thick, dark hair cascading down instantly reminded Cindy of her own eldest sister; her round face conjuring an image Cynthia had seen before, in photographs of Andrea at this age. An uncanny resemblance; a disquieting likeness she noted immediately evoked a memory from when she was only a toddler. Time and space seemed affected by this close encounter; confusing to the mortal soul. Watching intently, the spirit moved across the bedroom, crying for ***mommy*** over and over again before she left, walking through an unopened door into the eaves. Cindy was blown away. A young mind unprepared, she could not process what she'd just seen: the eye of the beholder, challenged to suspend disbelief again. It was beyond shocking to the youngster; she could not move or speak; locked in one position as if wedged in a vice of incomprehension. Wanting to scream "Go away!" the instant she had laid eyes on the little girl, Cindy's emotions began churning the second she heard the voice; pure and clear…and so very sad. The apparition made a sound which tore at Cynthia's soul; issuing this pathetic plea for her mother in the night. To be lost and so frightened, but lost where? As a shudder passed, rippling through her being, Cindy's eyes began filling with tears. This presence struck a chord; the little girl broke her heart.

It was not the only time Cynthia would cry for and with this child. She did not tell anyone about the encounter or an emotional reaction to it. Recovering her composure, rejoining her family downstairs, it had been too private and painful an experience to assign words to describe, too early to tell the truth. It would be months before other children began to disclose their experiences. Until then, Cindy kept it to herself.

This was only the first of many sightings over the better part of a decade. When Cindy is asked how frequently she saw this spirit, her reply sums it up with one word: *hundreds*. She was omnipresent…like God. At certain times she appeared solid in form, yet there were many manifestations when she'd appeared as a wispy figure, translucent; a shadow. This entity almost always spoke though there was never any interaction between them. She had seemed oblivious to the presence of a mortal in the room. Cindy made no overtures. A vague recollection of hearing her more often than seeing her, Cynthia still retains a vivid image of her in memory. Whenever the wee spirit manifested in form, she always carried something in her tiny hands, though Cindy was never able to determine exactly what it was; once she had passed through the room carrying a book tucked beneath her arm, an object Cindy had not seen before. At times it appeared to be a fine white piece of cloth, perhaps a lady's handkerchief. Occasionally, this child was dressed differently, formally, as if for a holiday or special event. It was a lovely outfit; a deep green velvet dress with a bright white pinafore fitted at the front, synched neatly at her waist. Whenever she appeared as such the girl seemed happy, laughing and playing: her voice was lighter. Then there were other times when darkness seemed to surround her; a pervasive sadness. When she cried her voice would tremble, the tears would flow like rain. Her domain relegated to the upper level of the house, only once was she seen on the main floor of the residence. Emerging from the eaves in Andrea's room, she would pass right through the door if it was closed, though she was perfectly capable of causing these doors to open and did so on numerous of occasions, as if it was announcing her presence. However, she did not interact with anyone and Cindy did not acknowledge her either, whether from a fear or a belief that she could not respond. Heard regularly playing in Andrea's closet, when this door was opened to see who was there, it silenced the child. Did she want to be discovered? Did she want to engage? A friend in need? Indeed. But Cynthia did not want to open *that* metaphorical door, preferring instead to watch her from a distance. In time, she'd learn to accept it. Adapting to this presence was only a small part of the new paranormal, what someone must be willing to endure when dwelling in a house alive with death. Cindy made the quantum leap of faith required. She welcomed this spirit into her world and tried not to intrude on her own. The sentiment was genuine; a kind-hearted soul acknowledging a spirit's plight.

Cynthia assumed she was the one playing with her toys. She began to care about the wee little one, watching over her as she moved through the portals; passages of the past. As Cindy grew older, this child appeared to grow sickly. Nurturing instincts kicked in. When she became a teenager, Cindy's attention to and affection for the entity increased precipitously. Because the apparition occurred with such frequency, becoming so familiar to a mortal soul, Cindy became confused by the presence, finding a discrepancy in her own thought process. Was this the *same* child? Was there a set of twins? Had she misread the situation? When a little cherub appeared to be healthy and happy, she was dressed in her best outfit, skipping carefree through the bedroom. When she appeared to be ill, it was always when she was wearing the drab gray cotton dress. With increased exposure Cindy began to see changes in the youngster: at times her face appeared hollow and sunken, her body emaciated, as if she was wasting away. These were the most miserable of encounters, times when Cindy cried too; it was obvious the child was dying. Cindy could not escape the pain of it and she could not bear to hear this child crying for her mother, suffering alone. It was a disturbing vision; hopeless...riddled with despair.

Was she sick or hurt? Lost and lonely? When Cindy discusses this series of events she cannot help but mention what role it played in her own emotional development. It sensitized her to the suffering of others and made her think about what some have endured in life and death. The visceral reaction Cindy had to the sound of this child's voice haunts her still. She has regrets. Why didn't she reach out to this entity? Was it such a foreign experience Cynthia could not bring herself to take that leap of faith? What would have happened had she done so? Because she heard the little girl many more times than she actually saw her, the voice is what now lingers in her consciousness, more so than the visual imagery; a memory of sound more vivid than sight. She could even be heard outside of the house, especially in their garden; as a haunting melody wafting on the breeze, intermingling with the wind. Carolyn knew all too well how distracting it could be: Downright dangerous.

As Cindy became more familiar with the apparition, she would often leave the bedroom, so to allow the child to play with her toys, something the spirit would never do while Cynthia was present. That's how the mortal discovered who'd been moving objects around her room. Upon her return, an hour or so later, everything had been rearranged. She could hear the child babbling and chattering, happily at play. This kind gesture yielded many valuable insights, reducing an initial resentment of having her things *toyed* with down to zero. Remember? To share and share alike: Do unto others as though you were the others. It only seemed right...because it was the only right thing to do.

With maturity came the ultimate realization. There was nothing to be done for or about it, nothing she could do to help this child...Cindy was and would always be the witness to her misery, unable to affect any positive change in a situation which occurred centuries before Cindy was born. The torture of it; listening and watching and knowing she was helpless. It was all too hopeless. The child died. It's why she was there. Once upon a time

Cindy was tempted to tell the little girl to go away and leave her alone, as if the youngster was invading her world. She grew to understand the true Nature of the dilemma. She learned to feel sympathy for the little darling then learned her sympathy was wasted. The poor creature did not know anyone was there or felt sorry for her; a painful ordeal was only hurting Cindy and comforting no one else.

With her understanding came an emotional withdrawal, severance as an act of self-protection. A mere mortal, the child whose heart was too big and too broken to care anymore began to remove herself from the bedroom whenever the girl appeared. Though the two had never interacted, Cynthia considered *her own* presence to be the intrusion, having changed her mind about who was invading whom. The spirit from the eaves had been there long before the Perron family moved into the farmhouse. In deference, as well as a need to extricate herself from the despair, Cindy took another bedroom...the instant her eldest sister left for college. Believing the change of venue would lessen her exposure and its impact, she was wrong. Still, when Nancy gave all their toys away to another family of deserving souls, without explicit permission to do so, Cynthia became absolutely furious. Though she had outgrown them those toys *belonged* to someone; a sick little girl not of this world. By taking them all away, an injustice was done, inadvertently depriving a spirit of what little the girl had to occupy eternity. Apparently, Cynthia still cared, after all.

"Just because *I* don't play with them anymore doesn't mean they weren't being played with! My God! You gave away all *our* childhood memories!"

Disheartened; devastated by her elder sister's misguided act of generosity, Cindy thought Nancy was too insensitive or too obtuse to conceive of this as an error in judgment; oblivious to the needs presenting in their own house. According to Cindy, the spirit children should have been their *first* priority: Misplaced loyalty. Adversely affected on behalf of the little girl from another time, Cynthia began a deliberate disengagement from an assortment of souls, living and dead. An evidently diminished capacity for tolerance, a prolonged period of quiet resentment followed. Far less attentive to others in her midst, Cindy went into seclusion; as self-imposed exile.

Isolating herself within the confines of a bedroom claimed, ignoring this spirit when she'd pass through, wandering their bedrooms as she always had before, Cindy blocked her out. Whenever she heard this tiny child crying at a distance, as a lone voice from deep within the eaves, she would pause and reflect upon the hopelessness of it all, then turn up the volume on her stereo and resume whatever it was she'd been doing: sad case dismissed. It was certainly not the end of supernatural experiences and in some ways, it was only the beginning. As one of several attempts made, plans concocted to remote-control a paranormal environment, this approach would ultimately prove to be ineffective. Cynthia's innocence had sadly disappeared with their treasured toys; remnants of a childhood lost with one grand, sweeping, pure-of-heart gesture of generosity.

Stepping across the threshold into adolescence, claiming another's bedroom as her own; it was a bold initial step toward adulthood, one Cynthia would be punished for taking, interpreted as a rejection. Forsaking childish things, the youngster focused her attention inward, spending more time alone in thought. During this introspective period she devised a plan to rid the house of spirits. Too confident at too early an age, Cynthia would discover what a mistake it was to assert herself, to presume any knowledge or control, as the foolhardy endeavor undertaken was bound to cost her dearly: hazardous to one's health.

***

April was equally disillusioned; hurt by Nancy's generous act of God. She withdrew as well. Cindy's response was prompt and to the point; anger. April reacted differently. She'd wept, though not for herself; she sobbed for a little boy she loved. Their sorrow was palpable; one could taste tears in the water and hear sighs in the air. So many pieces of their history were suddenly gone; a pathway into history instantly vanished. Their shared space was no longer cluttered with all the familiar objects of childhood. Nancy did not understand what she'd done to deserve being shunned. She was mourning the loss of her sisters. Nobody spoke to her for weeks…go away, little girl.

Carolyn had no choice but to intervene; the tension was intolerable, the rift, grown too wide. Dissention in the ranks, Carolyn ordered the end of uncivil discourse. Make peace-not war. No replacing what was gone, no way to make amends: reality. Accept it. Move on. Counting the losses... regrets all around.

Recalling this incident and its aftermath with sorrow transcending the years as they pass, it is beneath the weight of aged remorse that Cindy now reflects upon a sick little girl who cries for her mother. Perceived as a lonely child in life and death, the grown woman now looks back on a childhood riddled with doubts and irreconcilable emotions; questions never answered. Why had she responded so emotionally to the spirit's presence when she had already seen Manny and was not so adversely affected by him? Were there two children? Twins, perhaps? Why did she so eerily resemble Cynthia's eldest sister? Was there a cosmic connection between them, one familial in Nature? Oh, God!

"With all things and in all things, we are relatives."
American Indian Proverb

told you so

Katy was skeptical, in spite of the fact that she'd witnessed several unusual events occur in their old farmhouse. It never kept her from coming back but it always caused her to question the explanations. She was the pragmatic sort, like Roger in that respect. There were elements of Katy's personality Cynthia found annoying, as she'd all but accused her so-called friends of lying about what they were experiencing; of making it up as they went along. A figment of presumably overactive imaginations: Sticks and stones. Cindy remained as defensive; resentful of her callous attitude and thoughtless words. After a few years of unsolicited, often rude commentary, contrary opinions, the casting of aspersions and vapid doubts; at last... Redemption! Sweet, sweet revenge!

The ladies were preparing for school. Early morning light was filtered by a dense fog; then soft rain began falling. Cindy was seated at the kitchen table, brushing her hair in front of a portable makeup mirror. Katy spent the night, again. She and Nancy were in the bathroom. Nudging one another for space, bowing before the almighty mirror they playfully pilfered through cosmetics from Carolyn's collection, as teenage girls are prone to do from time to time.

From the corner of her eye, Cynthia noticed the telephone receiver... lifting itself off the cradle. Holding her breath, not making a sound, she observed as this manifestation continued; hovering, as something invisible manipulated the object. It was mesmerizing. In spite of the fact Cindy had seen it happen before, (on numerous occasions), it was still, as always, a remarkable sight. Suddenly their house guest emerged from the bathroom. Cindy stopped Katy with a flash of the eyes, having only time enough to whisper: "Look!" Katy's gaze was fixed on the floating phone. There it was. Proof. At last. Hallelujah!

Cindy was delighted! Admittedly taking certain perverse pleasure pointing it out, Katy stood in the doorway; transfixed and immobile. She watched as it happened; a telephone receiver, in midair, moved slowly away from the wall unit, floating like a feather on a breeze then lingered there, suspended in the thin spring air. An expression of pure panic on Kate's pale face: priceless. It didn't matter how much makeup she applied; she went as visibly white as *Casper*, another ghost she did *not* believe in! During this singular moment of total perfection, because timing is everything in life and in death, Cindy felt compelled to quickly quip, "Told you so!" As the gloating child spoke, an invisible co-conspirator assisted, deliberately drifting the receiver toward the wall unit, lining it up above then letting it drop with a jolt into the cradle with a distinctive sound uniformly produced. No mistaking it for something else. Cindy did not allow her smug satisfaction to surface...yet. Instead, she rolled her eyes disdainfully, returning to her task as if nothing unusual happened. Truth be told, it *was* nothing all that unusual.

Standing inside the alcove, Kate could not speak. She could not even move. After a few moments she bolted back into the bathroom, directly by Nancy's side, barely able to express what she'd just seen in the kitchen.

"Did you see that?" Frantic, Katy pulled Nancy away from her reflection.

"See what?" Distracted, preoccupied by meticulous application of mascara, Nancy showed no particular interest in whatever had spooked her friend.

"The telephone!" Kate explained at light speed while she still had Nancy's diverted attention. Shrugging her shoulders, Nancy ignored the alarm in her best friend's voice, presuming it to be another sign of arrested development. Kate knew she was a guest in the house of the spirits and no major newsflash was necessary just because the phone was floating in midair...again.

"Told you so; things like that happen all the time." Nancy refocused on her long, lovely eyelashes. Staring at her reflection in the mirror, she concluded: "Don't be scared. It's no big deal...don't make it one. They won't hurt you."

"I don't believe what I saw...and I don't believe in ghosts! It's a hoax!"

"Then *don't* believe it!" Nancy stopped what she was doing and turned to face a friend. "I don't care if you believe it or not, and neither do the ghosts! Think whatever you want. I really do not care!" Her statement was blunt but sincere; to the point. "I've never lied to you, Kate. Stop accusing me of it!"

Stunned, Kate quietly gathered her belongings from the vanity, repacking the bag she brought with her for the night. Quickly piling her books inside it, she left without saying another word. Cynthia reserved a satisfied smirk until the kitchen door closed, though it pained her to do so, wanting to gloat in the worst way. She deserved it; she had it coming and it finally arrived, courtesy of a playful spirit who'd yearned for acceptance from a skeptic: told ya so!

Walking to the bus stop alone gave Katy some time to think about many of the accusations she'd made; to reconsider a staunch, inflexible position she had maintained for several years. By the time the girls arrived, their friend had revised her overall approach, politely receiving them, chatting happily, as if nothing even happened. An attitude adjustment was called for and Katy appeared to comply. In time, she would admit that fear kept her in denial.

Katy really was freaked out and could not wait to get out of that farmhouse, leaving abruptly, with no intention of returning. Months later she came back with a newfound respect and a dangerous fascination. This bizarre incident she witnessed broadened a closed mind and she willingly accepted the word of her friends, shedding her skepticism as a snake sheds its skin. There were no further intimations of dishonesty, no more sarcastic comments...no future need of "told you so" among cohorts as a conciliatory, apologetic truce was struck between them. Kate would later admit she was too afraid to believe in *their* spirits because then she would have to accept what occurred in her *own* old house; forced to believe something it was far more comfortable to deny. Humbled as she was by this experience, she was likewise ashamed of a false accusation levied time and time again, testing the bounds of decency and true friendship, almost trashed. Comments were retracted. Charges were dropped. She took it all back, and rightfully so. There were no doubts left in her mind: this farmhouse had spooks. Oh God! They do exist! No one was lying to her.

Sticks and stones: For future reference, Katy was reminded that words are weapons, too; name-calling does hurt! Liar! A war of words was over as an obvious pause for reflection had done her some good. Friendships preserved in spite of this trial, Katy became a believer. In time, she would be the one to initiate some dangerous name-calling up of the spirits, without the benefit of a telephone, invoking the name Bathsheba. Anyone home? Leave a message!

"I have a great deal of company in the house, especially in the morning when nobody calls."
Henry David Thoreau

bloodbath

"Do the thing we fear and death of fear is certain."
Ralph Waldo Emerson

"Come on, girls. That wood won't cut itself." Too bad. Those were the few words everybody had come to dread, including the hard-working father who spoke them aloud. The novelty had worn off. Roger's gruff voice functioned as the clarion call to comrades in arms, weaponry consisting of an axe and an over-worked chainsaw; their mission involved the militaristic massacre of a dozen dead trees out in the woods. A surge ensued. Present arms! Carry logs. Load that truck. Heave Ho! Let's go! Charge! Their work was never done.

Sunday mornings held the quiet promise of loud and raucous football in the afternoon, along with a well-deserved nap and a sumptuous dinner... when all the chores were done. Cindy had already been out to the barn, tending to the horses. Actually, all the animals had been attended to well before anyone else was up. She was diligent about it, always mindful of their needs, regardless of the weather. Her blood was already pumping, though the same could not be said for anyone else, yet.

In the deep midwinter, those woods were nearly impenetrable. Autumn was the perfect time to forge out into the forest, to identify then retrieve fallen, seasoned logs. Once the underbrush had died back, retreating to the surface of the Earth with a first frostbite, briars were the only hazard. There was no shortage of firewood. Nature provided an abundant supply. Getting to it was not always easy; a veritable obstacle course of fallen limbs and soft, swampy spots creating booby traps for guerilla fighters out braving the elements; any soldier had to watch every step and in so doing, saw wondrous sights. On an important mission, there to capture not an enemy but a friend, there was time enough for mild diversions; watching a raven peck its way through the ice on a puddle to secure a sip of nectar beneath: Nature. It was so lovely, the only splendid aspect of an otherwise grueling task. They all knew what to expect and they all knew it had to be done. After suffering through the first, none of them were willing to face another brutal winter without the benefit of a fire in the place; Inconceivable! Once open, it provided warmth to a home sorely lacking it. There was a certain comfort associated with returning to the house after chopping wood for hours to find the smoke trickling, seeping from the chimney. It put them in the end zone; must be time for football. No; not yet.

"It's time to go!" If Roger was ready then everyone else had better be same as the general required his troops. Fall in...to the back of the truck. Carolyn cleared the dishes then headed for the only grocery store in the area open on Sundays. This too was a chore, KP duty...to stock the house with provisions; some bags as heavy as logs, but better than chopping wood. Her husband had arrived home the night before, flush with the profits from an exceptionally successful road trip. Hand it over. The kitchen pantry was virtually depleted of supplies. The woman on a mission of her own; Carolyn prepared to go out on patrol: shopping. Leaning over the table, passing back and forth between the food storage pantry and a pad and pen, she did a quick inventory; simple enough when the cupboard was bare...when there is nothing left to count up. Resentful of her husband in that moment, she hated living this way: feast or famine. Rather than the occasional hardship, it had become a lifestyle, one she did not savor in the least: Deprivation. Carolyn wrote her extensive list, beginning with the basics: *coffee milk bread butter cheese salt cereal oatmeal pasta potatoes onions carrots oranges grapes tomato sauce soups celery eggs bacon mayonnaise meats* Never one to cower from a challenge, she had about two hundred dollars at her disposal and the Scot in her could torture every dime of it, stretching money 'til it screamed, begging for mercy. No problem. No mercy. Tough times called for tougher measures. One did what one must just to survive, including tromping through the dense thicket of a forest with a chainsaw or buying what was on sale. Winter crops were in; replenishing vitamins with good healthy foods, she felt no remorse filling her cart with every fruit in season to feed her kids: a wise investment.

Coercing every penny to purchase its full worth, Carolyn returned home with few of them left in her pocket. She made it back to the house before the rest of her family emerged from beneath the canopy deep within the woods. Typically, their mother heard them before she saw them. As she built a fire they pulled the heavy woodshed door open and began off-loading their stash; a seasoned load ready to split and burn. They were a loud, rowdy crowd; blood pumping (thankfully that day none had yet to be spilled) and hearts pounding. Exertion showed on their faces. Ruddy cheeks and runny noses all around, five children were ready to take the well-deserved break they longed for but a general would not dismiss them until the job was done: task master.

As ominous clouds rolled in over the horizon, they had made it just in time. Storm troopers announcing a mission accomplished; it was time for a snack. The crowd came in through the woodshed and went straight into the kitchen. Large paper bags covered the surface of the table; some rummaging ensued. Carolyn then diverted their attention with a red mesh package full of oranges, slightly chilled from the journey; homeward bound. The kids tried tearing it open like ravenous creatures, clawing at fabric which would not give an inch. Enlisting a pair of scissors from the sideboard drawer, it solved the problem. Ripping tender skin away from its fruit, they devoured sweet meat in chunks, juice dripping from frostbitten chins. The oranges were luscious; deliciously ripe. Carolyn bought two bags...along with bananas and berries and grapes. Gratified, a mother watched as her children consumed half a bag before they had even removed their hats and coats.

Everyone disappeared into the parlor except Andrea, who remained behind to help her mother store an inordinately large order of groceries. Folding the paper bags, they too were then stored in the pantry. Carolyn recycled before it was fashionable. Popping a pork roast into the oven meant the chores were finished; mom was free to indulge in an orange of her own, poised in front of the fireplace, her vigilant spot. Andrea grabbed two of them, one for a weary father, along with several napkins, knowing what a juicy batch mom brought home. Carolyn pulled a serrated knife from the sideboard drawer. Arriving at the entrance of the parlor to quite a sight, the eldest counted her lazy sisters. All there; a bunch of frumpalumps, limp as rag dolls, scattered about in piles all over the furniture, spilling onto the floor. Roger was already half asleep, collapsed from exhaustion into his easy chair. Pretending to follow the game, he accepted the orange with thanks. It brought him back to life! Go Patriots! Down 14 points at the half: Ouch! That stinger: leaving a mark on their stats.

"Buncha bums." Stifling a smile, mom shook her head in feigned disgust. "Football bums." Carolyn did not bother to ask who was winning…she could not have cared less. Her interest was held in hand…her turn to sip the nectar. "Who wants to help me eat an orange?" A few takers in the crowd; settling in on the hearthstone, Carolyn assumed her *natural* position: (with legs folded beneath her torso *Indian style*, a trait of her Cherokee ancestors) their mother made herself comfy, so to begin the ancient ritual. Since childhood, Carolyn has eaten oranges in a specific way, preparing them with the same technique she learned from her mother. It requires a sharp knife, preferably serrated; a jagged cut is called for to release all of the juice. Christine, Cindy and April gravitated toward a fireplace, seating themselves in a semi-circle around her, each one anxious for a sip or a slice of the tasty morsel; a really sweet treat.

The trick is in the precision. Carolyn didn't think she needed to watch what she was doing…she had done it countless times before: cut a hole in the top, squeeze out the juice, drink from the fruit then eat its remains; supposedly a Southern tradition: the means of getting fresh-squeezed orange juice from a makeshift cup. The girls waited patiently, having seen this process unfold on many occasions, knowing it was worth the wait for a sip: Nectar of the gods. Plunging a knifepoint into the core of the orange, about a fingernail's length away from the stem, Carolyn impaled the piece of fruit on an angle, cutting it deeply inside. Sawing in a circular pattern, the width of more than an inch in radius, its juices began trickling then spurting up from the point of incision, gushing as projectile droplets from an open wound, one hell of a juicy orange indeed! Up, down and around she cut, carving out a flawless circle, creating a gaping hole. Practice makes perfect. She could've done it with eyes closed. Carolyn barely paid attention to this task-in-hand. Happily chatting with kids, discussing the deeds of their day, she impaled her fingernail beneath the skin, pulling the plug. Withdrawing it from the core, she sucked all the sweetness from the nub; the holy spot where a piece of fruit connects to the Creator, at the point of contact with its Mother Tree of Life. Playfully tossing the spent stem up and over her shoulder into the fire, she kept talking with the children while continuing a process which did not require her attention. She'd focused on her girls instead, gabbing about this or that, listening to them complaining about how cold it was in the woods, but also remarking about how beautiful it was, resplendent with colors of the season.

Squeezing the body of the fruit released its succulent nectar. She lifted it to her lips. The first few sips were marvelous; thoroughly refreshing. The ladies were right; true to initial reports from the field. It was a great batch of fruit! One more pinch should bring more to the surface for sharing. No one had yet to notice the blood.

Having pulled off her wet boots and equally moist socks minutes earlier, Carolyn appeared as a barefoot Indian princess squatting on her hearthstone. Christine cried out, shocked by the sight of it.

"Mom! You cut yourself!" Splotches of thick blood were splattered all over Carolyn's toes. Chris leapt up from the floor, rousing a father from his chair.

"Bad!" April yelled as well, panicked by the ghastly view; an ugly scene.

"The damn knife must have slipped!" Roger, awestruck by the spectacle.

"Oh, my God! Mom!" Cindy could not believe her eyes. Blood was oozing, literally dripping between her mother's toes, as if she had punctured a vein. Seeping down her arm to the elbow, it saturated the rolled cuff of her flannel shirt, spilling onto her blue jeans, staining them as well; what part of it was not absorbed into the fabric obeyed the law of gravity and dropped, forming puddles on the hearthstone. Evidence of carnage...everywhere around her!

"Jesus Christ!" Roger hovered over his wife, equally alarmed. "Where is it *all* coming from?" A wonder to behold.

Carolyn felt her heart pounding but could not feel the cut; that sharp sting of citric acid in an open wound. Holding her blood-drenched hand high into the air for further inspection first required juggling the orange into her other hand. In so doing, she identified the source of the blood. It was coming from inside the orange. "Roger. Look!" Carolyn squeezed the fruit. The prodigious amount of crimson liquid was gushed from within its gaping hole; more fluid than could come from a common orange, but this was an uncommon orange. The blood began to coagulate as soon as it hit open air, its hue turning from a rich, deep red tone to a rusty brown with auburn at the center of each droplet. It bubbled and seethed as she squeezed it, a constant stream trickling like teardrops along the surface of the pale skin on her arms. Thick and pasty to the touch, Carolyn became mesmerized. She sniffed at it, stuck between her fingertips. No doubt about it: blood. Perturbed by what was obviously some kind of supernatural interference, Carolyn grasped the orange, pressing into the skin so hard it left indentations. One final bubble of blood sprung to the surface, spilling onto her thoroughly soiled clothing then onto her feet. In an act of defiance; the woman refused to relinquish her orange. She squeezed it until the juice ran clear again...then sucked it dry. Pulling it apart, she tore it to shreds, eating every fiber of the fruit. Enraged, Carolyn heaved the hollow skin into an equally raging fireplace: It is finished.

The family was gathered all around her, but no one said a word. Every eye of each beholder was gazing in amazement, silently professing disbelief. She did *not* just do that! She did. Polka dot clots speckled all over her body, head to toes webbed with smooth gooey ooze, Carolyn's morbid fascination with the evidence was unsettling; a disturbing element of their mutual experience. She did not seem to be herself; appearing to be lost; elsewhere in mind. Her attention could not be diverted. Focused solely on the event, observing what was happening from within, transfixed by its aftermath, she was studying the Nature of the incident. There was a subtle, simmering fury present in her; the vicious way she'd attacked the orange, ripping it wide open with a vengeance then decimating it, flailing it into the fire. This behavior was out-of-character for a woman who suddenly appeared possessed by a savage mean streak. It was brutal. It was frightening. It was Bloody Hell...Wrath of God.

Once Carolyn had finished it off, so to speak, she stood then went into the bathroom to clean up and change her clothing. Peroxide saved the fabrics but what would save her soul from such an intrusive presence? Spots boiling up as white bubbles on the surface of stains, she'd meticulously removed them, blotting the blood with a cotton washrag; its coloring becoming diluted with each new application, dispersing any proof of her assertion with a treatment. Scrubbing off the streaks and droplets, Carolyn hovered over the bathroom sink for what must have been half an hour or more, cleansing her skin, speck by rusty speck; staring into a white porcelain basin as the residual evidence, squeezed from the washcloth, swirled away; out of sight but not out of mind. Sitting on the edge of their bathtub, she stared below at those ruddy red toes. According to her recollection, she'd been so struck by how much blood had been spilled, by the sheer volume accumulated on her feet, she studied these dried globules. Disoriented by this incident, the woman decided to leave both feet stained and soiled, covering them with a pair of white socks, for contrast. Later that night she would privately gaze at them again, touching the blood, tampering with evidence, marveling with the wonder of a child peering at the spots and blotches, drips and stains an uncommon orange left behind on her figure. Not until the following morning did she attempt to scrub them away; and scrub them she did, rubbing her tender skin raw with a hair brush; by that time, what was then required to remove remnants of an event she wished she could wash away from memory: a mortal wound which will never fully heal.

No one in the family knew quite how to react to what they had witnessed; how to express the dismay, having played a natural part in such an obviously supernatural event as well as its inexplicable aftermath. Returning to his easy chair, Roger made no further reference to the anomaly, pretending it didn't happen, but his dis/ease was evident to all. For the rest of that day the house remained quiet; its occupants subdued. Once voracious cravings for oranges abruptly subsided, a dramatic loss of appetite occurred, extending through an inordinately quiet dinner. Not one of them lifts an orange to their lips without remembering the Sunday afternoon one bled to death in their mother's hands.

Unlike most of the incidents and experiences they shared during that rather unusual decade, there are conflicting accounts among the family regarding this particular event. Carolyn recalls her reaction to it a certain way; the rest of the clan, quite another. Describing her behavior in far more benign terms than her five children do, each revisits the episode with identical detail and clarity. As far as her family is concerned, their mother's response was more bizarre than the actual incident. Even at her worst moment, this was entirely unlike her. They all recall her acute anger and frustration bubbling up like the blood itself...from within. At once accepting and rejecting the concept of an occurrence which defied any logical explanation, Carolyn's outburst of pure disdain was shocking for all. Her belligerence; a defiance of and resentment for whatever was causing the orange to bleed, was palpable, entirely contrary to her nature. But then to deliberately ingest the remains of the vile substance was transformative. With purpose; beyond reason: an act of war...taking no prisoners. An impulsive and equally repulsive act instantly impaled the mind and the memories of every witness. The animalistic tearing away at the flesh of the fruit: as symbolism, reflected on Carolyn as an altered entity in those moments; out-of-character...as if out of her mind, as if someone wicked had taken her place. An internal conflict: the struggle to retain control of her own life force. Heaving the carcass onto a funeral pyre bears its own significance. An incidental ordeal functions as multi-faceted metaphor: as a firm refusal to relinquish control to the living *or* the dead. The conquering of a demon: the battle of a lifetime. The drawing of a proverbial line in the sands of time then daring an evil presence to cross over it: there was much to extrapolate from a solitary event. A time to pause and reflect on the physical manifestation these spirits were capable of creating and manipulating, seemingly from thin air. A bloody orange spilling its contents on the intended victim; damage done was minimal, but the ominous message received was quite another spirit matter.

"The torment of human frustration, whatever its immediate cause,
is the knowledge that the self is in prism, its vital force and
'mangled mind' leaking away in lonely, wasteful self-conflict."
Elizabeth Drew

shared space

"A home is not a mere transient shelter:
its essence lies in the personalities of the people who live in it."
H. L. Mencken

Children are naturally selfish at birth; imbued with instincts geared toward self-preservation: basic survival techniques instilled prior to seeing the light. They frequently hoard, covet and claim as their own all objects and spaces they perceive to be personal in nature. In this way, children begin asserting themselves; establishing boundaries and developing an intrinsic sense of self. They are not prone to sharing and, in most situations, must be taught by their elders to be kind and conscientious, sensitive to others...as if they were the others. Of course, there are exceptions to every rule. There are some children who seem to come by these traits naturally without any prompting necessary.

Cindy was momentarily resentful of the little girl wandering her bedroom, touching and moving her toys. It was a harshness born of feeling threatened and did not persist for long. April did not appreciate having her things toyed with either. She was aggravated by the constant upheaval and rearrangements made in her absence. Andrea was a deeply disgruntled youngster, with good reason as her prized chalkboard was repeatedly tampered with then destroyed and Nancy was certain *someone* was reading her diary! Their precious and in some cases, irreplaceable things were being stolen or broken; misplaced and sometimes disappeared entirely. Theirs was not an environment conducive to an assumption of security for a child. It caused suspicions to brew; tempers to flare amongst the children from the start, within a few days of moving to the farm. There was always a sense of impending intrusion; odd perceptions of space being invaded, personalities being imposed upon; mutually claimed by a presence sensed but impossible to discern. As their disquieting existence became increasingly disruptive, they all made a choice: accept it or reject it. Deny it or acknowledge it. Without formulating any specific strategy (except for Cindy), each child gradually came to terms with her circumstances; each made an implicit decision based upon who they were as individuals, albeit young ones. Carolyn never had to tell her girls how to *be*; she marveled at who they were and, in time and space, what they would become. She did not have to tell them to "play nice"…they *were* nice…as a matter of character.

Cindy knew the little girl was sad and sickly. She likewise knew this spirit was the one playing with her toys, moving them all about the place when she was away from her bedroom. Having touched another child's tender heart with her mournful cries for a mother who never did come when called, Cindy soon began relinquishing her space to the little one whenever she appeared. Removing herself gave this spirit free reign. Cindy never left because she felt threatened and sometimes felt as if *she* was the intrusive presence. Leaving was a natural act; not fear-based. On the contrary, it was based in love; as a sympathetic gesture, kindness extended to a pitiful soul. Her exit had purpose and reason: she would want someone to do the same for her.

Their deference became habitual. Whenever Cindy entered her bedroom, if she was presented with evidence of a presence, some extrasensory indication the space was being shared, she'd immediately retreat; relinquishing a room to whomever rearranged an entire farmyard over the span of a few minutes. It was when she stepped back, giving another child a chance to play with toys. Cindy's natural persuasion was to give the wee little one time, whatever it was that *time* meant to her. These children were unfamiliar with the notion of boredom; there was always something else to do, someplace else to go and someone else to see, whereas the dispirited ghosts seemed trapped; no place to go but a memory. If they were capable of reaching through the cosmos, manipulating objects, Cindy considered her intentional act of kindness as an accommodation, a favor; an act of respect for the dead. It was obvious to her; their existence was an extraordinary occurrence which could and should be acknowledged with reverence. Her uniquely generous spirit was, in itself, a form of contact; like pouring seeds for wild birds then withdrawing into the shadows, at a safe distance, to watch them feast in morning light. There was something special, intrinsically satisfying about the practice of sharing for one too young to yet realize or appreciate the concept of good character she exemplified: an excellent trait. This escaped her; the good she had done as a child...for a child. Practicing the presence was essentially something sacred.

Of course, two adults had to adjust as well, particularly difficult when one of them refused to believe his eyes. Carolyn was frequently confronted with images constantly reassuring her that she was not alone...never alone. Many times she experienced identical sensations as those reported and complained about by her children; it was that distinct impression of being watched. Even when the spirits did not manifest in the corporeal realm of visual reality, they remained nonetheless real. A scent. A chill. Footsteps from where no mortal dared to tread. At times it felt downright crowded. Their constant barrage of sensations began as a confrontation, evolved into a distraction and eventually became a way of life: the new paranormal. In fact, it was only a matter of time before each of them discovered the space they supposedly owned was being shared with apparitions and entities which seemed to belong there as well; they did. Selfishness served no purpose and in the case of a child who cried too often, kindness extended seemed her only respite, her only glimpse of a childhood lost in the ether when left at play, even if the time was spent in solitary confinement while wandering the cosmos alone. The thought of it was too much to bear for a mortal soul who knew she had plenty to spare and time to share her belongings; perfectly willing to forfeit all of it on behalf of one far less fortunate than she. Little wonder then, when these treasured toys disappeared due to the generous act of a sibling, Cindy felt deeply conflicted and resentful of the offending sister. Yes, there were living children who had nothing, but she didn't *know* them! Cynthia had struggled with a loss on two fronts. The trinkets of childhood measured her time. An ethereal connection had been abruptly severed as the little girl stopped coming to play. From then on she only cried; the heartbreaking ramifications of one well-intended act. If she could have only stopped Nancy; counting the losses...regrets all around.

Bonds form in close quarters. Familiarity does not always breed contempt. Attachments between mortals and spirits are difficult to comprehend and will undoubtedly prompt much debate. In defense of relationship initially born of necessity, truth be told, *strangers* can be stranger than fiction and so can the truth. If a proper introduction is made and a positive attitude is maintained, the more crowded a neighborhood becomes, the more peaceful it will remain; one big happy family. If souls involved will simply try to get along, disputes can be amicably settled; working together in unity could result in a mutually beneficial conflict resolution. Down in the trenches, the gray space between black and white, the darkness and light of life and death, there is a light at the end of the tunnel: a pathway to heaven from hell. Reaching common ground requires uncommon valor. A truce declared in the midst of war brings respite for all involved. Space claimed can be space shared: Peace be with you, my friend. In death as in life, it only takes one bad apple: Bathsheba. As with the torches incident, she spoiled the bunch. A house divided will not stand for such nonsense. It does not matter who arrived first or lingered longest. What matters is the intention. Do no harm. Do only good. Do unto others as though they were the others…because it's the right thing to do. One needs no other reason to fulfill a purpose. Then say a prayer and give peace a chance. Amen.

"Change the changeable, accept the unchangeable,
and remove yourself from the unacceptable."
Denis Waitley

~ something sacred ~

Metamorphosis

"How many of our daydreams would darken into nightmares,
were there a danger of their coming true!"
Logan Pearsall Smith

Natural conversion: the transforming of this into that in the space and time required, according to all established laws of Nature. How long does it take a leaf to decompose in autumn; what variables exist which could conceivably impact or alter this process? How to factor the elements into these equations? Simple: "To every thing there is a season and a time for every purpose under Heaven." As beings in perpetual motion, ever-changing, consciously or not, in death we change yet again, morphing into something else: as pure energy, soul and spirit dispersed into the Cosmos. Metamorphosis is not an event but is instead an ongoing co-creative process which we remain actively involved in during each moment of existence. We are; always have been, always will be, in some form or another. Best we come to terms with Infinity and our own immortality. Accept it and move on across the Universe…at light speed.

No one could have predicted the outcome thus far; the consequences for mortal and immortal alike…bound together and bound to get worse before it got better. Something had drawn them to the home of their dreams, there to experience the nightmare of Reality. It was true. Whether being thrust across the threshold, pushed from behind or dragged in from the cold to the colder, Carolyn had been compelled to dwell within its walls; a sacred place in the country. As if the house itself functioned as a stern old schoolmarm ringing the bell, calling its students into class, it beckoned their assembly. Dutifully bringing everyone else along, soon the classroom was full to overflowing, all of them *present* and accounted for, there to learn their lessons well: "Here!" (**Geography Lesson #1:** On the existential map of life…we are here!) Even if one belligerent, non-complaint student refused to acknowledge the fact he was *in school*, frequently bunking the classes he had insisted did not exist, ultimately he absorbed by osmosis. Initially, no one was open to instruction, unwilling to accept a formal education they had specifically come to receive; disenchanted with the format in which it was presented. Eventually each one of them would learn to listen up! No syllabus had been provided for their complicated curriculum. Difficult to assess multiple messages coming all at once: as impossible to determine precisely who these multiple *personalities* were, appearing like so many guest lecturers on a busy convoluted campus. Carolyn was, by far, the most studious; the one who did all of the research: **home/work**. She had paid attention in class; took notes, followed directions, remained observant and kept a journal throughout this course as part of her reference materials for use later in life. At times it was utterly overwhelming, everyone teaching them something new simultaneously; challenging them to discern who had something of importance to impart and who was present merely to disrupt the class. In retrospect, it was *all* important: relevant and intense. At other times, the school/house appeared entirely vacant; students would sit there alone to worry, wondering which teacher was next destined to waltz in the classroom unannounced at any given moment in time and space. Such quiet time was welcome; a pause for reflection, like study hall. Best to be prepared for class; the test always came before the lesson. Some absorbed information with five senses; some relied on the sixth, while others depended on repetition; all learned their lessons well. One way or another, all teaching methodology required an element of memorization skills which qualified for credit toward completion of a course with no end. The student who had come to class most eager to learn was the one summarily dismissed; culminating in a rather odd combination of detention and attempted expulsion: punishment time. No apple for the teacher? Graduating to levels of higher learning; it was an unorthodox approach to education, one destined to terrorize and inspire in equal measure, quite like Catholic school!

Enlightenment is painful to observe; it stings the eyes of its beholders with images too bright to perceive, too difficult to focus on for long, until mortal eyes adjust to the Light. There was a period of maladjustment for this family who got more than they paid for in the bargain: what Carolyn once described as the real estate deal of the century. True enough; it was literally an estate with centuries of a history and what dwelled within the walls of that ancient edifice was far too real for her to abide. Had she known at the time what was yet to come Carolyn would have surely abandoned the dream. Soon enough others would arrive, hoping to help. When Ed and Lorraine Warren got wind of their predicament they came to the farm expressing a sincere desire to be of assistance and once the couple became involved it became quite apparent; Pandora had nothing on them. The energy Lorraine released; the compassion Ed harbored for the children, coupled to create a whirlwind of activity no one could have predicted. They knew…from the moment they stepped beyond the threshold. Both were perfectly capable of seeing in the dark…their eyes adjusting instantly to the Light in the midst of darkness: A wonder to behold.

***

Fear not the house, for it is not to blame. It remains as it has always been, a finely constructed piece of architecture with a personality or ten all its own; hard to keep count. If one must fear anything at all, best to fear the unknown, as life and death are apparently full of surprises. Fear the haunted woman who lurks in the night under cover of darkness then vanishes with the light of dawn. Fear fate or destiny which calls its pilgrims home to petrify them. Fear the knowledge that mortals know nothing. Fear the living…not the dead.

Bound they were, mortal to immortal alike. Yeats proved to be correct. He described spirits as being "Insipid as the dough before it is baked" and knew "they change their bodies at a word." The poet knew "Images can break the solitude of lovely, satisfied, indifferent eyes." Practically magical; he knew enough to tell the truth of them. It was not the end. It was only the beginning.

"The world is round and the place which may seem like the end may also be only the beginning."
Ivy Baker Priest

"*Mortals bask in the wonders of this world, sharing a desire to learn evermore of our place in the Universe, seeking meaning for our existence, all the while intrinsically knowing we know nothing at all. Yet, the intellect perseveres in pursuit of knowledge, yearning to discover that which defines limitations, serving to reveal our ignorance as an integral part of the learning process.*"

"Based upon numerous observations made in an old farmhouse, presumptions may be made of the Universe: We are not alone and what we are a part of is essentially invisible. It is Spiritual in Nature. It is something beyond ourselves, resembling ourselves when manifesting in form and substance; a profound discovery. A message received. We need only close our eyes to feel our spirits."

water
Stains
noted
726-22 NC

CPSIA information can be obtained at www.ICGtesting.com
Printed in the USA
LVOW08s1251310713

345573LV00003B/344/P

9 781456 747596

NE   8 - 13